1994

LYRICS OF THE AFRO-AMERICAN SPIRITUAL

THE GREENWOOD ENCYCLOPEDIA OF BLACK MUSIC

Bibliography of Black Music Volume 1: Reference Materials
Dominique-René de Lerma

Bibliography of Black Music Volume 2: Afro-American Idioms
Dominique-René de Lerma

Bibliography of Black Music Volume 3: Geographical Studies
Dominique-René de Lerma

Bibliography of Black Music Volume 4: Theory, Education, and Related Studies
Dominique-René de Lerma

Biographical Dictionary of Afro-American and African Musicians
Eileen Southern

African-American Traditions in Song, Sermon, Tale, and Dance, 1600s-1920:
An Annotated Bibliography of Literature, Collections, and Artworks
Eileen Southern and Josephine Wright, compilers

THE GREENWOOD ENCYCLOPEDIA OF BLACK MUSIC

LYRICS OF THE AFRO-AMERICAN SPIRITUAL

A Documentary Collection

Edited with introductory materials by
ERSKINE PETERS

Greenwood Press
Westport, Connecticut • London

Library of Congress Cataloging-in-Publication Data

Lyrics of the Afro-American spiritual : a documentary collection /
   edited with introductory materials by Erskine Peters.
      p. cm.—(The Greenwood encyclopedia of Black music, ISSN
0272-0264)
   Includes bibliographical references and indexes.
   ISBN 0-313-26238-1 (alk. paper)
   1. Spirituals (Songs)—Texts. I. Peters, Erskine. II. Series.
ML54.6.L96 1993
782.25—dc20   92-27574

British Library Cataloguing in Publication Data is available.

Library of Congress Catalog Card Number: 92-27574
ISBN: 0-313-26238-1
ISSN: 0272-0264

First published in 1993

Greenwood Press, 88 Post Road West, Westport, CT 06881
An imprint of Greenwood Publishing Group, Inc.

Printed in the United States of America

The paper used in this book complies with the
Permanent Paper Standard issued by the National
Information Standards Organization (Z39.48-1984).

10 9 8 7 6 5 4 3 2 1

Dedicated to
Hannah and Frederick Johnson, my
maternal great-great grandparents, who were
among the organizers of the Water Branch
Baptist Church of Bazilia, at Grovetown,
Columbia County, Georgia in 1874, a church
that had its true beginnings in the brush arbors
during the period of American slavery.

CONTENTS

PREFACE

This collection is designed to serve as a thematic reference that will be of particular use to literary and cultural historians, general historians, and theologians, all of whom frequently refer to the significance of the Afro-American spiritual in American life and culture. It is hoped that the collection will be as serviceable as those of blues lyrics and rap lyrics have been.

Many of these songs can be found in numerous musical collections, some only in a few collections, and some only in perhaps a single collection. The purpose of printing the lyrics without the music is to emphasize the substantial value of the words themselves, particularly since the words have had such a pervasive impact on Afro-American life. The lyrics without the musical scores make many more songs available in one volume. Indeed, the words alone tell a tremendous story of a people, while presenting, too, a theology of salvation.

This collection is not exhaustive (some scholars have estimated that the songs in all their variations number well over three or four thousand), but the collection does contain nine hundred seventy-eight spirituals, including variations. The word *variant* at the end of a song indicates that more than one version of the song appears in this collection. Many songs have numerous extant versions, but space limitations allow us to print here only a few of the more significant variants. In a few instances, I have included as many versions of a song as possible. In this way, I have been able to represent more of the phrasing, since it is, after all, the voluminous phras-

ing that I wish to make accessible. Codes are provided at the end of each song should the reader wish to go to the original source from which I have drawn the words. The keys to these codes are provided below.

I have not sought to replicate the various orthographies represented by the numerous collectors; instead I have tried to be somewhat consistent with spellings because as a future project I hope to create a concordance to the songs represented here. Readers interested in the original orthographies of the collectors may consult the sources from which the songs are drawn to see how the collectors thought they heard the pronunciations. Again due to space limitations, many of the songs are not presented here in the complete forms, that is, with all the repetitions. The essential lyrics are represented with as many of the repetitions as possible however.

I have separated the lyrics into nine categories in order to illuminate the great thematic richness of the songs. More categories and subcategories could be devised; for, of course, the categories as presented here are not intended to be absolute. Many songs could easily be moved from one of the presently constructed categories to another. Each thematic category is prefaced by an introductory statement, and the anthology opens with a historical and theoretical discussion in order to give further emphasis to the complexity of the songs and to enable the reader to explore the historical and theoretical ramifications of the Afro-American spiritual in American life and culture.

Publications on the spiritual are extensive, and several bibliographies have been compiled over the years. For that reason, only select bibliographies of song collections, histories, and rhetorical works are provided here. Each song is listed in the Title Index, and the first line from each song is alphabetized in the First Line Index. Numbers in parenthesis following the titles or first lines in the indexes indicate that there are several songs with the same title or the same first line. A general index provides access to topics, themes, persons, and places.

Many people gave me help and support throughout this project and I cannot name them all here, but I extend my heartfelt thanks. In particular I would like to acknowledge Professor Carl Stam, former Director of Choral Music at the University of Notre Dame, for his generosity in making his sheet music files available to me. For stenographic assistance I am especially indebted to Ms. Frances Carter, Administrative Assistant in the Department of Afro-American Studies at the University of California at Berkeley. She endured while typing the original manuscript, so many lines about death and sorrow, all the lines of repetition, and even my frenzied handwriting with grace. I would also like to acknowledge the assistance of Mrs. Stephanie Jackson for the stenographic relief she gave to Ms. Carter in the office at Berkeley; Ms. Nancy Kegler and Ms. Sherry Reichold in the Faculty Services Office at the University of Notre Dame for helping me to bring the project to completion; Ms. Nila Gerhold, Ms. Margaret Jasiewicz, and Ms. Cheryl Reed at the University of Notre Dame for their assistance; James Michael Leger and Troy Thibodeaux for their assistance with the copyediting and proof-reading; the staff of the Interlibrary Loan Division of the Main Library at the University of California at Berkeley and the Hesburgh Library at the University of Notre Dame for helping me to procure sources, and the late Professor William Davisson of Notre Dame for assistance with computer program transfers. The Institute for Scholarship in the Liberal Arts of the University of Notre Dame generously provided financial assistance. Above all, I thank all the composers and caretakers of the lyrics of the Afro-American spiritual.

To my regret, I was not able to include here all the spirituals I had wanted to represent. Due to difficulties with obtaining copyright permissions, versions of songs collected by notable figures like Miss Eva Jessye, Sterling A. Brown, William Dawson and a few others are not printed here. Nevertheless, it is my hope that the lyrics I have brought together will broaden our knowledge of the great range and amplitude of the spirituals as artistic, cultural, and historical repositories.

ACKNOWLEDGMENTS ─────────────────

We gratefully acknowledge the following publishers and publications as sources of the lyrics printed here, and we acknowledge the cooperation of publishers and individuals for their assistance in helping to clarify copyright regulations and in helping to secure permissions when necessary. Please refer to the "Codes" section of this preface as a reference for ascertaining the particular lyrics taken from the following sources.

AMS PRESS, INC., 56 East 13th Street, New York, NY 10003. For *Calhoun Plantation Songs*, collected and edited by Emily Hallowell. Boston: C. W. Thompson and Co., 1901, 1907. Reprinted by AMS Press, 1976. And for *Religious Folk Songs of the Negro*, arranged by the Musical Directors of The Hampton Normal and Agricultural Institute from the original edition by Thomas P. Fenner. Hampton Institute Press, 1874 and 1909. Reprinted by AMS Press, 1973.

BLACK AMERICAN LITERATURE FORUM, Indiana University, Terre Haute, IN 47809. A version of the introductory section on the poetics of the spiritual was published as "The Poetics of the Afro-American Spiritual" in *Black American Literature Forum*, Volume 23, Number 3 (Fall 1989) 560-578.

CROWN PUBLISHERS, 255 Park Avenue, South, New York, NY 10003, for United States and Canadian copyright clearances to reprint selections from John W. Work, *American Negro Songs and Spirituals: A Comprehensive Collection of 230 Folk Songs, Religious and Secular*, New York, 1940. Used by permission.

THE ESTATE OF E. A. MCILHENNY, Avery Island, LA 70513, for lyrics from *Befo' De War Spirituals: Words and Melodies*. Boston, 1933. Originally published by the Christopher Publishing House, 24 Rockland Street, Hanover, MA 02339. Selected songs reprinted with the permission of the Estate of E. A. McIlhenny. All rights reserved.

FORTRESS PRESS, Augsburg Fortress Publishers, 426 South Fifth Street, Minneapolis, MN 55440. Christa K. Dixon, *Negro Spirituals: From Bible to Folk Song*, 1976. Selections used with permission.

G. SCHIRMER, INC., Division of Macmillan, 866 Third Street, New York, NY 10002 for selections from Carl Diton, *Thirty-Six South Carolina Spirituals*, New York, 1930. International Copyright Secured. All rights reserved. Reprinted by permission. And for selections from Nicholas George Julius Ballanta-(Taylor), *Saint Helena Island Spirituals*. New York, 1925. International Copyright Secured. All rights reserved. Reprinted by permission. And for the following selections used by permission. International Copyrights Secured. All Rights Reserved.: "Ain't Got Time To Die." By Hall Johnson. Copyright © 1955 (Renewed) G. Schirmer, Inc.; "De Animals A-Comin'." By Marshall Bartholemew. Copyright © 1937. (Renewed) G. Schirmer, Inc.; "Guide My Head." By Fenno Heath. Copyright © 1971. G. Schirmer, Inc.; "Humble." By Marshall Bartholemew. Copyright © 1937. G. Schirmer, Inc.; "If I Got My Ticket I Can Ride." By Robert Shaw. Copyright © 1950 (Renewed) G. Schirmer,

Inc.; "Keep In The Middle Of The Road." By Marshall Bartholemew & Fenno Heath. Copyright © 1930 (Renewed) G. Schirmer, Inc. International Copyrights Secured. All Rights Reserved. Reprinted by Permission of G. Schirmer, Inc. And for "Never Saw Such a Man" from *Songs of the Soul* by Louis McGlohon. Copyright © 1980. Malcolm Music Ltd., a division of Shawnee Press, Inc. International Copyright Secured. All Rights Reserved. Used by Permission.

HARCOURT BRACE JOVANOVICH, INC., 6277 Sea Harbor Drive, Orlando, FL 32821. Linda Brent (nsee Harriet Jacobs), *Incidents in the Life of a Slave Girl*, 1973. Originally published in 1861. Selection used by permission. All rights reserved.

HARPERCOLLINS and THE SEABURY PRESS, New York, for permission to reprint "Death Ain't Nothing But a Robber" and "Soon One Morning" from James H. Cone, *The Spirituals and the Blues: An Interpretation*, 1972.

LAWSON-GOULD MUSIC PUBLISHERS, INC. Distributed by G. Schirmer, Inc. New York, NY. Used with permission of Lawson-Gould Music Publishers, Inc., 250 West 57th Street, Suite 932, New York, NY 10107. For "I Got A New Name" (1984, Whalum), "In the New Jerusalem" (1962, DeCormier), "Mount Zion" (1984, Whalum), "My God Is a Rock" (1963, Parker and Shaw), "Sometime I Feel" (1963, Shaw), "Sweet Home" (1960, Whalum). International copyrights secured. All rights reserved. Used by Permission.

J.B.T. MARSH, *The Story of the Jubilee Singers With Their Songs*. Originally published in 1881 by Houghton Mifflin Company, Boston. Selections used by permission of Houghton Mifflin Company, Two Park Street, Boston, MA 02108.

NEIL A. KJOS MUSIC COMPANY, San Diego, CA and Park Ridge, IL 60068 for "Ride the Chariot" (1015) by William Henry Smith. © Copyright 1939 by Max and Beatrice Krone, Neil A. Kjos Music Co., sole distributor, San Diego, CA. Used with Permission.

OLIVER DITSON/THEODORE PRESSER COMPANY for selections from William Arms Fisher, ed. *Seventy Negro Spirituals*. Boston: Oliver Ditson Company, 1926. International copyright secured. All rights reserved. Used by permission of Theodore Presser Company, Presser Place, Bryn Mawr, PA 19010.

SHAWNEE PRESS, INC., 49 Waring Drive, Delaware Water Gap, PA 18327-1099, for lyrics from *American Negro Spirituals: Jack Snyder's Collection of Favorite American Negro Spirituals*. Originally published by Jack Snyder Publishing Company, New York, 1926. Copyright © 1926 (Renewed) by Shawnee Press, Inc. International Copyright Secured. All rights reserved. Used by permission.

THEODORE PRESSER COMPANY, Presser Place, Bryn Mawr, PA 19010, for lyrics to "Toll the Bell, Angel" in R. E. Kennedy, "The Poetic and Melodic Gifts of the Negro." *Etude Music Magazine*, 41 (March, 1923), 159-60. Quotations used by permission. All rights reserved.

UNIVERSITY OF NORTH CAROLINA PRESS, P.O. Box 2288, Chapel Hill, NC 27515, for selections from Mary Allen Grissom, *The Negro Sings A New Heaven*; originally published as *The Negro Sings a New Song* by Mary Allen Grissom. © 1930 The University of North Carolina Press.

VIKING PENGUIN, INC., 40 West 23rd Street, New York, NY 10010, for selections from James Weldon Johnson and J. Rosamond Johnson, *The Books of American Negro Spirituals*, 1969. Originally published in 1925 and 1926 by The Viking Press, Inc.

WARNER/CHAPELL MUSIC, INC., 9000 Sunset Blvd., Penthouse, Los Angeles, CA 90069-1819, for use of "Daniel, Daniel Servant Of The Lord" by Undine S. Moore © 1953 Warner Bros., Inc. (Renewed). All rights reserved. Used by permission.

MRS. JOHN W. WORK III, c/o John W. Work IV, 276 Fifth Avenue, Suite #905, New York, NY 10001, for copyright permissions respecting the British Commonwealth to reprint selections from John W. Work, *American Negro Songs and Spirituals: A Comprehensive Collection of 230 Songs, Religious and Secular*. Published by Crown Publishers, New York, 1940. Selections used by permission of Mrs. John W. Work III.

Every reasonable effort has been made to authenticate the folk origins of materials included in this book. If there are any recognizable infractions, the author and publisher will be glad to receive information which will lead to more complete and accurate documentation in subsequent printings of this book.

CODES TO THE SOURCES OF THE LYRICS

"(Allen)" indicates that the source of the lyrics is William Francis Allen, Charles Pickard Ware, Lucy McKim Garrison, eds., *Slave Songs of the United States*. New York: A. Simpson and Company, 1867.

"(ANS)" indicates that the source of the lyrics is Jack Snyder, ed., *American Negro Spirituals: Jack Snyder's Collection of Favorite American Negro Spirituals*. New York: Jack Snyder Publishing Co., 1926.

"(ANSAS)" indicates that the source of the lyrics is John W. Work, *American Negro Songs and Spirituals: A Comprehensive Collection of 230 Folk Songs, Religious and Secular*. New York: Crown Publishers, Inc., 1940.

"(BANS)" indicates that the source of the lyrics is James Weldon Johnson and J. Rosamond Johnson, *The Books of American Negro Spirituals*. New York: The Viking Press, Inc., 1969.

"(BDWS)" indicates that the source of the lyrics is E. A. McIlhenny, *Befo' De War Spirituals: Words and Melodies*. Boston: Christopher Publishing House, 1933.

"(Brent)" indicates that the source of the lyrics is Linda Brent, *Incidents in the Life of a Slave Girl*. New York: Harcourt Brace and Jovanovich, Publishers, 1973. Excerpt taken from "The Church and Slavery" in *Incidents in the Life of a Slave Girl* by Linda Brent, copyright © 1973 by Walter Magnes Teller.

"(Calhoun)" indicates that the source of the lyrics is Emily Hallowell, *Calhoun Plantation Songs*. Boston: C. W. Thompson and Company, 1901 and 1907.

"(CD)" indicates that the source of the lyrics is Carl Diton, *Thirty-Six South Carolina Spirituals*. New York: G. Schirmer, Inc., Copyright 1930.

"(Cone)" indicates that the source of the lyrics is James H. Cone, *The Spirituals and the Blues: An Interpretation*. New York: The Seabury Press, 1972.

"(Dixon)" indicates that the source of the lyrics is Christa K. Dixon, *Negro Spirituals: From Bible to Folk Song*. Philadelphia: Fortress Press, 1976.

"(Fisher)" indicates that the source of the lyrics is William Arms Fisher, *Seventy Negro Spirituals*. Boston: Oliver Ditson Company, 1926.

"(FJS)" indicates that the source of the lyrics is J.B.T. Marsh, *The Story of the [Fisk] Jubilee Singers With Their Songs*. Originally published by Houghton Mifflin, Boston, 1881. Reprinted by Negro Universities Press, 1969.

"(Grissom)" indicates that the source of the lyrics is Mary Allen Grissom, *The Negro Sings A New Heaven*. Originally published as *The Negro Sings A New Song* by Mary Allen Grissom, © 1930, The University of North Carolina Press.

"(Hampton)" indicates that the source of the lyrics is *Religious Folk Songs of the Negro*, arranged by the Musical Directors of The Hampton Normal and

Agricultural Institute, Hampton Institute Press, 1909.

"(Hayes)" indicates that the source of the lyrics is *My Songs: Aframerican Religious Folk Songs Arranged and Interpreted* by Roland Hayes. Boston: Little, Brown and Company, 1948.

"(Kjos)" indicates the source of the lyrics is sheet music published by Neil A. Kjos Music Company, San Diego, CA and Park Ridge, Illinois 60068.

"(Krehbiel)" indicates the source of the lyrics is Henry Edward Krehbiel, *Afro-American Folksongs: A Study in Racial and National Music.* New York: Frederick Ungar Publishing Co., 1913.

"(L-G)" indicates that the source of the lyrics is sheet music published by Lawson-Gould Music Publishers, Inc., distributed by G. Schirmer, Inc., New York, New York.

"(Malcolm)" indicates that the source of the lyrics is sheet music published by Malcolm Music, Ltd., Shawnee Press, Inc., Delaware Water Gap, PA 18327, sole selling agent.

"(R. E. Kennedy)" indicates that the source of the lyrics is R. E. Kennedy, "The Poetic and Melodic Gifts of the Negro." *Etude Music Magazine*, XLI (March, 1923) 159-60.

"(Schirmer)" indicates that the source of the lyrics is sheet music published by G. Schirmer, Inc., New York, New York. Used by permission: "Ain't Got Time To Die." By Hall Johnson. Copyright © 1955 (Renewed) G. Schirmer, Inc.; "De Animals A-Comin'." By Marshall Bartholemew. Copyright © 1937. (Renewed) G. Schirmer, Inc.; "Guide My Head." By Fenno Heath. Copyright © 1971. G. Schirmer, Inc.; "Humble." By Marshall Bartholemew. Copyright © 1937. G. Schirmer, Inc.; "If I Got My Ticket I Can Ride." By Robert Shaw. Copyright © 1950 (Renewed) G. Schirmer, Inc.; "Keep In The Middle Of The Road." By Marshall Bartholemew & Fenno Heath. Copyright © 1930 (Renewed) G. Schirmer, Inc. International Copyrights Secured. All Rights Reserved. Reprinted by Permission of G. Schirmer, Inc.

"(St. Helena)" indicates that the source of the lyrics is *St. Helena Island Spirituals* recorded and transcribed by Nicholas George Julius Ballanta-(Taylor) published by G. Schirmer, Inc., New York, New York, 1925.

"(Traditional)" means that the lyrics are versions from my own cultural memory of growing up in Augusta, Georgia.

"(Variant)" indicates that there is a very similar version of the song which appears elsewhere in this collection.

INTRODUCTION AND HISTORICAL BACKGROUND TO THE AFRO-AMERICAN SPIRITUAL

Afro-American spirituals are not only sorrow songs, but are also jubilee songs, shout songs, chants, homilies, mantras, affirmations and collective, personal, and historical allegories. Spirituals tell part of the story of an embattled people. They are the heart of the text of traditional Afro-American Christian theology, and they contain, in general, crucial aspects of the Afro-American world view. As wisdom texts, they are instructional agents that functioned to controvert the distorted Christian catechesis that was created to indoctrinate the enslaved Africans into submission. To some extent, spirituals are allegories of experience, proverbs of understanding, and documents of quest. They are a premier corpus of documents commenting on the nature of chaos and they constitute the first major antidote for avoiding, and for countering, chaos. In the creation of the spirituals, the Afro-Americans were engaged in an ontologically and epistemologically mandated reconstitution of the self. They were engaged, too, in the arduous effort of salvaging what they could of their ancient African life-generating and life-affirming cosmology.

Every spiritual, which is a lyric of tremendous philosophical, emotive, and dramatic import, testifies to the discomfort or unrest in the enslaved African's state of being. Frederick Douglass characterized the spirituals as "tones, loud, long and deep, breathing the prayer and complaint of souls. . . . Every tone was a testimony against slavery, and a prayer to God for deliverance from chains" (quoted in Brewer, 459). To summarize points made by

Melvin Dixon in *Ride Out the Wilderness*, the spirituals functioned to delineate the religious and secular elements of conversion. This delineation of the religious and the secular elements provided for the enhancement of one's inner mobility and for the transformation of one's moral status (27). The composers' creativity with language helped them to construct a place of refuge where they might live out their transformation. The aggressive theology that the enslaved developed on their own stands, therefore, in significant contrast to the prescribed instructions of the slave masters. In the creation of the spirituals, the enslaved were, in effect, creating a territory in which they had some dominion and autonomy. And out of this basic creative experience would come the philosophical model through which one might explore other dimensions of free status and identity (13-15). By utilizing the songs, one could "initiate pilgrimages and other self-creating acts, including resistance and escape, that ultimately defeat the inertia of place and identity upon which the institution of slavery had thrived" (14). The spirituals propose three distinct localities of alternative refuge where one might find or forge a new identity: the wilderness, the lonesome valley, and the mountaintop (20). Consequently, of great significance to the fortification of the enslaved's self-esteem was their discovery of these alternatives of refuge, which essentially meant the "discovery of a geography of grace" (20). Although some of the narrative voices of the spirituals basically depicted themselves as wretched, there were many other voices that sought through language to exercise control over their geography and their identity. Dixon's analysis substantiates that "slave lore is filled with geographical references that parallel various states of mind. Here the physical geography links to spiritual landscape; if slaves were considered lowly creatures, for example, they seized upon opportunities to invest that state of being with enough mutability so that changes in the vernacular landscape—hillsides, valleys, swamp land, level ground—became references for the slave's feeling" (19).

As with all literature worthy of being called poetry, the spirituals, because of the way they utilize forms of language, definitely stimulate one to think of something far beyond their literal words. That is, the words carry figurative, symbolic, and anagogical implications. It is Arna Bontemps's assertion that the lyrics of spirituals, blues, and ballads are of equal vitality with the music itself and that these lyrical forms are themselves the source of an Afro-American poetic tradition (Bontemps, xx).

HISTORICAL BACKGROUND

In his pioneering and scientific study, *Afro-American Folksongs* (1914), distinguished musicologist Henry Edward Krehbiel, argues at length that "the only considerable body of song which has come into existence in the territory now compassed by the United States . . . are the songs of the former black slaves. . . . The songs of the black slaves of the South are original and native products. They contain idioms which were transplanted hither from Africa, but as songs they are the product of American institutions; of the social, political and geographical environment . . . of the joys, sorrows and experiences which fell to their lot in America" (Krehbiel, 22).

Significantly, too, in her discussion of the status of American poetry at the beginning of the twentieth century, Louise Bogan cites the Afro-American spiritual as holding a particular place of distinction for its oral and literary richness and energy. Bogan says, "The energy of folk poetry was . . . , at this time and for years to come, rigidly separated from the formal poetry of the period by barriers of taste. The one exception to this rule was the negro spiritual, which Stedman had recognized by including examples in his *American Anthology* (1900) and which had been mentioned by Thomas Wentworth Higginson in *The Atlantic Monthly* back in the sixties" (Bogan, 4-5).

As early as 1819, numerous references of varying degrees of appreciation had been made by writers regarding the existence and evolution of the Afro-American spirituals. Dena J. Epstein chronicles this evolution in significant detail in her notable study *Sinful Tunes and Spirituals*. In 1819 John F. Watson wrote in the *Methodist Error* criticizing camp meeting "excesses" caused by the "illiterate blacks": "In the blacks' quarter [of a camp meeting], the colored people get together, and sing for hours together, short scraps of disjointed affirmations, pledges, or prayers, lengthened out with long repetitious choruses. These are all sung in the merry chorus-manner of the southern harvest field" (cited in Epstein, 218). Levi Coffin who founded a Sunday school for slaves in 1821 in North Carolina describes an instance in which one "made a long and fervent prayer. . . . Then the negroes broke out with one of their plantation songs, or hymns, led by Uncle Frank; a sort of prayer in rhyme, in which the same words occurred again and again" (cited in Epstein, 220).

There was for some time a dispute concerning the origins of the Afro-American spirituals. Some denied their Afro-American origins believing that the African was incapable of such creativity, especially since the African made use of thematic elements that were basically Biblical materials borrowed from whites. However, the true proof of creativity in this dispute concerning historical origins and authenticity rests really in matters of style, both musical and thematic. Although numerous phrases and lines are borrowed from established Christian hymns, these phrases and lines, when molded and crafted into a new historical and spiritual time and space, become a new chronicle, a new music and a new poetry. The musical style is different from the European counterparts and the thematic elements are layered with dimensions that reflect the syncretism that was taking place between Christian and African spiritual cultures.

Krehbiel was the first music scholar to write a detailed analysis in defense of the authenticity of the Afro-American folksongs, of which the spirituals are just one category. He attributes the dispute over the Afro-American authenticity of the spirituals to "a foolish racial pride on the part of one class of Americans of more or less remote English ancestry, and a more easily understood and more pardonable prejudice on the part of former slaveholders and their descendants. . . ." (Krehbiel, 11). White Americans were not alone, however, in disputing the particular genius of early Afro-American song, as Krehbiel points out. In his book *Primitive Music* (1893), European scholar Dr. Richard Wallashek questioned the capabilities of Africans in America "under the influence of culture" (cited in Krehbiel, 11). Wallashek had contended that the Afro-American spiritual or folksong was highly overrated, being merely imitative or derivative of European compositions (Krehbiel, 11). Krehbiel makes two very fundamental points in defense of the Afro-American authenticity of these folksongs. One is that there are similarities between all peoples' folksongs, resulting from the proximity and intermingling of the groups. Further, if parallels found between Afro-American and other folksongs is evidence of the plagiarism of the African, then the Europeans are equally as culpable since folksongs, in general, share many of the same elements. Secondly, Krehbiel points out that if these folk song compositions that were held in dispute did not have Afro-American uniqueness, why did whites find it necessary to develop a tradition, a theatrical genre, of putting on "black face" in order to perform them if not in imitation? (Krehbiel, 14).

As a capstone to this dispute concerning the origins and authenticity of the spirituals, we might quote again from the work of Dena J. Epstein who writes: "Whatever it may have been initially (and that we may never know, for no missionary focused his attention on the transformation of this music), by the time the contemporary reporters described it, black sacred music shared many points of stylistic similarity with black secular music: rhythmic complexity, gapped scales, overlapping of leader and chorus, bodily movement, extended repetition of short melodic phrases—all now recognized as characteristics of African musics. These distinctive qualities presented insoluble problems to the early collectors of slave music, who were able to do little more than notate the general outline of the melody. Nineteenth-century transcriptions of the music by whites display few distinctive features that would differentiate it from white nineteenth-century music. Contemporary descriptions demonstrate, however, that there were widely perceived differences, although they could not be analyzed in those days before the invention of recording" (Epstein, 217).

The first substantial group of Afro-American spiritual lyrics was published in June of 1867 in *The Atlantic Monthly* by Thomas Wentworth Higginson, the Unitarian minister and editorial confidant of Emily Dickinson, who defended fugitive slaves in Boston, aided John Brown as one of Brown's "Secret Six," and commanded the first Civil War regiment made of formerly enslaved Afro-Americans. In his 1867 article, Higginson published the lyrics of thirty-seven songs. He sought in his article to introduce lyrics (without music) by discussing their musical and poetic nature, their themes, origin, performance context, frequency, and utility.

A few other persons had published brief descriptive statements on the spirituals a few years preceding Higginson, however. In 1862, James Miller McKim, former Presbyterian minister, a founder of the Anti-Slavery Society and close associate of abolitionist leader William Lloyd Garrison, published a report in *Dwight's Journal of Music* focusing on the serious and religious nature of the songs of the blacks of the Sea Islands off the coast of South Carolina. McKim not only recognized the music for its magnificent simplicity but also for its technical complexity and historical value, stating: "Each stanza contains but a single thought, set in perhaps two or three bars of music; and yet as they sing it, in alternate recitatives and choruses, with varying inflections and dramatic effect, this simple and otherwise monotonous melody will, to a musical ear and a heart susceptible of impression, have all the charm of variety. . . . I dwell on these songs not as a matter of entertainment but of instruction. They tell the whole story of these people's life and character" (cited in Sablosky, 274, 276).

Henry George Spaulding devoted a section of his article, "Under the Palmetto," published August 1863 in the *Continental Monthly*, to a description of the Afro-American religious shout, ritual-dance, and the shout songs. Spaulding was a Unitarian minister who had also visited the Sea Islands in 1863 as a member of the U.S. Sanitary Commission during the Civil War. Spaulding shows a great appreciation for the ritual or ring shout's complexity and for its significantly serious place in the Afro-American religious ceremony. In his description of the musical culture, Spaulding states that "with the adults, the shout always follows a religious meeting, and none but church members are expected to join. . . . I cannot help regarding it, in spite of many of its characteristics, as both a natural and a rational expression of devotional feeling" (Spaulding, 196-200).

Despite this appreciation, Spaulding had difficulty comprehending other aspects of the spiritual including difficulty discerning the thematic unity in the lyrics of some of the songs. He saw the words of the shout songs as "a singular medley of things sacred and profane" (Spaulding, 197). He attributed this to "the natural outgrowth of the imperfect and fragmentary knowledge of the Scriptures which the Negroes [had] picked up" (Spaulding, 199). While the Biblical knowledge of these songs' composers was without doubt fragmentary, the composers were also certainly influenced in their compositions by their African worldview that was not so extremely dualistic or Manichean as the Christian worldview in its schematization of the world with respect to the nature of the sacred and the secular and of good and evil. In his strongly Chrsitian vision, Spaulding probably could not see or simply had no knowledge that, in the African worldview, good and evil are more relative than polar, more complementary than oppositional; thus, we can see the derivation of his confusion of the sacred and profane. What Spaulding therefore characterizes as the "Scriptural patchwork" in the composition of some of the shout songs, sometimes is such but oftentimes it is not.

The earliest book-length collection of Afro-American spirituals containing both lyrics and music was published jointly in 1867 by William Francis Allen, Charles Pickard Ware, and Lucy McKim Garrison. Their collection, called *Slave Songs of the United States*, contains one-hundred thirty-six songs, including seven in Louisiana French and African creole. In addition to the songs, the book contains a significant thirty-eight page introduction. The introduction attempts to provide some information and analysis regarding the origins and historical development of the songs, their stylistic features as evinced in linguistic, rhetorical and imagistic usage, and their musical technique.

The second book-length collection was published in 1872 under the title *Jubilee Songs as Sung by the Jubilee Singers*. It was the famous Jubilee Singers of Fisk University who introduced the songs to thousands around the world. A similar collection of fifty songs was published in 1974 by Hampton Institute under the title *Hampton And Its Students*. Tuskegee Institute followed suit in 1884 with *Tuskegee Normal and Industrial Institute, Its Story and Its Songs*. These collections were revised several times, but were followed by many other collections through the next several decades, especially in the second decade of the twentieth century. The last major collections were perhaps James Weldon Johnson and J. Rosamond Johnson's *The Book of American Negro Spirituals* (1926) and *The Second Book of*

Negro Spirituals (1927), and also William Arms Fisher's *Seventy Negro Spirituals*, published also in 1926.

Concomitant with the growth of published collections of spirituals was also a significant increase in the scholarly attention given to the songs. Influential comments were made along with the statements of Krehbiel in the first quarter of the century by W.E.B. DuBois, John W. and F. J. Work, Thomas W. Talley, Howard W. Odum and Guy B. Johnson, Dorothy Scarborough, and Alain Locke.

SOURCES, THEMES AND FUNCTIONS

As Howard Thurman points out, the three major sources from which the Afro-American spirituals are derived are the Judaeo-Christian Bible, nature, and "personal experiences of religion that were the common lot of the people" (Thurman, 12). Aside from these sources, however, there must be added the everyday secular experiences and the memory of African culture. With reference to the identity of the composers themselves, Henry Krehbiel's explanation holds up very well. Krehbiel writes," . . . the creator of the folk song is an unindividualized representative of his people, himself a folk product. His idioms are taken off the tongue of the people; his subjects are the things which make for the joy and sorrow of the people. . . . Not only is his name forgotten, but his song enters at once upon a series of transformations, which . . . adapt it to varying circumstances of time and place without loss to its vital loveliness" (Krehbiel, 4).

The composers of the spirituals had an experiential and intellectual grasp of the Bible. The Bible provided a magnitude of materials that reflected their own conditions and aspirations. The composers syncretized personal experience and Biblical material to suit their own lyric, dramatic, and epic needs. Consequently, one sometimes finds Old and New Testament episodes and characters merged in the same time frame (Courlander, 38-39). The spirituals functioned to reassert and reaffirm the Afro-American's human significance, to be a source of psychic sustenance, regeneration, and potency. They served as chronicles, homilies, affirmations, mantras, and jubilations. Like mantras, the spirituals serve as positive-oriented thought, helping to neutralize the negative energies of the world. The making of the songs might well be what John Lovell suggests, that, inspired by the African tradition of poetry as magic, the folk composers and singers believed in the lyrics of the spirituals as one might believe in the power of incantations (Lovell, 197). While these songs function to lighten sorrow and toil, as Howard Thurman points out, "the human spirit makes a dual demand with reference to God—that God be vast, the Lord of Life, Creator, Ruler, King, in a sense imperial; and that He also be intimate, primary, personal" (Thurman, 20). It is perhaps this conceptualization which accounts for much of the epic quality of the spirituals. But the fundamental themes are: physical and spiritual deliverance, triumph over adversity, divinity at work in history, hope, faith, endurance, spiritual progress, transcendence, the suffering Christ and the suffering servant, atonement, mystical affirmation, alienation, apocalypse, and struggle.

THE POETICS OF THE AFRO-AMERICAN SPIRITUAL

[The black man] appreciates the rhythm of his speech and retains it in his songs by avoiding the melisma (many notes to one syllable of a word), as most of the Negro spirituals illustrate: "Little David Play On Your Harp"; "And I Couldn't Hear Nobody Pray"; "O! What A Beautiful City."[1]

A major contribution to the cultivation and preservation of the Afro-American poetic tradition has come through the legacy of the Afro-American spiritual. Characterized by its emphasis upon the transcendent and metaphysical, the spiritual is not only a record of the emotional reaction of the African in America, but the spiritual also contains aspects of a crystallized new and old world, in both content and form. The Afro-American spiritual in its form is both aesthetic and utilitarian. The development of this sacred vernacular poetry of the early Afro-American experience is sophisticated in its various syntheses of structural and semantic forms. Like the medieval European lyric, the Afro-American spiritual exerts a special charm for the modern reader in its adept mixture of naiveté and sophistication. In style the Afro-American spiritual spans the range from the obvious through various levels of the ambiguous to the generally confounding. As a profoundly verbal discipline within the magnificence of the music itself, the Afro-American spiritual establishes itself, along with the blues, field hollers and other vernacular forms, as one of the prototypic layers of verbal enrichment from which later modes and generations of Afro-American poetry would draw for their own evolution.

In his discussion of the style of the Afro-American spiritual, Alain Locke writes that these songs up through the first third of the twentieth century are the great folk-gift of Afro-Americans in the United States. For Locke, the spirituals "rank among the classic folk expressions in the whole world because of their moving simplicity, their characteristic originality, and their universal appeal . . . [U]nderneath broken words, childish imagery, peasant simplicity [are] an epic intensity and a tragic depth of religious emotion for which the only equal seems to have been the spiritual experience of the Jews, and for which the only analogue is the Psalms" (Locke, 18,20). Locke encourages us to remember that the spirituals are not sentimental or theatrical but are of epic stature, characterized by great and simple dignity. Essentially choral in origin and composition, "they are congregational outbursts . . . , choral improvisations on themes familiar to all the participants. Each singing of the piece is a new creation, and the changes, interpolations, [and] variations defy the most expert musician's recording" (Locke, 21). The congregational folk-singing which Locke describes is marked by unique breaks and tricks, syllabic quavers, off-tones and tone glides, and subtle rhythmic variation (Locke 22). Locke argues that over-emphasis on the melody [in the spirituals] would produce a sentimental ballad; over-emphasis on the harmony would produce a distortion approximating a barber-shop chorus; and over-emphasis on the rhythmic idiom would cause the tone and mood of succor to vanish and would produce instead a syncopated shout. Locke concludes on style in the spiritual: "It is only in a subtle fusion of these elements [-melody, harmony, and rhythmic idiom-] that the genuine folk spiritual exists or can be recaptured" (Locke, 22-23).

From the earliest periods in the evolution, development, and maturation of the Afro-American spiritual, some European-American observers have been fascinated by the uniqueness of the African-oriented song style as it has worked in conjunction with Biblical or secular themes. Since the nineteenth century there has been a dispute concerning the origins of the Afro-American folksong. Some have denied its Afro-American origins contending that the Africans and their descendants were incapable of such creativity. Henry Krehbiel was the first scholar to publish a detailed, book-length analysis in defense of the authenticity of the Afro-American folksong, of which the spiritual is a category. In his

1914 publication *Afro-American Folksongs*, Krehbiel takes on the European and American skeptics (Krehbiel, 11-18).

In general, though, African-oriented musical timing has been recognized as remarkable and even as exquisite. The Afro-American songster's adeptness at adjusting the metrics to unfamiliar words was especially singled out for praise. William Francis Allen writes in 1867, "The most obstinate Scripture phrases from hymns they will force to duty with any time they please, and will dash heroically through a trochaic tune at the head of a column of iambs with wonderful skills" (Allen, iv). The native or particular genius of the Afro-American spiritual song style was commented upon, too, as early as 1834 by Alexander D. Sims who wrote in *A View of Slavery, Moral and Political* that, "To hear at night . . . the songs of Zion, at a distance, caroled in tones of sweetest melody by many comingled voices, when native harmony instructed skill . . . , such is the melody with which night after night the Negroes charm the ear" (quoted in Epstein, 221).

In his eminent book-length study of the spiritual, John Lovell lists the basic principles of the Afro-American spiritual, many of which are poetic principles, into categories that he labels mechanical and nonmechanical elements. The nonmechanical elements, or aspects of the spiritual's style, include: (1) a simplicity which carries a core of subtlety, (2) a sense of immediacy in which very often the historical past is simultaneous with the present, (3) a critical approval or attitude toward the circumstance, (4) a use of the listener as a creative device, and (5) a great deal of strength in the song's first line, generally presenting a "summation of the community's and the poet's philosophical discovery" (Lovell, 204-14).

For Lovell, the spiritual is also characterized by twelve mechanical elements: (1) The assertion of, or reaction to, some philosophical or factual truth is emphasized through various forms of repetition. A spiritual often begins with the refrain or chorus lines, and from that point on the stanzas and refrains alternate. (2) The spiritual possesses clear, sharp phrasing through the predominant use of vigorous Anglo-Saxon words as a staple element. This element forms a striking rhetorical vehicle for the creative use of individual words, idioms, phrases and clauses, and for proposing resolutions and unanswerable questions. (3) The spiritual is characterized by the use of repetition, which functions to emphasize the most significant ideas. Often the

repeated words and phrases contain the coded instructions as well as the information which is of central importance to the members of culture. (4) There is a predominance of personal pronouns with terms suggesting a familial or communal relationship. (5) There is the emphatic use of the vocative. (6) There is the interchange of phrases, verses, and stanzas without difficulty. (7) There is the pervasive use of iambic tetrameter alternating with iambic trimeter, characterized by a rudimentary beat or rhythm, although a variety of other beats may be present. (8) The *abcb* rhyme scheme predominates, although one finds a variety of other rhyme schemes. And sometimes there is little or no rhyme. (9) There is the use of command and urgent request as part of the rhetorical strategy. The listener is, therefore, often used as a creative device because he or she is the one to whom the questions and commands are addressed. (10) There is the use of refrains and choruses, characteristically forming the second most important components of the spiritual in that they often provide a fulcrum from which the rest of the poetics of the lyrics radiate. (11) There is the use of careful organization with a vivid first line, a middle refrain line, and a chorus. And (12) there is the outstanding use of figures of speech (Lovell, 203-17).

Regarding the formal or structural features of the Afro-American spiritual, like many forms of Afro-American folk expression, the Afro-American spiritual is fundamentally antiphonal in structure; the verse and refrain or chorus are sung alternately (Wagner, 31).

In his 1926 Preface to *The Book of American Negro Spirituals*, James Weldon Johnson, like some earlier observers, pinpoints the African musical orientation of the spiritual. As did Henry Krehbiel and others, Johnson cites the spiritual's "striking rhythmic quality and the similarity to African songs in form and intervallic structure" (Johnson, 19). Johnson adds, however, that the spirituals, "upon the base of the primitive rhythms, go a step in advance of African music through a higher melodic and an added harmonic development" (Johnson, 19). The end result for Johnson is that the wonderful melodies which had been described so often are "hardly more wonderful than the harmonies" when heard in the "part singing of a large number of Negro voices" (Johnson, 19).

Johnson also sees the spirituals as marked by rhythmic intricacy and by a distinctive way of using musical time or beat. In Johnson's observation,

... the Negro loves nothing better in his music than to play with the fundamental time beat. He will, as it were, take the fundamental beat and pound it out with his left hand, almost monotonously; while with his right hand he juggles it. ... In listening to Negroes sing their own music it is often tantalizing and even exciting to watch a minute fraction of a beat balancing for a slight instant on the bar between two measures, and, when it seems almost too late, drop back into its own proper compartment (Johnson, 29-30).

These characteristics were present in the spirituals in their original folk form but were often lost in transcription due to the limitations of the European notation system. Johnson attributes the skepticism of early collectors of spirituals, concerning whether the songs were sung in harmony, to the fact that in the spiritual the Afro-American makes such frequent use of unison harmony: "The leading lines are always sung by a single voice or in unison harmony, and many of the refrains or choruses are sung in unison harmony down to the last phrase, and then in part harmony" (Johnson, 36).

He argues that the Afro-American developed a musical idiom "beyond his original African music" with respect to form, melody, and harmony (Johnson, 26). Nevertheless Johnson also argues that the majority of the spirituals are cast in the form he perceived as common to African songs, having leading lines and a response. He cites "Swing Low, Sweet Chariot" as having been originally composed in this manner:

Leader:	Swing low, sweet chariot,
Congregation:	Comin' for to carry me home.
Leader:	Swing low, sweet chariot,
Congregation:	Comin' for to carry me home.
Leader:	I look over Jordan, what do I see?
Congregation:	Comin' for to carry me home. ...

But Johnson argues that other spirituals bear witness to his thesis that the Afro-American developed the form a step further and cites the fact that in a significant group of spirituals, despite the retention of the lead and response, the latter develops into a "true chorus" which then takes precedence over the verses and dominates the whole song (Johnson, 26). As an example, Johnson cites the familiar "Steal Away to Jesus." First the congregation sings the chorus in part harmony:

Steal away, steal away,
Steal away to Jesus.

Steal away, steal away home,
I ain't got long to stay here.

The opening with the chorus is then followed by a verse sung either by the leader alone or by the congregation in unison:

My Lord, He calls me,
He calls me by the thunder,
The trumpet sounds within-a my soul.

Finally the response is sung in part harmony:

I ain't got long to stay here.
Steal away, steal alway. ...
        (Johnson, 26-27)

Johnson demonstrates that this development in form is carried even further in "Go Down, Moses," for example, where "the congregation opens with the powerful theme of the chorus, singing it in unison down to the last line, which is harmonized" (Johnson, 27). The form becomes even more complex, Johnson argues, in such songs as "Deep River" and "Walk Together Children"; the technique becomes "almost purely choral" (Johnson, 27).

In *Afro-American Folksongs*, Henry Krehbiel has also pointed to a possible relation between a type of African song form and the spiritual. Krehbiel observes that "there is a hint of an African relic in the allusion to the recitative-like character of the [African] feasting song" (Krehbiel, 40). According to Krehbiel, this characteristic is described as "recitative-like" or only resembling the recitative because "the recitative is broken by a full chorus" (Krehbiel, 44). With further regard to the spiritual's musical form, it is generally characteristic of nineteenth-century American commentators to mention the feature of repetition present in the songs, whether their comment is laudatory or derogatory. Their attention to this aspect of the spiritual itself signifies, whether the commentators fully comprehended it or not, that they discerned structural features and propensities in the Afro-American construction of song form which were at variance with the European orientation. The significant feature of repetition is found not only in the early Afro-American folk compositions but in the early literary compositions as well. In Jupiter Hammon's (b.1811) "An Evening Thought," for example, repetition functions as an integral part of the art of persuasion. As a general device, repetition not only functions to reiterate but also as an aesthetic device to create a sense of expectation. In addition, the full number of repetitions have the aesthetic function of giving a sense of completeness, satisfaction, and fulfillment to the work (Wiget, 6). Paradoxically, though, the repetitions can present a sense of yearning if that is the intention of the reiteration. Certainly repetition does not necessarily mean the same sounding or same hearing of a syllable, word, phrase, or line, but can mean, as well, a fresh sounding, improved sounding, or new hearing. Repetition can, of course, be manifold in its representations as well as in its functions. These representational facets include imitation, resemblance, vraisemblance, mirroring, overdetermination and underdetermination in description, collocation, association, complimentarity, similarity, simultaneity, and repetition interacting with displacement and opposition structures. Consequently, repetition affects the architectonics of the poem with respect to aspects of form, symmetry and balance (Orr, 121-22). In the spirituals, it is simply that sometimes a line is repeated to create the effect of rhymed couplet (Staley, 20).

In addition to citing the call-and-response form as the most common structure of the spiritual, "in which the solo verses alternate with refrain lines," music historian Eileen Southern points out that "there seems to be no typical pattern with regard to length of lines or to relationship between solo and refrain lines" (Southern, 189). Southern illustrates in her analysis that in some texts one may find all the lines having four metric feet (or four accents to a line), but that in other texts, as in the ballad meter, four-foot lines may alternate with three-foot lines. Furthermore, one may find that some texts have only two metric feet per refrain line (Southern, 189-90).

Southern's analysis also reveals the strophic form as common to the spiritual. In making use of the strophic form, a four-line stanza generally alternates with a four-line chorus. This chorus characteristically consists of three repeated lines and a refrain, as is illustrated above in Johnson's analysis of "Steal Away." The verse stanza, however, may have varying line structure. Southern points out that although the four-line stanza is conventional, some of the earliest spirituals recorded in writing do have three-line stanzas. She also finds it significant that all the three-line songs in Allen, Ware and Garrison's 1867 collection are sorrow songs, in contrast to shouts or jubilees (Southern, 190-91).

Southern argues, regarding form and style in the spiritual, that the opening verses of Afro-American folksong are generally syllabic; that is, there is one note for each syllable. This opening pattern, however, does not control succeeding verses. After the pattern has been established, varying numbers of syllables can be sung in a single pitch. Southern explains further that "one might expect that text repetition should be matched by musical repetition . . . but more often . . . exact repetition of poetic lines is not matched by repeating musical phrases" (Southern, 196-98).

Although there is not a one-to-one correspondence, the findings of American scholars regarding the structure of the spirituals compare easily with the three distinct forms of stanzaic structure that Nigerian scholar Romanus Egudu identifies in Igbo dance-poems. In presenting a general definition of a dance-poem, Egudu states that certain characteristics are common to all the forms of the Igbo dance-poems. First, they are dramatic in presentation. Normally, a singer leads while a number of people respond by singing the refrain; this gives the poems the color of dialogue and the spirit of communalism. Second, each of the poems is meant to accompany a dance (Egudu, 81). In addition, the three distinct stanzaic forms that Egudu finds in the dance-poem are: (1) the fixed-stanza form, (2) the growing-stanza type of which there are two variants: one in which the refrain follows every stanza and another in which the refrain follows every line of each stanza. Both types of growing-stanza poems share the common characteristics of incremental repetition, chain structure, and simplicity of narration. Chain structure means that several words from a preceding line are carried over into the succeeding line, not only providing musical sound repetition but also as a way of advancing the narrative and giving continuity to the tale. In general, in the chain structure, "with the exception of the first line and the last, the final word of every line is the first word of the following one" (Egudu, 76). (3) The third kind of Igbo dance-poem is marked by the varied-stanza form. Thus, in a poem in which there are three stanzas, the first and last stanzas may be the longest or may be the shortest, or somewhere in between. However, a major feature of the varied-stanza form is that it has different kinds of refrains within the same poem. The refrains, then, give distinction to the stanzas. In the varied-stanza form, rhythm and melody can also change from stanza to stanza (Egudu 78-80).

The use of semantic and structural repetition in

the spiritual is generally resolute or minimally variant, that is, substitutive (I got a robe, you got a robe;/I got a crown, you got a crown) as opposed to incremental. In addition to what was said earlier about repetition in the spiritual, repetition also aids in establishing the metrical pattern. The refrain repetitions often establish metrical patterns by standing in contrast to the meter of the verse lines. Repetition provides an increasing "insistence in sound and thought [which] tends to overcome the senses of the listener, producing an effect like that of the spell or incantation" (Staley, 15). Repetition also functions regularly to divide the thought or narrative of the spirituals into progressive segments. Repetition serves definitely as a unifying feature of the Afro-American spiritual and is a characteristic feature of many Afro-American musical forms. The use of repetition is integrally related to the call-and-response pattern, providing commentary upon the song's basic ideas. The refrain lines sometimes open the spiritual and are repeated after each verse. And, as has been stated, one of the most fundamental functions of repetition in the spiritual is in the reinforcement of meaning.

The use of *rhythmic rhyme* (my coinage), which is used often in traditional Afro-American folk seculars, is sometimes found in the spiritual. By rhythmic rhyme, I mean the marked use of beat in the repetition of a word. More often than not this repetition involves not a homophone but a single word used doubly. The rhythmic rhyme may be initial, medial, or terminal. We see, for example, that in the spiritual "The Winter" the rhythmic rhyme belongs only to one line, alternating from terminal to medial, and has no connection other than rhythmic with another line:

> 'Tis Paul and Silas bound in *chains chains*,
> And one did weep and the other did *pray pray*;
> You bend your knees on holy *ground ground*,
> Ask the *Lord, Lord*, for to turn you around;
> I turn my eyes toward the *sky, sky*,
> And ask the *Lord, Lord*, for wings to fly;
> for you see me going along *so, so*,
> I have my *tri - trials* here below. (emphasis added.)

A figure found frequently in the spiritual and sometimes in the blues is the invocative interjection. Although it is somewhat apostrophic in nature, the invocative interjection, such as *Lord* or *Oh, Lord*, functions as an outright cry of appeal or supplication in the spiritual. The prototypes for this type of invocative are found throughout the traditional African cultural forms. As Henry and Margaret Drewal have pointed out in their study of female power among the Yoruba, "Utterances, as expressions of the spiritual inner self of an individual, possess *ashe*, the power to bring things into actual existence" (Drewal and Drewal, 5). Janheinz Jahn also discusses this essential belief in invocative verbal power as an essential component of African cosmology (Jahn, 157-60).

The lyric invocatives of the Afro-American spiritual share this characteristic. Certainly, the lyric invocative, addressed in an implicit form, is what accounts for, in the Afro-American literary heritage, the profoundly spiritual tone of Jean Toomer's "Song of the Son" (1923) which opens with the invocative, active and visual phrase "Pour O Pour. . . ."

As in the blues tradition, the presence of the invocative interjection also makes the Afro-American spiritual more imperative in its tone. But in the blues, instead of serving so much as a form of appeal, this interjection has a more rhetorical function as a part of the response instead of the call. Thus, phrases like *Oh Lordy* and *Oh, yeah*, which are interjected into the blues are actually a type of self-commentary.

The forms of repetition which are pervasive in the spiritual may simply be remnants of the other ingenious aesthetic uses of repetition found in African oral traditions. In his study of what he calls the "expansible image" in the *ntsomi* story tradition of the Xhosa peoples of Transkei and Zululand in the Republic of South Africa, Harold Scheub provides illustrations and examples relevant to our discussion even though they are from prose narratives (Scheub, 113-18). In the *Ntsomi*, traditional use of continual repetition, the core images that move the plot along and aid in the development of character and setting are what may be thought of as expansible, that is, extending through a series of steps. While the expansibility of the image is characteristically narrative in its function, it is nevertheless quite poetic in effect. In essence, as is shown in the following examples, repetition in the *ntsomi* tradition of expansibility has a relay function. The repetitions serve as transitions for the thoughts, and as a kind of poetic continuity of movement for the narrator. That is, repetition can be phonological and/or semantic in its nature, dimensions, and functions:

1. When she had gone, the boy took the medicine and drank it. When he had drunk it, he went to the river,

and when he got to the river, he gave birth to two children, because he had consumed the medicine (Scheub, 118).

2. Time passed, time passed, and at this time there was a great drought. The grass was finished, everything dried up. The livestock could find nothing to eat, the rivers dried up, the pools dried up, the springs were dry, wilderness (Scheub, 122).

Should the *ntsomi* example seem geographically distant or farfetched, all one need do is to compare it with the repetition in the delivery style attributed to an Afro-American woman in 1862:

Once the time was that I cried all night. What's the matter? What's the matter? Matter enough. The next morning my child was to be sold, and she was sold, and I never expect to see her no more till the day of judgement. Now, no more that! no more that! no more that! With my hands against my breast I was going to my work, when the overseer used to whip me along. Now, no more that! no more that! When I think what the Lord done for us, and bought us thro' the troubles, I feel that I ought to go into his service. We are free now, bless the Lord! . . . No more that! no more that! no more that, now. . . .! (Aptheker, 10-11).

Or to use another example from African traditional verse, we may find a greater affinity to the formal repetition found in the spiritual in an excerpt from Yoruba divination poetry:

If I go on a distant journey,
Ifa look after my home well till I come.
Palm-tree, look after my home well till I come.
Metal lead looks after Oosaai's home in her absence.
If I go on a distant journey,
Ifa, look after my home well till I come.
Snail's home is always cold and pleasant.
If I go on a distant journey,

Ifa, look after my home well till I come.
Palm-tree, look after my home well till I come (quoted in Abimbola, 33).

Of course, in order to appreciate the Afro-American spiritual as literature, some detailed attention must be given to its utilization of, and creativity with, language itself. The songs have to be examined collectively and individually if one is to discover how it is that the verses and phrases often achieve and are characterized by an unsuspecting rhetorical power and how they achieve their tragic depth and epic intensity, while sustaining a simple dignity. Attention also needs to be given to the poetic derivations and to the uses of poetic tension in the songs. The language of the spiritual is made vivid by the frequent use of emphatic metaphor, forceful and direct diction and imagery, personification, rhyme and repetition (Southern, 192-96). The spiritual appears naive or has, to some degree, a naive quality because it generally does not display an overly literate texture nor an overly literate fabrication; that is, the spiritual is constructed not around grammatical and imagistic elaborations but around grammatical and imagistic essences. It has an ingenuity that is derived from its power to place bare essentiality in the realm of the metaphoric. This means, though paradoxically, that the materials selected to be used could not have been chosen naively by the composers.

The composers of the Afro-American spirituals shared a deep appreciation for the aesthetics of figurative magnanimity. They liked, for example, to imagine and construct imagery of supreme exaltation and exultation as is expressed in the following two fantastic lines from "Roll, Jordan Roll":

My brother sittin' on the tree of life,
And he heard when Jordan roll. . . .

The activity of exaltation described here, though beyond this world, is celebrated nevertheless as real. The magnanimity of the characters in the spiritual is characteristically drawn so as to be fixed in time, yet standing beyond time and terrestrial reality.

Although the Afro-American spiritual is quite 'choric' in both its compositional origins and performance, it is also in its nature and content extremely 'lyric.' It is choric in that many persons often contributed to its making and many were certainly generally a part of its performance; nevertheless, like the classical lyric, the Afro-American spiritual is highly subjective respecting its individual imaginative imagery, thought, and emotion. This quality is felt keenly even though one experiences at the same time a sense of the collective or of the historically representative. From these dual dimensions, the Afro-American spiritual derives much of its literary and philosophical intensity.

Composers of the spiritual often used words and phrases which approximate the *ideophone* functions evident in African oral traditions such as that of the Gbaya of Cameroun and the people of the Central African Republic. The primary ideophone "is a descriptive word that, unlike the verb (which merely states action) and the adjective (which only describes an item), creates an emotion. It creates a picture; it is sensual, enabling the listener to identify a feeling, a sound, color, texture, expression, movement, or silence through his own senses. The ideophone is poetic; it is in the purest sense imagery" (Noss, 75). In the Afro-American spiritual, for example, ideophonic words and phrases like "trembling" and "the blood ran twinkling down" in "He Never Said a Mumbling Word" function as important sensory elements in the poetics. The dimensions employed in the ideophone vary, depending on the composer and the context. Thus the ideophone may be layered in its dimensions with the comic, tragic, ironic, sarcastic, etc. . . . The employment of an ideophone may also, for example, aid the shift in poetic style from lyric to dramatic.

The Afro-American spiritual possesses a great range of artistry in its use of ambiguity, which enriches the range and levels of the literary experience, meaning, and interpretation. The literary experience in the spiritual begins at the level of magnificent simplicity and moves to other levels of complexity, employing historical allegory and allusion. Simplicity in this context is the virtually irreducible geometry of experience, of life, and of expression presented in the lyrics. In "Lay This Body Down," for example, the fundamental poetic dimension is achieved by the principal use of nature imagery and mere life experience. The meaning is minimally, if at all, dependent upon historical or Christian doctrinal context, as is so often the case with the spiritual:

O graveyard, O, graveyard,
I'm walking through the graveyard;
Lay this body down.

I know moonlight, I know starlight,
I'm walking through the starlight;

Lay this body down.

I walk in the moonlight, I walk in the starlight;
I lay this body down;
I know the graveyard, I know the graveyard,

When I lay this body down.

I lay in the graveyard and stretch out my arms;
I go to the judgement in the evening of the day,
And my soul and your soul will meet in the day,
When we lay this body down.

A basic stylistic element of the simplicity of the Afro-American spiritual is, of course, the simile. But

there is often an amplified use of this figure of speech. The basic comparison is made, as in the case of "Sometimes I feel like a motherless child," to establish the fundamental sense and image. However, the sense and image presented in the simile are amplified in the song by the use of the sense extension phrase "A long ways from home." It is the use of amplification techniques such as this that help to bring the dimension of magnificence to the spiritual's fundamental simplicity.

In another respect, regarding the magnificent simplicity of the spiritual, what we find is that the ordinary is turned into a vehicle of the astonishing. Lovell points out that, in employing mask and symbol, another feature of the imagery of the spiritual, the creators of the spiritual understood that "the real purpose of artistic inspiration is not expression but impact" (Lovell, 192). Demonstrating how mask and symbol are integral to the poetic impact of the Afro-American spiritual, Lovell provides a compelling analysis of the magnificent lyrics of "Lay This Body Down." Explaining that the form of the funereal poem is used as a guise by the speaker to portray his "unabashed confidence in the ability of life to conquer death" (Lovell, 192), Lovell reminds us that the language of the spiritual is not the language of an individual but of the persona of a folk community. We would thus be highly misdirected if we were simply to read the spiritual literally. Like the language of a close family or group, the language of any group living under peculiar social, political, and cultural circumstances necessarily develops according to its own semantic needs. A different routine for close communication is not then simply a matter of linguistic embellishment when constructed around "oral shorthand, symbol, meaningful but peculiar accent, irony, and significant silences," as is often evident in the lyrics of the spiritual (Lovell, 132). Consequently, one must be careful when encountering such frequent and seemingly basic or denotative terms as "death" in the spiritual. For example, the use of *death* for symbolic and ritualistic purposes was very fundamental to the African ancestors of Afro-Americans. The mask of death carried in Africa the connotation more of transition and opening than of finality and closure. In early Afro-America, *death* was perhaps more of a figurative or symbolic way of disguising one's yearnings to relocate or to transcend (Lovell, 112, 191).

Along other figurative lines, in "Daniel in the Lion's Den" the metaphoric functions are complicated by historical allusion, taking the song's literary range beyond the arena of magnificent simplicity found in "Lay This Body Down." However, this additional, historical dimension of complication does not necessarily make "Daniel in the Lion's Den" more beautiful or compelling than "Lay This Body Down":

    Oh-o Lord, Daniel's in the lion's den,
    Oh-o Lord, Daniel's in the lion's den,
    Oh-o-Lord, Daniel's in the lion's den,
    Come help him in a hurry,
    Help him in a hurry.

    Oh-o Lord, Daniel ain't got no friend,
    Come 'friend him in a hurry;
    Oh-o Lord, won't you ease my troubing mind,
    Come ease it in a hurry;
    Oh-o Lord, you know I ain't got no friend,
    Come 'friend me in a hurry;
    Oh-o Lord, you know what you promised me,
    Come give me in a hurry;
    Oh-o Lord, Jonah's in the belly of the whale,
    Come help him in a hurry;
    Oh-o Lord, three Hebrew children in the fiery
        furnace,
    Come help them in a hurry.

Further, "Pilgrim's Song" illustrates the fundamental metaphoric simplicity one might find in poetry constructed around the allegorical:

    I'm a poor, wayfaring stranger,
    While journeying through this world of woe,
    Yet there's no sickness, toil, and danger,
    In that bright world to which I go;
    I'm going there to see my father,
    I'm going there no more to roam,
    I'm just going over Jordan,
    I'm just going over home. . . .

On another figurative level, the song "Fix Me Jesus," whereas it is built around concrete, familiar imagery, complicates its imagery by a slight confounding of the reader's expectations with the dicta of the song's persona. The speaker wishes in death for a specific type of burial. He or she wants to be placed in solid ground at sufficient depth, all of which is normative, of course. But paradoxically he or she wants to be let down with the golden chain instead of the regular Christian doctrinal expectation of being taken upward by the chain:

    O, fix me, Jesus, fix me right,
    Fix me right, fix me right;

    Oh, fix me, Jesus, fix me right,
    Fix me so I can stand.

    Oh, place my feet on solid ground,
    Oh, place my feet on solid ground,
    Oh, when I die you must bury me deep;
    Oh, when I die you must bury me deep;
    Oh, dig my grave with a silver spade,
    Oh, dig my grave with a silver spade,
    And let me down with a golden chain,
    And let me down with a golden chain.

    Oh, fix me, Jesus, fix me right,
    Fix me right, fix me right;
    Oh, fix me, Jesus, fix me right,
    Fix me so I can stand.

With an even greater degree of complication, the song "Archangel, Open the Door" introduces in its second stanza an ostensibly irrelevant line which pushes the reader to a point of confusion and consequently into another type of experience with semantic ambiguity. Thus, as the theorist on literary ambiguity William Empson postulates, the reader "is forced to invent interpretations" (Empson, 176):

    I ask all them brothers around,
    Brothers, why can't you pray for me?
    I ask all them sisters around,
    Sisters, why can't you pray for me?

    I'm going to my heaven,
    I'm going home,
    Archangel, open the door;
    Brother, take off your knapsack, [italics mine]
    I'm going home,
    Archangel, open the door.

Some spirituals have an interesting rhetorical logic, involving a combination of call-and-response with a complicating correlative image or symbol. This style or technique is seen, for example, in the refrain of "Stand Still Jordan":

    Stand still, Jordan,
    Stand still, Jordan,
    Stand still, Jordan,
    Lord, I can't stand still.

The symbolic Jordan, while serving in an obvious manner as the focus of the rhetorical address, in a more crucial manner, functions as the emotive historical symbol from which the usurping "I" builds its definition. This use of the combination of figures provides for quite a compelling intellectuality as well as compelling style.

In some cases, even the forceful nature of the grammatical usage of one basic line of the refrain can carry a powerful poetic intensity. Such, for example, is the case in the line "Trouble Done Bore Me Down" where the "ungrammatical" verbal usage becomes an asset, serving as a poetic intensifier:

> Oh Lord, Oh Lord,
> What shall I do?
> Trouble done bore me down.
> I wander up, I wander down,
> Trouble done bore me down,
> I wonder where my Jesus gone,
> Trouble done bore me down. . . .

In addition to features such as alliteration, and vivid as well as metaphoric imagery, the poetic dimensions of the spiritual are sometimes derived from words, phrases and other constructions functioning as structural links and from semantic interplay, resulting in subtleties of wit, irony, humor, and paradox.

In the Afro-American spiritual, the poetic tension is frequently related to figurative time-possibility, time fusion, and syncretism. Again, "Roll, Jordan, Roll" is illustrative:

> O, march the angel march,
> O, march the angel march;
> O, my soul arise in Heaven, Lord,
> For to hear when Jordan roll.

In this verse poetic tension is derived or generated through faith-time or expectant-time as it works against actual or here-and-now time. This is illustrated poignantly in another example, "Jehovah Hallelujah," in which God's beneficence is celebrated, yet actual deprivation and desolation are intensely felt. Present here also is tension between the metaphysical and the physical realities:

> Jehovah, hallelujah,
> The Lord is providing,
> Jehovah, hallelujah,
> The Lord is providing.

The resolution of the disparity is in expectant-time, a time sense that pervades the imaginative style of the spiritual, necessarily postulating possible-time as fulfilled-time. This stretching of time, we might say, is what helps generate in the songs an extremely powerful and often tremendously transcendent

human posture. The Afro-American spirituals have a range in tone for that of extreme supplication and despondency, as in "Sometimes I Feel Like A Motherless Child," to that of exhortation, as in "You Better Get Ready for the Judgment Day."

Much of the poesis of the Afro-American spiritual is derived, however, from the interaction of the intra- and extra-metaphoric possibilities of the lyrics.[2] This intra- and extra-metaphoric possibility is a part of the Afro-American spiritual's most essential dynamism. Thus in "Keep Your Lamps Trimmed" the theology of salvation carries the intra-metaphoric emphasis with reference to the cultivation and maintenance of the soul. But the assertive force of the literalness of "lamps" cannot be ignored when juxtaposed with the anticipatory phrase "work's almost done" and with the both anticipatory and coaxing phrase "don't grow weary":

Keep Your Lamps Trimmed

> Keep your lamps trimmed and a-burning,
> Keep your lamps trimmed and a-burning,
> Keep your lamps trimmed and a-burning,
> For this work's almost done;
> Brothers, don't grow weary,
> Brothers, don't grow weary,
> For this work's almost done.
>
> 'Tis religion makes us happy,
> 'Tis religion makes us happy,
> We are climbing Jacob's ladder,
> Every round goes higher and higher.
>
> Keep your lamps trimmed and a-burning,
> Keep your lamps trimmed and a-burning,
> Keep your lamps trimmed and a-burning,
> For this work's almost done;
> Brothers, don't grow weary,
> Brothers, don't grow weary,
> For this work's almost done.

The phrases push toward the extra-metaphoric possibilities of physical deliverance. The initially intra-metaphoric "lamps" then follows the logic of the extra-metaphoric, carrying the connotation of an instrument useful for seeing one's way after the work is done when one has not allowed oneself to succumb to weariness. The extra-metaphoric possibility is evident without obscuring the intra-metaphoric connotation on which the extra-metaphoric is built.

It is indeed the poetic originality of the Afro-American spiritual that Sidney Finkelstein draws upon to refute George Jackson Pullen's and Guy Johnson's argument that the Afro-American spiritual is a mere borrowing and aesthetically substandard relative of various white spirituals and hymns. In creating a distinctive body of verse that could be recognized as their own, Afro-American composers not only created a new music but also a characteristically fresh imagery and manner of phrasing. Some lines they borrowed, some they re-cast, and some they simply created. But the Afro-American composers' sense of poetics accounts for a substantial part of the differences in the Euro-American and Afro-American forms, as Finkelstein demonstrates by citing the very examples Pullen uses to discount Afro-American originality. In contrast to their white counterparts, the following verses from Afro-American spirituals illustrate a decided generic style that is predominant in the Afro-American spiritual, but not in Euro-American spirituals. This style reflects the poetic principles of the Afro-American spiritual as stated earlier. These principles of immediacy, personal involvement, and dramatic appeal are not predominant in Pullen's white examples, even though the Afro-American composers may have retained some of the exact lines from the white hymns:

I. White Form:

Saw ye my Savior, saw ye my Savior,
Saw ye my Savior and God?

O He died on Calvary, to atone for you and me
And to purchase our pardon with blood.

Black Form:

Were you there when they crucified my Lord?
Were you there when they crucified my Lord?
O sometimes it causes me to tremble, tremble,
    tremble,
Were you there when they crucified my Lord?

II. White Form:

Ah poor sinner, you run from the rock,
When the moon goes down in blood,
To hide yourself from the mountain top,
To hide yourself from God.

Black Form:

There's no hiding place 'round here,
There's no hiding place 'round here,
O I went to the rock to hide my face,
The rock cried out; No hiding place!
There's no hiding place 'round here.

(quoted in Finkelstein, 20-21.)

In each instance of these examples the sense of immediacy, personal involvement, and the dramatic appeal are heightened in the Afro-American form and become consistent in the Afro-American tradition. This is so even when the Euro-American form itself is quite imagistic as in the second example above.

Grammatical idiosyncrasy is often of special importance for establishing a functionally Afro-beat or rhythm in the spiritual. For example, in addition to the extra-semantic emphasis given to the "ungrammatical" negative in the line "Trouble done bore me down," additional semantic emphasis is also generated by the graver accent carried by the initial "d" than certainly would be generated by the more grammatical statement "Trouble has born me down." Grammatical inconsistency is not a pervasive principle of meaning in the spiritual, but it is sometimes a significant one. This use of the "ungrammatical" becomes consistently significant, however, in the evolution of Afro-American poetry with poets who are bi-dialectal, that is, who are consciously using standard English and an Afro-American vernacular as their idiom. Reknowned concert tenor Roland Hayes, who was the first international operatic singer to make the spirituals a regular part of his performance, saw in the use of dialect the mastery of a high art form that enhanced the tradition of the Afro-American spiritual. Hayes referenced these masters as "high priests of folk song utterance" who were "very discriminating in their taste, choice and use of dialect," having developed an extraordinary skill at making dialect word forms coalesce with the thought to be expressed" (Hayes, 8).

The prototypic lyricism of the spiritual certainly cannot be discussed without giving particular attention to the Afro-American folk cry, for the folk cry is the ultimate archetypal source of Afro-American lyricism. The folk cry is the index to the Afro-American soul urge. It is simultaneously religious and secular. It is toward this unmatched, archetypal lyricism that so much of Afro-American poetic genius aspires and by which that genius is also inspired. The folk cry is the expression of the soul toward the divine and cosmic genesis. It is from this frame of reference that the Afro-centric soul is always expressing and examining its cosmic connection through moans, chants, and wails. The Afro-American folk cry works in the true sense of the lyrical, heavily marked by the primary lyric features of subjectivity, emotion, imagination, and melody.

In its most essential form, the Afro-American folk cry is a type of "free music in which every sound, line and phrase is exploited for itself in any fashion that appeals to the crier to evoke that great depth of emotion so characteristic of the spirituals and the blues. The dynamic of the folk cry may be short and sharp, with an abrupt end, or . . . can waver, thin out, and gently disappear into the air. It may consist of a single musical statement or a series of statements, and may reflect any one of a number of moods—homesickness, loneliness, lovesickness, contentment, exuberance" (Courlander, 82). The words may or may not be discernible. There may not be any words per se. The meaning is, above all, in the tone of the sounds.

Having its primary origins in Africa, the Afro-American folk cry may still be heard there as well as in the rural, southern United States at various times during the day in the open countryside, in a church, or in a prison. As with the spiritual, the folk cry could serve as a way of communicating with God, nature, the cosmos, the self, or a neighbor whom one suspects to be working at an invisible distance on the other side of a wooded range or over on some distant hill. Like its descendant, the spiritual, the folk cry could be a way of calling for assistance. It could be a way of bidding good morning or goodnight (Courlander, 80-84).

In his excellent discussion of the Afro-American folk cry, Willis James states that "anyone who takes the time can easily see that the Negro has taken his cries—'whoops,' 'hollers,' 'calls' and grafted them on to present-day song patterns whose practice goes back hundreds of years" (James, 24). James's assertion certainly has significant implications for Afro-poetics in the United States and is especially relevant to Afro-poetics considering the range of classifications which James gives to the folk cries: calls, selling or street cries, religious, field, night, dance and water cries and calls (James, 25). From these forms the primal or prototypic lyricism of the Afro-American poetic tradition is certainly derived. Attention has been brought to this factor by R. Emmett Kennedy when in 1923 he wrote concerning the poetic and melodic gifts of the Afro-American, that what he called the Afro-American's "partiality for high-sounding words, his wonderful way of mispronouncing them, his splendid gift of euphony, and his fluency in making what the French call 'liaison,' help materially to make the negro a little more than passingly interesting. He is a noteworthy factor when it comes to summing up literary values,

and his original melodies and delightful dialect can never fail to bring him his just right to immortality" (R. E. Kennedy, 159).

The magnificent simplicity and lyrical achievement of the Afro-American spiritual established the prototypic standard of artistic and lyrical fulfillment for many Afro-American writers. The depth of personal emotion that is captured in the corpus of spirituals such as "Nobody Knows the Trouble I've Seen," "A Balm in Gilead," and "Sometimes I Feel Like a Motherless Child" has been considered unrivaled by writers like Langston Hughes and Adrienne Kennedy, who were certainly aware of and impressed by the lyrical acheivement of classic English writers like Keats, Wordsworth, and Shakespeare. But no matter that Paul Laurence Dunbar's "Compensation" is written as a standard English poem, it is nevertheless doubtful that Dunbar drew simply upon English literary classics as the exclusive standard-bearers of lyricism when he set out to write that poem. Only in relation to the poem's form might one say that the standard was definitely British. But in terms of theme, lyrical depth, and simplicity, one cannot overlook the resemblance of Dunbar's "Compensation" to the Afro-American spiritual. The same could be said, of course, for Dunbar's "Sympathy," as well as a number of his other lyrical poems. In effect, then, it is not only the highly celebrated rhythmic mode that has established prototypes in the Afro-American literary tradition.

Both Langston Hughes and Adrienne Kennedy have referred specifically to the spiritual as the lyrical prototype for much of their work. Hughes, for example, affirms the prototypic influence of the spiritual for the composing of his celebrated "The Negro Speaks of Rivers" while on a train ride for Cleveland to Mexico at the age of seventeen:

I looked out of the Pullman at the great muddy river flowing down toward the heart of the South, and I began to think what that river, the old Mississippi, had meant to Negroes in the past . . . how Abraham Lincoln had made a trip down to New Orleans and how he had seen slavery at its worst, and had decided within himself that it should be removed from American life. Then I began to think about the rivers in our past—the Congo, and the Niger, and the Nile in Africa—and the thought came to me: "I've known rivers," and I put it down on the back of an envelope I had in my pocket . . . (Meltzer, 63).

Hughes continues by stating that the "lyric beauty

of the living poetry in the spirituals'' had profoundly influenced him (Meltzer, 66). And, of course, in a very specific sense for Hughes in the composition of this poem, the river itself had been well-honed by the Afro-American spiritual into a predominant symbol representing the depth of the Afro-American experience. This is seen in such favored phrases and lines as ''Deep river, Lord'' and ''I want to cross over Jordan,'' coupled with such a strong allusion to ''Nobody Knows the Trouble I've Seen.'' As Arnold Rampersad says of ''The Negro Speaks of Rivers'' in his biography of Hughes, ''The diction of the poem is simple and unaffected either by dialect or rhetorical excess; its eloquence is like that of the best black spirituals'' (Rampersad, 40).

Giving her testimony to the undisputed influence of the spirituals in her work, OBIE Award winning playwright Adrienne Kennedy, who thinks of herself actually as a dramatic, lyric poet, has said: ''I learned that I belonged to a race of people who were in touch with a kingdom of spirituality and mystery beyond my visible sight'' (A. Kennedy, 14). ''[In my childhood and youth] I had a slim yellow book on the piano that contained many Negro spirituals, 'Go Down, Moses,' 'Sometimes I Feel Like a Motherless Child,' 'Nobody Knows the Trouble I've Seen,' 'He Knows Just how Much We Can Bear' '' (A. Kennedy, 97). Kennedy adds, ''The sound of Mrs. Rosenbaugh, [my high school Latin teacher], reading Latin is a sound I strive for when I write, just as I strive for the emotional level of the spirituals. Nobody Knows the Trouble I've Seen, Nobody Knows but Jesus. And, Sometimes I Feel Like a Motherless Child. And, Go Down Moses, Way Down to Egypt Land, Tell Old Pharaoh to Let My People Go'' (A. Kennedy, 90-91).

Certainly, the magnificent spirituals were among the most significant nurturing materials for Afro-American artists of all varieties for several generations after slavery. One who is aware of the depth of this lyrical tradition in Afro-American culture cannot therefore overlook its impact even upon the creation of passion and emotion in works, for example sonnets, whose form is definitely European derived. No matter how formally European are the sonnets of Countee Cullen (''Yet Do I Marvel''), Claude McKay (''If We Must Die''), and Gwendolyn Brooks (''What Shall I Give My Children''), the lyricism is nevertheless grounded in the legacy of emotions of skepticism, doubt, alienation, resistance, and beleagueredness, etc. . . . , so splendidly uttered in the most celebrated of the Afro-American spirituals.[3]

The Afro-American spiritual in its artistic richness is not only therefore a bedrock of the Afro-American musical tradition, but is, as well, a seedbed for the development of Afro-poetics in the United States. And as an historical record of Afro-American experience, the spiritual is, of course, irreplaceable.

CONCLUSION

Characterized by its emphasis upon the transcendent and metaphysical, the spiritual is not only an ostensible record of the emotional reaction of the African in America, but the spiritual also contains aspects of a new and old worldview and forms crystallized. Noted composer Anton Dvorak applauded the monumental thematic range of the spiritual when he stated, concerning his *New World Symphony*, that ''the so-called plantation songs are indeed the most striking and appealing melodies that have been found this side of the water. There is nothing in the whole range of composition that cannot be supplied with themes from this source'' (quoted in C. O. Jackson, 27). The Afro-American spiritual exerts a special charm for the modern reader in its adept mixture of naiveté and sophistication.[4] In style, the Afro-American spiritual spans the range from the obvious through various levels of the ambiguous to the generally confounding. Taken collectively, the Afro-American spiritual is like a cabalistic text, a key to the human heart that represents the chakra of being, the source of the directive and corrective energy of existence, the generating and preserving life-force that emphasizes the metaphysical and the physical by showing how these two aspects of reality in their totality are one. Collectively, the spirituals serve as a large shield upon which is written the hieroglyphs for the preservation of human essence, each spiritual itself representing a key to the exploration of existence. As a profoundly verbal discipline operating in cooperation with, although independently enough of the magnificence of the music itself, the Afro-American spiritual establishes itself, along with the blues and other vernacular forms, as one of the prototypic layers of verbal enrichment for which later modes and generations of Afro-American poetry would draw.

NOTES

1. Elkin T. Sithole, ''Black Folk Music'' in Thomas Kochman, ed., *Rappin' and Stylin' Out*, University of Illinois Press, 1972, p. 70.

2. The intra-metaphoric figure is grounded in or based upon internal reality, signifying, for example, the light of faith, the light of the spirit, the light of the mind-soul force.

The extra-metaphoric figure is the generating figure or image grafted from the outer or physical world which is posited, transformed or molded into a reflection of the inner world.

3. See especially pages 11-13.

4. Among many examples, one may wish to think about the roots of the lyricism in poems like "A Black Man Talks of Reaping" by Arna Bontemps, "Song of the Son" and "Brown River Smile" by Jean Toomer.

WORKS CITED:

Abimbola, Wande. "Stylistic Repetition in Ifa Divination Poetry." Lagos: University of Lagos Mimeograph Series, n.d.

Allen, William Francis, et al. *Slave Songs of the United States.* New York: Books for Libraries Press, 1971.

Aptheker, Herbert. "The Negro Woman." *Masses and Mainstream.* (February, 1949): 10-11.

Bogan, Louise. *Achievement in American Poetry.* Chicago: Henry Regency and Company, 1951.

Bontemps, Arna. *American Negro Poetry.* New York: Hill and Wang, 1974.

Brewer, J. Mason. *American Negro Folklore.* Chicago: Quadrangle Books, 1968.

Courlander, Harold. *Negro Folk Music, U.S.A.* New York: Columbia University Press, 1963.

Dixon, Melvin. *Ride Out the Wilderness: Geography and Identity in Afro-American Literature.* Urbana: University of Illinois Press, 1987.

Drewal, Henry and Margaret. *Gelede: Art and Female Power Among the Yoruba.* Bloomington: Indiana University Press, 1983.

Egudu, Romanus. "The Art of Igbo Dance-Poems." *The Conch: A Sociological Journal of African Cultures and Literatures* 1 (1971): 76-81.

Empson, William. *Seven Types of Ambiguity.* New York: New Directions Press, 1966.

Epstein, Dena J. *Sinful Tunes and Spirituals.* Urbana: University of Illinois Press, 1977.

Finkelstein, Sidney. *Composer and Nation: The Folk Heritage of Music.* New York: International Publishers, 1960.

Holman, C. Hugh, et al. *A Handbook to Literature.* New York: The Odyssey Press, 1960.

Jackson, Clyde Owen. *The Songs of Our Years.* Exposition Press, 1968. Originally published in *Century Magazine,* 1895.

Jahn, Janheinz. *Neo-African Literature: A History of Black Writing.* New York: Grove Press, 1968.

James, Willis Laurence. "The Romance of the Negro Folk Cry in America." *Phylon* 1 (1955): 24-25.

Johnson, James Weldon and Johnson, J. Rosamond. *The Books of American Negro Spirituals.* New York: Viking Press, 1969.

Kennedy, Adrienne. *People Who Led to My Plays.* New York: Alfred A. Knopf, 1987.

Kennedy, R. Emmett. "The Poetic and Melodic Gifts of the Negro." *The Etude* (March, 1923): 159.

Krehbiel, Henry Edward. *Afro-American Folksongs.* New York: Fredrick Ungar Publishing Company, 1914.

Locke, Alain. *The Negro and His Music.* Port Washington: Kennikat Press, 1968.

Lovell, John. *Black Song: The Forge and The Flame: The Story of How The Afro-American Spiritual was Hammered Out.* New York: Collier-Macmillan, 1972.

Noss, Philip A. "Description of Gbaya Literary Art." In Dorson, Richard, ed. *African Folklore.* New York: Doubleday Anchor Books, 1972.

Orr, Leonard. *Problems and Poetics of the Non-Aristotelian Novel.* Lewisburg, PA: Bucknell University Press, 1991.

Sablosky, Irving. *What They Heard: Music in America, 1852-1881.* Baton Rouge: Louisiana State University Press, 1986.

Scheub, Harold. "The Art of Nongenile Mazithathu Zenan, A Caleka Ntsomi Performer." In Richard Dorson, ed., *African Folklore.* New York: Doubleday Anchor Books, 1972.

Southern, Eileen. *The Music of Black Americans: A History.* New York: W. W. Norton and Company, 1971.

Spaulding, Henry George. "Under the Palmetto." *Continental Monthly.* (August 1863): 196-200.

Staley, Sister Mary Roberta. "The Rhythmic Art of the American Negro Poet." Unpublished Master's Thesis, University of Notre Dame, 1933.

Thurman, Howard. *Deep River.* New York: Harper and Brothers, 1955.

Toomer, Jean. *Cane.* New York: Liveright, 1973.

Wagner, Jean. *Black Poets of the United States,* trans. by Kenneth Douglas. Urbana: University of Illinois Press, 1973.

Wiget, Andrew. *Instructor's Guide for the Heath Anthology of American Literature,* ed. by Judith Stanford. Lexington, MA: D. C. Heath and Company, 1990.

LYRICS OF SORROW, ALIENATION, AND DESOLATION _____

Lyrics of sorrow constitute a significant portion of the body of the Afro-American spirituals. Lyrics of sorrow can be further broken down into several subcategories such as lyrics of alienation, desperation, and desolation, all of which are included in this section. The lyrics of sorrow are, in general, a record of the anguish and ontological stress of early Afro-Americans. W.E.B. DuBois has referred to this stress as the weariness of the heart. The phrases of these songs are often so weighted with despair that they exhibit a haunting effect that is suggestive of one's having been plunged into an inexorable moral abyss. These lyrics frequently evoke terror in the soul that receives them. They record unhappiness, abuse, disappointment, disillusionment with humanity, longing, yearning, exile, loss, and beleaguerment.

The traditional African was very well aware that the world was inhabited by evil and that evil produced sorrow. However, this awareness notwithstanding, the extensive malevolence of the enterprise of the Atlantic slave trade struck the African with the power of a devastating thunderbolt. For surely, the Africans, belonging to one of the oldest parts of world culture had known slaves and slave systems, but they had not been familiar with a culture built upon the institution of bondage--and bondage into perpetuity, at that. Moreover, the Africans could not understand the reasons why enslavement had happened with such enormity of scale. Unable to answer this enigma, it is no wonder they could so readily identify with the crucified Jesus; for both had undergone cruel suffering and punishment without any apparent malevolence of character perpetrated by them upon their victimizers. It is from being confronted with this new and unfathomable experience that what Sterling Stuckey characterizes as the "unearthly moans and piercing shrieks,"[1] arises in Afro-American song. Thus, the enslaved Afro-Americans captured in words, handed down from generation to generation, their troubled wondering about their identity, their place in the universal order, and their relationship to the Great Force which decreed order in the cosmos. The one thing the Africans in America knew for certain was that they were now experiencing, face to face, some new aspect of the profound mystery of the world and of human existence.

Among those spirituals dominated by sorrowful language is a significant group of songs which are concerned specifically with the themes of alienation and desolation. Bereft of the communal autonomy and personal esteem that was the birthright granted through the traditional African social structure, and finding their spiritual autonomy under constant challenge, these songs reveal that it is often easy for the Africans in

_____

1. Sterling Stuckey, SLAVE CULTURE. New York: Oxford University Press, 1987, p. 3.

America to be overtaken by a feeling of alienation. This is true even though they can see that their personal situation is not unique or singular to their individual selves.

The lyrics of this group of songs often express the anguish of being distant from humanity, not simply of being distant from human beings. The world is cold and inhumane. It is an uncomfortable place in which to dwell. The reign of chaos sometimes makes it difficult to find anyone with whom a link can be forged to make an appeal even in prayer. Too often there is no spiritual company. Frequently, one has no sense of direction, and wanders about, burdened with humiliation, bewilderment, and the fear of absolute abandonment by the universe. To indicate the intensity of this chaotic state of being, hell and midnight are conjoined in one of the songs. "It's always midnight way down in hell," the song says. The anguish and desolation in the songs are derived certainly from the feeling of separation and exile from the African cultural home and from the very terrible knowledge that separation has perhaps become that by which their lives will perpetually be defined.

Adam's In the Garden Pinning Leaves

First time God called Adam,
Adam refused to answer,
Adam's in the garden laying low;
Second time God called Adam,
Adam refused to answer,
Adam's in the garden laying low.

Eve, where is Adam,
Oh, Eve, where is Adam?
Oh, Eve, where is Adam?
Lord, Adam's in the garden pinning leaves.

Next time God called Adam,
God hollered louder,
Adam in the garden pinning leaves;
Next time God called Adam,
God hollered louder,
Adam's in the garden pinning leaves.
You, Eve, can't see Adam,
You, Eve, can't see Adam,
Oh, Eve, can't see Adam,
Lord, Adam's behind the fig tree pinning leaves.   (BDWS)

All I Do, The Church Keep A-Grumbling

All I do, the church keep a-grumbling,
All I do, Lord, all I do.
All I do, the church keep a-grumbling,
All I do, I do, I do.

Try my best to serve my Master,
Try my best to serve my Lord;
Try my best to follow my Leader,
Try my best to serve my Lord;
Kneel and pray so the devil won't harm me,
Try my best to serve my Lord;
I'm going to cling to the ship of Zion.

Hallelujah,
Hallelujah,
Hallelujah.   (BANS)

All I Do, The People Keep A-Grumbling

All I do, the people keep a-grumbling,
All I do, all I do,
All I do, the people keep a-grumbling,
All I do, I do, all I do.

All I do, the doctor gives me over,
All I do, my wife's not satisfied,
All I do, I do, all I do.All I do in the days of trouble,
All I do, all I do, all I do,

All I do in the days trouble,
All I do, I do, I do, all I do.   (CD)

Am I Born To Die?

Dark was the night and cold the groun'
On which the Lord was laid:
His sweat like drops of blood ran down,
In agony he prayed
Am I born to die,
Am I born to die,
Am I born to die
To lay this body down.

Father, remove this bitter cup,
If such thy sacred will;
If not, content to drink it up
Thy pleasure to fulfill.

Go to the garden, sinner see
Those precious drops there flow,
The heavy load He bore for thee,
For there He lie so low.

Then leave of Him the cross to bear
Thy Father's will obey,
An' when temptations press thee near
Awake, to watch an' pray.

Am I born to die,
Am I born to die,
Am I born to die,
Am I born to die?   (Calhoun)

The Angels Done Bowed Down

O, the angels done bowed down,
O, the angels done bowed down,
O, the angels done bowed down,
O, yes, my Lord.

While Jesus was hanging upon the cross,
The angels kept quiet till God went off,
And the angels hung their harps on the willow trees,
To give satisfaction till God was pleased.

His soul went up on the pillar of cloud,
O, God he moved and the angels did bow,
Jehovah's sword was at His side,
On the empty air he began to ride.

"Go down angels to the flood,
Blow out the sun, turn the moon into blood!
Come back angels bolt the door,
The time that's been will be no more!"   (ANS)

Been A-Listening

Been a-listening all night long,
Been a-listening all night long,
Been a-listening all night long,
To hear some sinner pray.

Some say John the Baptist was nothing but a Jew.
But the Holy Bible tells us he was a preacher, too.
Go read the third of Matthew,
And read the chapter through;
It is the guide for Christians
And tells them what to do.

Been a-listening all night long,
Been a-listening all night long,
Been a-listening all night long,
To hear some sinner pray.   (FJS)

Before This Time Another Year

Before this time another year I may be gone,
Out in some lonely graveyard,
O, Lord, how long?

My mother's broke the ice and gone,
O, Lord, how long?
By the grace of God I'll follow on,
O, Lord, how long?

My father's broke the ice and gone,
O, Lord, how long?
By the grace of God I'll follow on,
O, Lord, how long?

My Savior's broke the ice and gone,
O, Lord, how long?
By the grace of God I'll follow on,
O, Lord, how long?   (ANS)

Be With Me

Be with me, Lord! Be with me!
Be with me, Lord! Be with me!

When I'm in trouble, be with me!
When I'm in trouble, be with me!

When I'm dying, be with me!
When I'm dying, be with me!

When I'm on my lonesome journey,
I want Jesus to be with me.   (ANS)

Blind Man Lying At The Pool

Blin' man lying at the pool,
Blin' man lying at the pool,
Blin' man lying at the pool,
Blin' man lying at the pool.

Lying there for to be heale',
Lying there for to be heale',
Lying there for to be heale',
Blin' man lying at the pool.

Crying: O Lord save me,
Crying: O Lord save me,
Crying: O Lord save me,
Blind man lying at the pool.

Save my weary soul,
Save my weary soul,
Save my weary soul,
Blind man lying at the pool.

Pray remember me,
Pray remember me,
Pray remember me,
Blind man lying at the pool.   (Calhoun)

The Blind Man Stood On The Road

O, the blind man stood on the road and cried,
O, the blind man stood on the road and cried,
Crying "O, my Lord, save-a me";
The blind man stood on the road and cried.
Crying that he might receive his sight,
Crying that he might receive his sight'
Crying "O, my Lord, save-a me";
The blind man stood on the road and cried.   (BANS)

By And By (1)

O, by and by, by and by,
I'm going to lay down my heavy load,
O, heavy load,
I know my robe's going to fit me well,
I tried it on at the gates of hell.

O, hell is deep and a dark despair,
I'm going to lay down my heavy load,
O, stop sinner and don't go there,
I'm going to lay down my heavy load.

O, by and by, by and by,
I'm going to lay down my heavy load,
O, heavy load.   (BANS)

By and By (2)

By and by we all shall meet again,
By and by we all shall meet again,
O, by and by, we all shall meet again,
And I wouldn't mind dying if dying was all.

After death got to fill an empty grave,
After death got to fill an empty grave,
After death got to fill an empty grave,
And I wouldn't mind dying if dying was all.   (ANSAS)

City Called Heaven

I am a poor pilgrim of sorrow.
I'm in this wide world along.
No hope in this world for tomorrow.
I'm trying to make heaven my home.

Sometimes I am tossed and driven.
Sometimes I don't know where to roam.
I've heard of a city called heaven.
I've started to make it my home.

My mother's gone on to pure glory.
My father's still walking in sin.
My sisters and brothers won't own me
Because I'm trying to get in.

Sometimes I am tossed and driven.
Sometimes I don't know where to roam,
But I've heard of a city called heaven,
And I've started to make it my home.   (Hayes)

Come Here Jesus If You Please

No harm have I done you on my knees,
No harm have I done you on my knees.

O, Lord, have mercy on poor me,
O, Lord, have mercy on poor me.

When you see me on my knees,
Come here, Jesus, if you please.   (ANS)

Come Here, Lord!

Come here, Lord!
Come here, Lord!
Sinner crying,
Come here, Lord!

O, little did I think He was so nigh,
He spoke and made me laugh and cry;
O, mourners, if you believe,

The grace of God you will receive;
Some seek God's face but don't seek it right,
They pray a little by day and none by night;
O, sinner, you had better pray,
For Satan's 'round you every day.

Come here, Lord!
Come here, Lord!
Sinner crying,
Come here, Lord!   (BANS)

Cruel Jews

Cruel Jews, just look at Jesus,
Cruel Jews, just look at Jesus,
Cruel Jews, just look at Jesus,
See how He died on Calvary.
He died one time, He'll die no more;
They nailed Him to the cross, just look at Jesus;
And the blood ran down, just look at Jesus;
They riveted His feet, just look at Jesus;
They hanged Him high, just look at Jesus;
And they stretched Him wide, just look at Jesus;
He died for me, He died for you;
O, the cruel Jews, done took my Jesus,
See how He died on Calvary.   (BDWS)

Death Ain't Nothin' But A Robber

Death ain't nothin' but a robber, don't you see.
Death ain't nothin' but a robber, don't you see.
Death came to my house, he didn't stay long,
I looked in the bed an' my mother was gone,
Death ain't nothin' but a robber, don't you see.

Death came to my house, he didn't stay long,
I looked in the bed an' my father was gone,
Death ain't nothin' but a robber, don't you see.

Death came to my house, he didn't stay long,
I looked in the bed an' my brother was gone,
Death ain't nothin' but a robber, don't you see.   (Cone)

Do Don't You Weep For The Baby

Do don't you weep for the baby,
My heart,
Oh, my heart.
Do don't you weep for the baby,
For my heart's so sorry.

Do don't you weep for the baby,
My heart,
Oh, my heart.

Do don't you weep for the baby,
For my heart's so sorry.

(Fisher)

Do, Lord Remember Me (1)

Do, Lord, remember me.
Do, Lord, remember me.
When I'm in trouble,
Do, Lord, remember me.

When I'm low down,
Do, Lord, remember me.
Oh, when I'm low down,
Do, Lord, remember me.

Don't have no cross,
Do, Lord, remember me.
Don't have no crown,
Do, Lord, remember me.

Do, Lord, remember me.
Do, Lord, remember me.

(BDWS)

Do, Lord Remember Me (2)

Do, Lord, O, do Lord,
Do remember me
Oh, Lordy
Do, Lord, O, do Lord,
Do remember me
Do Lord, O, do Lord
Do remember me
Way beyond the sea.

I've got a home in glory land
And you can have one, too
Oh, I've got a home in glory land
And you can have one, too
I've got a home in glory land
And you can have one, too
When I am called to go.

(Traditional)

Don't You Hear The Lambs A-Cryin'?

Don't you hear the lambs a-cryin'
Way over on the other shore?
Don't you hear the lambs a-cryin'?
Oh, Shepherd, feed my sheep.
One for Mary and one for Martha,
One for to make my heart rejoice.
Don't you hear the lambs a-cryin'
Way over on the other shore?

One for Paul and one for Silas,
One to make my heart rejoice.

Don't you hear the lambs a-cryin'
Way over on the other shore?   (St. Helena)

Down On Me

Down on me, down on me,
Looks like everybody in the whole round world
Is down on me.

Talk about me as much as you please,
I'll talk about you when I get on my knees;
Sometimes I'm up, sometimes I'm down,
Sometimes I'm almost on the ground;
Heaven's so high, I am so low,
Don't know if I'll ever get to heaven or no.

Looks like everybody in the whole round world
Is down on me.   (ANS)

The Downward Road Is Crowded

Oh, the downward road is crowded,
                crowded, crowded,

Oh, the downward road is crowded,
                with unbelieving souls.
Come, all ye wayward travellers,
And let us all join and sing,
The everlasting praises,
Of Jesus Christ our King.
Old Satan's mighty busy,
He follows me night and day,
And everywhere I'm appointed,
There's something in my way.

When I was a sinner
I loved my distance well,
But when I came to find myself,
I was hanging over Hell.

Oh, the downward road is crowded,
                crowded, crowded,
Oh, the downward road is crowded,
                with unbelieving souls.   (Hampton)

Every Hour In The Day

One cold freezing morning,
I will lay this body down,
I will pick up my cross,
And follow my Lord,
All around my Father's throne.

Every hour in the day, cry holy,
Cry holy, my Lord!

Every hour in the night, cry Jesus,
Oh, show me the crime I've done.   (ALLEN)

Ezekiel Said Here Was A Wheel In A Wheel

Wheel, wheel, wheel,
Oh, wheel, my Lord, a wheel, wheel!
Ezekiel said there was a wheel in a wheel,
O, the wheel in a wheel in a wheel.

I wonder where was Moses
        when the church burned down,
I wonder where was Moses
        when the church burned down;
Standing over Jordan with his head hung down.

I wonder where is Moses,
        He must be dead,
I wonder where is Moses,
        He must be dead;
Children of the Israelites crying for bread.

Dark clouds rising,
        It looks like rain,
Dark clouds rising,
        It looks like rain;
Sun drawing water from Emanuel's vein.

Get your bundle ready,
        I know it's time,
Get your bundle ready,
        I know it's time;
I can't tell winter from the summer time.

Wheel, wheel, wheel,
Oh, wheel, my Lord, a wheel, wheel!
Ezekiel said there was a wheel in a wheel,
O, the wheel in a wheel in a wheel.   (CD)

The Graveyard

Who's going to lay this body, Member,
O, shout glory,
And who's going to lay this body,
Oh, ring Jerusalem.

O, call all the members to the graveyard,
O, graveyard ought to know me,
O, grass grow in the graveyard,
O, I reel and I rock in the graveyard,
O, I walk and toss with Jesus,
My mother reel and toss with the fever,
I have a grandmother in the graveyard,
O, where do you think I find them?
I find them, Lord, in the graveyard

I reel, and I rock, and I'm going home,
O, repeat that story over.

Graveyard, you ought to know me,
Who's going to lay this body, Member,
O, shout glory,
And who's going to lay this body,
Oh, ring Jerusalem.   (ALLEN)

Hammering

Those cruel people! Those cruel people!
Those cruel people! Those cruel people!
They crucified my Lord, they crucified my Lord,
They crucified my Lord, they crucified my Lord;
They nailed Him to the tree, they nailed Him to the tree,
They nailed Him to the tree, they nailed Him to the tree;

You hear the hammer ringing, you hear the hammer ringing,
You hear the hammer ringing, you hear the hammer ringing;
The blood came trickling down, the blood came trickling down,
The blood came trickling down, the blood came trickling down.

Hammering   !Hammering!
Hammering   !Hammering!   (ANS)

The Hammer Keeps Ringing

Oh, the hammer keeps ringing
On somebody's coffin,
Oh, the hammer keeps ringing
On somebody's coffin,
Oh, the hammer keeps ringing
On somebody's coffin:
Good Lord, I know my time ain't long.   (Traditional)

Hard Trials

The foxes have holes in the ground,
The birds have nests in the air,
The Christians have a hiding place,
But we poor sinners have none.
Now ain't them hard trials, tribulations?

Ain't them hard trials?
I'm going to live with God!

Old Satan tempted Eve,
And Eve, she tempted Adam;
And that's why the sinner has to pray so hard
To get his sins forgiven.

Oh, Methodist, Methodist is my name,
Methodist till I die;

I'll be baptized on the Methodist side,
And a Methodist will I die.

Oh, Baptist, Baptist is my name,
Baptist till I die;
I'll be baptized on the Baptist side,
And a Baptist will I die,

While marching on the road,
A-hunting for a home,
You had better stop your differences
And travel on to God.

The foxes have holes in the ground,
The birds have nests in the air,
The Christians have a hiding place,
But we poor sinners have none.
Now ain't them hard trials, tribulations?
Ain't them hard trials?
I'm going to live with God!   (FJS)

He Arose

The Jews killed poor Jesus,
The Jews killed poor Jesus,
The Jews killed poor Jesus,
And laid him in a tomb.
He arose, he arose,
He arose and went to heaven in a cloud.

Then came down an angel,
Then came down an angel,
Then came down an angel,
He rolled away the stone.
He arose, he arose,
He arose and went to heaven in a cloud.

Then Mary she came weeping,
Then Mary she came weeping,
Then Mary she came weeping,
A-looking for her Lord.
He arose, he arose,
He arose and went to heaven in a cloud.   (FJS)

Hear The Lambs A-Crying

You hear the lambs a-crying,
Hear the lambs a-crying,
Hear the lambs a-crying,
Oh, shepherd, feed-a my sheep.

Our Savior spoke these words so sweet:
"Oh, shepherd, feed-a my sheep,
Said, "Peter if you love me, feed my sheep."
Oh, shepherd, feed-a my sheep.
Oh, Lord, I love Thee, Thou dost know;

Oh, shepherd, feed-a my sheep;
Oh, give me grace to love Thee more;
Oh, shepherd, feed-a my sheep.

I don't know what you want to stay here for,
For this vain world's no friend to grace;
If I only had wings like Noah's dove,
I'd fly away to the heavens above.
When I am in an agony,
When you see me, pity me,
For I am a pilgrim travelling on
The lonesome road where Jesus gone.

Oh, see my Jesus hanging high,
He looked so pale and bled so free;
Oh, don't you think it was a shame,
He hung three hours in dreadful pain.

You hear the lambs a-crying,
Hear the lambs a-crying,
Hear the lambs a-crying,
Oh, shepherd, feed-a my sheep   (Hampton)

Heaven Bells A-Ringing In My Soul

Nobody knows who I am,
Who I be till the coming day,
Nobody knows who I am,
Who I be till the coming day.
O the heaven bells ringing,
The sing-sol singing,
Heaven bells a-ringing in my soul.

Going away to see my Jesus,
Going away to see my Lord.
Walked around from door to door,
What to do I did not know.

I'm a-coming to the Lord,
Coming up till heaven I view.

Heaven's a high and lofty place,
But you can't get there,
If you ain't got grace.

Nobody knows who I am,
Who I be till the coming day,
Nobody knows who I am,
Who I be till the coming day.

The sing-sol singing.
Heaven bells a-ringing in my soul.   (Fisher)

He Never Said A Mumbling Word (1)

Oh, they whipped Him up the hill, up the hill, up the hill,
Oh, they whipped Him up the hill, and He never said a mumbling
    word,
Oh, they whipped Him up the hill, and He never said a mumbling
    word,
He just hung down His head, and He cried.

Oh, they crowned Him with a thorny crown, thorny crown, thorny
    crown,
Oh, they crowned Him with a thorny crown, and He never said a
    mumbling word,
Oh, they crowned Him with a thorny crown, and He never said a
    mumbling word,
He just hung down His head, and He cried.

Well, they nailed Him to the cross, to the cross, to the cross,
Well, they nailed Him to the cross, and He never said a mumbling
    word,
Well, they nailed Him to the cross, and He never said a mumbling
    word,
He just hung down His head, and He cried.

Well, they pierced Him in the side, in the side, in the side,
Well, they pierced Him in the side, and the blood came
    a-twinkling down,
Well, they pierced Him in the side, and the blood came
    a-twinkling down,
Then He hung down His head, and He died.   (Hayes)

He Never Said A Mumbling Word (2)

They led him to Pilate's bar,
They led him to Pilate's bar;
They all cried, "Crucify Him,"
They all cried, "Crucify Him,"
But he never said a mumbling word.

They nailed Him to the tree,
They nailed Him to the tree;
They pierced Him in the side,

They pierced Him in the side;
But he never said a mumbling word.

He hung His head and died,
He hung His head and died;
They laid Him in the tomb,
They laid Him in the tomb,
Wasn't that a pity and a shame,
Wasn't that a pity and a shame.

But he never said a mumbling word.
Not a word, not a word, not a word, not a word.   (ANS) (Variant)

Holy Bible

Holy Bible, Holy Bible,
Holy Bible, book divine, book divine;
O, what weeping, O, what weeping,
O, what weeping over me, over me;

Weeping Mary, weeping Mary,
Weep no more, weep no more.

Before I'd be a slave, I'd be buried in my grave,
And go home to my Father and be saved.

Doubting Thomas, doubting Thomas,
Doubting Thomas, doubt no more, doubt no more;
Great Jehovah, Great Jehovah,
Great Jehovah, over all, over all.

Before I'd be a slave, I'd be buried in my grave,
And go home to my Father and be saved.   (ANS)

Holy, Holy, You Promised To Answer Prayer

Holy, holy, you promised to answer prayer,
Holy, holy, you promised to answer prayer,
In that morning when the Lord said holy.

John! John! this is a barren land,
John! John! this is a barren land;
Who locked, Who locked,
Who locked the lion's jaw?
Lord, Lord, this is a needed time.

Holy, holy, you promised to answer prayer,
Holy, holy, you promised to answer prayer,
In that morning when the Lord said holy.   (CD)

How Long?

When the clouds hang heavy and it looks like rain,
     O Lord, how long?
Well the sun's drawing water from every vein,
     O Lord, how long?

About this time another year
     I may be gone
Within some lonely graveyard-
     O Lord, how long?

If I had prayed when I was young,
     O Lord, how long?
Well, I would not've had such a hard race to run.
     O Lord, how long?   (R.E. Kennedy)

I Been A-Listening

I been a-listening all the night time,
Been a-listening all the day,
Been a-listening all the night time,
For to hear some sinner pray.

One day when I was walking,
Along that lonesome road,
My Savior spoke unto me
And filled my heart with love.
Oh, some say John the Baptist
Was nothing but a Jew,
But the holy Bible testifies
Saint John was a preacher too.

When I was a sinner,
I love my distance well,
But when I came to find out
I was hanging over hell.
When I was a turn-back,
I sinned both night and day,
But now I'm a Christian
I'll shout myself away.   (BDWS)

I've Been 'Buked

I've been 'buked and I've been scorned,
  O, Lord--
I've been 'buked and I've been scorned,
  Children--
I've been 'buked and I've been scorned,
I've been talked about sure's you're born.

But, ain't goin' to lay my 'ligion down,
  No, Lord--
Ain't goin' to lay my 'ligion down,
  Children--
No, ain't goin' to lay my 'ligion down,
Ain't goin' to lay my 'ligion down.   (Traditional)

I Can't Stand The Fire

I can't stand the fire,
Dear sister, I can't stand the fire,
While Jordan there rolls so swift.
I can't stand the fire,
Dear sister, I can't stand the fire,

O Lord, I can't stand the fire,
While Jordan there rolls so swift.   (ALLEN)

I Couldn't Hear Nobody Pray

In the valley on my knees!
With my burden and my Savior!
And I couldn't hear nobody pray,
O, way down yonder by myself,
And I couldn't hear nobody pray.
Chilly waters in the Jordan!
Crossing over into Canaan!
And I couldn't hear nobody pray,
O, way down yonder by myself,
And I couldn't hear nobody pray.

Hallelujah! Troubles over!
In the kingdom with my Jesus!
And I couldn't hear nobody pray,
O, way down yonder by myself,
And I couldn't hear nobody pray.   (Hampton)

I Feel Like My Time Ain't Long

Went to the graveyard the other day,
I looked at the place where my mother lay;
Sometimes I'm up, sometimes I'm down,
And sometimes I'm almost on the ground,
Mind out, my brother, how you walk on the cross,
Your foot might slip and your soul get lost.

I feel like, I feel like,
I feel like my time ain't long;
I feel like, I feel like,
I feel like my time ain't long.   (ANS)

I Love My Blessed Savior

I love my blessed Savior,
And sorry when he died;
It hurt me to my heart
To see Him crucified.

He cried how long,
He cried how long,
He cried how long,
For my Lord told me so.

When Jesus was hangin' on the cross,
And the Jews was standin' round,
One picked up the sword and plunged it
        in his side,
And the blood came tricklin' down.

Then they said it wasn't no sun,
And one said it wasn't no moon,
And one said it wasn't no stain,
And the whole world was silent.
Silent, silent, silent,

For the space of a hour and a half;
God called the welcome soldiers
To take home the welcome Soul.

Then Joseph begged for his body,
And the body was given to him,
He wrapped it up in a linen cloth
And buried Him in the ground.   (St. Helena)

I'm All Wore Out A-Toiling For The Lord

I'm all wore out a-toiling for the Lord,
My bones done tremble on the brink of the grave,
O Jerusalem is nigh,
And I ain't a bit afraid.

Come on, sinner,
There is time to save.
Come on, sinner, come!
Come on, sinner, come!
Oh, oh,
Come on, sinner, come!

I'm all wore out a-toiling for the Lord,
My days are numbered and I'm ready to go,
In the evening time
I pray to see the open door.

Come on, sinner,
There is time to save.
Come on, sinner, come!
Come on, sinner, come!
Oh, oh,
Come on sinner, come!   (Fisher)

I'm A-Rolling (1)

I'm a-rolling, I'm a-rolling,
I'm a-rolling through an unfriendly world;
I'm a rolling, I'm a-rolling,
I'm a-rolling through an unfriendly world.

O, brothers, won't you help me to pray?
O, sisters, won't you help me in the service of the Lord?

I'm a-rolling, I'm a-rolling,
I'm a-rolling through an unfriendly world;
I'm a rolling, I'm a-rolling,
I'm a-rolling through an unfriendly world.   (BANS)

I'm A Rolling (2)

I'm a-rolling,
     I'm a-rolling,
I'm a-rolling through an unfriendly world.

O brothers, won't you help me to pray?
O sisters, won't you help me to pray?
O preachers, won't you help me to fight?
Won't you help me in the service of the Lord?
I'm a-rolling,
        I'm a-rolling,
I'm a-rolling through an unfriendly world.   (FJS)

I'm Going To Tell God All My Troubles

I'm going to tell God all my troubles,
I'm going to tell God all my troubles,

I'm going to tell God all my troubles,
When I get home.

I'm going to tell God how you treat' me,
I'm going to tell God how you treat' me,
I'm going to tell God how you treat' me,
When I get home.   (Traditional)

I'm Going Where There Ain't No More Dying

Joshua fought the battle 'round Jerico's wall,
I'm going where there ain't no more dying;
And he kicked a brick out of Satan's hall,
I'm going where there ain't no more dying;
Children, A-amen
Children, A-amen
I'm going where there ain't no more dying.

And the second time around the sun stopped sitting,
The sun stopped sitting down;
The third time around the children were a-blowing,
The children were a-blowing strong;
The fourth time around the wall came a-tumbling,
The wall came a-tumbling down.

Children, A-amen,
Children, A-amen,
I'm going where there ain't no more dying.   (BDWS)

I'm In Trouble

I'm in trouble, Lord,
        I'm in trouble,
I'm in trouble, Lord,
        Trouble about my grave.

Sometimes I weep,
        Sometimes I mourn;
I'm in trouble about my grave;
Sometimes I can't do neither one,
I'm in trouble about my grave.   (ALLEN)

I'm Troubled In The Mind

I am a-troubled in the mind,
O, I am a-troubled in the mind,

I ask my Lord what shall I do,
I am a-troubled in the mind.

I'm a-troubled in the mind,
What you doubt for?
I'm a-troubled in the mind.

(ALLEN)

I Must Walk My Lonesome Valley

I must walk my lonesome valley,
I got to walk it for myself,
Nobody else can walk it for me,
I got to walk it for myself.

I must go and stand my trial,
I got to stand it for myself,
Nobody else can stand it for me,
I got to stand it for myself.

Jesus walked his lonesome valley,
He had to walk it for himself,
Nobody else could walk it for him,
He had to walk it for himself.

(ANS)

In This Land

Lord, help the poor and needy,
In this land, in this land,
Lord, help the poor and needy,
In this land, in this land.

In that great getting-up morning,
We shall face another sun.

Lord, help the widows and the orphans,
Lord, help the motherless children,
Lord, help the hypocrite members,
Lord, help the long tongue liars.

In that great getting-up morning,
We shall face another sun.

(ANS)

Is Massa Going To Sell Us Tomorrow?

Mammy, is massa going to sell us tomorrow?
Yes, yes, yes!
Mammy, is massa going to sell us tomorrow?
Yes, yes, yes.
Mammy, is massa going to sell us tomorrow?

Yes, yes, yes!
Oh watch, watch and pray.

Mammy, don't you grieve after me,
No, no, no!
Mammy, oh, don't you grieve after me,
No, no, no!
Mammy, oh, don't you grieve after me,

No, no, no!
Oh, watch, watch and pray.   (Fisher)

Is There Anybody Here?

Is there anybody here who loves my Jesus?
Anybody here who loves my Lord?
I want to know if you love my Jesus;
I want to know if you love my Lord.

This world's a wilderness of woe,
So let us all to glory go;
Religion is a blooming rose,
And none but them who feel it know;
When I was blind and could not see,
King Jesus brought the light to me;
When every star refuse to shine,
I know King Jesus will be mine.   (ANSAS)

I Stood Outside The Gate

I stood outside the gate;
They would not let me in--me in.
I prayed to my good Lord,
To cleanse me from all sin--all sin.

Lord Jesus Christ, I seek to find,
Pray tell me where He dwells-He dwells.
Oh, you go down in yonder fold
An' search among the sheep--the sheep.
There you will find Him, I am told,
He's where he loves to be--to be.
An' if I find Him how'll I know
Round any other man--other man?

He has Salvation on His brow,
He has a wounded han'--wounded han'.
I thank you for your advice--
I'll find Him if I can--if I can.   (Grissom)

It's Me, O, Lord

It's me, it's me, it's me, O Lord,
Standing in the need of prayer,
It's me, it's me, it's me, O Lord,
Standing in the need of prayer.

Tain't my mother or my father,
But it's me, O, Lord,
Standing in the need of prayer.

Tain't my deacon or my leader,
But it's me, O, Lord,
Standing in the need of prayer.   (BANS)

I've Been In The Storm So Long

I've been in the storm so long,
I've been in the storm so long, children,
I've been in the storm so long,
Oh, give me little time to pray.

Oh, let me tell my mother
How I come along,
Oh, give me little time to pray,
With a hung down head and a aching heart,
Oh, give me little time to pray.

Oh, when I get to heaven,
I'll walk all about,
Oh, give me little time to pray,

There'll be nobody there to turn me out,
Oh, give me little time to pray.

I've been in the storm so long,
I've been in the storm so long, children,
I've been in the storm so long,
Oh, give me little time to pray.   (Fisher)

I've Been Listening All The Night Long

I've been listening all the night long,
Been listening all the day,
I've been listening all the night long,
To hear some sinner pray.

Some said that John the Baptist,
Was nothing but a Jew,
But the Bible doth inform us,
That he was a preacher too.

Go read the fifth of Matthew,
And read the chapter through.
It is the guide to Christians,
And tells them what to do.

There was a search in heaven,
And all the earth around,
John stood in sorrow hoping
That a Savior might be found.

I've been listening all the night long,
Been listening all the day,
I've been listening all the night long,
To hear some sinner pray.   (Hampton)

I Want To Go Home

There's no rain to wet you,
O, yes, I want to go home,
Want to go home.

There's no sun to burn you,
O, yes, I want to go home;
There're no hard trials,
O, yes, I want to go home;
There're no whips a-cracking,
O, yes, I want to go home;
There's no tribulation,
O, yes, I want to go home;
There's no more slavery in the kingdom,
O, yes, I want to go home;
There're no evil-doers in the kingdom,
O, yes, I want to go home;
All is gladness in the kingdom,
O, yes, I want to go home.   (ALLEN)

I Wish I Had Died In Egypt Land

"O, I can't stay away,
"I can't stay away,
"I can't stay away,
"I wish I had died in the Egypt land."

Children grumbled on the way,
"Wish I had died in the Egypt land";
Children they forgot to pray,
"Wish I had died in the Egypt land."

Now they wept, now they moaned,
"Wish I had died in the Egypt land";
Then they turned around and groaned,
"Wish I had died in the Egypt land."

Yes, the children they did right,
"Wish I had died in the Egypt land";
When they went and had that fight,
"Wish I had died in the Egypt land."   (ANS)

The Jews, They Took Our Savior

The Jews, they took our Savior
And they buried him in a sepulchre,
They placed the watchman 'side His grave
For to see Him when He rose,

I believe they said,
"To see Him when He Rose."

Go low down in the valley,
Go low down in the valley,
Go low down in the valley,
Good Lord,
For to easy my trouble in mind,
I believe they said,
"To easy my trouble in mind."

A-yonder comes ole Satan
With a black Bible under his arm,
He said unto ole Moses:
"Now one half of them people is mine,
"One half of them people is mine."
I believe he said,
"One half of them people is mine."   (Fisher)

John, John, Of The Holy Order

John, John, with the holy order,
Sitting on the golden altar;
John, John, with the holy order,
Sitting on the golden altar,
To view the promised land.

O, Lord, I weep, I mourn,
Why don't you move so slow?
I'm hunting for some guardian angel,
Gone along before.
Mary and Martha,
Feed my lamb, feed my lamb,
Simon Peter, feed my lamb,
A-sitting on the golden order.

John, John, with the holy order,
Sitting on the golden altar;
John, John, with the holy order,
Sitting on the golden altar
To view the promised land.   (Allen)

The Last Supper

Jesus was a-sittin' at the last Passover.
John, he rested upon His shoulder.
Jesus said one word that seemed to blight.
He said, "One of you goin' to betray me to-night."
Mark cried out,"Lord, is it I?"
James cried out, "Lord, is it I?"
Then Jesus said,
"A-look an' see him that dip in the dish with me."

My time is come, my time is come,
O, my time is come!

Then Jesus with His disciples Simon-Peter
And others went into the garden.
Jesus said to them,
"Tarry ye here, while I go and pray."
Then when Jesus on returning found his disciples asleep, He said:
"Simon! Simon!
"Sleep-est thou?
"Simon! Coulds't thou not watch one hour?
"Simon! The spirit is willing but the flesh is weak."

My time is come, my time is come,
Oh, my time is come,
I'm boun' to pay the debt I owe.   (Hayes)

Listen To The Lambs

Listen to the lambs,
Listen to the lambs,
Listen to the lambs all a-crying,
I want to go to heaven when I die.

Come on sister with your ups and downs,
Angels waiting for to give you a crown;
Come on sister, and don't be ashamed,
Angels waiting to write your name;
Mind out brother how you walk on the cross,
Foot might slip and your soul get lost.
Listen to the lambs,
Listen to the lambs,
Listen to the lambs all a-crying,
I want to go to heaven when I die.   (Hampton)

Look-a How They Done My Lord

Look-a how they done my Lord,
Look-a how they done my Lord,
Look-a how they done my Lord,
He never said a mumbling word,
Not a word, not a word;
The blood it came twinkling down.

They saw him when he rose and fell,
They carried him to Calvary;
He had to wear a thorny crown,
They carried him to Pilate's Hall;
They licked him with violence,
And they nailed him to the tree.

Thomas said I won't believe,
Thomas said I won't believe;
He said Thomas saw my hand,
He said Thomas see my hand;
He bowed his head and died,
He bowed his head and died.

Look-a how they done my Lord,
Look-a how they done my Lord.   (BANS)

Look Away In The Heaven

Look away, look away, look away,
Look away, look away in the heaven,
Look away, look away, look away,
Look away, look away in the heaven.

One of these days, I am going away,
Look away in the heaven!
I won't be back till Judgement Day,
Look away in the heaven!

There ain't but one thing grieves my mind,
Look away in the Heaven!
The Christian going to heaven
Leave the sinner behind.

Look away, look away, look away,
Look away, look away in the heaven,
Look away, look away, look away,
Look away, look away in the heaven.   (CD)

Lord, I Cannot Stay Here By Myself

Lord, I cannot stay here by myself, by myself,
Lord, I cannot stay here by myself, by myself.

My mother has gone and left me here,
My father has gone and left me here,
I'm going to weep like a willow
And mourn like a dove,
Oh Lord, I cannot stay here by myself.

Yes, I am a poor little motherless child,
Yes, I am a poor little child of God
In this world alone,
Oh Lord, I cannot stay here by myself.

I got my ticket at the low depot,
Low depot,
Yes I got my ticket at the low depot,
Low depot,

Yes, I got my ticket at the low depot,
Oh Lord, I cannot stay here by myself.   (BDWS)

Lord, I Wish I Had A-Come

Lord, I wish I had a-come

Lord, I wish I had a-come   when you called me,

                                       when you called me,

Lord, I wish I had a-come

                              when you called me,

Sitting by the side of my Jesus,
Way over in the heavens,
Way over in the heavens,
Way over in the heavens,
Sitting by the side of my Jesus.

There's no temptations in the heavens,
There's no temptations in the heavens,
My father and my mother in the heavens,
My father and my mother in the heavens,
Sitting by the side of my Jesus,
Way over in the heavens,
Way over in the heavens,
Way over in the heavens,
Sitting by the side of my Jesus.

                                                        (FJS)

Mary Had A Baby, Yes, Lord

Mary had a baby,
Yes, Lord!
Mary had a baby,
Yes, Lord;
Mary had a baby,
Yes, Lord!
The people keep a-coming
And the train done gone.

Mary had a baby,
Yes, Lord!
What did she name him?
She named him King Jesus,
She named him Mighty Counselor.
Where was he born?
Born in a manger,
Yes, Lord.

Mary had a baby,
Yes, Lord!
The people keep a-coming
And the train done gone.

                                                        (BANS)

Master Going To Sell Us Tomorrow

Mother, is master going to sell us tomorrow?
Yes, yes, yes!
Mother, is master going to sell us tomorrow?
Yes, yes, yes!
Mother, is master going to sell us tomorrow?
Yes, yes, yes,
O, watch and pray!

Going to sell us down in Georgia?
Yes, yes, yes!
Going to sell us down in Georgia?

Yes, yes, yes!
O, watch and pray!

Farewell, mother, I must leave you.
Yes, yes, yes!
Farewell, mother, I must leave you.
Yes, yes, yes!
O, watch and pray!

Mother, don't grieve after me.
No, no, no!
Mother, don't grieve after me
No, no, no!
O, watch and pray!

Mother, I'll meet you in heaven.
Yes, my child!
Mother, I'll meet you in heaven.
Yes, my child!
O, watch and pray!

                                                        (Hampton)

May Be The Last Time

I don't know, I don't know, I don't know;
May be the last time, I don't know,
I don't know.

May be the last time you'll hear me pray,
May be the last time, I don't know;
May be the last time you'll hear me pray,
May be the last time, I don't know.

I don't know, I don't know, I don't know;
May be the last time, I don't know,
I don't know.

                                                        (CD)

Most Done Travelling

Oh, my mother's in the road,
Most done travelling,
My mother's in the road,
Most done travelling,
My mother's in the road,
Most done travelling;
I'm bound to carry my soul to the Lord.
I'm bound to carry my soul to Jesus.

Oh, my sister's in the road,
Oh, my brother's in the road,
Oh, the preacher's in the road,
All the members are in the road,
Most done travelling;
I'm bound to carry my soul to the Lord.
I'm bound to carry my soul to Jesus.

                                                        (Hampton)

Motherless Children Have A Hard Time

Motherless children have a hard time
when mother's gone;

Motherless children have a hard time
when mother's gone;

Father'll do the best he can,
He don't really understand;
Motherless children have a hard time
when mother's gone.

Mother said I must obey
when mother's gone;

Mother said I must obey
when mother's gone;

Mother said I must obey,
Let religion have her sway;
Motherless children have a hard time
when mother's gone.

Mother told me I must pray
when mother's gone;

Mother told me I must pray
when mother's gone;

Mother told me I must pray,
Keep my feet in Jesus' way;
Motherless children have a hard time
when mother's gone.   (CD)

My Body Rocked A Long Fever

Wait, my brother, better true believe,
Better true,
Be a long time getting over cross;
Wait, my sister, better true believe,
And you'll get up to heaven at last.
O, my body rocked a long fever,
O! with a pain in the head!
I wish I'd been in the kingdom,
To sit along side my Lord!

By the help of the Lord we rise up again,
O, the Lord he comforts the sinner;
By the help of the Lord we rise up again,
And we'll get to heaven at last.

O, my body rocked a long fever,
O! with a pain in the head!
I wish I'd been in the kingdom,
To sit along side my Lord!   (ALLEN)

My Soul Wants Something That's New

My soul wants something that's new, that's new,
My soul wants something that's new, that's new,
My soul wants something that's new.

Dark was the night and cold the ground,
On which the Lord was laid,
His sweat like drops of blood ran down,
In agony He prayed.

Was it for the crimes that I had done,
He groaned upon the tree?
Amazing pity, grace unknown,
And love beyond degree.

My soul wants something that's new, that's new,
My soul wants something that's new, that's new,
My soul wants something that's new.   (Hampton)

My Time Is Come

Jesus was settin' at the last Passover,
John he rested upon his shoulder,
He spoke one word and it seemed to blight,
He said one of you will betray me tonight.

My time is come,
O, my time is come;
My time is come,
I'm bound to pay the debt I owe.

Mark cried out, Lord is it I?
Luke cried out, Lord is it I?
Jesus said look and see,
He that sup in the dish with me.

The cruel Jews they took my Lord,
They bound Him with a purple cord.
They led Him up to Pilate's Hall,
The council met and the roll was called.

Pilate's wife she had dream,
The innocent Lam' I never seen,

Bring me water to wash my han',
I will not be guilty of the innocent Lam'.   (St. Helena)

My Way Is Cloudy (1)

O, brethren, my way,
My way's cloudy, my way,
Go send them angels down,
O, brethren.

There's fire in the east,
And fire in the west,
There's fire among them Methodists,
O, send them angels down.

Satan's mad
And I am glad,

He missed the soul
He thought he had.

Oh, send them angels down,
My way's cloudy, my way,
Go send them angels down,
O, brethren,
Send them angels down.   (BANS)

My Way's Cloudy (2)

Oh! brethren, my way, my way's cloudy,
                                        my way,
Go send them angels down,
Oh! brethren, my way, my way's cloudy,
                                        my way,
Go send them angels down.

There's fire in the east and fire in the west
And fire among the Methodists;
Old Satan's mad and I am glad,
He missed the soul he thought he had.
I'll tell you now as I told you before
To the promised land I'm bound to go;
This is the year of Jubilee,
The Lord has come to set us free.

Oh! brethren, my way, my way's cloudy,
                                        my way,
Go send them angels down.
Oh! brethren, my way, my way's cloudy,
                                        my way,
Go send them angels down.   (FJS)

Nobody Knows The Trouble I Feel

Nobody knows the trouble I feel,
Nobody knows but Jesus,
Nobody knows the trouble I feel,
    Glory in-a my soul.

Sometimes I'm up, sometimes I'm down,
    Glory in-a my soul,
Sometimes I'm almost to the groun',
    Glory in-a my soul.

One mornin' I was walkin' along,
    Glory in-a my soul,
I heard a noise, I saw no one,
    Glory in-a my soul.

One day as I was walkin' roun',
    Glory in-a my soul,
I saw some grapes was hangin' down,
    Glory in-a my soul.

I picked some fruit and sucked the juice,
   Glory in-a my soul,
The juice was sweet as the honey comb,
   Glory in-a my soul.

Satan he whisper in my ear,
   Glory in-a my soul,
Said he done broke my kingdom down,
   Glory in-a my soul.

By the grace of God I rise again,
   Glory in-a my soul,
By the grace of God I rise again,
   Glory in-a my soul.

            (St. Helena)

Nobody Knows The Trouble I See (1)

Nobody knows the trouble I see,
Lord,
Nobody knows the trouble I see,
Nobody knows the trouble I see,
Lord,
Nobody knows like Jesus.

   Brothers, will you pray for me?
   Sisters, will you pray for me?
   Mothers, will you pray for me?
   Preachers, will you pray for me?

Nobody knows the trouble I see,
Lord,
Nobody knows the trouble I see,
Nobody knows the trouble I see,
Lord,
Nobody knows like Jesus.

   Sometimes I'm up.
   Sometimes I'm down.
     Oh, yes, Lord;
   Sometimes I'm almost to the ground
     Oh, yes, Lord.

Nobody knows the trouble I see,
Lord,
Nobody knows the trouble I see,
Nobody knows the trouble I see,

Lord,
Nobody knows like Jesus.

            (Traditional)

Nobody Knows The Trouble I've Seen (2)

Oh, nobody knows the trouble I've seen,
Nobody knows but Jesus,
Nobody knows the trouble I've seen,
Glory Hallelujah!

Sometimes I'm up, sometimes I'm down;
Oh, yes Lord;
Sometimes I'm almost to the ground,
Oh, yes, Lord.

Although you see me going along so,
I have my trials here below;
One day I was walking along,
The element opened, and the Love came down;

I shall never forget that day,
When Jesus washed my sins away.

Oh, nobody knows the trouble I've seen,
Nobody knows but Jesus,
Nobody knows the trouble I've seen.
Glory Hallelujah!   (Hampton) (Variant)

Nobody Knows Who I Am

O, nobody knows who I am,
Who I am till the judgment morning!
Heaven bells a-ringing, the saints all a-singing,
Heaven bells a-ringing in my soul.

Want to go to Heaven, want to go right,
Want to go to Heaven all dressed in white;
Don't want to stumble, don't want to fall,
Want to be in Heaven when the roll is called;
If you don't believe that I've been redeemed,
Follow me down to Jordan's stream.   (ANSAS)

Now We Take This Feeble Body

Now we take this feeble body,
And we carry it to the grave,
And we all leave it there,
Hallelujah, hallelujah, hallelujah.

Now we take the dear old Father,
And we carry him to the grave,
And we all leave him there,
Hallelujah, hallelujah, hallelujah.

Now we lift our mournful voices,
As we gather 'round the grave,
And we weep as we sing,
Hallelujah, hallelujah, hallelujah.   (FJS)

Oh Lord, Have Mercy On Me

Yes, we'll all fall on our knees,
And face the rising sun,
Yes, we'll all fall on our knees,

And face the rising sun,
Oh Lord, have mercy on me.

If we never pray together anymore,
If we never pray together anymore,
Yes, we'll fall on our knees,
And face the rising sun;
Oh Lord, have mercy on me.

If we never meet together anymore,
If we never groan together anymore,
If we never preach together anymore,
Yes, we'll fall on our knees,

And face the rising sun;
Oh, Lord have mercy on me.   (BDWS)

Oh, Po' Little Jesus

Oh, po' little Jesus,
Oh, po' little Jesus,
Oh, po' little Jesus,
This world gonna break Your heart,
There'll be no place to lay your head, my Lord.

Oh, Mary she bow down and cry,
Oh, Mary she bow down and cry,
For there's no place to lay His head.

Oh, po' little Jesus,
Oh, po' little Jesus.

Come down all you holy angels,
Sing 'roun' Him with your golden harps,
For some day He will die to save this world.

Oh, po' little Jesus,
Oh, po' little Jesus.   (L-G)

O, Lord, I'm Hungry

O, Lord, I'm hungry,
I want to be fed,
O, Lord, I'm hungry,
I want to be fed,
O, feed me, Jesus, feed me,
Feed me all my days,
O, feed me all the days of my life,
O, feed me, Jesus, feed me,
Feed me all my days,
O, feed me all the days of my life.

O, Lord, I'm naked,
I want to be clothed,
O, Lord, I'm naked,
I want to be clothed,

O, clothe me, Jesus, clothe me,
Clothe me all my days,
O, clothe me all the days of my life,
O, clothe me, Jesus, clothe me,
Clothe me all my days,
O, clothe me all the days of my life.

O, Lord, I'm sinful,
I want to be saved,
O, Lord, I'm sinful,
I want to be saved,
O, save me, Jesus, save me,
Save me all my days,
O, save me all the days of my life,
O, save me, Jesus, save me,
Save me all my days,
O, save me all the days of my life.   (ANS)

O, Wretched Man

O, wretched man that I am,
O, wretched man that I am,
O, wretched man that I am,
O, who will deliver poor me?
I'm bowed down with a burden of woe,
I'm bowed down with a burden of woe,
I'm bowed down with a burden of woe,
O, who will deliver poor me?   (ANS)

Poor Me

I'm sometimes up, I'm sometimes down,
Trouble will bury me down;
But still my soul feels heavenly bound,
Trouble will bury me down;
O, brethren, poor me, poor me,
Trouble will bury me down;

Hallelujah to the Lamb!
Trouble will bury me down;
The Lord is on the giving hand,
Trouble will bury me down;
O, brethren poor me, poor me,
Trouble will bury me down;

Sometimes I think I'm ready to drop,
Trouble will bury me down;
But thank my Lord, I do not stop,
Trouble will bury me down;
O, brethren, poor me, poor me,
Trouble will bury me down.   (ANS)

Rain Fall And Wet Becca Lawton

Rain fall and wet Becca Lawton,
Oh, rain fall and wet Becca Lawton,
Oh! Brother, cry holy!

Do, Becca Lawton, come to me yonder,
Say, brother Tony, what shall I do now?
Beat back holy and rock salvation.

Rain fall and wet Becca Lawton
Oh, rain fall and wet Becca Lawton,
Oh! Brother, cry holy!

(ALLEN)

Rough And Rolling Sea

Farewell, farewell to my only child,
Like a rough and a rolling sea,
Like a rough and a rolling sea.

The lightings flashed,
And the thunders rolled,
Like a rough and rolling sea.

The storms beat high,
And the winds blew fierce,
Like a rough and rolling sea.

(Hampton)

Scandalize My Name

I met my mother the other day,
I gave her my right hand,
An' jus' as soon as ever my back was turned,
She scandalize' my name,
Scandalize' my name,
Scandalize' my name,
No, no. Scandalize' my name.

I met my brother the other day;
I met my deacon the other day;
I met my elder the other day,
I gave him my right hand,
An' jus' as soon as ever my back was turned,
He scandalize' my name,
Scandalize' my name,
Scandalize' my name,
No, no. Scandalize' my name.

(Calhoun)

Shall I Die?

Believer, O, shall I die?
O, my army, shall I die?
Jesus died, shall I die?
Died on the cross, shall I die?

Die, die, die, shall I die?
Jesus is there a-coming, shall I die?
Run for to meet him, shall I die?
Weep like a weeper, shall I die?
Mourn like a mourner, shall I die?
Cry like a crier, shall I die?   (Allen)

Shepherd, Shepherd

Shepherd, Shepherd, where'd you lose your sheep?
Shepherd, Shepherd, where'd you lose your sheep?
Shepherd, Shepherd, where'd you lose your sheep?
O, the sheep all gone astray,
The sheep all gone astray.

Shepherd, Shepherd, where'd you lose your lambs?
Shepherd, Shepherd, where'd you lose your lambs?
Shepherd, Shepherd, where'd you lose your lambs?
O, the sheep all gone astray,
The sheep all gone astray.

I pray to the Lord to bring them back someday,
I pray to the Lord to bring them back someday,
I pray to the Lord to bring them back someday,
O, the sheep all gone astray,
The sheep all gone astray.   (ANS)

Sister Mary Had-a But One Time

Sister Mary had-a but one child,
Born in Bethlehem.
And-a every time-a the-a baby cried,
She'd-a rocked Him in the weary land.
O, three wise men-a to Jerusalem came,
They'd travelled very far.
They said, "Where is He born King of the Jews
For we have seen His star?"

King Herod's heart was troubled,
He marvelled but his face was grim.
He said, "Tell me where the Child may be found,
I'll go and worship Him,
I'll go and worship Him."

Sister angel appeared to Joseph,
And gave him-a this-a command,
"Arise ye, take your wife and child,
Go flee into Egypt land.
For yonder comes old herod,
A wicked man and bold.

He's slayin' all the children
From six to eight days old."
Sister Mary had-a but one child,
Born in Bethlehem,
And-a every time-a the-a baby cried,

She'd-a rocked Him in the weary land,
She'd-a rocked Him in-a the weary land.   (Hayes)

The Social Band

Bright angels on the water,
Hovering by the light;
Poor sinner standing in darkness
And cannot see the light.

I want Aunty Mary to go with me,
I want Aunty Mary to go with me,
I want Aunty Mary to go with me,
To join the social band.   (ALLEN)

Somebody Got Lost In The Storm

Somebody got lost in the storm,
In the storm,
Somebody got lost in the storm,
Somebody got lost,
Somebody got lost,
Somebody got lost,
Somebody got lost in the storm,
In the storm.

A mourner got lost in the storm,
In the storm,
A mourner got lost in the storm,
In the storm,
A mourner got lost,
A mourner got lost,
A mourner got lost in the storm,
In the storm.

A sinner got lost in the storm,
In the storm,
A sinner got lost in the storm,
In the storm,
A sinner got lost,
A sinner got lost,
A sinner got lost in the storm,
In the storm.

A gambler got lost in the storm,
In the storm,
A gambler got lost in the storm,
In the storm,
A gambler got lost,
A gambler got lost,
A gambler got lost in the storm,
A gambler got lost in the storm.   (Fisher)

Sometimes I Feel

Sometimes I feel like a moanin' dove,
Sometimes I feel like a moanin' dove,
Sometimes I feel like a moanin' dove,
Sometimes I feel like a moanin' dove;
Wring my hands an' cry, cry, cry,
Wring my hands an' cry, cry, cry,
Wring my hands an' cry, cry, cry;
Sometimes I feel like a moanin' dove,
Wring my hands and cry, cry, cry.

Sometimes I feel like a motherless child,
Sometimes I feel like a motherless child,
Sometimes I feel like a motherless child,
Wring my hands and cry, cry, cry,
Wring my hands and cry, cry, cry.

Sometimes I feel like I gotta no home,
Sometimes I feel like I gotta no home,
Sometimes I feel like I gotta no home,
Wring my hands and cry, cry, cry,
Wring my hands and cry, cry, cry.

Sometimes I feel like a eagle in the air,
Sometimes I feel like a eagle in the air,
Sometimes I feel like a eagle in the air,
Spread my wings and fly, fly, fly.

Sometimes I feel like a moanin' dove,
Sometimes I feel like a moanin' dove.
Wring my hands and cry, cry, cry.   (L-G)

Sometimes I Feel Like A Motherless Child

Sometimes I feel like a motherless child,
Sometimes I feel like a motherless child,
Sometimes I feel like a motherless child,
A long way from home,
A long way from home;
True believer;
A long way from home.

If this was judgment day,
If this was judgment day,
If this was judgment day,
Every little soul would pray,
Every little soul would pray;
True believer;
Every little soul would pray.

Sometimes I feel like I'm almost gone,
Sometimes I feel like I'm almost gone,
Sometimes I feel like I'm almost gone,

Way up in the heavenly land!
Way up in the heavenly land;
True believer;
Way up in the heavenly land.   (Hampton)

Sometimes My Trouble Make Me Tremble

Were you there when they crucified my Lord?
Were you there when they crucified my Lord?
O, sometimes my trouble make me tremble, tremble, tremble,
Were you there when they crucified my Lord?
Were you there when they whipped Him up Calvary?
Were you there when they led Him to Pilate's bar?
Were you there when they nail Him to the cross?
Were you there when they pierced Him in the side?
Were you there when He hung His head and died?
Were you there when they laid Him in the tomb?
Were you there when He rose up from the dead?

O, sometimes my trouble make me tremble, tremble, tremble.
O, sometimes my trouble make me tremble, tremble, tremble. (St. Helena)

Soon One Morning

Soon one mornin', death comes a-creepin' in my room.
O my Lord, O my Lord, what shall I do?

Death done been here, took my mother an' gone,
O my Lord, O my Lord, what shall I do?

Death done been here, left me a motherless child,
O my Lord, O my Lord, what shall I do?   (Cone)

Sorry To Tell

Sorry to tell you,
Lord, Lord,
Sorry to tell you.
Lord, Lord,
Sorry to tell you,
Sorry to tell you,
Sorry to tell you, Lord.   (Calhoun)

Sweet Home

Sweet home,
Sweet home,
Sweet home,
Sweet home,
Lord, I wonder if I'll ever get home.
I heard the voice of Jesus say,
"Come unto me and rest;
Lay down thy weary one,
Lay down thy head upon my breast."

I came to Jesus as I was,
Weary, worn, and sad,
And I found in Him a resting place,
And he has made me glad.

Sweet home,
Sweet home,
Sweet home,
Sweet home,
Lord, I wonder if I'll ever get home.   (L-G)

Swing Low, Sweet Chariot

Oh swing low, sweet chariot,
Swing low, sweet chariot,
Swing low, sweet chariot,
I don't want you to leave me behind.

Oh the good old chariot swings so low,
Good old chariot swings so low,
Oh the good old chariot swings so low,
I don't want it to leave me behind.

Oh the good old chariot will take us all home,
I don't want it to leave me behind.
Oh swing low, sweet chariot,
Swing low, sweet chariot,
Swing low, sweet chariot,
I don't want you to leave me behind.   (Hampton) (Variant)

There's A Man Going Round Taking Names

There's a man going round taking names,
There's a man going round taking names,
He's a-taken my mother's name,
And he has left my heart in pain,
There's a man going round taking names.

Oh, Death is the man taking names;
Oh, Death is the man taking names;
He's a-taken my father's name,
And left my heart in pain,
There's a man going round taking names.   (Fisher)

There's Something On My Mind

There's something on my mind that's
    worrying me,
There's something on my mind that's
    worrying me,
There's something on my mind that's
    worrying me,
So let us watch, Lord, and pray as we live.

Father's drinking with their sons that's what's
    worrying me,
Father's drinking with their sons that's what's
    worrying me,
Father's drinking with their sons that's what's
    worrying me,
So let us watch, Lord, and pray as we live.

The church is out of union that's what's
    worrying me,
The church is out of union that's what's
    worrying me,
The church is out of union that's what's
    worrying me,
So let us watch, Lord, and pray as we live.   (ANSAS)

They Led My Lord Away

They led my Lord away, away,
They led my Lord away, away,
O, tell me where to find Him, find Him.

The Jews and Romans in one band,
They crucified the Son of Man;
They led Him up to Pilate's bar,
But the Jews could not condemn Him there;
Old Pilate said, "I wash my hands,"
"I find no fault in this just Man."
They led my Lord away, away,
They led my Lord away, away,
O, tell me where to find Him, find Him.   (ANS)

This Is The Trouble Of The World

I asked Father Georgy for religion,
Father Georgy wouldn't give me religion;
You give me religion
For to run to my elder,
O, this is the trouble of the world.
This is the trouble of the world,
O, this is the trouble of the world.   (ALLEN)

This May Be The Last Time

This may be the last time,
This may be the last time,
This may be the last time,
Oh, it may be the last time,
I don't know.
I went in the valley,
And I didn't go to stay,
Oh, it may be the last time,
I don't know.
My soul got happy
And I stayed all day,

Oh, it may be my last time,
I don't know.   (Fisher)

'Tis Me

'Tis me, 'tis me, O Lord,
Standing in the need of prayer;
'Tis me, 'tis me, O Lord,
Standing in the need of prayer.

Not my brother, but 'tis me, O Lord,
Not my sister, but 'tis me, O Lord,
Not my mother, but 'tis me, O Lord,
Not my elder, but 'tis me, O Lord,
Standing in the need of prayer.   (Hampton)

Trouble Done Bore Me Down

Oh Lord, oh Lord,
What shall I do?
Trouble done bore me down.
Oh Lord, oh Lord,
What shall I do?
Oh, trouble done bore me down.

He's gone on high to prepare a place,
Trouble done bore me down,
For to prepare a place for me and you,
Trouble done bore me down.

Oh Lord, oh Lord,
Have mercy on me,
Trouble done bore me down;
Oh Lord, oh Lord,
Have mercy on me,
Oh, trouble done bore me down.

I've seen some strangers quite unknown,
Trouble done bore me down;
I'm a child of misery,
Trouble done bore me down.

I'm sometimes up and sometimes down;
Trouble done bore me down;
I'm sometimes level with the ground,
Trouble done bore me down.

Oh Lord, oh Lord,
What shall I do?
Trouble done bore me down.
Oh Lord, oh Lord,
What shall I do?
Trouble done bore me down.

I bent my knees and smote the ground,
Trouble done bore me down;

I asked God almighty for to run me 'round.
Trouble done bore me down.

Oh Lord, Oh Lord,
What shall I do?
Trouble done bore me down.
Oh Lord, oh Lord,
What shall I do?
Trouble done bore me down.

When I was a moaner just like you,
Trouble done bore me down,
I moaned 'til the Lord God set me free,
Trouble done bore me down.

Oh Lord, oh Lord,
Take pity on me,
Trouble done bore me down;
Oh Lord, oh Lord,
Take pity on me,
Trouble done bore me down.

This bed of sin on which I lie,
Trouble done bore me down.
I lay my body down to die,
Trouble done bore me down.

Oh Lord, oh Lord,
Take pity on me,
Trouble done bore me down;
Oh Lord, Oh Lord,
Take pity on me,
Oh, trouble done bore me down.   (BDWS)

The Trouble Of The World

I want to be my Father's children,
I want to be my Father's children,
I want to be my Father's children,
Roll, Jordan, roll.
O, say, ain't you done with the trouble of this world?
Ah, say, ain't you done with the trouble of this world?
Ah, roll, Jordan, roll.

I ask the Lord how long I hold them,
Hold them to the end;
My sins so heavy I can't get along,
My sins so heavy I can't get along,
I cast my sins in the middle of the sea,
I cast my sins in the middle of the sea.

O, say, ain't you done with the trouble of this world?
O, say, ain't you done with the trouble of this world?
I wish I was in jubilee,
I wish I was in jubilee.   (ALLEN)

Trouble's Going To Weigh Me Down

Trouble's going to weigh me down in the morning,
Trouble's going to weigh me down.
Trouble's going to weigh me down in the morning,
Trouble's going to weigh me down!

Just so the tree fall,
Just so he lie,
Just so the sinner live,
Just so he die,
Well-a trouble's going to weigh me down,
God knows it.   (Fisher)

Up On The Mountain

Way up on the mountain, Lord!
Mountain top, Lord!
I heard God talking, Lord!
Children, the chariot stopped, Lord!

One day Lord, one day, Lord,
Walking 'long, Lord,
With hung down head, Lord!
Children, an aching heart, Lord!   (BANS)

Way Down In Hell

It's always midnight way down in hell,
It's always midnight way down in hell,
Let me tell you,
It's always midnight way down in hell,
It's always midnight way down in hell,
Evangelist Job done spoke and said,
How can a man live once he's dead?
I remember the day, I remember it well,
My dungeon shook and my chain fell off.
Satan's mad and I'm glad,
I trust the Lord I'm going to keep him mad;
Oh! the test is on every where I go,
I got some faith, Lord, but I ask for more.   (BDWS)

Weep No More For Baby

Weep no more for baby, my heart;
Weep no more for baby,
My heart's so sorry.

Weep no more for baby, my heart;
Weep no more for baby,
My heart's so sorry.   (CD)

Were You There?

Were you there when they crucified my Lord?
                              Were you there?
Were you there when they crucified my Lord?
                              Were you there?
Oh, sometimes it causes me to tremble, tremble.
Were you there when they nailed Him to the tree?
                              To the tree?
Were you there when they nailed Him to the tree?
                              To the tree?
Oh, sometimes it causes me to tremble, tremble.

Were you there when they pierced Him in the side?
                              In the side?
Were you there when they pierced Him in the side?
Oh, sometimes it causes me to tremble, tremble.

Were you there when the sun refused to shine?
                              Refused to shine.
Were you there when the sun refused to shine?
Refused to shine.
Oh, sometimes it causes me to tremble, tremble.

Were you there when they laid Him in the tomb?
                              In the tomb?
Were you there when they laid Him in the tomb?
                              In the tomb?
Oh, sometimes it causes me to tremble, tremble;
Were you there when they laid him in the tomb?   (Hampton)

What A Trying Time

O, Adam, where are you?
Adam, where are you?
Adam, where are you?
O, what a trying time!

Lord, I am in the garden;
Adam, you ate that apple;
Lord, Eve she gave it to me;
Adam, it was forbidden;
Lord said, walk out of the garden.

O, Adam, where are you?
Adam, where are you?
Adam, where are you?
O, what a trying time!   (ALLEN)

What Harm Has Jesus Done?

Oh, what harm Jesus done you,
What harm Jesus done you,
What harm Jesus done you,
The sinners all hate him so?

Nothing 'tall that was wrong,
He gave me Faith to believe,
For to bear my spirit home.

Done no harm at all,
Gave me Faith to conquer,
To bear my spirit home.

Nothing 'tall that was wrong,
He died for all of mankind,
For to prepare a heavenly home.   (BDWS)

Wheel In A Wheel

Wheel, wheel, wheel,
O, wheel, my Lord,
Wheel, wheel, Ezekiel said.
'Twas a wheel in a wheel,
Wheel in a wheel.

Dark cloud risin', it looks like rain--
Dark cloud risin', it looks like rain--
The sun drawin' water from Emanuel's veins.
Get your bundle ready, I know it's time,
Get your bundle ready, I know it's time,
Get your bundle ready, I know it's time,
You can tell the winter from the summer time.

I wonder where is Moses, he must be dead,
The children of the Israelites cryin' for bread.
I wonder where was Moses when the church burn down,
I wonder where was Moses when the church burn down,
Standin' over yonder with His head hung down.   (St. Helena)

When I'm Gone

When I'm gone,
When I'm gone,
When I'm gone,
Lord, when I'm gone,
Somebody's going to miss me,
When I'm gone, gone, gone.

Going to miss me for my moan,
Miss me for my groan,
Somebody's going to miss me.
When I'm gone.
Going to miss me for my walk,
Miss me for my talk;
Going to miss me for my shout,
For I'm shouting all about;
Going to miss me for my praise
Miss my Christian ways.

When I'm gone,
When I'm gone,

Somebody's going to miss me,
When I'm gone.   (BDWS)

When You Hear My Coffin Sound

When you hear my coffin sound,
Good Lord, Good Lordy,
Good Lord, I'm coming home!

Pray, don't touch my garment,
Good Lord, Good Lordy,
Good Lord, I'm coming home!

Tell my mother to meet me,
Good Lord, Good Lordy,
Good Lord, I'm coming home!

When you hear my funeral preached,
Good Lord, Good Lordy,
Good Lord, I'm coming home!

When you hear my coffin sound,
Good Lord, Good Lordy,
Good Lord, I'm coming home!   (CD)

Where Shall I Go?

Where shall I go?
Where shall I go?
Where shall I go?
To ease my troubling mind?

I went to the rock to hide my face,
The rock cried out "No hiding place."
The man who loves to serve the Lord
Will surely get his just reward.

Where shall I go?
Where shall I go?
Where shall I go?
To ease my troubling mind?   (ANS)

Who's Going To Close My Dying Eyes?

O who's going to close my dying eyes?
                                        O Lord!
Who's going to close my dying eyes?

                                        O angel, O angel!
Who's going to close my dying eyes?   (R.E. Kennedy)

LYRICS OF
CONSOLATION AND FAITH _____

Confronted with a harsh reality and its bitter odds, the enslaved Afro-Americans sought arduously to maintain a quality of spiritual wholeness and health for their inner being. Many songs were composed, therefore, for the purpose of consolation and fortification, as bulwarks against bewilderment. This group of songs is especially representative of those spirituals which James Cone has spoken of as uniting joy and sorrow, hope and despair. These songs are a testament of faith to the transforming power of the spirit. They speak of the healing potion and the agents available to those who have undergone and withstood the insufferable. They seek to convey the formulas for invoking the mediating agents, and they starkly affirm that the healing balms do exist.

These songs speak, however, to more than the personal. Songs of this category are often oriented towards the collective group to encourage communal uplift. Songs like "Let Us Praise God Together On Our Knees" convey a sense of petition for communal consolation and gratitude for the existence of the spirit world. On the other hand, songs like "Sit Down, Servant" convey a communal understanding and collective sympathy for the needs of the individual. Yet, in addition to the emphasis on the personal and communal anguish of the ostensible victims, beneath all the suffering communicated in these songs, there is a deep concern and compassion for the tragic nature of the whole of humankind.[1]

_____

1. James Cone, THE SPIRITUALS AND THE BLUES. New York: Seabury Press, 1972, p.5.

Anchor In The Lord

Anchor, believer, anchor,
Anchor in the Lord,
Throw your anchor any way,
Anchor in the Lord.

Throw it to my dear mother's door,
    Anchor in the Lord,
Throw it to my dear father's door,
    Anchor in the Lord,
Throw it to my dear sister's door,
    Anchor in the Lord,

King Jesus says he'll come again,
    Anchor in the Lord,
King Jesus makes the cripple walk,
    Anchor in the Lord,
King Jesus makes the blind to see,
    Anchor in the Lord.
Anchor, believer, anchor,
Anchor in the Lord,
Throw your anchor any way,
Anchor in the Lord.   (FJS)

The Angels Are Watching Over Me

All night, all night,
    the angels are watching over me.
All night, all night,
    the angels are watching over me.

Someday Peter and someday Paul,
    The angels are watching over me--
Ain't but one God made us all,
    The angels are watching over me.

You get there before I do,
    The angels are watching over me--
Tell all my friends I'm coming too.
    The angels are watching over me.   (St. Helena)

Arkangel

Who is the ruler, Arkangel?
Who is the ruler, Arkangel?
Who is the ruler, Arkangel?
Who is the ruler, Arkangel?

Jesus is the ruler,
Jesus is the ruler;
He rules my soul,
He rules my soul;
He rules the heaven,
He rules the heaven;
He rules the sinner,

He rules the sinner;
He ruled little David,
He ruled little David;
He ruled old Goliath,
He ruled old Goliath.
Who is the ruler, Arkangel?
Who is the ruler, Arkangel?

(BDWS)

Balm In Gilead

There is a balm in Gilead
To make the wounded whole,
There is a balm in Gilead
To heal the sin-sick soul.

Sometimes I feel discouraged
And think my work's in vain,
But then the Holy Spirit
Revives my soul again.

Don't ever feel discouraged,
For Jesus is your friend,
And if you lack for knowledge,
He'll never refuse to lend.

If you cannot sing like angels,
If you cannot preach like Paul,
You can tell the love of Jesus,
And say "He died for all."

(ANS)

Bright Sparkles In The Churchyard

May the Lord,
        He will be glad of me,
May the Lord,
        He will be glad of me,
May the Lord,
        He will be glad of me.
In the heaven, He'll rejoice,
In the heaven twice,
In the heaven, He'll rejoice.

Bright sparkles in the churchyard,
Give light unto the tomb,
Bright summer, Spring's over,
Sweet flowers in their bloom.
My mother once, my mother twice,
My mother, she'll rejoice,
In the heaven once,
In the heaven twice,
In the heaven, she'll rejoice.

Mother, rock me in the cradle all the day,
Mother, rock me in the cradle all the day,
All the day, all the day,
Oh, rock me in the cradle all the day.

Oh, mother don't you love your darling child,
Mother, rock me in the cradle all the day;
You may lay me down to sleep,
    my mother dear,
You may lay me down to sleep,
    my mother dear,
Oh, rock me in the cradle all the day.

(FJS)

Chilly Water

Chilly water, chilly water,
Hallelujah to that Lamb, to that Lamb.

I know that water is chilly and cold,
But I have Jesus in my soul;
O, in that ark the little dove moaned,
Christ Jesus standing as the corner stone;
Old Satan's just like a snake in the grass,
He's watching to bite you as you pass;
O, brothers and sisters, come one and all,
You'd better be ready when the roll is called.
Hallelujah to that Lamb, to that Lamb,
Chilly water, chilly water,
Hallelujah to that Lamb, to that Lamb.

(BANS)

The Church Of God

The church of God,
    That sounds so sweet,
The church of God,
    That sounds so sweet.

Oh, look up yonder what I see,
Bright angels coming after me.

Oh, Jesus told you once before,
To go in peace and sin no more;
Oh, Paul and Silas bound in jail,
Then one did sing and the other pray.

Oh, did you hear my Jesus say,
"Come unto me, I am the way";
Oh, come along, Moses, don't get lost,
Oh, stretch your rod and come across.

The church of God,
    That sounds so sweet,
The church of God,
    That sounds so sweet.

(Hampton)

Come By Here, My Lord

Come by here, my Lordy,
Come by here,

Come by here, my Lordy,
Come by here,
Come by here, my Lordy,
Come by here,
O, Lord,
Come by here.

Somebody's dying, Lord,
Come by here,
Somebody's dying, Lord,
Come by here,
Somebody's dying, Lord,
Come by here,
O, Lord,
Come by here.
Somebody's praying, Lord,
Come by here,
Somebody's praying, Lord,
Come by here,
Somebody's praying, Lord,
Come by here,
O, Lord, come by here.

Somebody needs you, Lord,
Come by here,
Somebody needs you, Lord,
Come by here,
Somebody needs you, Lord,
Come by here,
O, Lord,
Come by here.

(Traditional)

Come Down Sinner

Come down, come down,
Come down, sinner, you're none too late;
Come down, come down,
O, come down, sinner, you're none too late.
O, come down, sinner, you're none too late.
Some seek the Lord,
But don't seek Him right,
Little at day and none at night.

Pray hard, pray hard,
Pray hard, sinner you're none too late;
Pray hard, pray hard,
O, pray hard, sinner, you're none too late.
Times ain't like they used to be,
I for you and you for me.

Bow low, bow low,
Bow low, sinner, you're none too late;
Went down the hill to say my prayer,
When I got there old Satan was there.

Seek hard, seek hard,
Seek hard, sinner, you're none too late;

What do you think old Satan say?
"Jesus dead, and God gone away."

Shout hard, shout hard,
Shout hard, sinner, you're none too late;
What to do, I did not know,
Right back home I had to go.
Mourn hard, mourn hard,
Mourn hard, sinner, you're none too late;
Something spoke unto my soul
"Go in peace and sin no more."

Come down, come down,
Come down, sinner, you're none too late.   (Hampton)

Come Trembling Down

Come trembling down, go shouting home,
Safe in the sweet arms of Jesus,
Come Jesus;
'Twas just about the break of day,
King Jesus stole my heart away.

Come trembling down, go shouting home,
Safe in the sweet arms of Jesus,
Come Jesus.   (Krehbiel)

Daniel, Daniel, Servant Of The Lord

Oh, the king cried,
"Oh, Daniel, Daniel, oh!
Daniel, Daniel, oh!
A-that-a Hebrew Daniel,
A-that-a Hebrew Daniel,
Daniel, Daniel, oh!
Oh, Daniel, Daniel,
Servant of the Lord!"

Among the Hebrew nation,
One Hebrew, Daniel, was found.
They put him in the lion's den.
He stayed there all night long.

Now, the king in his sleep was troubled,
And early in the morning he rose
To find God had sent a-his angel down
To lock the lion's jaws!

Oh, the king cried,
"Oh! Daniel, Daniel,
Servant of the Lord!"

(Undine S. Moore)
©1953 Warner Bros.
Inc. (Renewed)
All rights reserved.
Used by Permission.

Do Lord, Remember Me (1)

Oh, do Lord, do Lord, do remember me,
Oh, do Lord, do Lord, do remember me,
Oh, do Lord, do Lord, do remember me,
Oh, do Lord, remember me.

Oh, when my enemies are behind me,
When the hell hounds are behind me,
When the sinners are all around me,
When I'm dead and gone to judgement.

Oh, do Lord, do Lord, do remember me,
Oh, do Lord, do Lord, do remember me,
Oh, do Lord, do Lord, do remember me,
Oh, do Lord, remember me.

(BDWS)

Do Lord, Remember Me (2)

Do Lord, do Lord, do remember me,
Do Lord, do Lord, do remember me,
Do Lord, do Lord, do remember me,
Do Lord, remember me.
When I'm sick an' by myself,
Do remember me;
When I'm sick an' by myself,
Do remember me.
When I'm sick an' by myself,
Do remember me,
Do, Lord, remember me.

When I'm crossing Jordan,
Do remember me;
If I ain't got no frien's at all,
Do remember me;
Paul and Silas bound in jail,
Do remember me;
One did sing while the other one prayed,
Do remember me,
When I'm bound in trouble,
Do remember me;
When I'm goin' from do' to do',
Do remember me.

(Grissom)

Done Found My Lost Sheep

Done found my lost sheep,
Done found my lost sheep,
Done found my lost sheep, hallelujah.

My Lord had a hundred sheep,
One of them did go astray;
That just left him ninety-nine,
To go to the wilderness to seek and find.

If you find him, bring him back,
Cross the shoulders across your back;
Tell the neighbors all around,
That lost sheep has done been found.

In that Resurrection Day
Sinner can't find no hiding place;
Go to the mountain, the mountain moves,
Run to the hill, the hill runs too.

Sinner man traveling on trembling ground,
Poor lost sheep ain't ever been found;
Sinner, why don't you stop and pray,
Then you'd hear the Shepherd say:

Done found my lost sheep,
Done found my lost sheep,
Done found my lost sheep.   (BANS)

Done Found The Way At Last

Been a long time praying for this-a way,
Thank God almighty,
Done found the way at last.

Oh, dig, dig, for the meeting done broke,
I and you must part;
Part in body, but not in mind,
I love you in-a my heart.
Oh, good night
For the meeting done broke,
I and you must part;
Part in body
But not in mind.
I love you in-a my heart.   (BDWS)

Don't Get Weary

Members, don't get weary,
Members, don't get weary,
Members, don't get weary,
For the work's almost done.

O, keep your lamps trimmed and a-burning,
Keep your lamps trimmed and a-burning,
Keep your lamps trimmed and a-burning,
For the work's almost done.   (St. Helena)

Don't Leave Me, Lord

Don't leave me, Lord,
Don't leave me, Lord,
Lord, don't leave me behind;
Don't leave me, Lord,
Don't leave me, Lord,

Lord, don't leave me behind.

Jesus, Jesus is my friend,
He will go with me to the end;
No use talking about what you going to do,
Don't tend to deny my God for you;
I don't want to stumble,
And I don't want to stop,
I don't want to be no stumbling block.

Don't leave me, Lord,
Don't leave me, Lord,
Lord, don't leave me behind.

(Hampton)

Don't You Grieve After Me

Oh, who is that a-coming?
Don't you grieve after me;
Oh, who is that a-coming?
Don't you grieve after me;
Oh, who is that a-coming?
Don't you grieve after me;
Lord, I don't want you to grieve after me.

It looks like Gabriel,
    Don't you grieve after me;
Oh, who is that behind him?
    Don't you grieve after me;
It looks like Jesus,
    Don't you grieve after me;
Go, blow your trumpet, Gabriel,
    Don't you grieve after me;

How loud must I blow it?
    Don't you grieve after me;
Loud as seven claps of thunder,
    Don't you grieve after me;
To wake the sleeping nations,
    Don't you grieve after me.

Oh, who is that a-coming?
Don't you grieve after me;
Oh, who is that a-coming?
Don't you grieve after me;
Oh, who is that a-coming?
Don't you grieve after me;
Lord, I don't want you to grieve after me.

(FJS)

Don't You Let Nobody Turn You Around

Don't you let nobody turn you around,
Turn you around, turn you around,
Don't you let nobody turn you around,
Turn you around, turn you around,
Keep the straight and narrow way.

I was at the river of Jordan,
Baptism was begun,
John Baptized the multitude,
But he sprinkled narry one.
The Baptists, they go by water,
The Methodists, they go by land,
But when they get to heaven
They'll shake each other's hand.

You may be a good Baptist,
And a good Methodist as well,
But if you ain't the pure in heart
Your soul is bound for hell.

Don't you let nobody turn you around,
Turn you around, turn you around,
Don't you let nobody turn you around,
Turn you around, turn you around.   (ANS)

Early In The Morning

I met little Rosa early in the morning,
And I asked her,
How're you doing, my daughter?

O, Jerusalem, early in the morning,
Walk 'em easy around the heaven,
Walk 'em easy around the heaven,
O, Jerusalem, early in the morning,
Walk 'em easy around the heaven,
'Till all living may join that band.   (Allen)

Elijah Rock

Elijah, rock! shout! shout!
Elijah, rock! shout! shout!
Elijah, rock! calling up the Lord;

Elijah, rock! shout! shout!
Elijah, rock! shout! shout!
Elijah, rock! calling up the Lord;

Elijah _____,
Elijah _____;

Elijah, rock! shout! shout!
Elijah, rock! calling up the Lord;
Elijah, rock! shout! shout!
Elijah, rock! calling up the Lord.   (Traditional)

Get On The Boat Little Children

Angel came from heaven,
I thought I heard him say,
"Just you raise them diamond curtains.

"And hear them Christians pray."

When I was a moaner,
I moaned both night and day,
But now I am a Christian,
I'll shout myself away.

One day when I was walking,
Along the lonesome road,
My Savior spoke unto me
And filled my heart with love.

Going 'round the mountain,
Think we'll make a stand,
Heard the voice of Jesus,
Thank God He's in the land

Just get on the boat, little children,
Just get on the boat, little children,
And we will sail away.

(BDWS)

The Gift Of God Is Eternal Life

Oh, the gift of God is eternal life,
Eternal life, eternal life;
Oh, the gift of God is eternal life,
And the wages of sin is death.

The very first blessing sister Mary had,
She had that blessing of one:
Think that her son Jesus Christ
Suckled at the breast so young.

The very next blessing sister Mary had,
It was the blessing of two:
To think that her son Jesus Christ is
Chief of the heavenly crew.

The very next blessing sister Mary had,
It was the blessing of three:
To think that her son Jesus Christ,
Could set a poor sinner free.

The very next blessing sister Mary had,
It was the blessing of four:
To see that her son Jesus Christ
Could preach to the poor.

(BDWS)

Give Me Jesus

O, when I come to die,
⠀⠀⠀O, when I come to die,
O, when I come to die,
Give me Jesus,
Give me Jesus,
You may have all this world;

Give me Jesus.
In the morning when I rise,
          In the morning when I rise
You may have all this world;
Give me Jesus.

Dark midnight was my cry,
          Dark midnight was my cry,
O, when I come to die,
Give me Jesus.
I heard the mourner say,
          I heard the mourner say,
You may have all this world;
Give me Jesus.
Give me Jesus.

                                                                    (FJS)

Give Me Jesus When I Die

Oh, soon in the morning,
Give me Jesus when I die,
Soon in the morning,
Give me Jesus when I die.

Give me Jesus' spirit for the comfort,
Give me Jesus' talk for the comfort
Oh, Lord, you know my heart's desire,
Give me Jesus when I die.

Give me Jesus when I'm dying,
Give me Jesus when the sinners are all around me,
Give me Jesus when the moaners are all around me,
Give me Jesus when I die.

Give me Jesus when the day is breaking,
Give me Jesus when the world's on fire,

Oh, give me Jesus when the world's on fire,
Give me Jesus when I die.   (BDWS) (Variant)

Give Me That Old Time Religion

Give me that old time religion,
Give me that old time religion,
Give me that old time religion,
It's good enough for me.

It was good for the Hebrew children,
It was good for the Hebrew children,
It was good for the Hebrew children,
And it's good enough for me.

It will do when the world's on fire,
It will do when the world's on fire,
It will do when the world's on fire,
And it's good enough for me.

Oh, give me that old time religion,
Give me that old time religion,
Give me that old time religion,
It's good enough for me.   (BANS)

Give Me Your Hand

O, give me your hand,
Give me your hand,
All I want is the love of God;
Give me your hand, give me your hand,
You must be loving at God's command.

You say you're aiming for the skies,
Why don't you quit telling your lies?
You say the Lord has set your free,
Why don't you let your neighbor be?
You seek God's grace but don't seek it right,
You pray in the day, but none at night.

O, give me your hand,
Give me your hand,
All I want is the love of God;
Give me your hand, give me your hand,
You must be loving at God's command.   (BANS)

Glory And Honor

Glory and honor, praise Jesus,
Glory and honor, praise the Lamb,
Got glory and honor, praise Jesus,
Glory and honor, praise, Amen.

Adam and Eve in the garden for to see,
Eve picked the apple off God's little tree;
God called to Adam,"You sinner man
"Leave my garden as fast as you can."

Some say Noah was a foolish man,
Built his ark in Sinai land,
Done got out the notion of dying at all.
Old uncle Noah,
Don't you do that again.

Steady, Christian, steady yourself,
Come on let me tell you about God Himself, how he died,
Christians cried,
God almighty walking in paradise.   (BDWS) (Variant)

God Is A God

God is a God!
God don't never change!
God is a God,
And He always will be God!

He made the sun to shine by day,
He made the sun to show the way,
He made the stars to show their light,
He made the moon to shine by night, saying,

God is a God!
God don't never change!
God is a God,
And He always will be God!

The earth's His footstool and heaven's his throne,
The whole creation, all His own,
His love and power will prevail,
His promises will never fail, saying,

God is a God!
God don't never change!
God is a God,
And He always will be God!   (ANS)

God's Got Plenty Of Room

God's got plenty of room,
        got plenty of room,
'Way in the kingdom,
God's got plenty of room my Jesus says,
'Way in the kingdom.
Brethren, I have come again,
'Way in the kingdom,
To help you all to pray and sing,
'Way in the kingdom.

So many-a weeks and days have passed
Since we met together last;
Old Satan trembles when he sees
The weakest saints upon their knees;
Prayer makes the darkest cloud withdraw,
Prayer climbed the ladder Jacob saw.
Daniel's wisdom may I know,
Stephen's faith and spirit sure;
John's divine communion feel,
Joseph's meek and Joshua's zeal.

There is a school on earth begun,
Supported by the Holy One;
We soon shall lay our school books by,
And shout salvation as I fly.

God's got plenty of room,
        got plenty of room,
'Way in the kingdom,
God's got plenty of room my Jesus says,
'Way in the kingdom.   (Allen)

Going To Set Down And Rest A While

Going to set down and rest a while,
Going to set down and rest a while,
Going to set down and rest a while,
When my good Lord calls me.

Sister Mary went to heaven,
And she went there to stay,
And she didn't go to come back no more;
She sang a song that the angels couldn't sing:
"Hoseanna, carry on."

Little children, don't you moan,
Little children, don't you moan,
Little children, don't you moan,
When my good Lord calls me.
O, Zion!
O, Zion!
O, Zion!
When my good Lord calls me.   (Fisher)

The Golden Altar

John saw-r-O,
John saw-r-O,
John saw the holy number
Sitting on the golden altar!

It's a little while longer here below,
Here below, here below,
It's a little while longer here below,
Before the Lamb of God!

And home to Jesus we will go,
        we will go,
We are the people of the Lord;
There's a golden slipper in the heavens for you,
        in the heavens for you,
Before the Lamb of God;
I wish I'd been there when prayer begun,
        when prayer begun,

To see my Jesus about my sins,
Home to glory we will go,
        we will go.

John saw-r-O,
John saw-r-O,
John saw the holy number
Sitting on the golden altar!   (Allen)

Goodbye, Brother

Goodbye, brother, goodbye, brother,
If I don't see you more;

Now God bless you,
Now God bless you,
If I don't see you more.

We part in the body,
But we meet in the spirit,
We'll meet in the heaven
In the blessed kingdom.

So goodbye, brother, goodbye, sister
Now God bless you,
Now God bless you.   (Allen)

Goodbye, Brothers

Goodbye, brothers, goodbye, sisters,
If I don't see you anymore;
I'll meet you in heaven
        in the blessed Kingdom,
If I don't see you any more.
We'll part in the body,
        We'll meet in the spirit,
If I don't see you any more;
So now God Bless you,
        God bless you,
If I don't see you any more.   (FJS)

Good Lord Done Been Here

Adam in the garden,
Eve, she disobeyed,
She broke the covenant,
And we got her debt to pay.

But my good Lord done been here,
Blessed my soul and gone away.

Don't you pay no mind to a woman,
She's a tempting thing,
She rigs herself in a deceiving way
To trick the heart of a man.

When I get to heaven,
I'm going to stand on the sea of glass,
Going to holler to you sinners down below
Done got my home at last.

And my good Lord done been here,
Blessed my soul and gone away.   (BDWS)

A Great Campmeeting In The Promised Land

Oh, walk together, children,
Don't you get weary;
Oh, walk together, children,

Don't you get weary;
Oh, talk together children,
Don't you get weary;
Oh, sing together children,
Don't you get weary;
There's a great campmeeting in the promised land.

Going to mourn and never tire,
Going to mourn and never tire,
Going to mourn and never tire,
There's a great campmeeting in the promised land.

Oh, get you ready children,
For Jesus is a-coming,
Going to have a happy meeting,
Going to pray and never tire.

Going to have it in heaven,
Don't you get weary;
Going to shout in heaven,
Oh, will you go with me;
Don't you get weary,
Going to shout and never tire.

There's a better day a-coming,
Don't you get weary;
Oh, slap your hands, children,
Oh, pat your feet, children,
Don't you get weary,
There's a great campmeeting in the promised land.

Oh, feel the Spirit a-moving,
Oh, now I'm getting happy,
Don't you get weary;
I feel so happy
Going to fly and never tire,
Going to live with God forever,
Don't you get weary,
There's a great campmeeting in the promised land.   (Hampton)

A Happy New Year

What a happy new year,
What a happy new year,

What a happy, what a happy,
What a happy new year.

I'm running through grace
To that happy place;
Through grace I'm determined
To see my Lord's face.

One thing I do find,
I'll keep it in my mind,
He won't live in glory
And leave me behind.

O sinner, believe
Christ will you receive,
For all things are ready,
And you stand in need.

What a happy new year,
What a happy new year,
What a happy, what a happy,
What a happy new year.   (FJS)

Heaven Is A Beautiful Place (1)

Heaven is a beautiful place,
I believe, I believe;
Heaven is a beautiful place,
I believe, I believe;
Heaven is a beautiful place,
I believe, I believe.

Ain't no liars over there,
I believe, I believe;
Ain't no gamblers over there,
I believe, I believe;
Ain't no sickness over there,
I believe, I believe;
All good people over there,
I believe, I believe;
No backsliders over there,
I believe, I believe;
No back biters over there,
I believe, I believe.   (St. Helena)

Heaven Is A Beautiful Place (2)

Heaven is a beautiful place,
I know;
It ain't no liars in Heaven,
I know.
If you wanta get to heaven on time,
You sho' got to plumb the line.
Heaven is a beautiful place,
I know.

Heaven is a beautiful place,
I know;
It ain't no gamblers in Heaven,
I know;
It ain't no drunkards in Heaven,
I know;
It ain't no sinners in Heaven,
I know;
It ain't no troubles in Heaven,
I know.   (Grissom)

He Raised Poor Lazarus

Oh, He raised poor Lazarus,
Raised him up,
He raised him from the dead,
I told you so,
While many were standing by;
Jesus loosened the man from under the ground,
And told him, "Go prophesy,"
And told him, "Go prophesy."
He gave healing unto the sick,
Yes, He did,
He gave sight unto the blind,
I know He did,
He done abled the crippled to walk,
Oh, he raised the dead from under the ground,
And gave them permission to talk.

Oh, moan along, moan along,
Oh, ye moaning souls! ye moaning souls,
Heaven is my home;
Jesus has been here one time,
Lord, He's coming again,
Get ready and let us go home.

(Hampton)

He's A Mighty Good Leader

He's a mighty good leader,
He's a mighty good leader,
He's a mighty good leader,
Jesus Christ, God's Son, God's Son,
He's a mighty good leader,
He's a mighty good leader,
He's a mighty good leader,
Jesus Christ, God's Son.

He is my Captain,
He's a mighty good leader;
In time of trouble,
He's a mighty good leader.
Jesus Christ, God's Son, God's Son,
He's a mighty good leader,
He's a mighty good leader,
He's a mighty good leader,
Jesus Christ, God's Son.

(ANSAS)

He's Got The Whole World In His Hands

He's got the whole world in his hands,
He's got the big round world in his hands;
He's got the whole world in his hands,
He's got the whole world in his hands.

He's got the wind and the rain in his hands,
He's got the sun and moon in his hands;

He's got the wind and the rain in his hands,
He's got the whole world in his hands.

He's got the little bitsy baby in his hands,
He's got the tiny little baby in his hands;
He's got the itsy bitsy baby in his hands,
He's got the whole world in his hands.

He's got you and me, brother, in his hands,
He's got you and me, sister, in his hands;
He's got you and me, brother, in his hands,
He's got the whole world in his hands.

He's got everybody in his hands,
He's got everybody in his hands,

He's got everybody in his hands,
He's got the whole world in his hands.   (Dixon)

He's Just The Same Today

When Moses and his soldiers,
From Egypt land did flee,
His enemies were in behind him,
And in front of him to see.

God raised the waters like a wall,
And opened up the way,
And the God that lived in Moses' time
Is just the same today.

Daniel faithful to his God
Would not bow down to men,
And by God's enemy he was hurled
Into the lion's den.

God locked the lion's jaw we read,
And robbed him of his prey,
And the God that lived in Daniel's time
Is just the same today.   (BANS)

He's The Lily Of The Valley (1)

He's the lily of the valley,
    Oh! my Lord;
He's the lily of the valley,
    Oh! my Lord;
King Jesus in the chariot rides,
    Oh! my Lord;
With four white horses side by side
    Oh! my Lord.
What kind of shoes are those you wear,
That you can ride upon the air?
These shoes I wear are gospel shoes,
And you can wear them if you choose.

He's the lily of the valley,
    Oh! my Lord;
He the lily of the valley,
    Oh! my Lord;
King Jesus in the chariot rides,
    Oh! my Lord;
With four white horses side by side
    Oh! my Lord.

(FJS)

He's The Lily Of The Valley (2)

He's the Lily of the valley,
He's my Lord;
He's the white Rose of Sharon,
He's my Lord.

He's the Great Physician,
He's my Lord;

He heals your sorrows,
He's my Lord.

He's the Alpha and Omega, the beginning and the end,
He's my Lord;
He's the Shepherd of the Flock, the door to enter in,
He's my Lord.

He's the Lord that was an' is to come,
He's my Lord;
He's the Rock the church is built upon,
He's my Lord.

He's the Bread of Heaven, the Truth, the Way,
He's my Lord;
He's the light that shines to a perfect day,
He's my Lord.

He's the Balm of Gilead, the Great Physician,
He's my Lord;
By His stripes we are healed of all diseases,
He's my Lord.

(Grissom)

Hope I Join The Band

Oh, sinner going to sing around
The new burying ground,
Oh, sinner going to sing around
The new burying ground,
Oh, sinner going to sing around
The new burying ground,
Hope I join the band.

Oh, the moaners going to mourn around,
The new burying ground,
Oh, the prayers going to pray around,
The new burying ground,

Oh, the distorters going to distort around,
The new burying ground,
Oh, when I'm dead and buried in
The new burying ground,
Hope I join the band.   (BDWS)

House What's Built Without Hands

I want a house what's built without hands,
I want that house what's built without hands,
I want that house what's built without hands,
Oh, built by the hammer of the angels,
Built by the hammer of the angels,
Built by the hammer of the angels.
I want my mother to come and go with me,
I want my mother to come and go with me,

I want my mother to come and go with me,
For to show me Jerusalem and Canaan.
He died for me and He died for you,
He died for me and He died for you,
Oh, He died with the angels all around Him,
He died with the angels all around Him.   (BDWS)

I Am Not Afraid To Die

I am not afraid to die,
I am not afraid to die,
I am not afraid to die,
I am not afraid to die.
Jesus rides the milk white horse,
Jesus rides the milk white horse,
I am not afraid to die.

Satan Rides the iron gray,
Satan rides the iron gray,
I am not afraid to die.

I am bound for the promised land,
I am bound for the promised land,
I am not afraid to die.   (St. Helena)

I Believe This Is Jesus

I believe this is Jesus,
Come and see, come and see,
O, I believe this is Jesus,
Come and see, come and see.
The light of God shines in His face,
He offers all His pardoning grace;
The love of God shines in His eyes,
He tells of mansions in the skies;
Did you ever see such love before,
Saying, "Go in peace and sin no more."   (ANS)

I Can't Stay Away

Moaner, why don't you pray?
Moaner, why don't you pray?
Moaner, why don't you pray?
I can't stay away.

Give-a my life to live with Jesus,
Give-a my life to live with Jesus,
Give-a my life to live with Jesus,
I can't stay away.

I'm going home to live with Jesus,
Long white robe in the heaven for me,
Golden girdle in the heaven for me,
Golden slippers in the heaven for me,
Starry crown in the heaven for me,
I can't stay away.

(BDWS)

I Do Know God Don't Lie

I do know God don't lie,
I do know God don't lie,
I do know God don't lie,
The heaven pass away.

Just want tell what a liar will do,
He always come with something new,
Steal your horse with false pretense,
And claim that he is your bosom frien'.

Every day when you look out,
You will see that liar comin' to your house,
Then that liar will have his way,
And take a seat and stay all day.
Just about time you goin' change your min',
Tell you a little truth and make it shine.

Just about time he gets his business fix,
He'll sweeten that rock with a little trick,
If your Aunt Julia don't tell Aunt Jane,
Do for God's sake don't you call my name.

Just about time for liar to leave,
He'll cause your heart and mind to grieve,
But he'll strictly tell you before he go,
If he ask you do you tell him I tell you so.

(St. Helena)

I Got A Home In That Rock

I got a home in that Rock,
Don't you see?
I got a home in that Rock,
Don't you see?

Between the earth and sky,
Thought I heard my Savior cry,
You got a home in that Rock,
Don't you see?

Poor man Lazarus, poor as I,
Don't you see?
Poor man Lazarus, poor as I,
Don't you see?
Poor man Lazarus, poor as I,
When he died he found a home on high;
He had a home in that Rock,
Don't you see?

Rich man, Dives,
He lived so well,
Don't you see?
Rich man, Dives,
He lived so well,
Don't you see?
Rich man, Dives,
He lived so well,
When he died he found a home in Hell,
He had not home in that Rock,
Don't you see?

God gave Noah the rainbow sign,
Don't you see?
God gave Noah the rainbow sign,
Don't you see?
God gave Noah the rainbow sign,
No more water but fire next time.
Better get a home in-a that Rock,
Don't you see?   (BANS)

I Got A Mother In The Bright Shinin' World

I got a mother in the bright shinin' world,
I got a mother in the bright shinin' world,
Dear mother, I hope to meet you over there
        in the bright shinin' world.
In the bright shinin' world,
In the bright shinin' world,
I hope to meet you over there
In the bright shinin' world.

I got a father in the bright shinin' world,
I got a father in the bright shinin' world,
Dear father, I hope to meet you over there
        in the bright shinin' world.

Jesus call me in the bright shinin' world,
Jesus call me in the bright shinin' world,
I hope to meet Him over there
In the bright shinin' world.   (St. Helena)

I Have Another Building

I know I have another building,
I know it's not made with hands, O brethren;
I want to go to Heaven and I want to go right,
O, I want to go to heaven all robed in white.

I haven't been to Heaven but I've been told,
O, the gates are pearl and the streets are gold;
I look over yonder and what do I see?
A hold band of angels coming after me.

I know I have another building,
I know I have another building,
I know it's not made with hands.

(ANSAS)

I Hope My Mother Will Be There

I hope my mother will be there,
In that beautiful world on high;
Oh, I will be there, I will be there,
In that beautiful world on high,

With the palms of victory,
        crowns of glory,
In that beautiful land on high.
I hope my sister will be there,
That used to join me in prayer;
I hope my brother will be there,
I know my Savior will be there,
That used to listen to my prayer,
In that beautiful world on high.

(Hampton)

I Know That My Redeemer Lives

Oh, I know, I know, my Lord,
And I know that my Redeemer lives.
Just stand right still
        and steady yourself,
Oh, just let me tell you
        about the God Himself;
Oh, Daniel in the Lion's den,
Oh, none but Jesus is Daniel's friend;
Oh, Caleb and Joshua,
        the very ones,
That prayed to God for to stop the sun;
Just watch the sun
        and see how it runs,
Oh, don't let it catch you with your work undone.

Oh, I know, I know, my Lord,
I know that my Redeemer lives.

(FJS)

I'm A-Going To Eat At The Welcome Table

I'm a-going to eat at the welcome table,
I'm a-going to eat at the welcome table,
      some of these days.
I'm a-going to feast on milk and honey,
I'm a-going to feast on milk and honey,
      some of these days.
I'm a-going to fly all around in heaven,
I'm a-going to fly all around in heaven,
      some of these days.
I'm a-going to wade across Jordan's river,
I'm a-going to wade across Jordan's river,
      some of these days.   (CD)

I'm Going To Live With Jesus

I'm going to live with Jesus,
A soldier of the Jubilee;
I'm going to live with Jesus,
A soldier of the cross.

I've started out for heaven,
A soldier of the Jubilee;
I know I love my Jesus,
A soldier of the cross.

Oh! when you get there remember me,
A soldier of the Jubilee,
Oh! when you get there remember me,
A soldier of the cross.   (FJS)

I'm 'Most Done Traveling

Yes, I'm bound to carry my soul to my Jesus,
I'm bound to carry my soul to my Lord,
I'm bound to carry my soul to my Jesus,
I'm bound to carry my soul to my Lord.
The preacher's on the way,
I'm 'most done traveling;
The preacher's on the way,
I'm 'most done traveling.

Poor sinner's on the way,
That moaner's on the way,
My mother's on the way,
Rough, rocky, road,
I'm 'most done traveling.   (BDWS)

I'm Troubled In Mind

I'm troubled, I'm troubled,
I'm troubled in mind;
If Jesus don't help me,
I surely will die.

O, Jesus, my Savior,
      On thee I'll depend,
When troubles are near me,
You'll be my friend.

When ladened with trouble
      And burdened with grief,
To Jesus in secret I'll go for relief;
In dark days of bondage
      To Jesus I prayed,
To help me to bear it,
      And he gave me his aid.

I'm troubled, I'm troubled,
I'm troubled in mind;
If Jesus don't help me,
I surely will die.

          (FJS)

In The Kingdom

My mother has gone to journey away,
My father has gone to journey away,
My sister has gone to journey away,
In the kingdom in the kingdom today.

In the kingdom, in the kingdom,
In the kingdom, in the kingdom,
In the kingdom, in the kingdom,
In the kingdom, sweet kingdom,
In the kingdom, in the God-blessed kingdom,
In the kingdom, in the holy, bright kingdom,
In the kingdom, in the kingdom today.

          (Hampton)

I've Got a Mother In The Heavens

I've got a mother in the heavens,
Outshines the sun,
Outshines the sun, outshines the sun,
I've got a mother in the heavens,
Outshines the sun,
Way beyond the moon.

I've got a father in the heavens,
Outshines the sun,
Outshines the sun, outshines the sun,
I've got a father in the heavens,
Outshines the sun,
Way beyond the moon.

I've got a sister in the heavens,
Outshines the sun,
Outshines the sun, outshines the sun,
I've got a sister in the heavens,
Outshines the sun,
Way beyond the moon.

When we get to heaven,
We will outshine the sun,
Outshine the sun, outshine the sun,
When we get to heaven,
We will outshine the sun,
Way beyond the moon.   (Hampton)

Jesus Done Just What He Said

Jesus done just what he said,
Healed the sick and he raised the dead.
Yes, he did.
Oh, yes, he did.

Up on the mountain my Lord spoke,
Out of his mouth came fire and smoke.
Yes, he did.
Oh, yes, he did.

John the Baptist he declared,
Ain't but the righteous shall get there.
Yes, he did.
Oh, yes, he did.
I remember the hour, I remember it well.
When Jesus wash my sins away.
Yes, he did.
Oh, yes, he did.

You can tell the world about that,
You can tell the nation about that.
Tell them my Lord has come,
Tell them what the Comforter has done.
That he brought joy, joy, joy to my soul.   (St. Helena)

Jesus' Going To Make Up My Dying Bed

You needn't mind my dying,
You needn't mind my dying,
You needn't mind my dying,
Jesus's going to make up my dying bed.

In my dying room I know,
Somebody's going to cry,
All I ask you to do for me,
Just close my dying eyes.

I'll be sleeping in Jesus,
I'll be sleeping in Jesus,
I'll be sleeping in Jesus,
Jesus's going to make up my dying bed.
In my dying room I know,
Somebody's going to mourn,
All I ask you to do for me,
Just give that bell a tone.

I'll be resting easy,
I'll be resting easy,
I'll be resting easy,
Jesus's going to make up my dying bed.
When I get to heaven,
I want you to be there too,
When I cry out "holy,"
I want you to say so too.

I'll be talking with the angels,
I'll be talking with the angels,
I'll be talking with the angels,
Jesus's going to make up my dying bed.   (ANS)

Jesus Locked the Lion's Jaw

Baptist, Baptist, unbeliever,
Baptist, Baptist, when I'm dead and gone.
Jesus lock the lion, lock the lion, lock the lion jaw.

Methodist, Methodist, unbeliever,
Methodist, Methodist, when I'm gone.
Jesus lock the lion, lock the lion, lock the lion jaw.

Good ol' Daniel, faithful servant,
Good ol' Daniel, when I'm dead and gone.
Jesus lock the lion, lock the lion, lock the lion jaw.   (Calhoun)

Jesus On The Waterside

Heaven's bell a-ringing,
        I know the road;
Heaven's bell a-ringing,
        I know the road;
Heaven's bell a-ringing,
        I know the road,
Jesus is sitting on the waterside.

Do come along,
        Do let us go,
Do come along,
        Do let us go,
Do come along,
        Do let us go,
Jesus is sitting on the waterside.   (Allen)

Jesus Rolling In-a His Arms

Great God He rules all around the mountain,
Great God He rules all around the mountain,
Great God He rules all around the mountain,
Jesus rolling in-a His arms.

May the Lord bless the moaner,
May the Lord bless the moaner,

May the Lord bless the moaner,
Jesus rolling in-a His arms.

May the Lord bless the sinner,
May the Lord bless my sister,
May the Lord bless my turn-back,
May the Lord bless my brother.
Great God He rules all around the mountain,
Jesus rolling in-a His arms.   (BDWS)

John Saw

John saw, Oh, John saw,
John saw the holy number
Sitting on the golden altar.
Worthy, worthy is the Lamb, is the Lamb, is the Lamb,
Worthy, worthy is the Lamb,
Sitting on the golden altar.

Mary wept and Martha cried
To see their Savior crucified,
Weeping Mary, weep no more
Jesus say He gone before.

Want to go to heaven when I die,
Shout salvation as I fly;
It's a little while longer here below,
Then a-home to glory we shall go.

John saw, Oh, John saw,
John saw the holy number,
Sitting on the golden altar.   (Hampton) (Variant)

Join Them

On Sunday morning I seek my Lord,
Join them, join them, oh!
Oh join them believer, join them so,
Join them, join them, oh!
Join, brethren, join us oh,
Join us, join us, oh!
We meet tonight to sing and pray,
In Jesus' name we'll sing and pray.   (ALLEN)

King Emanuel

Oh, who do you call the King Emanuel;
I call my Jesus King Emanuel.
Oh, the King Emanuel is a mighty Emanuel;
I call my Jesus King Emanuel.

Oh, some call Him Jesus; but I call Him Lord,
Let's talk abut heaven and heaven's fine things,
Oh steady, steady, a little while;
I will tell you what my Lord done for me;

He plucked my feet out of the miry clay;
He set them on the firm Rock of Ages.

Oh, who do you call the King Emanuel;
I call my Jesus King Emanuel.
Oh, the King Emanuel is a mighty Emanuel;
I call my Jesus King Emanuel.   (Hampton)

King Jesus Built Me A House Above

King Jesus built me a house above,
King Jesus built me a house above,
King Jesus built me a house above,
And he built it without a hammer or nail.

King Jesus built me a house above,
King Jesus built me a house above,
King Jesus built me a house above,
And he built it on Jerusalem lane.

I want my sister to go with me,
I want my sister to go with me,
I want my sister to go with me,
To feast on the heavenly manna.   (ANSAS)

King Jesus Is My Only Friend

King Jesus is my only friend,
King Jesus is my only friend,
King Jesus is my only friend,
King Jesus is my only friend.

When the doctor, the doctor done give me over,
When the doctor, the doctor done give me over,
When the doctor, the doctor done give me over,
King Jesus is my only friend.

When the preacher, the preacher done give me over,
King Jesus is my only friend.
When my house, my house become a public hall,
King Jesus is my only friend.
When my face, my face become a looking glass,
King Jesus is my only friend.   (St. Helena)

Let Us Cheer The Weary Traveler

Let us cheer the weary traveler,
Cheer the weary traveler;
Let us cheer the weary traveler,
Along the heavenly way.

I'll take my gospel trumpet,
And I'll begin to blow,
And if my Savior helps me,
I'll blow wherever I go.

And if you meet with crosses,
And trials on the way,
Just keep your trust in Jesus,
And don't forget to pray.

Let us cheer the weary traveler,
Cheer the weary traveler;
Let us cheer the weary traveler,
Along the heavenly way.   (Hampton)

Lit'l Boy

"Lit'l Boy, how ole are you?
"Lit'l Boy, how ole are you?
"Lit'l Boy, how ole are you?"
"Sir, I'm only twelve years old."

This Lit'l Boy had them to remember
That He was born the twenty-fifth of December,
Lawyers and doctors were amazed,
And had to give the Lit'l Boy praise.

"Lit'l Boy, how ole are you?
"Lit'l Boy, how ole are you?
"Lit'l Boy, how ole are you?"
"Sir, I'm only twelve years old."

Lawyers and doctors stood and wondered,
As though they had been struck by thunder;
Then they decided while they wondered,
That all mankind must come under.

"Lit'l Boy, how ole are you?
"Lit'l Boy, how ole are you?
"Lit'l Boy, how ole are you?"
"Sir, I'm only twelve years old."

The last time the Lit'l Boy was seen,
He was standin' on Mount Olivet Green.
When He'd dispersed of the crowd,
He entered up into a cloud.

"Lit'l Boy, how ole are you?
"Lit'l Boy, how ole are you?
"Lit'l Boy, how ole are you?"
"Sir, I'm only twelve years old."   (Hayes)

Little David

The Lord called David,
And He called three times,
David came a-running:
Lord what's troubling your mind?
Little David, play on your harp, hallelujah.

Little David was a shepherd boy,
He killed Goliath and shouted for joy,
Little David, play on your harp, hallelujah.
Little David, play on your golden harp, hallelujah.

The Lord loved David,
And he loved him well;
He sent Goliath right down to hell.
Little David, play on your harp, hallelujah.
Little David, play on your golden harp, hallelujah.   (BDWS)

A Little Talk With Jesus Makes It Right

O, a little talk with Jesus makes it right,
          all right;

Little talk with Jesus makes it right,
          all right.

Lord, troubles of every kind,
Thank God, I'll always find
That a little talk with Jesus makes it right.

My brother, I remember
When I was a sinner lost,
I cried, "Have mercy Jesus,"
But still my soul was tossed;
Till I heard King Jesus say,
"Come here, I am the way."

Sometimes the forked lightning,
And muttering thunder, too,
Of trials and temptation
Make it hard for me and you;
But Jesus is our friend,
He'll keep up till the end.
And a little talk with Jesus makes it right,
O, a little talk with Jesus makes it right.   (BANS)

The Lord Is My Shepherd

The Lord, the Lord, the Lord is my shepherd,
The Lord, the Lord, the Lord is my shepherd,
The Lord, the Lord, the Lord is my shepherd,
The Lord is my shepherd and I shall not want.

He maketh me to lie down in green pastures,
He maketh me to lie down in green pastures,
He maketh me to lie down in green pastures,
The Lord is my shepherd and I shall not want.

He leadeth me beside the still water,
He leadeth me beside the still water,
He leadeth me beside the still water,
The Lord is my shepherd and I shall not want.   (ANSAS)

Love-Feast In Heaven

There's a love-feast in heaven,
        by and by, children,
There's a love-feast in heaven,
        by and by, children,
Yes, a love-feast in heaven,
        by and by, children,
There's a love-feast in heaven,
        by and by.

Oh! run up, children,
        get your crown,
And by your savior's side sit down;
Old Satan told me not to pray,
He wants my soul at the Judgement Day;
Oh, brethren and sisters, how do you do,
And does your love continue true?
Oh, brethren, brethren, how do you know?
Because my Jesus told me so.

There's a love-feast in heaven,
        by and by, children,
There's a love-feast in heaven,
        by and by.   (FJS)

Members, Don't Get Weary

Members, don't get weary,
Members, don't get weary,
Members, don't get weary,
For the work's most done.

O, keep your lamp trimmed and burning,
Keep your lamp trimmed and burning,
Keep your lamp trimmed and burning,
For the work's almost done.

I'm going down to the river of Jordan,
When my work is done;
I'm going to sit at the welcome table,
When my work is done;
I'm going to feast on milk and honey,
When my work is done;
I'm going to march with the tallest angel,
When my work is done.

Members, don't get weary,
Members, don't get weary,
Members, don't get weary,
For the work's most done.   (BANS)

My Brethren, Don't Get Weary

My brethren, don't get weary,
Angels brought the tidings down;

Don't get weary,
I'm hunting for a home, home.

You'd better be a-praying,
I do love the Lord;

For judgment day's a-coming,
I do love the Lord, Lord.

Oh where you running, sinner?
The judgment day is coming!
You'll see the world on fire!
You'll see the element a-melting
You'll see the moon a-bleeding,
You'll see the stars a-falling.
I do love the Lord, Lord.

My brethren, don't get weary,
Angels brought the tidings down;

Don't get weary,
I'm hunting for a home, home.

(Hampton)

My God Is A Man Of War

My God He is a Man--a Man of war,
My God He is a Man--a Man of war,
My God He is a Man--a Man of War,
An' the Lord God is His name.

He tol' Noah to build an ark,
By His Holy plan;
He tol' Moses to lead the children,
From Egypt to the Promised Lan'.

Long befo' the flyin' clouds,
Befo' the heavens above,
Befo' creation ever was made,
He had redeemin' love.

He made the sun an' moon an' stars,
To rule both day an' night;
He placed them in the firmament,
An' tol' them to give light.
He made the birds of the air,
An' made the earth aroun';
He made the beasts of the field,
An' made the serpents on the groun'.

(Grissom)

My God Is A Rock

My God is a rock in a weary land,
My God is a rock in a weary land,
My God is a rock in a weary land,
Shelter in time of storm.

I know He is a rock in a weary land,
I know He is a rock in a weary land.

Stop 'n let me tell you about Chapter One,
Hallelu, Hallelu,
When the Lord God's work was just begun,
Stop 'n let me tell you about Chapter Two,
When the Lord God's written His Bible through.
Stop 'n let me tell you about Chapter Three,
When the Lord God died on Calvary.

My God is a rock in a weary land,
Shelter in time of storm.
Stop 'n let me tell you about Chapter Four,
When the Lord God visit among the po'.
Stop 'n let me tell you about Chapter Five,
When the Lord God brought the dead alive.
Hallelu, Hallelu.

Stop 'n let me tell you about Chapter Six,
He went in Jerusalem and healed the sick.
O, my Jesus,

O, I know Him;
He's a rock in a weary land.
Stop 'n let me tell you about Chapter Seven,
Died and risen and went to Heav'n;
O, my Jesus,
O, my Jesus.

Stop 'n let me tell you about Chapter Eight,
John seen him standin' at the Golden Gate,
He was knockin' at the Golden Gate,
Hallelujah, Jesus,
O, my Jesus.

Stop 'n let me tell you about Chapter Nine,
Lord God turned the water to wine,
Stop 'n let me tell you about Chapter Ten,
John says He's comin' in the world again.

My God is a rock in a weary land,
My God is a rock in a weary land;
Shelter in time of storm.
Hallelu, Hallelu.

(L-G)

My Mind Stayed On Freedom

I woke up this morning with my mind
    Stayed on freedom,
I woke up this morning with my mind
    Stayed on freedom,
I woke up this morning with my mind
    Stayed on freedom,
Hallelu! Hallelu! Hallelu!

My mother got her mind
  Stayed on freedom,
My father got his mind
  Stayed on freedom,
My brother got his mind
  Stayed on freedom,
My sister got her mind
  Stayed on freedom,
Hallelu! Hallelu! Hallelu!

(Traditional)

Never Leave Me Alone

Never leave me alone, alone,
Never leave me alone, alone,
My Jesus promised
Never leave me alone.

When my health is weakening,
Never leave me alone;
When I am dying,
Never leave me alone;
If you see me failing,
Never leave me alone;

My Jesus promised,
Never leave me alone.

(CD)

Never Saw Such A Man

Never saw such a Man before,
Never saw such a Man before,
Never saw such a Man before,

Never saw such a Man before,
That'd give up His only Son to die.

I never saw such a Man.
Did you ever see such a Man?
Oh, I never saw such a Man before,
That'd give up His only Son to die.

(Malcolm)

The New Born Baby

Baby, born in Bethlehem,
Oh, when I get in glory,
Oh, when I get in glory,
Oh, when I get in glory,
Glory be to the new-born Baby.

The world reel,
But I get in glory,
Oh, when I get in glory,
Oh, when I get in glory,
Glory be to the new-born Baby.

My trials rise,
But I get in glory,
Oh, when I get in glory,
Oh, when I get in glory,
Glory be to the new-born Baby.

The wind blow,
But I get in glory,
Oh, when I get in glory,
Oh, when I get in glory,
Glory be to the new-born Baby.   (Fisher)

O, Brothers, Don't Get Weary

O, brothers, don't get weary,
O, brothers, don't get weary,
O, brothers, don't get weary,
We're waiting for the Lord.

We'll land on Canaan's shore,
We'll land on Canaan's shore,
When we land on Canaan's shore,
We'll meet forever more.   (Allen)

O, Glory

O, glory, O, glory
O, glory, O, glory
There is room enough in Paradise
To have a home in glory.

O, glory, O, glory,
O, glory, O, glory,
I'm going to see my mother,
I'm going to see my sister,
I'm going to see my father,
I'm going to see my brother.

O, glory, O, glory
O, glory, O, glory
There is room enough in Paradise
To have a home in glory.   (Traditional)

Oh, Mary, Don't You Weep

Oh, Mary, don't you weep, don't you moan,
Oh, Mary, don't you weep, don't you moan,
Pharaoh's army already got drowned,
Oh, Mary, don't you weep.

One of these mornings bright and fair,
Gonna take my wings and cleave the air,
Pharaoh's army already got drowned
Oh, Mary don't you weep.   (Traditional)

Oh Mary, Oh Marthy

Oh! Mary, Oh! Marthy, go tell my disciples,
Goin' to meet Him in Galilee,
Goin' to meet Him in Galilee.
Yes, bless the Lord, meet Him in Galilee.
Goin' to meet Him in Galilee.

Oh! yonder come the chariot,
The horses dressed in white,
The fo' wheels a-runnin' by the grace of God,
An' the hin' wheels a-runnin' by love;
An' the hin' wheels a-runnin' by love.

Oh! Yonder come ole Satan
With a black book under his arm;
A hollerin' "Give me justice,
"More'n half them people am mine,
"More'n half them people am mine.
"Yes, bless the Lord, half them people am mine;
"More'n half them people am mine."

Oh! yonder come Brother Peter,
An' how do you know it's him?
With a crown upon his fo'head
An' the keys of Bethlehem,
An' the keys of Bethlehem.
Yes, bless the Lord, keys of Bethlehem;
An' the keys of Bethlehem.

Oh! yonder come Sister Mary,
An' how do you know it's her?
A shoutin' Hallelujah
An' praises to the Lamb,
An' praises to the Lamb.

Yes, bless the Lord, praises to the Lamb;
An' praises to the Lamb.

(Grissom)

Oh, My Lord, What Shall I Do?

Hush, oh hush, somebody's calling me,
Hush, oh hush, somebody's calling me,
Hush, oh hush, somebody's calling me,
Oh my Lord, oh my Lord, what shall I do?

I think, I think, the angels calling me,
I think, I think, the angels calling me,
Oh, my Lord, oh my Lord, what shall I do?

It sounds just like my mother's voice to me,
It sounds just like my mother's voice to me,
Oh, my Lord, oh my Lord, what shall I do?

Run, sinner, run, and find your hiding place,
Run, sinner, run, and find your hiding place,

Oh, my Lord, oh my Lord, what shall I do?

What you going to do when death comes creeping
     at your door?
What you going to do when death comes creeping
     at your door?
Oh, my Lord, oh my Lord, what shall I do?

Going to close my eyes, and sleep away in death,
Going to close my eyes, and sleep away in death,
Oh, my Lord, Oh, my Lord, what shall I do?

Going to lay my head, yes my head, on Jesus' breast,
Going to lay my head, yes my head, on Jesus' breast,
Oh, my Lord, oh my Lord, what shall I do?

I'm so glad I got my religion in time,
I'm so glad I got my religion in time,
Oh, my Lord, oh my Lord, what shall I do?   (BDWS)

The Old Ark's Moving Along

Just wait a little while,
I'm going to tell you about the old ark, old ark,
The old ark moving along, moving along,
Oh, the old ark moving, moving, moving,
The old ark moving, moving along.

The Noah and his sons
Went to work upon dry land,
They built an ark just according to command,
Noah and his sons went to work upon the timber,
The proud began to laugh,
And the silly to point their finger.

When the ark was finished just according to plan,
Master Noah took his family,
Both animal and man;
When the rain began to fall --
And the ark began to rise,

The wicked hung around
With their groans and their cries.

Forty days and forty nights,
The rain it kept falling;
The wicked climbed the trees,
And for help they kept calling;
That awful rain, she stopped at last,
The waters they subsided
And that old ark with all on board
On Ararat she rided.

Oh, the old ark moving, moving, moving,
The old ark moving, moving along.   (Hampton)

O, Mary, Don't You Weep Don't You Mourn (2)

O, Mary, don't you weep, don't you mourn,
O, Mary, don't you weep, don't you mourn;
Pharaoh's army got drowned,
O, Mary, don't you weep.

Some of these mornings bright and fair,
Take my wings and cleave the air;
When I get to heaven going to sing and shout,
Nobody there for to turn me out;
When I get to heaven going to put on my shoes,
Run about glory and tell all the news.

(ANSAS) (Variant)

O, Mother, Don't You Weep

When I'm gone, when I'm gone,
When I'm gone, gone, gone,
O, Mother, don't you weep when I'm gone.

For I'm going to heaven above,
Going to the God I love,
O, Mother, don't you weep when I'm gone.

O, Mother, meet me there,
Mother, meet me in the air,
O, Mother, don't you weep when I'm gone.

(ANS)

Over The Crossing

Bending knees a-aching,
Body racked with pain,
I wish I was a child of God,
I'd get home by and by.
Keep praying, I do believe
We've a long time wagging over the crossing;
Keep praying, I do believe
We'll get home to heaven by and by.
O, yonder's my old mother,
Been a wagging at the hill so long,
It's about time she crossed over,
Get home by and by.

O hear that lumbering thunder
A-roll from door to door,
A-calling the people home to God;
They'll come home by and by.
O see that forked lightning
A-jump from cloud to cloud,
A-picking up God's children;
They'll get home by and by.
Pray mourner, I do believe,
Little children, I do believe,
We'll get home to heaven by and by.

(ALLEN)

Plenty Good Room

There's plenty good room, there's plenty good room,
Way in the Kingdom;
There's plenty good room, there's plenty good room,
Way in the kingdom.

My Lord's done just what he said,
Healed the sick and raised the dead;
One of these mornings bright and fair,
Going to hitch my wings and cleave the air;
When I was a mourner just like you,
I prayed and prayed till I came through.
Come on mourner, make a bound,
The Lord will meet you on the half-way ground.   (ANSAS)

Poor Mourner's Got A Home At Last

Poor mourner's got a home at last,
Mourner's got a home at last.

O, mourner, mourner,
Ain't you tired of mourning?
Bow down on your knees
And join the band with the angels.

O, no harm, Lord, no harm,
Go tell brother Elijah,
No harm, Lord, no harm,
Poor mourner's got a home at last.

O gambler, gambler,
Ain't you tired of gambling?
Bow down on your knees
And join the band with the angels.
Poor mourner's got a home at last
Their mourner's got a home at last.   (BANS)

Religion Is A Fortune

Oh, religion is a fortune,
        I really do believe,
Oh, religion is a fortune,
        I really do believe,
Oh, religion is a fortune,
            I really do believe,
Where Sabbaths have no end.
Where you been, poor mourner,
Where you been so long?
Been low down in the valley for to pray,
And I ain't done praying yet.

Going to sit down in the kingdom,
Going to walk about in Zion,
Going to see my sister Mary,
Going to see my brother Jonah,

Going to talk with the angels,
Going to see my master Jesus,
I really do believe.

(Hampton)

Religion So Sweet

O, walk Jordan's long road,
And religion so sweet;
O, religion is good for anything,
And religion so sweet.

Religion makes you happy,
Religion gives me patience,
O, member, get religion;
I've a long time been hunting,
I'm seeking for my fortune,
O, I'm going to see my Savior,
Going to tell him about my trials;
They call me a boasting member,
They call me a turnback Christian,
They call me instruction maker;
But I don't care what they call me,
Lord, trials belong to a Christian;
O, tell me about religion,
I weep for Mary and Martha,
I seek my Lord and I find him.
O, walk Jordan's long road,
And religion so sweet;
O, religion is good for anything,
And religion so sweet.

(ALLEN)

The Religion That My Lord Gave Me

O, the religion that my Lord gave me,
Shines like a morning star;
O, the religion that my Lord gave me,
Shines like a morning star.

O, Brother, you'd better believe, believe,
To shine like a morning star;
O, Mourner, you'd better believe, believe,
To shine like a morning star;
O, sinner, you'd better believe, believe,
To shine like a morning star.

O, the religion that my Lord gave me,
Shines like a morning star;
O, the religion that my Lord gave me,
Shines like a morning star.

(ANS)

Ring The Bells

Ring the bells!
All God's children, ring the bells!
So they say;

Not today, not tomorrow,
Ring the bells!

Ring the bells!
When in trouble, ring the bells!
Ring the bells and tell the Savior,
Ring the bells!
Ring the bells and let Him hear you.
Ring the bell!
So they say;
Not today, not tomorrow,
Ring the bells!   (CD)

Rocka My Soul

Rocka my soul
In the bosom of Abraham,
Rocka my soul
In the bosom of Abraham,
Lord, rocka my soul.

He toted the young lambs
In his bosom,
And left the old sheep alone.

Rocka my soul
In the bosom of Abraham,
Rocka my soul.
In the bosom of Abraham,
Lord, rocka my soul.   (ALLEN)

Rock of Ages

My loving brother,
When the world's on fire,
Don't you want Christ's bosom for your
        pillow?
O, hide me over in the Rock of Ages,
O, Rock of Ages cleft for me.

My loving sister,
When the world's on fire,
Don't you want Christ's bosom for your
        pillow?
O, hide me over in the Rock of Ages,
O, Rock of Ages cleft for me.   (ANS)

Roll And Rock

Roll and rock,
        Can't you come along,
Roll and rock,
        Can't you come along,

Roll and rock,

Can't you come along,
My soul wants to go home to glory.
Tell me brother, tell me now,
Where you been so long one.
Been rising and falling at the old church door,
And my soul wants to go home to glory.
Tell me brother better still,
I know you got more besides,
Been praying the good Lord for to turn me around,
And my soul wants to go home to glory.   (BDWS)

Rolling In Jesus' Arms

I'm a-rolling in Jesus' arms,
I'm a-rolling in Jesus' arms;
On the other side of Jordan,
I'm a-rolling in Jesus' arms.

One day when I was walking,
Along that lonesome road,
My Savior spoke unto me,
And filled my heart with love.

He chose me for a watchman,
To blow the trumpet of God,
To join the weary traveler
Along that heavenly road.

Why do you tarry, sinner,
Why do you wait so long?
Your Savior is a-waiting for you,
Why don't you come along?

You need not look for riches,
Nor either dress so fine,
The robe that Jesus gives you,
Outshines the glittering sun.   (BDWS)

Roll On

Roll on, roll on, sweet moments roll on,
And let these poor pilgrims go home, go home.
When I was blind and could not see,
King Jesus brought that light to me.
The heavenly land bright and fair,
There are very few seen going there.

Roll on, roll on, sweet moments roll on,
And let these poor pilgrims go home, go home.   (ANS)

Room Enough

Oh, brothers, don't stay away,
    Brothers, don't stay away,
    Brothers, don't stay away,

Don't stay away,
For my Lord says there's room enough,
Room enough in the heavens for you,
My Lord says there's room enough,
Don't stay away.

Oh, mourners, don't stay away,
For the Bible says there's room enough,
Oh, sinners, don't stay away,
For the angel says there's room enough,
Oh, children, don't stay away,
For Jesus says there's room enough,
Room enough in the heavens for you,
My Lord says there's room enough.   (FJS)

'Round About The Mountain

Round about the mountain,
O, 'round about the valleys,
O, 'round about the mountain,
And she'll rise in His arms.

The Lord loves the sinner,
The Lord loves the sinner,
The Lord loves the sinner,
And she'll rise in His arms.   (Krehbiel)

Sailing Over Yonder

We are sailing over yonder,
We are sailing over yonder,

We are sailing over yonder,
On the other side of the shore.

Some for Silas, some for Peter,
Some for to make my heart rejoice;
Some for Silas, some for Peter,
Good Shepherd, feed my lamb.

You may travel to the gates of hell,
But if you look unto the Lord,
Old hell will never get you,
You'll come home straight to God.   (BDWS)

Shout On, Children

Shout on, children, you'll never die,
Glory hallelu!
You're in the Lord,
And the Lord's in you;
Glory hallelu!
Shout and pray both night and day;
How can you die, you're in the Lord?

Come on, children, let's go home;
O, I'm so glad you're in the Lord.

(ALLEN)

Singing On The Old Church Ground

We're singing, singing tonight,
We're singing on the ol' church groun',
We're singing, singing to night,
We're singing on the ol' church groun'.

We're praying, praying tonight,
We're praying on the ol' church groun',
We're praying, praying tonight,
We're praying on the ol' church ground.

We're mourning, mourning tonight,
We're mourning, mourning tonight,
O, sinners tonight, sinners tonight,
We're mourning on the ol' church groun'.

We must leave you, leave you tonight,
We must leave you, leave you tonight,
We must leave you, leave you tonight,
We must leave you on the ol' church groun'.

O, good bye, good bye tonight,
O, good bye, good bye tonight,
Good by on the ol' church groun',
Good bye on the ol' church groun'.

(Calhoun)

Sinner, Please Don't Let This Harvest Pass

Sinner, please don't let this harvest pass,
Sinner, please don't let this harvest pass;
Sinner, please don't let this harvest pass
And die, and lose your soul at last.

Sinner, O, see that cruel tree,
See that cruel tree, Lord!
Where Christ has died for you and me, Lord!
I know that my redeemer lives,
My redeemer lives, Lord!
Sinner, please don't let this harvest pass.

My God is a mighty man of war,
A mighty man of war, Lord!
Sinner, please don't let this harvest pass.

(BANS)

Sit Down

Sit down, servant; sit down, servant;
Sit down and rest a little while.
Sit down, servant; sit down, servant;
Sit down and rest a little while.
I know you are tired; sit down, servant;

You come over mountain; sit down servant;
I know you had trouble; sit down, servant;
I know you been crying; sit down, servant;

I know you been praying; sit down, servant;
I know you been afflicted; sit down, servant;
It a tiresome journey; sit down, servant;
It a long journey; sit down, servant.   (Dixon)

Sitting Down Side Of My Jesus

O, Lamb!
Sitting down side of my Jesus,
O, Lamb!
Sitting down side of my Jesus.

O, Holy!
Sitting down side of my Jesus,
Paul and Silas,
Sitting down side of my Jesus,
Mary and Martha,
Sitting down side of my Jesus,
In the kingdom,
Sitting down side of my Jesus,
Little children,
Sitting down side of my Jesus.   (Calhoun)

Some Of These Mornings

Going to see my mother some of these mornings,
See my mother some of these mornings,
See my mother some of these mornings,
Look away in the heaven
Look away in the heaven,
Hope I'll join the band.

Oh, sitting in the kingdom some of these mornings,
Sitting in the kingdom some of these mornings,
Look away in the heaven,
Hope I'll join the band.

Going to see my brother some of these mornings;
Oh, shouting in the heaven some of these mornings;
Going to walk about in Zion some of these mornings,
Going to talk with the angels some of these mornings.
Going to talk the trouble over some of these mornings.
Look away in the heaven,
Hope I'll join the band.   (Hampton)

Soon I'll Be Done

Soon I'll be done with the trouble of this world,
Soon I'll be done with the trouble of this world,
Soon I'll be done with the trouble of this world,
Going to live with God.

Come, my brother, go with me,
Come, my brother, go with me,
Come, my brother, go with me,
Let King Jesus make you free.

When I get to heaven I will sing and tell,
When I get to heaven I will sing and tell,
When I get to heaven I will sing and tell,
How I did shun both death and hell.   (ANS)

The Sun Mows Down

Hurry mourner! hurry mourner!
Hurry mourner! Going to pray until I die.
The sun mows down, the sun mows down,
Going to pray until I die.

Now what do you think about dying children?
Now what do you think about dying children?
I think its mighty trying, children,
I think its mighty trying, children;
My Jesus will meet me in that morning,
My Jesus will meet me in that morning.   (ANSAS)

Tell All The World, John

Tell all the world, John,
Tell all the world, John,
I know the other world's not like this.

What kind of shoes are those you wear,
That you can walk up in the air?
When Jesus shook the manna tree,
He shook it for you and He shook it for me.
Going to talk to the Father, talk to the Son,
Going to talk about the work that I left undone.   (ANSAS)

Tell It

Father Abraham sitting down side-a the holy Lamb,
Way up on the mountaintop,
Tell it, tell it, tell it.
My Lord spoke and the chariot stop,
Sitting down side-a the holy Lamb.
Father Abraham sitting down side-a the holy Lamb.

Good bye an' fare you well,
Meet me aroun' the throne of God;
Weep like a willow an' mourn like a dove,
If yo want to go to heaven, you got to go by love.

M for Michael, G for Golia',
D for little David done kill Golia',
M for Mary, P for Paul,
C for Christ, He die for us all.

When I get to heaven going to sit an' tell
The three Arcangels to ring the bell;
When I get to heaven going to sit an' choose,
Going to ask my Lord for the silver shoes;
Sitting down side-a the holy Lamb,
Jeremiah sitting down side-a the holy Lamb.   (Calhoun)

There Is Rest For The Weary Traveller

There is rest for the weary traveller,
There is rest for the weary traveller,
O, there is rest for the weary traveller,
There is rest, there is rest for me.

There is rest when I come over Jordan;
There is rest when the doctor give me over;
There is rest for the Hebrew children.
There is rest, there is rest for me.   (St. Helena)

There's A Meeting Here Tonight

I take my text in Matthew,
And by the Revelation,
I know you by your garment,
There's a meeting here tonight.
There's a meeting here tonight,
There's a meeting here tonight,
I hope to meet again.

Brother John was a writer,
He wrote the laws of God,
Sister Mary say to brother John,
"Brother John, don't write no more";
There's a meeting here tonight,
There's a meeting here tonight,
I hope to meet again.

I see brother Moses yonder,
And I think I ought to know him,
For I know him by his garment,
He's a blessing here tonight,
He's a blessing here tonight,
I think I ought to know him,
He's a blessing here tonight.   (ALLEN)

This Is The Man

This is the Man who made this earth,
This is the Man -
This is the Man who died for you,
This is the Man -

This is the Man you call Jesus Christ,
This is the Man -
This is the Man who rose again,

This is the Man -
This is the Man,
You talk about the Man,
This is the Man.

(CD)

This Old Time Religion

Oh! this old time religion,
This old time religion,
      This old time religion,
It is good enough for me.

It is good for the mourner,
It will carry you home to heaven,
It brought me out of bondage,
It is good when you are in trouble,
It is good enough for me.

Oh! this old time religion,
This old time religion,
      This old time religion,
It is good enough for me.

(FJS)

To See God's Bleedin' Lamb

Want to go to heaven when I die,
When I die, when I die;
Want to go to heaven when I die
To see God's bleedin' Lamb.

Jacob's ladder deep and long,
Deep and long, deep and long;
Jacob's ladder deep and long,
To see God's bleedin' Lamb.

See God's Angel comin' down,
To see God's bleedin' Lamb;
Comin' down in a sheet of blood,
To see God's bleedin' Lamb;
Sheet of blood all mingle' with fire,
To see God's bleedin' Lamb;
Then you raise your voice up higher,
To see God's bleedin' Lamb;
An' you join the heavenly Choir,
To see God's bleedin' Lamb.

(St. Helena)

Two Wings

Got two wings to veil your face,
Two wings for to sail away,
Got two wings to veil your face,
Two wings for to sail away.

Oh Lordy, Oh angel,
Let me tell you about God Himself,

How he traveled here below, healed the sick and raised the dead,
Cast out devils in His name.
If ever I get to heaven's door,
Going to make my bow and walk right in;
Going to choose my seat and sit right down;
Going to chatter with the Father,
And argue with the Son.

Ain't but one thing grieves my mind,
My mother's gone to heaven and left me behind,
And when she gets to that heavenly door,
Going to make one bow and walk right in,
Cause she don't expect to come here no more.

Poor little dove, you creeping thing,
Got up on the ark and begun to sing:
Redeem, redeem, I'm born of God,
Think of the things Master Jesus done,
Brought me home before the setting of the sun.   (BDWS)

Wait A Little While

Wait a little while,
Then we'll sing the new song;

Wait a little while,
Then we'll sing the new song.

My heavenly home is bright and fair,
No pain or sorrows enter there;
Jesus my Lord to heaven is gone,
He whom I fix my hopes upon.
Wait a little while,
Then we'll sing the new song;
Wait a little while,
Then we'll sing the new song.   (FJS)

Walk About Elders

Walk about Elders, Jesus a listenin';
Walk about Elders, Jesus died.

Paul an' Silas bound in Jail,
Paul an' Silas a-bound in jail;
Paul an' Silas a-bound in jail,
Nothin' but the blood of Jesus can pay their bail.
Walk about Elders, Jesus is a-listenin';
Walk about Elders, Jesus died.

Good ole Daniel in the lion's den,
Good ole Daniel in the lion's den;
Good ole Daniel in the lion's den,
None but the lowly Jesus was his frien'.
Walk about Elders, Jesus a-listenin';
Walk about Elders, Jesus died.

While the rich man lived he lived so well,
While the rich man lived he lived so well;
While the rich man lived he lived so well,
When he died he made his home in Hell.
Walk about Elders, Jesus a-listenin';
Walk about Elders, Jesus died.

When you see me standin' round,
When you see me standin' round;
When you see me standin' round.
You jus' can know that I'm Heaven bound.
Walk about Elders, Jesus a-listenin';
Walk about Elders, Jesus died.

(Grissom)

Walk God's Heavenly Road

March along,
    Oh, Canaan land,
    Oh, Canaan land,
March along,
    Oh, Canaan land,
Walk God's heavenly road.

If you don't love your brother,
Don't you take his name abroad,
Take him as a bosom friend,
And carry him to God.

Yes, on this rock I'll build my church,
There I mean to stand.
Stand on the wayside,
'Til God almighty gives command.
Oh the Father looked at the Son and smiled,
And the Son did look at Him.
Father redeem my soul from hell,
And the Son did set me free.
March along,
    Oh, Canaan land,
Walk God's heavenly road.

(BDWS)

Walk You In The Light

Walk you in the light,
Walk you in the light,

Walk you in the light,
Walking in the light of God.

Oh, children, do you think it true,
That Jesus Christ did die for you,
Yes, He died for me and He died for you,
For the Holy Bible does say so.

I think I heard some children say,
That they never heard their parents pray,

O, parents, that is not the way,
But teach your children to watch and pray.

I love to shout, I love to sing,
I love to praise my heavenly King,
Oh, sisters can't you help me sing
For Moses' sister did help him.

Oh, the heavenly land so bright and fair,
A very few that enter there,
For good Elijah did declare,
That nothing but the righteous shall go there.

Walk you in the light,
Walk you in the light,
Walk you in the light,
Walking in the light of God.   (Hampton)

Way Bye And Bye

Way bye and bye,
Oh, way bye and bye,
We goin' to have a good time,
Way bye and bye.

I'm goin' to meet my brother there,
I'm goin' to meet my brother there,
We goin' to have a good time,
Way bye and bye.

I'm goin' to meet my Father there.
We don't need no gamblers there.
We don't need no drunkards there.
We don't need no hypocrites there.
We need good Christians there,
Way bye and bye.   (St. Helena)

Way In The Heaven By And By

Way in the heaven by and by,
Way in the heaven by and by,
We're going to have a good time,
Way in the heaven by and by.

There will be no liars there,
There will be no liars there;
There will be no hypocrites there,
There will be no hypocrites there;
There will be no troubles there,
There will be no troubles there;
We're going to have a good time,
Way in the heaven by and by.   (CD)

We Are Building On A Rock

We are building on a Rock,
On high, on high,
It's a mighty true Rock,
On high, on high,
It's a mighty solid Rock,
On high, on high.
Christ Jesus is the Rock,
On high, on high,
The very gates of hell,
On high, thank God,
Will not prevail against it,
On high, thank God,
Help me to build on the Rock.
On high, on high.

(Hampton)

Weeping Mary

Weeping Mary, weeping Mary,
Weeping Mary, weep no more,
Weep no more, weep no more,
Weeping Mary, weep no more:
They nailed Him to the cross,
With a spear they pierced His side.
While the blood trickled down,
He bowed His head.
He bowed His head.

Weeping Mary, weeping Mary,
Weeping Mary, weep no more,
Weep no more, weep no more,
Weeping Mary, weep no more.
He bowed his head to die no more,
He rose from the dead;
He's a-coming again on the Judgment Day.
Doubting Thomas, doubting Thomas,
Doubting Thomas, doubt no more,
Doubt no more, doubt no more,
Doubting Thomas, doubt no more.

(Fisher)

We'll Stand The Storm

Oh, stand the storm,
     It won't be long,
We'll anchor by-and-by;
Stand the storm,
     It won't be long,
We'll anchor by-and-by.

My ship is on the ocean,
We'll anchor by-and-by;

My ship is on the ocean,
We'll anchor by-and-by.

She's making for the kingdom,
I've a mother in the kingdom.
Oh, stand the storm,
  It won't be long;
We'll anchor by-and-by.   (FJS)

A Wheel In A Wheel (2)

A wheel in a wheel,
Oh, my Lord,
A wheel in a wheel,
Oh, my Lord,
Going to take a ride
On the chariot wheel.

It runs by love,
Oh, my Lord,
It runs by faith,
Oh, my Lord,
Chariot's a-coming,
Oh, my Lord,
Going to take a ride,
On the chariot wheel.   (Hampton)

When I Fall On My Knees

Let us break bread together
On our knees, yes, on our knees;
Let us break bread together
On our knees, yes, on our knees.

When I fall on my knees,
With my face to the rising sun,
Oh, Lord, have mercy on me.

Let us break bread together
On our knees, yes, on our knees;

Let us break bread together
On our knees, yes, on our knees.   (BANS)

When I'm Dead

When I'm dead don't you grieve after me,
When I'm dead don't you grieve after me,
When I'm dead don't you grieve after me,
By and by don't you grieve after me.

Pale Horse and Rider have taken my mother away,
Pale Horse and Rider have taken my mother away,
Pale Horse and Rider have taken my mother away,
By and by don't you grieve after me.

Pale Horse and Rider stop at every door,
Pale Horse and Rider stop at every door,

Pale Horse and Rider stop at every door,
By and by don't you grieve after me.
Cold icy hand took my father away,
Cold icy hand took my father away,
Cold icy hand took my father away,
By and by don't you grieve after me.   (ANS)

When We Do Meet Again

When we do meet again,
When we do meet again,
When we do meet again,
'Twill be no more to part.

Brother Billy, fare you well,
Brother Billy, fare you well,
We'll sing hallelujah,
When we do meet again.   (ALLEN)

Who'll Be A Witness For My Lord?

My soul is a witness for my Lord,
My soul is a witness for my Lord,
My soul is a witness for my Lord,
My soul is a witness for my Lord.

You read in the Bible and you understand,
Methuselah was the oldest man;
He died nine-hundred and sixty nine,
He died and went to heaven, Lord, in due time.

You read in the Bible and you understand,
Samson was the strongest man;
Samson went out at one time,
And he killed about a thousand of the Philistines.

Delilah fooled Samson, this we know,
For the Holy Bible tells us so;
She shaved his head as clean as your hand,
And his strength became the same as any natural man.

Now, Daniel was a Hebrew child,
He went to pray to his God awhile;
The King at once for Daniel did send,
And put him right down in the lion's den;
God sent his angels, the lions to keep
And Daniel laid down and went to sleep.

My soul is a witness for my Lord,
My soul is a witness for my Lord,
My soul is a witness for my Lord,
My soul is a witness for my Lord.   (BANS)

Witness

My soul is a witness for my Lord,
My soul is a witness for my Lord,
My soul is a witness for my Lord,
My soul is a witness for my Lord.

You read in the Bible and you understand,
Methuselah was the oldest man,
He lived nine hundred and ninety-nine,
He died and went to heaven, Lord, in due time.
Now Methuselah was a witness for my Lord,
Methuselah was a witness for my Lord.

You read in the Bible and you understand,
Samson went out at one time,
And he killed about a thousand of the Philistines.
You read in the Bible and you understand,
Samson was the strongest man;
Delilah fooled Samson this we know,
For the Holy Bible tells us so;
She shaved off his head just as clean as your hand,
And his strength became as any other man's.

Now Daniel was a Hebrew child,
He went to his Lord to pray a while;
The King at once for Daniel did send,
And he put him right down in the lion's den;
God sent his angels the lions for to keep,
And Daniel lay down and went to sleep

Now, who will be a witness for my Lord?
Now, who will be a witness for my Lord?   (ANSAS)

Wonder Where Is Good Old Daniel

Wonder where is good old Daniel,
Wonder where is good old Daniel,
Wonder where is good old Daniel,
Way over in the Promised Land.

He was cased in the den of lions,
By and by we'll go and meet him,
Wonder where're those Hebrew children,
They came through the fiery furnace,
By and by we'll go and meet them,
Wonder where is doubting Thomas,

Wonder where is sinking Peter.
Way over in the Promised Land.   (Hampton)

You Go, I'll Go With You (1)

Lord, when I go and tell them what you say,
They will not believe in me;
Oh, you go, I'll go with you,

Open your mouth, I'll speak for you.

Father, I stretch my hands to Thee,
No other help I know,

If Thou should turn Thyself away,
Oh, whither shall I go.

Oh, He gave me a ticket
And He told me to go,
He gave me a horn
And he told me to blow
And if I blow my lungs away,
The Lord will fix it in the coming day.

Oh, you go, I'll go with you,
Open your mouth, I'll speak for you.   (CD)

You May Bury Me In The East

You may bury me in the East,
You may bury me in the West,
But I'll hear the trumpet Sound
In that morning;
In that morning, my Lord,
How I long to go,
For to hear the trumpet sound
In that morning.

Good ol' Christians on that day,
Dey'll take the wings and fly away
For to hear the trumpet sound
In that morning.
In that morning, my Lord,
How I long to go,
For to hear the trumpet sound
In that morning.   (ANS)

You're Tired, Chil'

Oh, sit down, sister, sit down!
I know you're tired, sit down!
'Cause you come a long way;
Sit down, chile,
Sit down, an' res' a lit'l while.
Oh, res' a lit'l while.
Oh, you come a long way,
An' you had hard trials,
An' I know you're tired,
Sit down, chile!
Sit down an' res' a lit'l while!
Oh, you come a long way,
An' you had hard trials,
An' I know you're tired,
Sit down, chile!
Sit down, an' res' a lit'l while.

Tell me what you're waitin' for.
I'm waitin' for my mother,
'Cause I want to tell her howdy.
Sit down, chile!
Sit down, an res' a lit'l while.
Oh, you come a long way,
An' the road is dark,
An' I know you're tired.

Sit down, chile!
Sit down an' res' a lit'l while;
Oh, sit down, sister, sit down!
I know you're tired, sit down!
'Cause you've come a long way,
Sit down, chile!
Sit down and res' a lit'l while.
Oh, you come a long way,
An' you had hard trials,
I know you're tired,
Sit down, chile!
Sit down, an res' a lit'l while.   (Hayes)

LYRICS OF
RESISTANCE AND DEFIANCE _____

Despair is not the dominant emphasis in the lyrics of the Afro-American spiritual. There are as many or more compositions that speak specifically of resistance and defiance. For certain, in overall numbers, counting all the categories, songs of utter despair form only a minor segment of the total corpus of the spirituals. The numerous lyrics of resistance and defiance demonstrate the significant endeavor of the Afro-Americans not to be overcome by enslavement in any of its various dimensions: physical, spiritual, or psychological. While the direction of the Africans in America might have been complicatedly obscured, one thing was clear: in whatever form one might manage, one must continue to struggle. The lyrics in this group, therefore, often express audacity, dynamism, valiance, and dogged determination. Also, the themes are numerous. To endeavor to endure slavery, one must fortify oneself, through some form of symbolic or literal breastplate. Unification and organization are called for. One must encourage others in resistance. One must be alert to the use and availability of subtle types of strategy and trickery. One has to learn how to strategize in the wilderness and to meet secretively, some of the songs say. Even rehearsal for freedom was seen as a type of defiance and resistance. Thus, one might in the present circumstance of enslavement try on the clothes of liberty by imagining, for instance, how it would be to move about in freedom's shoes or freedom's robe. It was clear to many of the enslaved that they were living under a condition of war, and they often spoke of their reality specifically in those terms.

Ain't Going To Tarry Here

Sweep it clean,
Ain't going to tarry here;
Sweep it clean,
Ain't going to tarry here;
I sweep my house with the gospel broom.

Ain't going to tarry here,
I sweep my house with the gospel broom,
Ain't going to tarry here.

Sweep it clean,
Ain't going to tarry here,
Sweep it clean,
Ain't going to tarry here.

Going to open my mouth to the Lord,
Ain't going to tarry here,
Going to open my mouth to the Lord,
Ain't going to tarry here.

O-o-o- Lordy,
Ain't going to tarry here
O-o-o Lordy,
Ain't going to tarry here.

Cause he's digging down in the grave,
Ain't going to tarry here;
Cause he's digging down in the grave,
Ain't going to tarry here.

The big bell's tolling in Galilee,
Ain't going to tarry here;
The big bell's tolling in Galilee,
Ain't going to tarry here.

O-o-o Lordy,
Ain't going to tarry here,
O-o-o Lordy,
Ain't going to tarry here.   (BDWS)

Ain't Got Time To Die

Lord, I keep so busy praising my Jesus,
    Keep so busy praising my Jesus,
    Keep so busy praising my Jesus,
    Keep so busy praising my Jesus,
    Keep so busy praising my Jesus,
Ain't got time to die.

'Cause when I'm healing the sick,
    When I'm healing the sick,
    When I'm healing the sick,
    When I'm healing the sick,
Ain't go time to die.
'Cause it takes all of my time,

It takes all of my time,
It takes all of my time,
To praise my Jesus,
Ain't got time to die.

If I don't praise Him,
If I don't praise Him,
If I don't praise Him,
The rocks gonna cry out,
Glory and honor, glory and honor,
Ain't got time to die.

Lord, I keep so busy working for the kingdom,
Keep so busy working for the kingdom,
Keep so busy working for the kingdom,
Keep so busy working for the kingdom,
Ain't got time to die.

'Cause when I'm feeding the po',
When I'm feeding the po',
When I'm feeding the po',
I'm working for the kingdom,
And I ain't got time to die.

Lord, I keep so busy serving my Master.
Keep so busy serving my Master,
Keep so busy serving my Master,
Ain't got time to die.

'Cause when I'm giving my all,
When I'm giving my all,
When I'm giving my all,
I'm serving my Master,
Ain't got time to die.   (BMC)

Bear Your Burden

Bear your burden, bear your burden,
Bear your burden, bear your burden,
Bear your burden in the heat of the day.

Hypocrite, hypocrite God despise,
Tongue so clean and he'll tell lies.

One of these days about twelve o'clock,
This ole world's going to reel and rock.

One of these mornin' bright and fair,
Goin' to take my flight in the middle of the air.

Bear your burden, bear your burden,
Bear your burden, bear your burden,
Bear your burden in the heat of the day.   (St. Helena)

Bye and Bye

O, Lord, I wonder,
Bye and bye,
O, Lord, I wonder,
Bye and bye.

'Twas a wonder in the heaven,
Bye and bye,
'Twas a wonder in the heaven,
Bye and bye.

O, God tol' Joseph,
Bye and bye,
To take Mary and the baby,
Bye and bye;

An' go down in Egyp',
Bye and bye,
Until Herod is dead,
Bye and bye.

When Herod was dead,
Bye and bye,
O, out of Egypt',
Bye and bye,

Have I called my Son,
Bye and bye,
O, Lord, I wonder,
Bye and bye;

God tol' Moses,
Bye and bye,
To go down in Egyp',
Bye and bye,

And tell ol' Pharaoh,
Bye and bye,
To loose my children,
Bye and bye.

I want to cross Jordan,
Bye and bye,
Good Lord, I wonder,
Bye and bye.

(Calhoun)

Children, You'll Be Called On

Children, you'll be called on
    To march in the field of battle,
When this warfare'll be ended,
Hallelu,
When this warfare'll be ended.

I'm a soldier of the jubilee,
This warfare'll be ended;
I'm a soldier of the cross.

Children, you'll be called on
        To march in the field of battle
When this warfare'll be ended,
Hallelu,
When this warfare'll be ended.   (FJS)

Coming Again By and By

Ain't no more dodging in the bushes,
In-a God's army by and by,
Ain't no more dodging in the bushes,
In-a God's army by and by.

I bow out here and bow out there,
Everywhere I went to bow,
Something there was in my way,
It's nothing but the devil
But he cannot stay.

Oh, He's coming again on the mountain top,
Coming again by and by,
He's coming to judge this whole round world,
Coming again by and by,
Oh, He's coming again
Coming again by and by,
He's coming this time and He'll come no more,
Coming again by and by.   (BDWS)

Daniel Saw The Stone

Daniel saw the stone,
Rolling, rolling,
Daniel saw the stone,
Cut out the mountain without hands.

Never saw such a man before,
Preaching gospel to the poor;
Daniel prayed in the lion's den,
'Spite of all those wicked men;
Daniel prayed three times a day,
Drove the devil far away.

Daniel saw the stone,
Rolling, rolling,
Daniel saw the stone,
Cut out the mountain without hands.   (Hampton)

Die In The Field

Oh, what you say, seekers?
Oh, what you say, seekers?

Oh, what you say, seekers?
About that Gospel war?

And what you say, brothers?
Oh, what you say, brothers?
Oh, what you say, brothers?
About that Gospel war.

And I will die in the field,
Will die in the field,
Will die in the field,
I'm on my journey home.   (BANS)

Don't You Grieve After Me

When I'm dead and buried,
Don't you grieve after me;
When I'm dead and buried,
Don't you grieve after me;
When I'm dead and buried,
Don't you grieve after me.
Oh, children, A-Amen.
Oh, my sister and brother,
Don't your grieve after me;
When I'm gone to judgement,
Don't you grieve after me;
Oh, how he traveled,
Don't you grieve after me;
Rock them hills and valleys down,
Don't you grieve after me;
Drop them sins and rally 'round,
Don't you grieve after me.
Oh, children, A-Amen.   (BDWS) (Variant)

Down By The River

Oh, we'll wait till Jesus comes,
Down by the river,
We'll wait till Jesus comes,
Down by the riverside.

Oh, hallelujah to the Lamb,
The Lord is on the giving hand,
Oh, we are pilgrims here below,
Oh, soon to glory we will go;
Oh, little did I think that He was so nigh,
He spake, and made me laugh and cry.

Down by the river,
Down by the riverside,
Oh, we'll wait till Jesus comes,
Down by the river,
We'll wait till Jesus comes,
Down by the riverside.   (FJS)

The Enlisted Soldiers

Hark! listen to the trumpeters,
They call for volunteers,
On Zion's bright and flowery mount,
Behold the officers.
They look like men, they look like men,
They look like men of war,
All armed and dressed in uniform,
They look like men of war.

Their horses, white with their armor bright,
With courage bold they stand,
Enlisting soldiers for their King,
The march to Canaan's land.
They look like men, they look like men,
They look like men of war,
All armed and dressed in uniform,
They look like men of war.

It set my heart in quite a flame,
A soldier thus to be,
I will enlist, gird on my arms,
And fight for liberty.
They look like men, they look like men,
They look like men of war,
All armed and dressed in uniform,
They look like men of war.
We want no cowards in our band,
That will their colors fly;
We call for valiant-hearted men,
Who're not afraid to die.
They look like men, they look like men,
They look like men of war,
All armed and dressed in uniform,
They look like men of war.

To see our armies on parade,
How martial they appear,
All armed and dressed in uniform,
They look like men of war.
They look like men, they look like men,
They look like men of war,
All armed and dressed in uniform,
They look like men of war.

They follow their great General,
The great Eternal Lamb,
His garment stained in His own blood,
King Jesus is his name.
They look like men, they look like men,
They look like men of war,
All armed and dressed in uniform,
They look like men of war.

The trumpets sound, the armies shout,
They drive the host of Hell,
How dreadful is our God to adore,

The great Immanuel.
They look like men, they look like men,
They look like men of war,
All armed and dressed in uniform,
They look like men of war.   (Hampton)

Fighting On

Fighting on, hallelujah!
We're almost down to the shore;
Fighting on, fighting on, hallelujah!
We're almost down to the shore.

Hallelujah to the Lamb,
Jesus died for every man.
He died for you, He died for me.
He died to save the whole world free.

In my room by my bed,
Jesus take me when I'm dead;
When I get on that other shore,
I'll bless my Lord for ever more.
Fighting on, hallelujah!
We're almost down to the shore;
Fighting on, fighting on, hallelujah!
We're almost down to the shore.   (Hampton)

Go, Chain The Lion Down

Go, chain the lion down,
Go, chain the lion down,
Go, chain the lion down,
Before the heaven doors close.

Do you see that good old sister,
Come a-wagging up the hill so slow?
She wants to get to heaven in due time,
Before the heaven doors close.

Do you see the good old Christians?
Do you see the good old Christians?

Go, chain the lion down,
Go, chain the lion down,
Go, chain the lion down,
Before the heaven doors close.   (FJS)

Going To Pull My War-Clothes

Going to pull my war-clothes,
Down by the riverside,
Down by the riverside;
Going to pull my war-clothes,
Down by the riverside,
Study war no more.

Going to meet my brethren,
Down by the riverside,
Down by the riverside;
Going to meet my brethren,
Down by the riverside,
Study war no more.

Going to meet my sister,
Down by the riverside,
Down by the riverside;
Going to meet my sister,
Down by the riverside,
Study war no more.

(CD)

Great Day

Great day, the righteous are marching,
Great day!
God's going to build up Zion's walls.

The chariot rode on the mountain top,
My God he spoke and the chariot stopped;
This is the day of jubilee,
The Lord has set his people free.

Going to take my breast-plate, sword in hand,
And march out boldly in the field;
We want no cowards in our band,
We call for valiant hearted men.

Great day, the righteous are marching,
Great day!
God's going to build up Zion's walls.

(BANS)

Hail, Mary

I want some valiant soldier here,
I want some valiant soldier here,
I want some valiant soldier here,
To help me bear the cross.

O, hail, Mary, hail!
O, hail, Mary, hail!
O, hail, Mary, hail!
To help me bear the cross.

Done with the driver's driving
Done with massa's hollering
Done with missus' scolding.
I want some valiant soldier here,
I want some valiant soldier here,
I want some valiant soldier here,
To help me bear the cross.

(ALLEN)

Hold Out

Oh, your religion never make you shame,
Oh, your religion never make you shame,
Oh, your religion never make you shame,
Hold out.

Oh, I'm going down to the Jordan, hold out,
    Hold out.

Oh, if that is your aim, hold out,
    Hold out.

I think my mother say hold out,
    Hold out.

(St. Helena)

Hold Out To The End (1)

I'm going to hold out to the end,
Going to hold out to the end,
It's my determination to hold out to the end.

Sometimes I was in trouble,
Did not know the way;
I'm going to hold out to the end,
Until the judgment day.

Sometimes I'm discouraged,
Look unto the Lord,
And the Holy Spirit inspires me,
And fills my soul with love.

Sometimes I feel discouraged,
And think my work's in vain,
But I look to my Savior
And revive my soul again.

Mary set her table
'Spite of all her foes.
Jesus sitting in the middle of the table,
And the cup done overflowed.

You need not look for riches,
Or either dress so fine,
The robe that Jesus gives you
Outshines the glittering sun.

(BDWS) (Variant)

Hold Out To The End (2)

All the Mount Zion members,
Have many ups and downs;
But cross come or no come,
For to hold out to the end.

Hold out to the end,
Hold out to the end,

It is my determination,
For to hold out to the end.

                                                          (ALLEN)

Hold The Wind (1)

Hold the wind! Hold the wind!
Hold the wind, don't let it blow!
Hold the wind! Hold the wind!
Hold the wind, don't let it blow!

I got my Jesus, going to hold Him fast,
Hold the wind, don't let it blow!
I'm going to stand on a sea of glass,
Hold the wind, don't let it blow!
Thund'ring and light'ning and it looks like rain,
Hold the wind, don't let it blow.

                                           (ANSAS) (Variant)

Hold The Wind, Don't Let It Blow

Hold the wind, hold the wind,
Hold the wind, don't let it blow;
Hold the wind, hold the wind,
Hold the wind, don't let it blow.

Talk about me just as much as you please,
The more you talk I'm going to bend my knees;
You ask me why I can shout so bold,
The love of Jesus is in my soul;
You ask me why I am always so glad,
The devil missed the soul he thought he had;
I'm going to heaven and I'm going there right,
I'm going to heaven all dressed in white.

Hold the wind, hold the wind,
Hold the wind, don't let it blow;
Hold the wind, hold the wind,
Hold the wind, don't let it blow.

                                                          (BANS)

Hold Your Light

What makes old Satan
  to follow me so?

Satan hasn't nothing at all
  for to do with me;
Run, seeker,
Hold your light,
Sister Mary,
Hold your light,
Seeker, turn back,
Hold your light,
  on Canaan shore.

                                                          (ALLEN)

Hunting For The Lord

Hunt till you find him,
Hallelujah,
And a-hunting for the Lord;
Till you find him,
Hallelujah,
And a-hunting for the Lord.   (ALLEN)

I Ain't Got Weary Yet

And I ain't got weary yet,
And I ain't got weary yet;
Been down in the valley so long,
And I ain't got weary yet.

Been praying for the sinner so long,
And I ain't got weary yet;
Been praying for the mourner so long,
And I ain't got weary yet;
Been going to the sitting-up so long,
And I ain't got weary yet.

And I ain't got weary yet,
And I ain't got weary yet;
Been down in the valley so long,
And I ain't got weary yet.   (FJS)

I Am Free

I am free,
I am free, my Lord,
I am free,
I'm washed by the blood of the Lamb.

You may knock me down,
I'll rise again,
I'm washed by the blood of the Lamb;
I fight you with my sword and shield,
I'm washed by the blood of the Lamb.

Remember the day, I remember it well,
My dungeon shook and my chain fell off;
Jesus cleaned and made me white,
Said go in peace and sin no more;
Glory to God, let your faith be strong,
Lord, it won't be long before I'll be gone.   (BDWS)

I And Satan Had A Race

I and Satan had a race,
Hallelujah, hallelujah,
I and Satan had a race,
Hallelujah, hallelujah.

Win the race against the course,
Satan tells me to my face,
He will bring my kingdom down;
Jesus whispers in my heart,
He will build it up again.

Satan mounts the iron-grey,
Rides half way to Pilot-Bar;
Jesus mounts the milk-white horse,
Says you cheat my Father's children,
Says you cheat them out of glory;
Trouble like a gloomy cloud
Gathers thick and thunders loud.

I and Satan had a race,
Hallelujah, hallelujah,
I and Satan had a race,
Hallelujah, hallelujah.

(ALLEN)

I Can't Stay Behind

I can't stay behind, my Lord,
I can't stay behind,
There's room enough in the heaven, my Lord,
Room enough, room enough,
I can't stay behind!

I been all around, all around,
Been all around in the heaven, my Lord,
I've searched every room,
In the heaven, my Lord,
The angels singing all around the throne,
My father call--and I must go
Shout backwards, member, shout backwards!

O, my mother is gone! my mother is gone!
My mother is gone into heaven, my Lord!
I can't stay behind;
My father is gone! my father is gone!
I can't stay behind!

O, I'se been on the road!
I'se been on the road!
I'se been on the road into heaven, my Lord!
I can't stay behind!
O, room in there, room in there,
Room in there in the heaven, my Lord,
I can't stay behind!

(ALLEN)

I Don't Feel Noways Tired

I am seeking for a city,
Hallelujah, seeking for a city,

Hallelujah, city into the heavens,
Hallelujah, city into the heavens.

Lord, I don't feel noways tired,
Children, I don't feel noways tired,
Oh, glory Hallelujah,
For I hope to shout glory
When this world's on fire.

We will travel on together, hallelujah,
Going to war against the devil, hallelujah,
Going to pull down Satan's kingdom, hallelujah,
Going to build up the wall of Zion, hallelujah.
There is a better day a-coming, hallelujah,
When I leave this world of sorrow, hallelujah,
For to join the holy number, hallelujah,
Then we'll talk the trouble over, hallelujah.
Going to walk about in Zion, hallelujah,
Going to talk with the angels, hallelujah,
Going to tell God about my crosses, hallelujah,
Going to reign with him forever, hallelujah.

Love, I don't feel noways tired,
Children, I don't feel noways tired.   (Hampton)

I Don't Feel Weary

I don't feel weary and noways tired,
O, glory hallelujah;
Just let me in the kingdom,
While the world is all on fire,
O, glory hallelujah.

Going to live with God forever,
While the world is all on fire,
And keep the ark a-moving,
While the world is all on fire.

I don't feel weary and noways tired,
O, glory hallelujah;
Just let me in the kingdom,
While the world is all on fire.   (ALLEN)

I Got My Sword In My Hand

I got my sword in my han',
In my han', Lord;
I got my sword in my han',
Help me sing it.
I got my sword in my han',
In my han', Lord;
I got my sword in my han'.

I'm a-prayin', Lord,
I got my sword in my han';
I'm a-preachin', Lord,
I got my sword in my han';

I'm a-shoutin', Lord,
I got my sword in my han'.

My sister's in one place
An' I in another;
My mother's in one place
An' I in another;
My father's in one place
An' I in another;
My frien's are in one place
An' I in another;
Judgment Day's a-gonna
Bring us all together.   (Grissom)

I Know When I'm Going Home

Old Satan told me to my face,
O, yes, Lord,
The God I seek I'll never find,
O, yes, Lord;
True believer,
I know when I'm going home,
True believer,
I know when I'm going home,
True believer,
I know when I'm going home,
I've been afraid to die.   (ALLEN)

I Love The Lord

I love the Lord;
He heard my cry,
And pitied every groan.

Long as I live,
While troubles 'rise,
I'll hasten to his throne.   (Traditional)

I'm A Soldier In The Army Of The Lord

I'm a soldier in the army of the Lord,
I'm a soldier in the army,
I'm a soldier in the army of the Lord,
I'm a soldier in the army.

I won't retreat back in the army of the Lord,
I'm a moaner in the army of the Lord,
Going to fight against Satan in the army of the Lord,
I'm a worrier in the army of the Lord.

I wouldn't tell a lie in the army of the Lord,
Brother Stephen died in the army of the Lord,
The old doctor died in the army of the Lord,
I'm a soldier in the army of the Lord.   (BDWS)

I'm Going Home

I sought my Lord in the wilderness,
In the wilderness, in the wilderness,
I sought my Lord in the wilderness,
For I'm going home,
For I'm going home,
For I'm going home,
I'm just getting ready,
For I'm going home.

I found free grace in the wilderness,
In the wilderness, in the wilderness,
My father preaches in the wilderness,
For I'm going home,
For I'm going home.

(ALLEN)

I'm Going To Do All I Can

I'm going to do all I can for my Lord,
For my Lord;
I'm going to do all I can for my Lord,
For my Lord
I'm going to do all I can for my Lord,
'Til I can't do no more.
I'm going to pray all I can for my Lord,
For my Lord;
I'm going to bear all I can for my Lord,
For my Lord;
I'm going to sing all I can for my Lord,
For my Lord,
'Til I can't sing no more.

(ANSAS)

I'm Going To Stay In The Battlefield

I'm going to stay in the battlefield,
I'm going to stay in the battlefield,
I'm going to stay in the battlefield 'til I die.

I'm going to watch, fight and pray,
I'm going to watch, fight and pray,
I'm going to watch, fight and pray 'til I die.

I'm going to treat everybody right,
I'm going to treat everybody right,
I'm going to treat everybody right 'til I die.

I'm going to march that heavenly road,
I'm going to march that heavenly road,
I'm going to march that heavenly road 'til I die.

(BDWS)

I'm Going Up To Heaven Anyhow

Anyhow, anyhow, anyhow, my Lord!
Anyhow, yes, anyhow;
I'm going up to heaven anyhow.

If your brother talks about you,
And scandalizes your name,
Down at the cross you must bow;
If your sister talks about you,
And scandalizes your name,
Down at the cross you must bow;
If your preacher talks about you,
And scandalizes your name,
Down at the cross you must bow;
If your deacon talks about you,
And scandalizes your name,
Down at the cross you must bow.

Anyhow, anyhow, anyhow my Lord!
Anyhow, yes, anyhow;
I'm going up to heaven anyhow.   (BANS)

I'm Running For My Life

I'm running for my life,
I'm running for my life,
I'm running for my life,
I'm running for my life,
I'm running for my life.

If anybody asks you what's the matter with me,
Just tell him I say
I'm running for my life.

I'm moaning for my life,
If anybody ask you what's the matter with me,
Just tell him I say
I'm moaning for my life.

I'm praying for my life,
If any body asks you what's the matter with me,
Just tell him I say
I'm praying for my life.   (St. Helena)

I'm Working On The Building

I'm working on the building for my Lord,
                    for my Lord, for my Lord,
I'm working on the building for my Lord,
                    for my Lord, for my Lord,
I'm working on the building for my Lord,
                    working on the building too.

If I was a sinner, I tell you what I would do,
I'd throw away my sinful ways and work on the building too;

If I was a dancer, I tell you what I would do,
I'd throw away my dancing shoes and work on the building too;
If I was a gambler, I tell you what I would do,
I'd throw away my gambling dice and work on the building too.

I'm working on the building for my Lord,
                              for my Lord, for my Lord,
I'm working on the building for my Lord,
                              for my Lord, for my Lord. (ANS)

Inching Along

Keep a-inching along,
Keep a-inching along;
Jesus will come by and by;
Keep a-inching along
Like a poor inch worm,
Jesus will come by and by.

'Twas inch by inch
I sought the Lord;
And inch by inch
He blessed my soul;
The Lord is coming to take us home,
And then our work will soon be done;
Trials and troubles are on the way,
But we must watch and always pray;
We'll inch and inch along,
And inch and inch till we get home.

Keep a-inching along,
Keep a-inching along;
Jesus will come by and by;
Keep a-inching along,
Like a poor inch worm,
Jesus will come by and by.   (FJS)

I Never Intend To Die In Egypt Land

I cannot stay away,
I cannot stay away,
I cannot stay away,
I never intend to die in Egypt land.

Come all the world and you shall know,
How you was save' from in this sword.
I strove indeed but I could not tell
How to shun the gates of hell.
What to do I did not know,
I thought to hell I would surely go;
I looke' this way and that to fly,
I tried salvation for to buy it;
I prayed in the Eas' and I prayed in the Wes',
Seeking for that eternal res'.

At las' I looked to Calvary:
I saw my Jesus on the tree.
I felt the parting, I heard his voice.
My soul got happy and I rejoice'.
If ever I reach the mountain top,
I will praise my lord and never stop.
Go down to the water when you dry
An' then you'll get your full supply.

You pray fo' me and I pray fo' you,
That is the way the Christians do.
Run up Christians and get yo' crown,
An' by your Savior's side sit down.
You can't get los' in the wilderness
With a lighted candle in yo' breas'.

I'm going down to the Jordan to pay my fare:
Jesus' life-boat will meet me there.
Jesus calls "Come unto Me,
Poor sinner, I will set you free."
He called His bretheren on the sea,
Sayin', "Leave yo' nets an' follow Me."
On the cloud to Heaven He rode,
Now He dwells in the light with God.
Bye an' bye he will come fo' me.
When from sin I am wholly free.

I am borned of God, indeed I am.
Sinner, deny me if you can.
While shepherds at their flock atten',
The Angel brought good news to them.
Over in Jerusalem at the post,
See Simon filled with the Holy Ghost.
Lord, let thy servant go:
Jesus Christ is born, I know.
The widow of Aneril came to see,
Who should bleed and die fo' me.

O, there's a time when I must die
To stand befo' my God on high.
As I go down the stream of time,
I will leave this sinful world behin'.
There's no repentance in the grave,
Nor pardon offered for the dead.
Hell is ready to receive
The dying man who won't believe.
O, bless the Lord, i was born to die,
To stand befo' my God on high.

Through heat and cold Christ had to go,
To institute his church below.
My father's fought the battle at las',
And all the days on earth are pas'.
My mother has broke the ice and gone,
And now she sings a heavenly song.
I hope to eat my mother there,
Who used to kneel with me in prayer.

Religion is like a blooming rose.
And none but them that feel it knows.

Way over yonder in the harvest fiel'
The angel's working at the chariot wheel;
The chariot's down by the Jo'dan side,
In the chariot i expect to ride.
Some say I'll not make it so,
But I'll land my soul on Heaven sho'.

The ol' ship's a-coming jus' like a whirl
To take God's children safe out of this worl'.
When I'm happy I'll shout an' sing
And make the heavenly welkin ring.
The very time I thought I was los'
The dungeon shook an' my chains fell off.
An angel with bright wings of gol'
Brought the glad tidings to my soul.

Here we walk the golden streets,
We tells to all the saints we meets.
The chariot runs on the mountain top,
My Lord bid the chariot stop.
My head was wet with the midnight dew;
The morning star was a witness, too.
I never will give up the shield
Until the Devil has made to yield.   (Calhoun)

In The Army Of The Lord

I'm a soldier in the Army of the Lord,
I'm a soldier in this Army;
I'm a soldier in the Army of the Lord,
I'm a soldier in this Army.
I'll live again in the Army of the Lord,
I'll live again in this Army;
I'll live again in the Army of the Lord,
I'll live again in this Army.

If a man dies in the Army of the Lord,
If a man dies in this Army;
If a man dies in the Army of the Lord,
I f a man dies in this Army.
He'll live again in the Army of the Lord,
He'll live again in this Army;
He'll live again in the Army of the Lord,
He'll live again in this Army.

I've had a hard time in the Army of the Lord,
Had a hard time in this Army;
I've had a hard time in the Army of the Lord,
Had a hard time in this Army.
I'm fightin' for my rights in the Army of the Lord,
I'm fightin' for my rights in this Army;
I'm fightin' for my rights in the Army of the Lord,
I'm fightin' for my rights in this Army.

I've come a long way in the Army of the Lord,
Come a long way in this Army;
I've come a long way in the Army of the Lord,
Come a long way in this Army.
Some day I'll rest in the Army of the Lord,
Some day I'll rest in this Army;
Some day I'll rest in the Army of the Lord,
Some day I'll rest in this Army.

My soul died in the Army of the Lord,
My soul died in this Army;
My soul died in the Army of the Lord,
My soul died in this Army.
It'll live again in the Army of the Lord,
It'll live again in this Army;
It'll live again in the Army of the Lord,
It'll live again in this Army.

Hoseanna, in the Army of the Lord,
Hoseanna, in this Army;
Hoseanna, in the Army of the Lord,
Hoseanna, in this Army.

We'll live again in the Army of the Lord,
We'll live again in this Army.
We'll live again in the Army of the Lord,
We'll live again in this Army.

My mother died in the Army of the Lord,
My mother died in this Army;
My mother died in the Army of the Lord,
My mother died in this Army.
She'll live again in the Army of the Lord,
She'll live again in this Army;

She'll live again in the Army of the Lord,
She'll live again in this Army.   (Grissom)

In The Mansions Above

Good Lord, in the mansions above,
Good Lord, in the mansions above,
My Lord, I hope to meet my Jesus
In the mansions above.

If you get to heaven before I do,
Lord, tell my Jesus I'm a-coming too,
To the mansions above.

My Lord, I've had many crosses and tribulations
    here below;
My Lord, I hope to meet you
In the mansions above.

Fight on, my brother, for the mansions above,
For I hope to meet my Jesus there
In the mansions above.

Good Lord, in the mansions above,
Good Lord, in the mansions above,
My Lord, I hope to meet my Jesus
In the mansions above.   (ALLEN)

I Wish I Had Been There

My mother, you follow Jesus,
My sister, you follow Jesus,
My brother, you follow Jesus,
To fight until I die.

I wish I had been there,
To climb Jacob's ladder,
I wish I had been there
To wear the starry crown.   (ALLEN)

I Won't Stop Praying

And I won't stop praying,
And I won't stop praying,
And I won't stop praying,
That's what Satan's grumbling about.

Old Satan's mad and I am glad,
He missed the soul he thought he had;
Old Satan's a liar and a conjurer too,
And if you don't mind he'll conjure you;
The Bible is our engineer,
It points the way to heaven clear.

And I won't stop praying,
And I won't stop praying,
And I won't stop praying,
That's what Satan's grumbling about.   (ANS)

John's On The Island On His Knees

John's on the Island on his knees,
John's on the Island on his knees,
John's on the Island,
John's on the Island.

Oh, he's praying to his Father on his knees,
Oh, he's praying to his Father on his knees,
Sinner dead, a-starving on his knees.
Sinner dead, a-starving on his knees.

You can't starve a Christian on his knees,
You can't harm a Christian on his knees,
He's crying Lord have mercy on his knees,
John saw the number on his knees.   (BDWS)

Join The Angel Band

If you look up the road,
You'll see father Moses,
Join the angel band;
If you look up the road,
You'll see father Moses.
Join the angel band.

Do, father Moses, gather your army,
O, do more souls gather together
O, do join them, join them for Jesus,
O, do join them, join them archangel.   (ALLEN)

'Listed In The Battlefield

Pray on, my brother,
Don't you get tired,
I'm lying in the arms of the Lord.
Pray on, my brother,
Don't you get tired,
I'm lying in the arms of the Lord.

Come and 'listed in the field of, field of battle,
I'm getting in the field of, field of battle,
I'm getting in the field of, field of battle,
Lying in the arms of the Lord.

Pray on, my sister,
Don't you get tired;
Pray on,. my mother,
Don't you get tired;
Pray on, my elder,
Don't you get tired;
Pray on, my aunty,
Don't you get tired;
I'm lying in the arms of the Lord.   (Calhoun)

Listen To The Angels

Where do you think I found my soul,
Listen to the angels shouting,
I found my soul at hell's dark door,
Listen to the angels shouting,
Before I lay in hell one day,
Listen to the angels shouting,
I sing and pray my soul away,
Listen to the angels shouting.
Run all the way, run all the way,
Run all the way my Lord,
Listen to the angels shouting,
Blow, Gabriel, blow,
Blow, Gabriel, blow,
Tell all the joyful news,
Listen to the angels shouting.

I don't know what
  sinner want to stay here for,
Listen to the angels shouting,
Blow, Gabriel, blow,
Blow, Gabriel, blow,
Tell all the joyful news,
Listen to the angels shouting.   (FJS)

Little Innocent Lamb

Little Lamb,
Little Lamb,
Little innocent Lamb,
I'm gonna serve God till I die,
I'm gonna serve God till I die,
I'm gonna serve God till I die.
Little Lamb,
Little Lamb,
Little innocent Lamb,
I'm gonna serve God till I die.

Hypocrite, tell you what he do,
He'll talk about me,
And he'll talk about you.

The devil's got a slippery shoe,
Now, if you don't mind
He's gonna slip it on you.
I'm gonna serve God till I die,
'Cause there ain't no dying over there
In that heavenly land,
In that heavenly land.

There'll be joy, joy, joy!
In that heavenly land.

Just take one brick from Satan's wall,
Satan's wall gonna tumble and fall,
I'm gonna serve God till I die.
Little Lamb,
Little Lamb,
Little innocent Lamb,
I'm gonna serve god till I die.   (Schirmer)

Lord, Until I Reach My Home

Lord, until I reach my home,
Until I reach my home,
I never expect to give the journey over,
Until I reach my home.

Old Satan's mighty busy,
He follows night and day,
And every time I go to pray,
I find him in my way.

Now don't you mind old Satan
With all his tempting charms,
He want to steal your soul away,
And fold you in his arms.

When I was lying at hell's dark door,
No one to pity poor me,
Master Jesus He come riding by,
And bought my liberty.

Lord, until I reach my home,
Until I reach my home,
I never expect to give the journey over,
Until I reach my home.   (Hampton)

Many Thousand Gone

No more auction block for me
No more, no more;
No more auction block for me,
Many thousand gone.

No more peck of corn for me,
No more driver's lash for me,
No more pint of salt for me,
No more hundred lash for me,
No more mistress' call for me.

Many thousand gone
Many thousand gone
No more, no more.   (Douglass)

Marching Up The Heavenly Road

Marching up the heavenly road,
Marching up the heavenly road,
I'm bound to fight until I die;
Marching up the heavenly road.

My sister, have you got your sword and shield,
I got'em fo' I left the field;
O, come along, Moses, don't get lost,
I stretch your rod and come across;
O' fare you well friends, fare you well foes,
I leave you all my eyes to close.   (ANSAS)

March On

Way over in the Egypt land,
        You shall gain the victory;
Way over in the Egypt land,
        You shall gain the day.
March on, and you shall gain the victory;
March on, and you shall gain the day.

When Peter was preaching at the Pentecost,
He was endowed with the Holy Ghost;
When Peter was fishing in the sea,
He dropped his net and followed me;
King Jesus on the mountain top,
King Jesus speaks and the chariot stops.

Way over in the Egypt land,
        You shall gain the victory;
Way over in the Egypt land,
        You shall gain the day.
March on, and you shall gain the victory;
March on, and you shall gain the day.   (FJS)

My Sister, You'll Be Called On

When this warfare is ended,
I'm a soldier of the Jubilee,
When this warfare is ended,
I'm a soldier of the cross,
My sister, you'll be called on,
For to march in that field of battle.

My brother, you'll be called on,
For to march in that field of battle,
When this warfare is ended, hallelu.

Moaner, you'll be called on,
For to march in that field of battle
When this warfare is ended, hallelu.

Oh elder, you'll be called on,
For to march in that field of battle,
When this warfare is ended, hallelu.   (BDWS)

My Soul's Determining

Oh, my little soul, soul's determined,
Oh, my little soul, soul's determined,
God's going to raise heaven a little higher,
God's going to raise heaven a little higher,
God's going to raise heaven a little higher.

Oh, my little soul, soul's determined,
Oh, my little soul, soul's determined,
I pray determined,
Soul's determined.

God's going to sink hell a little lower,
God's going to sink hell a little lower,
I've grown determined.

You may bury my body in the east,
You may bury my body in the west,
I moan determined.

You may bury my body in the distant sea,
You may bury my body in the distant sea,
I pray determined.

Oh, my little soul, soul's determined,
Oh, my little soul, soul's determined,
I don't care where you bury my body,
I don't care where you bury my body,
I don't care where you bury my body.
Oh, my little soul, soul's determined,
Oh, my little soul, soul's determined.
I walk determined,
Soul's determined,
I walk determined,
Soul's determined.

(BDWS)

No Man Can Hinder Me

Walk in, kind Saviour,
No man can hinder me!
Walk in, sweet Jesus,
No man can hinder me!

See what wonder Jesus done,
Jesus make the dumb to speak,
Jesus make the cripple walk,
Jesus give the blind his sight,
Jesus do most anything.
Rise, poor Lazarus, from the tomb,
Satan ride an iron-gray horse,
King Jesus ride a milk-white horse.

Walk in, kind Saviour,
No man can hinder me!
Walk in, sweet Jesus,
No man can hinder me!

(ALLEN)

Not Weary Yet

O, I'm not weary yet,
O, I'm not weary yet,
I have a witness in my heart,
I'm not weary yet.
Since I been in the field to fight,
I have a heaven to maintain,
The bond of faith is on my soul;
Old Satan toss a ball at me,
He thinks the ball would hit my soul,
The ball's for hell and I'm for heaven.

O, I'm not weary yet,
O, I'm not weary yet,
I have a witness in my heart,
I'm not weary yet.

(ALLEN)

Oh, Freedom

Oh, freedom, oh, freedom,
Oh, freedom over me!
And before I'd be a slave,
I'll be buried in my grave,
And go home to my Lord and be free.

No more moaning, no more moaning,
No more moaning over me.
No more weeping, no more weeping,
No more weeping over me!
There'll be singing over me!
There'll be shouting, there'll be shouting,
There'll be shouting over me!
There'll be praying, there'll be praying,
There'll be praying over me.

Oh, freedom oh, freedom,
Oh, freedom over me!
And before I'd be a slave,
I'll be buried in my grave,
And go home to my Lord and be free.   (Hampton)

Oh, Give Way, Jordan

Oh, give way, Jordan, give way, Jordan,
Oh, give way, Jordan,
I want to go across to see my Lord.
Oh, I heard a sweet music up in the air,
I want to go across to see my Lord;
And I wish that music would come here,
I want to go across to see my Lord.

Oh, stow back, stow back the powers of hell,
And let God's children take the field,
Now stand back, Satan, let me go by,
Going to serve my Jesus till I die.

Soon in the morning by break of day,
See the Old Ship of Zion sailing away,
Now I must go across, and I shall go across,
This sinful world I cannot but cross.
Oh, I heard such a lumbering in the sky,
It made me think my time was nigh,
Yes, it must be my Jesus in the cloud,
I never heard him speak so loud;
Oh, give way, Jordan, give way, Jordan,
I want to go across to see my Lord.   (Hampton)

Oh, Lord, Answer My Prayer

Hum---m, Lordy, chained in hell and can't come out,
Hum---m, Lordy, chained in hell and can't come out,

Wonder what Satan's grumbling about,
Wonder what Satan's grumbling about,
Oh Lord, answer my prayer.

He's drained in hell and can't get out,
He's drained in hell and can't get out,

He's drained in hell and can't get out,
Oh Lord, answer my prayer.

I tried on shoes that John tried on,
Tried on shoes that John tried on,
Oh Lord, answer my prayer;
Done tried on the robe that John tried on,
Tried on the robe that John tried on,
Oh, Lord, answer my prayer.

I've been tried by the waters and didn't get lost,
Tried by the waters and didn't get lost,
Tried by the waters and didn't get lost,
Oh Lord, answer my prayer.

Been tried by the fire and didn't get burnt,
Tried by the fire and didn't get burnt,
Tried by the fire and didn't get burnt,
Oh Lord, answer my prayer.   (BDWS)

Peter On The Sea

Peter, Peter,
Peter on the sea, sea, sea!
Peter, Peter,
Peter on the sea, sea, sea!

Gabriel, Gabriel,
Gabriel, blow your trump, trump, trump!
Gabriel, blow your trumpet,
Gabriel, blow your trumpet loud!

Daniel, Daniel,
Daniel in the lions', lions',
Daniel in the lions',
Daniel in the lions' den.

Who did, who did,
Who did swallow Jonah, Jonah?
Who did swallow Jonah?
Who did swallow Jonah whole?

Whale did, whale did,
Whale did swallow Jonah, Jonah,

Whale did swallow Jonah,
Whale did swallow Jonah whole!

Peter, Peter,
Peter on the sea, sea, sea!

Peter, Peter,
Peter on the sea, sea, sea!   (Hampton)

Pilgrim's Story

I'm a poor, wayfaring stranger,
While journeying through this world of woe,
Yet there's no sickness, toil, and danger,
In that bright world to which I go;
I'm going there to see my father,
I'm going there no more to roam,
I'm just going over Jordan,
I'm just going over home.

I know dark clouds will gather 'round me,
I know my way is rough and steep,
Yet bright fields lie just before me,
Where God's redeemed their vigils keep;
I'm going there to see my mother,
She said she'd meet me when I come,
I'm just going over Jordan,
I'm just going over home.

I'll soon be free from every trial,
My body will sleep in the old churchyard,
I'll drop the cross of self denial,
And enter on my great reward;
I'm going there to see my Savior,
To sing His praise in heaven's dome,
I'm just going over Jordan,
I'm just going over home.   (Hampton)

Pray All The Members

Pray, all the members,
O, Lord!
Pray all the members,
Yes, my Lord!
Pray a little longer,
O, Lord!
Pray a little longer,
Yes, my Lord!

Jericho done worried me,
O, Lord!
Jericho, Jericho.
I've been to Jerusalem,
O, Lord!
Patroller around me,
Yes, my Lord!
Thank God he didn't catch me,
O, Lord!
Went to the meeting,
O, Lord!
Met brother Hercules,
What do you think he told me?

Yes, my Lord!
Told me to turn back
O, Lord!
Jump along Jericho.

Pray, all the members,
O, Lord!
Pray, all the members,
Yes, my Lord!

(Allen)

Ride On, King Jesus

Ride on, King Jesus,
No man can hinder me;
Ride on, King Jesus,
No man can hinder me.
I was young when I begun,
But now my race is almost done;
King Jesus ride on a milk-white horse,
The river of Jordan he did cross;
If you want to find your way to God,
The gospel highway must be trod.

Ride on, King Jesus,
No man can hinder me;
Ride on, King Jesus,
No man can hinder me.

(FJS)

Road Is Rugged, But I Must Go

Road is rugged, but I must go.
I must go to see my Lord;
Road is rugged, but I must go,
I must go to see my Lord.

It's a field of battle, but I must go,
I must go to see my Lord;
It's a field of battle, but I must go,
I must go to see my Lord!

Got to pray so hard, but I must go,
Oh, I must go to see my Lord!
Jesus died, and I must go,
I must go to see my Lord!
Road is rugged, but I must go,
I must go to see my Lord;
Road is rugged, but I must go,
Oh, I must go to see my Lord.

(CD)

Roll, Jordan, Roll

Roll, Jordan, roll,
        roll, Jordan, roll,
I want to go to heaven when I die
To hear Jordan roll.

Oh, brothers, you ought to been there
A sitting in that Kingdom
To hear Jordan roll,
Yes, my Lord!

Roll, Jordan, roll,
      roll, Jordan, roll,
I want to go to heaven when I die
To hear Jordan roll.   (ANS)

Run Here Jeremiah

Run here, Jeremiah,
      Ho, my Lord,
Run here, Jeremiah,
Hey, hey, Lord --

Run here with your hammer,
Run here with your hammer --
What you going to do with the hammer?
Hammer on the heart of the wicked --
Hammer on the heart of the wicked --
Hey, Hey, Lord --

Run Here Jeremiah
      Ho, my Lord --
Look over yonder,
Hey, hey, Lord --
Yonder come Jeremiah.
How you know it's Jeremiah?
Ho, my Lord,
I know him by his vestment,
Hey, hey, my Lord.   (BDWS)

Run, Mary, Run

Run, Mary, run; Run, Mary, run,
Oh, run, Mary run.
I know the other world is not like this;
Fire in the east, and fire in the west,
I know the other world is not like this
Bound to burn the wilderness,
I know the other world is not like this.

Jordan river is a river to cross,
I know the other world is not like this;
Stretch your rod and come across,
I know the other world is not like this.

Swing low, chariot, into the east,
Let God's children have some peace;
Swing low, chariot, into the west,
Let God's children have some rest.

Swing low, chariot, into the north,
Give me the gold without the dross;
Swing low, chariot, into the south,
Let God's children sing and shout.

If this day was judgement day,
Every sinner would want to pray;
That trouble it comes like a gloomy cloud,
Gathers thick, and thunders loud.
Run, Mary, run; Run, Mary, run,
Oh, run, Mary, run.
I know the other world is not like this.   (Hampton)

Run To Jesus

Run to Jesus,
        Shun the danger,
I don't expect to stay much longer here.

He will be our dearest friend,
And will help us to the end;
Oh, I thought I heard them say,
There were lions on the way;
Many mansions there will be,
One for you and one for me.

Run to Jesus,
        Shun the danger,
I don't expect to stay much longer here.   (FJS)

Singing With A Sword In My Hand

Singing with a sword in my hand,
Lord, Singing with a sword in my hand,
Singing with a sword in my hand, Lord,
Singing with a sword in my hand.

Prettiest singing ever I heard,
Way over on the hill,
The angels sing and I sing, too.

Prettiest shouting ever I heard,
Way over on the hill,
The angels shout and I shout, too.

Prettiest preaching ever I heard,
Way over on the hill,
The angels preached and I preached, too.

Prettiest praying ever I heard,
Way over on the hill,
The angels prayed and I prayed, too.

Prettiest mourning ever I heard,
Way over on the hill,
The angels mourned and I mourned, too.

Mourning with a sword in my hand, Lord,
Mourning with a sword in my hand, Lord,
Mourning with a sword in my hand.   (BANS)

Sitting Down Beside The Lamb

New Jerusalem! New Jerusalem!
Sitting down beside the Lamb.

Before I'd lay in hell one day, good Lord!
I'd sing and pray myself away, good Lord!
The tallest tree in Paradise, good Lord!
The Christians call the tree of life, good Lord!
I'll let you know before I go,
Whether I love the Lord or no.

Sitting down beside the Lamb,
O, mourner, mourn along!
Sitting down beside the Lamb.   (ANS)

Stand By Me

When the storm of life is raging,
Stand by me, stand by me.
When the storm of life is raging,
Stand by me, stand by me.
When the world is tossing me
Like a ship upon the sea,
Thou who rulest wind and water,
Stand by me, stand by me.
Thou who rulest wind and water,
Stand by me, stand by me!

In the midst of tribulation,
Stand by me, stand by me.
When the hosts of hell assail me,
And my strength begins to fail me,
Thou who never lost a battle,
Stand by me, stand by me,
Oh, stand by me.
Thou who never lost a battle,
Stand by me, stand by me.

In the midst of faults and failures,
Stand by me, stand by me.
When I do the best I can,
Stand by me, stand by me.
And my friends misunderstand,
Thou who knowest all about me,
Thou who knowest all about me,
Stand by me, stand by me,
Oh, stand by me.
Thou who knowest all about me,
Stand by me, stand by me.

In the midst of persecution,
Stand by me.
When my foes in battle array,
Stand by me,
Undertake to stop my way,
Thou who stood by Paul and Silas,
Stand by me!

When I'm growing old and feeble,
Stand by me.
When my life becomes a burden,
Stand by me,
And I'm nearing chilly Jordan,
O, thou Lily of the Valley,
Stand by me!

(Fisher)

Standing On The Sea Of Glass

Standing on the sea of glass,
Standing on the sea of glass,
Standing on the sea of glass,
With the gospel sword in my hand.

I'll let you know before I go,
Whether I love my Lord or no;
Come along brother one and all,
Let's get ready against Gabriel's call;
If you get to heaven before I do,
Tell my Lord I'm coming too,
With the gospel sword in my hand.

Standing on the sea of glass,
Standing on the sea of glass,
With the gospel sword in my hand.

(BDWS)

Stand Still, Jordan

Stand still, Jordan,
Stand still, Jordan,
Stand still, Jordan,
Lord, I can't stand still.

I got a mother in heaven,
I got a mother in heaven,
I got a mother in heaven,
Lord, I can't stand still.

When I get up in glory,
When I get up in glory,
When I get up in glory,
Lord, I can't stand still.

Jordan river, Jordan river,
Jordan river is chilly and cold.
It will chill my body,
It will chill my body,

It will chill my body,
But not my soul.

(BANS)

Stand The Storm

O, stand the storm, it won't be long,
We'll anchor by and by, O brethren!
Stand the storm, it won't be long,
We'll anchor by and by.

My ship is on the ocean,
We'll anchor by and by;
She's making for the kingdom,
We'll anchor by and by;

I've a mother in the kingdom,
We'll anchor by and by.

(ANSAS)

Stay In The Field

Stay in the field,
Stay in the field,
O, Warrior, stay in the field,
Until the war is ended.

Mine eyes are turned to the heavenly gate,
I'll keep on my way or I'll be late;
The tallest tree in Paradise,
The Christians call the Tree of Life;
Green trees burning, why not the dry,
My savior died, why not I?

Stay in the field,
Stay in the field,
O, warrior, stay in the field,
Until the war is ended!

(Hampton)

Steal Away And Pray

O, steal away and pray,
I'm looking for my Jesus;
Steal away and pray,
I'm looking for my Jesus,
Can't stay away.

I prayed so hard
When looking for my Jesus,
Prayed so hard
When looking for my Jesus,
Can't stay away.

Sinners, sinners, why don't you pray?
Seekers, seekers, why don't you pray?
Mourners, mourners, why don't you pray?

Brothers, brothers, why don't you pray?
I can't stay away.   (ANS)

There's A Meeting Here Tonight

Get you ready,
        there's a meeting here tonight,
Come along,
        there's a meeting here tonight.
I know you by your daily walk,
There's a meeting here tonight.

Camp meeting down in the wilderness,
I know its among the Methodists;
Those angels wings are tipped with gold,
That brought glad tidings to my soul;
My father says it is the best,
To live and die a Methodist;
I'm a Methodist bred and a Methodist born,
And when I'm dead there's a Methodist gone.
Get you ready,
        there's a meeting here tonight.
Come along,
        there's a meeting here tonight,
I know you by your daily walk,
There's a meeting here tonight.   (FJS)

These All Of My Father's Children

These all of my Father's children,
These all of my Father's children,
These all of my Father's children,
All in one band.
I soon shall be done with the trouble of the world,
Trouble of the world, trouble of the world,
I soon shall be done with the trouble of the world,
Going home to live with God.

Oh, my sister, where's your counter seal,
Oh, my sister, where's your counter seal?
I had it before I left the field,
I had it before I left the field;
I got my breastplate, sword and shield,
I got my breastplate, sword and shield;
I'm boldly marching through the field,
I'm boldly marching through the field.   (BDWS)

Travel On

Sister Rosy,
You get to heaven before I go,
Sister,
You look out for me,
I'm on the way.

Travel on, travel on.
You heaven bound soldier,
Travel on, travel on,
Go hear what my Jesus says.   (ALLEN)

Trying To Get Home

Lord, I'm bearing heavy burdens,
Trying to get home;
Lord, I'm bearing heavy burdens,
Trying to get home;
Lord, I'm bearing heavy burdens,
Trying to get home.

Lord, I'm climbing high mountains,
Trying to get home;
Lord, I'm climbing high mountains,
Trying to get home;
Lord, I'm climbing high mountains,
Trying to get home.
Lord, I'm standing hard trials,
Trying to get home;
Lord, I'm standing hard trials,
Trying to get home;
Lord, I'm standing hard trials,
Trying to get home.   (ANS)

Turn Back Pharaoh's Army

Gwine to write to Massa Jesus
        To send some valiant soldier
To turn back Pharaoh's army,
Hallelu!
If you want your souls converted,
        You'd better be a-praying
To turn back Pharaoh's army,
Hallelu!

You say you are a soldier,
        Fighting for your Savior,
To turn back Pharaoh's army,
Hallelu!
When the children were in bondage
        They cried unto the Lord,
He turned back Pharaoh's army,
Hallelu!

When Moses smote the water,
        The children all passed over,
He turned back Pharaoh's army,
Hallelu!

When Pharaoh crossed the water,
        The waters came together
And drowned ole Pharaoh's army,
Hallelu!   (FJS)

Until I Reach My Home

Until I reach my home,
Until I reach my home,
I never intend to give the journey over,
Until I reach my home.
True believer.

O, some say give me silver
And some say give me gold,
But I say give me Jesus,
Most precious to my soul.

They say that John the Baptist
Was nothing but a Jew,
But the Holy Bible tells us
The he was a preacher too.

Until I reach my home,
Until I reach my home,
I never intend to give the journey over,
Until I reach my home.

(BANS)

Wade In The Water

Wade in the water,
Wade in the water, children,
Wade in the water,
God's gonna trouble the water.

Wade in the water,
Oh, wade in the water, children,
Wade in the water,
God's gonna trouble the water.

(Traditional)

Walk, Mary, Down The Lane

Three long nights and three long days,
Jesus walking down the lane.
Three long nights and three long days,
Jesus walking down the lane.
In the morning down the lane,
In the morning down the lane,

Walk, Mary, down the lane,
Walk, Mary, down the lane.

Jesus calls you down the lane,
Jesus calls you down the lane;
In the heaven, down the lane,
In the heaven, down the lane;
I'm afraid of nobody, down the lane,
'Fraid of nobody, down the lane.

Walk, Mary, down the lane,
Walk, Mary, down the lane,

Walk, Mary, down the lane,
Walk, Mary, down the lane.   (BANS)

We Are Climbing The Hills Of Zion

We are climbing the hills of Zion,
    The hills of Zion, the hills of Zion,
We are climbing the hills of Zion,
    With Jesus in our souls.

O, brethren, do get ready,
O, seeker, do get ready,
O, sinner, do get ready.

We are climbing the hills of Zion,
    The hills of Zion, the hills of Zion,
We are climbing the hills of Zion,
    With Jesus in our souls.   (FJS)

We'll Die In The Field

O, what do you say, seekers,
    O, what do you say, seekers,
O, what do you say, seekers,
    About the Gospel war?

And I will die in the field,
    Will die in the field,
    Will die in the field,
I'm on my journey home.

O, what do you say, brothers?
O, what do you say, Christians?
O, what do you say, preachers?
I'm on my journey home.

And I will die in the field,
    Will die in the field,
    Will die in the field,
I'm on my journey home.   (FJS)

We'll Overtake The Army

We'll overtake the army,
     Overtake the army,
     Overtake the army,
     Yes, my Lord.

I've 'listed, and I mean to fight,
     Yes, my Lord,
Till every foe is put to flight,
     Yes, my Lord,
Though I may fall I'll bless His name,
     Yes, my Lord,
I'll trust in God and rise again
     Yes, my Lord;
The God I serve is a man of war,
     Yes, my Lord,
He fights and conquers ever more,
     Yes, my Lord.

We'll overtake the army,
     Overtake the army,
     Overtake the army,
     Yes, my Lord.   (FJS)

We're Almost Home

We're almost home,
     We're almost home,
We're almost home to ring those charming bells.

Oh, come along brothers
     Come along, come along;
Oh, come along sisters,
     Come along, come along;
Come along, come along,
Come along, come along,
To ring those charming bells.   (FJS)

When Shall I Get There

There's a heavenly home up yonder,
There's a heavenly home up yonder,

There's a heavenly home up yonder,
Oh! when shall I get there?

Old Pilate says,
      I wash my hands,
I find no fault in this just man;
John and Peter ran to see,
But Christ had gone to Galilee;
Paul and Silas bound in jail,
They sang and prayed both night and day;
I'm bred and born a Methodist,
I carry the witness in my breast.

There's a heavenly home up yonder,
There's a heavenly home up yonder,

There's a heavenly home up yonder,
Oh! when shall I get there?   (FJS)

Wrestle On, Jacob

I hold my brother with trembling hand,
The Lord will bless my soul,
Wrestle on, Jacob, Jacob,
Day is a-breaking,
Wrestle on, Jacob,
Oh, he would not let him go.

I will not let you go, my Lord,
Fisherman Peter out at sea.
He cast all night and he cast all day,
He catch no fish but he catch some soul;
Jacob hang from a trembling limb,
I looked to the East at the breaking of the day,
The old ship of Zion went sailing away.

Wrestle on, Jacob, Jacob,
Day is a-breaking,
Wrestle on, Jacob,
Oh, he would not let him go.   (ALLEN)

Wrestlin' Jacob (1)

All night, wrestlin' Jacob,
All night, all night
Till the break of day;
O, we wrestle, wrestle
All the night till the break of day.

All night, dear young convert, all night,
All night till the break of day;
O, we will wrestle, wrestle all the night
Till the break of day.

All night, my dear brother, all night,
All night, my dear brother, all night.   (St. Helena)

Wrestling Jacob (2)

Wrestling Jacob, let me go,
Wrestling Jacob, let me go,
Wrestling Jacob, let me go,
I will not let you go.

Day is breaking, Jacob, let me go,
Day is breaking, Jacob, let me go,
Day is breaking, Jacob, let me go,
I will not let you go.

If you'll bless my soul,
I'll let you go,
If you'll bless my soul,
I'll let you go,
I will not let you go.

When I'm sinking down, pity me,
When I'm sinking down, pity me,
When I'm sinking down, pity me,
I will not let you go!

Wrestling Jacob, let me go,
Wrestling Jacob, let me go
I will not let you go.

(Hampton)

You Better Run, Run, Run

You better run, run, run,
You better run, run, run,
You better run, run, run,
And run in time--
Keep your hand upon the throttle--
And your eyes on the prize.

If you can't sing like angels,
And you can't preach like Paul,
You can tel the love of Jesus,
You can say He died for all.

Oh, when my mother give me over,
Goin' to let God's bosom be my pillow,
Hide me, Oh, thou Rock of Ages,
Rock of Ages cleft for me.

(St. Helena)

You Got A Right

You got a right, I got a right,
We all got a right to the tree of life.
Yes, tree of life.

The very time I thought I was lost,
The dungeon shook and the chain fell off.
You may hinder me here,
But you can't hinder me there

'Cause God in the heaven's
Going to answer prayer.

O, brother, O, sister,
You got a right, I got a right,
We all got a right to the tree of life.   (BANS)
Yes, tree of life.

Zion's Children

Oh! Zion's children coming along,
Coming along, coming along,
O, Zion's children coming along,
Talking about the welcome day.
I hail my mother in the morning,
Oh! don't you want to live up yonder?
I think they are mighty happy,
Coming along, coming along;
Oh! Zion's children coming along,
Talking about the welcome day.   (FJS)

LYRICS OF DELIVERANCE _____

Deliverance is a pervasive theme of the spirituals. The spirituals speak of freedom through means of escape, through death in the form of a transition, through resurrection and immortality, and through general modes of spiritual salvation. Deliverance lyrics appeal for release from obstacles and physical and mental victimization. That is, they call for release from the entrapments of slavery and from the maze of cages that slavery constructs. Deliverance is also stimulated by the need to reunite with former members of the community.

Although one may not be able to be physically delivered in this life, one is nevertheless continually proclaiming the need for spiritual readiness to move into a better after-life. Spiritual uprightness may be one's best mode of escape from such a troubled world. The ultimate deliverance called for is from the world of woe-stricken humanity. With virtually no legal redress through which they could effectively petition and gain their freedom, the enslaved Africans had to contemplate and deliberate upon their deliverance through whatever mechanisms they could imagine or contrive. One would most likely have to *take* one's freedom, though some gained it through manumission, and some few had the dubious option of buying it. Focus on deliverance often concerned with alerting others regarding opportunities and strategies for escaping their condition. Very specifically, one's deliverance might be assisted by attaining some degree of literacy so that one might more easily find his or her way in the right direction when running toward freedom. The general worldview of the enslaved Africans seems to have held that deliverance required assistance of spiritual agents. Some of the songs represented in this group are themselves pleas to spiritual agents for attention, resistance, and remembrance. The plea is not always for the act of remembrance to be made at the time of the will of God, but in some instances it is called for "in a hurry." In Howard Thurman's words, these songs record, in essence, the belief that "God was at work in all history: He manifested himself in certain specific acts that seemed to be over and above the historic process itself."[1]

_____

1. Howard Thurman, DEEP RIVER: REFLECTIONS ON THE RELIGIOUS INSIGHT OF CERTAIN OF THE NEGRO SPIRITUALS. New York: Harper and Brothers, 1955, p. 13.

After A While

After 'while, after 'while,
Some sweet day after while,
I'm going up to see my Jesus,
O, some sweet day after 'while.

Pray on! Pray on!
Some sweet day after 'while,
Pray and time will soon be over,
O, some sweet day after 'while.

Shout on! Shout on!
Some sweet day after 'while,
Shout and time will soon be over,
O, some sweet day after 'while   (ANS)

Almost Over

Some seek the Lord
And they don't seek him right,
Pray all day and sleep all night,
And I'll thank God,
Almost over, almost over, almost over,
And I'll thank God, almost over.

Sister, if your heart is warm,
Snow and ice will do you no harm;
I done been down,
And I done been tried,
I been through the water,
And I been baptized.

O, sister, you must mind
How you step on the cross,
Your foot might slip,
And your soul get lost.

When you get to heaven
You'll be able to tell
How you shunned the gates of hell;
Wrestled with Satan
And wrestled with sin,
Stepped over hell
And came back again.

Almost over, almost over,
Almost over, almost over.   (ALLEN)

The Angel Rolled The Stone Away

The angel rolled the stone away,
The angel rolled the stone away;
'Twas a bright and shiny morn,
When the trumpet began to sound;

The angel rolled the stone away,
The angel rolled the stone away.

Sister Mary came running at the break of day,
Brought the news from heaven,
I'm looking for my Savior,
Tell me where he lay,
High up on the mountain,
The stone done rolled away.

The soldiers were a-plenty,
Standing by the door,
But they could not hinder
The stone done rolled away.

Old Pilate and his wise men,
Didn't know what to say,
The miracle was on them,
The stone done rolled away.

(BANS)

Angel's Waiting At The Door

My sister's took her flight
        and gone home,
And the angel's waiting at the door.
My sister's took her flight
        and gone home,
And the angel's waiting at the door.
Tell all my father's children,
        Don't grieve for me;
Tell all my father's children
        Don't grieve for me.

She has laid down her cross
        and gone home,
She has taken up her crown,
        and gone home,
And the angel's waiting at the door.
Tell all my father's children,
Don't grieve for me;
Tell all my father's children
Don't grieve FOR ME.

(FJS)

Aye Lord, Don't Leave Me

Cryin', aye Lord, don't leave me,
Cryin', aye Lord, don't leave me,
Cryin', aye Lord, don't leave me,
But guide me on my way.
When I was a sinner,
I loved my distance well,
But when I came to find myself
I was hangin' over hell.

I went down to the river of Jordan,
And stepped onto the sea of glass;

Ole Satan thought that I fell in,
But I got to heaven at las'.

The train at the station,
Blowin' for rich and poor;
Them that have their tickets ready
Will jump on the train and go.   (St. Helena)

The Band of Gideon

Oh, the band of Gideon, band of Gideon,
Band of Gideon over in Jordan,
Band of Gideon, band of Gideon,
O, how I long to see that day.

I hail to my sister,
My sister she bows low,
Say, don't you want to go to heaven,
How I long to see that day.

Oh, the twelve white horses, the twelve white horses,
Oh, the twelve white horses over in Jordan;
Twelve white horses over in Jordan,
How I long to see that day.

Oh, the milk white horses, the milk white horses,
Oh, hitch 'em to the chariot,
Oh, hitch 'em to the chariot,
How I long to see that day.   (BANS)

Bell Done Rung

I know, member, know Lord,
I know I heard the bell ring.

Want to go to the meeting,
Bell done rung;
Road so stormy,
Bell done rung;
The church is most over,
The heaven-bell's a heaven-bell,
Bell done rung,
The heaven bell, I'm going home.

I shout for the heaven-bell
It's heaven enough for me,
Brother ain't you member?
Bell done rung.   (ALLEN)

The Blind Man Stood On The Road And Cried

O, the blind man stood on the road and cried,
O, the blind man stood on the road and cried,
Crying, "O my Lord, save me."

The blind man stood on the road and cried,
Crying, "What kind of shoes are those you wear?"
Crying, "What kind of shoes are those you wear?"

O, the blind man stood on the road and cried,
Crying that he might receive his sight,
Crying that he might receive his sight.

The blind man stood on the road and cried,
Crying, "These shoes I wear are gospel shoes,"
Crying, "These shoes I wear are gospel shoes."

O, the blind man stood on the road and cried,
O, the blind man stood on the road and cried,
Crying, "O my Lord, save me."

                                                (BANS) (Variant)

Blow Your Trumpet, Gabriel

The tallest tree in Paradise,
The Christian calls the tree of life;
And I hope that trumpet might blow me home,
To the new Jerusalem.

Blow your trumpet, Gabriel,
Blow louder, louder;
And I hope that trumpet might blow me home,
To the new Jerusalem.

Paul and Silas bound in jail,
Sing God's praise both night and day,
Christians pray both night and day;
And I hope that trumpet might blow me home,
To my new Jerusalem.

So blow the trumpet, Gabriel,
Blow the trumpet, louder;
And I hope that trumpet might blow me home,
To my new Jerusalem.

                                                (ALLEN)

Can't You Live Humble?

Can't you live humble?
Praise King Jesus!
Can't you live humble
To the dying Lamb?
Lightning flashes, thunders roll,
Make me think of my poor soul.
Come here, Jesus, come here, please,
See me Jesus, on my knees.

Everybody come and see,
A man's been here from Galilee.
Came down here, and he talked to me,
Went away and he left me free.

Can't you live humble?
Praise King Jesus!
Can't You live humble
To the dying Lamb?   (BANS)

Come Down

Come down,
Come down, my Lord!
Come down,
Way down in Egypt land.

Jesus Christ, He died for me,
Way down in Egypt land.
Jesus Christ, He set me free,
Way down in Egypt land.
Born of God I know I am,
Way down in Egypt land;

I'm purchased by the dying Lamb,
Way down in Egypt land.

Peter walked upon the sea,
Way down in Egypt land;
And Jesus told him, "Come to me,"
Way down in Egypt land.

Come down,
Come down, my Lord!
Come down,
Way down in Egypt land.   (ANS)

Daniel In The Lion's Den (1)

Daniel in the lion's den,
Daniel in the lion's den,
Daniel in the lion's den,
Daniel in the lion's den,
Daniel in the lion's den,
Daniel in the lion's den.

Oh, the Angel lock the lion's jaws.
Oh, how-a could Daniel pray.
Daniel pray three times a day.   (St. Helena)

Daniel's In The Lion's Den (2)

Oh-o Lord, Daniel's in the lion's den,
Oh-o Lord, Daniel's in the lion's den,
Oh-o Lord, Daniel's in the lion's den,
Come help him in a hurry,
Help him in a hurry.

Oh-o Lord, Daniel ain't got no friend,
Come 'friend him in a hurry;

Oh-o Lord, won't you ease my troubling mind,
Come ease it in a hurry;
Oh-o Lord, you know I ain't got no friend,
Come 'friend me in a hurry;
Oh-o Lord, you know what you promised me,
Come give me in a hurry;
Oh-o Lord, Jonah's in the belly of the whale,
Come help him in a hurry;
Oh-o Lord, three Hebrew children in the fiery furnace,
Come help them in a hurry.   (BDWS)

The Danville Chariot

Oh swing low, sweet chariot,
Pray let me enter in,
I don't want to stay here no longer.
I done been to heaven,
    And I done been tried,
I been to the water,
    And I been baptized,
I don't want to stay here any longer.
Oh down to the water I was led,
My soul got fed with the heavenly bread,
I don't want to stay here any longer.

I had a little book,
    And I read it through,
I got my Jesus as well as you;
Oh I got a mother in the promised land,
I hope my mother will feed them lambs.
Oh, some go to church to holler and shout,
Before six months they're all turned out;
I don't want to stay here any longer.
Oh, some go to church to laugh and talk,
But they know nothing 'bout that Christian walk;
I don't want to stay here any longer.

Oh, shout, shout, the devil is about,
Oh shut your door and keep him out;
I don't want to stay here any longer.
For he is so much like a snake in the grass,
If you don't mind he will get you at last,
I don't want to stay here any longer.   (Hampton)

Death's Going To Lay His Cold Icy Hands On Me

Death is going to lay his cold icy hands on me,
Death is going to lay his cold icy hands on me.
One morning I was walking along,
I heard a voice and saw no man;
Said go in peace and sin no more,
Your sins forgiven and your soul set free.

One of these mornings it won't be long,
You'll look for me and I'll be gone,

Yes, one of these mornings about twelve o'clock,
This old world's going to reel and rock.

Death is going to lay his cold icy hands on me,
Death is going to lay his cold icy hands on me, Lord!   (BANS) (Variant)

Deep River

Deep river,
    My home is over Jordan,
Deep river,
Lord,
    I want to cross over into camp ground,
Lord,
    I want to cross over into camp ground,
Lord,
    I want to cross over into camp ground.

Oh, don't you want to go to that Gospel feast,
That promised land where all is peace;
I'll go into heaven and take my seat,
Cast my crown at Jesus' feet;

Oh, when I get to heaven,
    I'll walk about,

There's nobody there
    For to turn me out.

Deep river,
    My home is over Jordan,
Deep river, Lord,
    I want to cross over into camp ground,
Lord,
    I want to cross over into camp ground.   (FJS)

Didn't My Lord Deliver Daniel

Didn't my Lord deliver Daniel,
Deliver Daniel, Deliver Daniel,
And why not every man?

He delivered Daniel from the lion's den,
Jonah from the belly of the whale,
And the Hebrew children from the fiery furnace,
And why not every man.
The moon run down in a purple stream,
The sun forbear to shine
Every star disappear,
King Jesus shall be mine.

The wind blows East,
And the wind blows West;
It blows like the Judgement Day;
Every soul that never did pray
Will be glad to pray that day.

I set my foot on the Gospel ship,
And the ship it begin to sail;
It landed me over on Canaan shore,
I'll never come back anymore.

Didn't my Lord deliver Daniel,
Deliver Daniel, deliver Daniel,
Didn't my Lord deliver Daniel,
And why not every man?   (FJS)

Don't Call the Roll

Oh, don't call the roll,
Don't call the roll,
Don't call the roll,
Don't call the roll till I get there.

Jacob's ladder's slim and tall,
Ain't got no faith,
Surely you must fall.

Two white angels come a-walking down,
Long white robe and a starry crown.
Oh, don't call the roll,
Don't call the roll,
Don't call the roll,
Don't call the roll till I get there.   (Hampton)

Don't You View That Ship A-Come A-Sailing?

Don't you view that ship a-come a-sailing?
Hallelujah, don't you view that ship a-come a-sailing?
Don't you view that ship a-come a-sailing?
Don't you view that ship a-come a-sailing? Hallelujah.

That ship is heavy loaded, Hallelujah,
That ship is heavy loaded,
She neither reels nor totters, Hallelujah.
She is loaded with bright angels, Hallelujah.
Oh, how do you know they're angels? Hallelujah.
I know them by their mourning, Hallelujah.
Oh, yonder, comes my Jesus, Hallelujah.
Oh, how do you know it is Jesus? Hallelujah.
I know him by his shining, Hallelujah.

Don't you view that ship a-come a-sailing?
Hallelujah, don't you view that ship a-come a-sailing?   (Hampton)

Down By The Riverside

Going to lay down my burden,
Down by the riverside,
Down by the riverside,

Down by the riverside,
I ain't going to study war no more.

I ain't going to study war no more,
I ain't going to study war no more,
I ain't going to study war no more,
I ain't going to study war no more.

Going to lay down my sword and shield,
Down by the riverside,
Down by the riverside,
Down by the riverside,
Going to lay down my sword and shield,
Down by the riverside,
Ain't going to study war no more.   (Traditional)

Every Day'll Be Sunday

By and by, by and by, good Lord!
By and by,
Every day'll be Sunday by and by.
One of these mornings bright and fair,
Going to take my winds and cleave the air;
One day, one day walking along,
I thought I heard the angel's song.   (ANSAS)

Farewell, My Brother

Farewell, my brother, farewell forever,
Fare you well, my brother, now
For I am going home.
Oh, goodbye, goodbye,
For I am bound to leave you,
Oh, goodbye, goodbye,
For I am going home.
Shake hands, shake hands,
For I am bound to leave you,
Oh, shake hands, shake hands,
For I am going home.   (FJS)

For The Lord

For the Lord, for the Lord,
I'm going to lay down my life for the Lord.

One day as I was walking along,
The elements opened and the love came down,
I'm going to lay down my life for the Lord.

I shall never forget that day
When Jesus washed my sins away,
I'm going to lay down my life for the Lord.

You can hinder me here but you cannot there,
For the Lord in heaven's going to answer prayer,
I'm going to lay down my life for the Lord.

I wonder what satan's grumbling about,
He's chained in hell an' he can't come out,
I'm going to lay down my life for the Lord.   (Calhoun)

Gideon's Band

Oh, the band of Gideon,
        band of Gideon,
Over in Jordan,
        band of Gideon,
How I long to see that day.

I hail to my sister,
My sister she bow low,
Say, the twelve white horses,
        twelve white horses,
Over in Jordan;
Oh, hitch 'em to the chariot,
        hitch 'em to the chariot,
Over in Jordan.

I hail to my brother,
My brother he bow low,
Say, don't you want to go to heaven?
How I long to see that day!
Oh, ride up in the chariot,
Over in the chariot,
It's a golden chariot,
Over in Jordan.

I hail to the mourner,
The mourner he bow low,
Say, don't you want to go to heaven?
How I long to see that day!
Oh, the milk and the honey;
Over in Jordan,
Oh, the healing water,

Healing water over in Jordan,
How I long to see that day.   (FJS)

Give-A Way, Jordan

Give-a way, Jordan,
Give-a way, Jordan, Lord,
Give-a way, Jordan,
I mus' go for to see my Lord.

Give-a way, Jordan,
Give-a way, Jordan, Lord,
Give-a way, Jordan,
I mus' go for to see my Lord.

Nebuchadnezzar sat on his royal seat,
I mus' go for to see my Lord.
He saw the three Hebrew children boun' hands an' feet.
I mus' go for to see my Lord.
Give-a way, Jordan,
Give-a way, Jordan, Lord,
Give-a way, Jordan,
I mus' go for to see my Lord.   (Hayes)

Give Up the World

The sun gives a light in the heaven all around,
The sun gives a light in the heaven all around,
The sun gives a light in the heaven all around,
Why don't you give up the world?

My brother, don't you give up the world?
My brother, don't you give up the world?
My brother, don't you give up the world?
My brother, don't you give up the world?
We must leave this world behind.   (ALLEN)

Go, Chain The Lion Down

Go, chain the lion down,
Go, chain the lion down,
Go, chain the lion down,
Before the heaven doors close.

Do you see that good old sister,
Come a-wagging up the hill so slow?
She wants to get to heaven in due time,
Before the heaven doors close.

Do you see the good old Christians?
Do you see the good old preachers?
Come a-wagging up the hill so slow?
They want to get to heaven in due time,
Before the heaven doors close.   (FJS)

Go Down, Moses

Go down, Moses,
Way down in Egypt Land,
Tell ole Pharaoh,
Let my people go.

When Israel was in Egypt Land,
Oppressed so hard they could not stand;
"Thus saith the Lord," bold Moses said,
"If not I'll smite your first born dead;

"No more shall they in bondage toil,
Let them come out with Egypt's spoil."
When Israel out of Egypt came,

And left the proud oppressive land;
O, 'twas a dark and dismal night,
When Moses led the Israelites;
'Twas good old Moses and Aaron, too,
'Twas they that led the armies through;
The Lord told Moses what to do,
To lead the children of Israel through;
O come along Moses, you'll not get lost,
Stretch out your rod and come across;
As Israel stood by the water side,
At the command of God it did divide.
When they had reached the other shore,
They sang a song of triumph o'er;
Pharaoh said he would go across,
But Pharaoh and his host were lost;
O, Moses, the cloud shall cleave the way,
A fire by night, a shade by day;
You'll not get lost in the wilderness,
With a lighted candle in your breast;
Jordan shall stand up like a wall,
And the walls of Jericho shall fall,
Your foes shall not before you stand,
And you'll possess fair Canaan's land;
'Twas just about in harvest time,
When Joshua led his host divine.

O let us all from bondage flee,
And let us all in Christ be free;
We need not always weep and moan,
And wear these slavery chains forlorn;
This world's a wilderness of woe,
O, let us on to Canaan go;
What a beautiful morning that will be,
When time breaks up in eternity;
O bretheren, bretheren, you'd better be engaged,
For the devil he's out on a big rampage;
The Devil he thought he had me fast,
But I thought I'd break his chains at last;
O take your shoes from off your feet,
And walk into the golden street;
I'll tell you what I likes the best,
It is the shouting Methodist;
I do believe without a doubt,
That a Christian has the right to shout.

Go down, Moses,
Way down in Egypt land,
Tell ole Pharaoh,
Let my people go.   (FJS)

Going To Ride Up In The Chariot

Going to ride up in the chariot,
    Sooner in the morning,
Going to ride up in the chariot,
    Sooner in the morning,

And I hope I'll join the band;
O, Lord, have mercy on me.

Going to meet my brother there,
Going to chatter with the angels,
Going to meet my Master Jesus,
    Sooner in the morning,
    Sooner in the morning,
O, Lord, have mercy on me.

(FJS)

Go In The Wilderness

I wait upon the Lord,
I wait upon the Lord,
I wait upon the Lord, my God,
Who takes away the sin of the world.

If you want to find Jesus,
Go in the wilderness,
Go in the wilderness,
Go in the wilderness,
Mourning brother,
Go in the wilderness
To wait upon the Lord.
You want be a Christian,
Go in the wilderness,
You want to get religion,
Go in the wilderness,
If you expect to be converted,
Go in the wilderness
To wait upon the Lord.

O, weeping Mary,
Go in the wilderness,
Afflicted sister,
Go in the wilderness,
Say, you ain't a member?
Go in the wilderness,
Half-done Christian,
Go in the wilderness,
Come backslider,
Go in the wilderness,
Baptist member,
Go in the wilderness,
O, seek, brother Bristol,
Jesus a-waiting to meet you
    in the wilderness.

I wait upon the Lord,
I wait upon the Lord,
I wait upon the Lord, my God,
Who takes away the sin of the world.

(ALLEN)

Goodbye

Goodbye, my brother, goodbye,
Hallelujah!
Goodbye, sister Sally, goodbye,
Hallelujah!
Going home,
Hallelujah! Jesus calls me,
Hallelujah! Linger no longer,
Hallelujah! Tarry no longer,
Hallelujah!   (ALLEN)

Good Lord, Shall I Be The One?

Good Lord, shall I be the one,
Good Lord, shall I be the one,
Good Lord, shall I be the one,
Good Lord, shall i be the one,
Good Lord, shall i be the one?

I see my mother coming, coming, coming,
I see my mother coming,
Making for the Promise' Lan'.

I see my sister coming, coming, coming;
I see my brother coming, coming, coming;
I see my elder coming, coming, coming,
Making for the Promise' Lan'.   (Calhoun)

Good News, The Chariot's Coming

Good news, the chariot's coming,
Good news, the chariot's coming,
Good news, the chariot's coming,
And I don't want her to leave me behind.

Going to get up in the chariot,
Carry me home;
Get up in the chariot,
Carry me home,
And I don't want her to leave me behind.

There's a long white robe in the heaven, I know;
And I don't want her to leave me behind;
There's a golden crown in the heaven, I know;
And I don't want her to leave me behind;
There's a golden harp in the heaven, I know;
And I don't want her to leave me behind;
There's silver slippers in the heaven, I know;
And I don't want her to leave me behind.

Good news, the chariot's coming,
Good news, the chariot's coming ,
And I don't want her to leave me behind.   (Hampton)

Good Old Chariot

Swing low, sweet chariot,
Swing low, sweet chariot,
Swing low, sweet chariot,
Don't you leave me behind,
Oh, don't you leave me behind.

Good old chariot, swing so low,
Good old chariot, swing so low,
Good old chariot, swing so low,
Don't you leave me behind.

Good old chariot, take us all home,
Good old chariot, take us all home,
Good old chariot, take us all home,
Oh, don't you leave me behind.

Swing low, sweet chariot,
Swing low, sweet chariot,
Swing low, sweet chariot,
Oh, don't you leave me behind.   (FJS)

Gospel Train (1)

The gospel train is coming through,
The sun is getting out of view,
And if you get there before I do,
Tell them I'm coming by and by.

Stars in the heaven
Number one, number two,
Number three, number four,
Good Lord, good Lord, good Lord,
By and by.

There was a camp meeting,
Way down in the swamp,
Oh, Lord, hallelujah!
Got so dark they had to get a lamp.
The preacher he was long
And the preacher he was loud,
Along came an alligator,
And scared away the crowd.
Oh, Lord, hallelu!

Said the black bird
To the crow,
Oh Lord, hallelujah!
What makes the farmer hate us so,
Oh Lord, hallelu!
Ever since Adam and Eve
Were made, Oh, Lord, Hallelujah!
Pulling up the corn
Is just our trade.
Oh, Lord, hallelujah!

The gospel train is coming through,
The sun is getting out of view,
And if you get there before I do,
Tell them I'm coming by and by.   (BDWS) (Variant)

The Gospel Train, or Get on Board, Little Children (2)

The gospel train is coming,
        I hear it just at hand;

I hear the car wheels moving,
        And rumbling through the land.
Get on board, children,
        Get on board;
Get on board, children,
There's room for many more.

I hear the bell and whistle,
        The coming round the curve;
She's playing all her steam and power,
        And straining every nerve.

No signal for another train
        To follow on the line;
O, sinner, you're forever lost,
        If once you're left behind.

This is the Christian banner,
        The motto's new and old;
Salvation and Repentance
        Are burnished there in gold.

She's nearing now the station,
        O, sinner, don't be vain,
But come and get your ticket,
        And be ready for the train.

The fare is cheap and all can go,
        The rich and poor are there;
No second-class on board the train,
        No difference in the fare.

Get on board, children,
        Get on board;
Get on board, children,
There's room for many more.

There's Moses, Noah and Abraham,
        And all the prophets, too,
Our friends in Christ are all on board,
        O, what a heavenly crew.

We soon shall reach the station,
        O, how we then shall sing;
With all the heavenly army,
        We'll make the welkin ring.

We'll shout o'er all our sorrows,
  And sing forever more,
With Christ and all his army
  On that celestial shore.

Get on board, children,
  Get on board;
Get on board, children,
There's room for many more.   (FJS)

Guide My Head

Guide my head while I run this race,
Guide my head while I run this race,
Guide my head while I run this race,
Guide my head while I run this race,
"Cause I don't want to run this race in vain.

Guide my hands while I run this race,
Guide my hands while I run this race,
Guide my hands while I run this race,
Guide my hands while I run this race,
'Cause I don't want to run this race in vain.

Guide my feet while I run this race,
Guide my feet while I run this race,
Guide my feet while I run this race,
Guide my feet while I run this race,
'Cause I don't want to run this race in vain.

Guide my heart while I run this race,
Guide my heart while I run this race,
Guide my heart while I run this race,
Guide my heart while I run this race,
'Cause I don't want to run this race in vain.   (Schirmer)

Hail John's Army Bend Down

Hail, John's army bend down and die,
Hail, John's army bend down and die,
Clock up in heaven done struck one.
Bend down and die,
The good Lord Jesus was Mary's son,
Bend down and die.

Clock up in heaven done struck two,
Jesus Christ was born a Jew;
Clock up in heaven done struck three,
Jesus Christ can make a blind man see;
Clock up in heaven done struck four,
Jesus Christ can make a rich man poor;
Clock up in heaven done struck five,
Jesus Christ can make a dead man alive.

Clock up in heaven done struck six,
Jesus Christ can help you in a fix;

Clock up in heaven done struck seven,
Jesus Christ got the key of heaven;
Clock up in heaven done struck eight,
Jesus got the key to the pearly gate.

Clock up in heaven done struck nine,
Jesus Christ turned water to wine.
Clock up in heaven done struck ten,
Jesus died on the cross to save all men;
Clock up in heaven done struck eleven,
Jesus shows sinners the way to heaven;
Clock up in heaven done struck twelve,
Jesus Christ says do all things well.

Hail, John's army bend down and die,
Hail, John's army bend down and die.   (BDWS)

Has Anybody Here Seen My Lord?

Has anybody here seen my Jesus,
Anybody here seen my Lord?
I want to know have you seen-a my Jesus,
I want to know have you seen-a my Lord.

This world's a wilderness of woe,
Then let us all to heaven go.

That gospel train is moving fast,
We's all going to glory,
Lord, at last.

Has anybody here seen my Jesus,
Anybody here seen my Lord?
I want to know have you seen-a my Jesus,
I want to know have you seen-a my Lord.   (Fisher)

Hold On!

Keep you hand on-a that plow!
Hold on!
Hold on! Hold on!
Keep your hand right on-a that plow!
Hold on!

Noah, let me come in,
Doors all fastened and the windows pinned.
Keep your hand on-a that plow!
Noah said, You done lost your track,
Can't plow straight and keep-a lookin' back.

Sister Mary had a gold chain;
Every link was my Jesus' name.
Keep you hand on-a that plow!
Keep on plowin' and don't you tire;
Every row goes higher and higher.

If you want to get to Heaven
I'll tell you how:
Keep your right hand on-a that plow!
If that plow stays in-a your hand,
Land you straight in the Promise' Land.   (Dixon)

How Long The Train Been Gone

How long the train been gone--
How long the train been gone--
How long the train been gone--
O, yes, Lord.

Train been gone a long time,
Train been gone a long time,
Train been gone a long time,
O, yes, Lord.

Wave down the gospel train,
Wave down the gospel train,
Wave down the gospel train,
O, yes, Lord.
Hand me down my walkin' cane,
Hand me down my walkin' cane,
Hand me down my walkin' cane,
O, yes, Lord.

Better get your ticket sign,
Better get your ticket sign,
Better get your ticket sign,
O, yes, Lord.

You better fall in line,
You better fall in line,
You better fall in line,
O, yes, Lord.   (St. Helena)

Hunting For A City

I am hunting for a city,
To stay awhile,
I am hunting for a city,
To stay awhile,
I am hunting for a city,
To stay awhile.
O, believer got a home at last.   (Allen)

I Am Hunting For A City

I am huntin' for a city for to stay a while,
I am huntin' for a city for to stay a while,
I am huntin' for a city for to stay a while,
True believer has a home at last.

Oh, run, dear young converts, go and tell my Lord,
Oh, run, dear young converts, go and tell my Lord,
True believer got a home at last.

Oh, run, my lovin' sister, go and tell my Lord,
Oh, run, my lovin' sister, go and tell my Lord,
True believer got a home at last.   (St. Helena)

I Can't Stay Behind

I can't stay behind,
My Lord, I can't stay behind;
I can't stay behind,
My Lord, I can't stay behind.

The roses bloom, the roses bloom,
The roses bloom in the heaven I know;
The lilies bloom, the lilies bloom,
The lilies bloom in the heaven I know;
There's room enough, there's room enough,
There's room enough in the heaven I know;
The angels sing, the angels sing,
The angels sing in the heaven I know.
I can't stay behind,
My Lord, I can't stay behind;

I can't stay behind,
My Lord, I can't stay behind.   (CD)

If I Got My Ticket, Can I Ride?

Lord, if I got my ticket,
Can I ride?
Lord, If I got my ticket,
Can I ride?
Lord, if I got my ticket,
Can I ride,
Ride away to heaven that mornin'?

Hear a big talk of the Judgment Day,
You got no time to projic away!
Away by and by without a doubt!
Jehovah will order his train about,
Clean out the world and leave no sin,
Tell me, please, where have you been?

Lord, if I got my ticket,
Can I ride?
Lord, if I got my ticket,
Can I ride,
Ride away to heaven that mornin'?

Hear a big talk about the Gospel Train,
Yeah, that's my aim.
Stand at the station patient and wait,
The train is comin' and it's never late.

So long comin' that it worried my mind;
I thought it was late
But was just on time.

Lord, if I got my ticket,
Can I ride?
Lord, if I got my ticket,
Can I ride,
Ride away to heaven that mornin'.   (Schirmer)

I Know I Would Like To Read

I know I would like to read, like to read,
Like to read a sweet story of old,
I would like to read, like to read,
I would like to read a sweet story of old.

Come on, brother, and help me sing,
The story of King Emanuel;
If ever I get up on the other shore,
By the grace of God I'll come here no more;
I just want to get up on the mountain top,
I'll praise my God and never stop.

I know I would like to read, like to read,
Like to read a sweet story of old,
I would like to read, like to read,
I would like to read a sweet story of old.   (Hampton)

I'll Meet You Way Up Yonder

I'll meet you way up yonder in a few day,
        in a few day;
I'll meet you way up yonder,
An' I'm going home.

Heaven so high an' I'm so low,
An' then I'm going home.
Don't know whether I'll ever reach it or no,
An' then I'm going home.

Ol' satan's mad an' I am glad,
He missed a soul he thought he had,
If you get there befo' I do,
You may tell them all I'm coming, too.
An' then I'm going home,
I'll meet you way up yonder,
An' then I'm going home.   (Calhoun)

I'm Going Back With Jesus

I'm going back with Jesus when He comes, when He comes,
And I'm going back with Jesus when He comes, when He comes,
O, He may not come today,
But He's coming anyway,

And I'm going back with Jesus when He comes.
And we won't die any more when He comes, when He comes,
And we won't die any more when He comes, when He comes;
And He's going to bring my mother with Him when He comes,
And He's going to bring my mother with Him when He comes.

I'm going back with Jesus when He comes, when He comes,
And I'm going back with Jesus when He comes, when He comes,
O, He may not come today,
But He's coming anyway,
And I'm going back with Jesus when He comes.   (ANS)

I'm So Glad

I'm so glad done just got out of that Egypt land,
I'm so glad done fell in love with the Son of Man.

I remember the day, I remember it well,
Done fell in love with the Son of Man,
My dungeon shook and my chain fell off,
Done fell in love with the Son of Man.
I'm going to heaven on the eagle's wing,
All don't see me, going to hear me sing,
Done fell in love with the Son of Man,
When I get there, I'll shortly tell,
How I whipped Satan at the gate of hell.

I'm so glad done just got out of that Egypt land,
I'm so glad done fell in love with the Son of Man.   (BDWS)

I'm Traveling To The Grave

I'm traveling to the grave,
I'm traveling to the grave,
My Lord,
    I'm traveling to the grave
For to lay this body down.
My master died shouting,
    Singing glory hallelujah;
The last word he said to me
    Was about Jerusalem.

My misses died shouting,
    Singing glory hallelujah;
The last word she said to me
    Was about Jerusalem.

My brother died shouting,
    Singing glory hallelujah;
The last word he said to me
    Was about Jerusalem.

My sister died shouting,
    Singing glory hallelujah;

The last word she said to me
   Was about Jerusalem.

I'm traveling to the grave,
I'm traveling to the grave,
   I'm traveling to the grave,
For to lay this body down.   (FJS)

In Bright Mansions Above

In bright mansions above,
In bright mansions above,
Lord, I want to live up yonder,
In bright mansions above.

My father's gone to glory,
My brother's gone to glory,
The Christian's gone to glory,
I want to live there, too, Lord,
I want to live up yonder,
In bright mansions above.   (FJS)

In The Army

God knows 'tis a better day than this a-coming,
In the army by and by.
God knows 'tis a better day than this a-coming,
In the army by and by.

When we shall see our sister,
In the army by and by;
When we shall see our brother,
In the army by and by;
When we shall see brother Michael,
In the army by and by;
When we shall see King Jesus,
In the army by and by.
God knows 'tis a better day than this a-coming,
In the army by and by.
God knows 'tis a better day than this a-coming,
In the army by and by.   (Calhoun)

I Want To Join The Band

What is that up yonder I see?
Two little angels coming after me;
I want to join the band,
I want to join the band,
I want to join the band.   (ALLEN)

I Will Overcome

I will overcome,
I will overcome,

I will overcome,
I will overcome,
Down in my heart,
I do believe
I will overcome some day.

Jesus take me by the hand,
Jesus take me by the hand,
Jesus take me by the hand,
Jesus take me by the hand,
Down in my heart,
I do believe
I will overcome some day.

I will be all right,
I will be all right,
I will be all right,
I will be all right,
Down in my heart,
I do believe
I will be all right some day.
I will see the Lord,
I will see the Lord,
I will see the Lord,
I will see the Lord,
Down in my heart,
I do believe
I will see the Lord some day.

(Traditional, Sea
Islands)

Join The Army Of The Lord

Reign, oh! reign, oh, reign, my Savior,
Reign, oh! reign, oh, reign, my Lord.

Takes a faithful soul to join us in the army of the Lord,
Takes a faithful soul to join us in the army;
You must bow low to join us in the army of the Lord,
You must pray to join us in the army of the Lord,
Takes a winning soul to join in the army of the Lord.

No liar can join us in the army of the Lord,
You must walk right to join us in the army of the Lord;
Didn't he deny the world to join us in the army of the Lord,
Didn't he hunt the hills to join us in the army of the Lord?

Reign, oh! reign, oh, reign, my Savior,
Reign, oh! reign, oh, reign, my Savior.

(BDWS)

Just Above My Head

Just above my head,
I hear music in the air;
Just above my head,
I hear music in the air;
Just above my head,

I hear music in the air;
There must be a God somewhere.   (Traditional)

Keep Your Lamps Trimmed

Keep your lamps trimmed and a-burning,
Keep your lamps trimmed and a-burning,
Keep your lamps trimmed and a-burning,
For this work's almost done;
Brothers, don't grow weary,
Brothers, don't grow weary,
For this work's almost done.

'Tis religion makes us happy,
'Tis religion makes us happy,
We are climbing Jacob's ladder,
Every round goes higher and higher.

Keep your lamps trimmed and a-burning,
Keep your lamps trimmed and a-burning,
Keep your lamps trimmed and a-burning,
For this work's almost done;
Brothers don't grow weary,
Brothers don't grow weary,
For this work's almost done.   (FJS)

Kind Savior

Hallelujah, kind Savior,
Let this warfare be ended,
Hallelu!
If my sister want to go,
Why don't she come along?
Let this warfare be ended,
Hallelu!

If my brother want to go,
If my mother want to go,
If my elder want to go,
Why don't he come along?
Let this warfare be ended,
Hallelu!   (Calhoun)

A Little More Faith In Jesus

All I want, all I want,
All I want is a little more faith in Jesus.
Whenever we meet you here we say,
A little more faith in Jesus;
Pray, what's the order of the day?
A little more faith in Jesus.

I tell you now as I told you before,
To the promised land I'm bound to go;
Oh! Hallelujah to the Lamb,

The Lord is on the giving hand;
I do believe without a doubt,
That Christians have a right to shout;
Shout, you children, shout, you're free,
For Christ has bought this liberty.
All I want, all I want,
All I want is a little more faith in Jesus.
Whenever we meet you here we say,
A little more faith in Jesus,
Pray, what's the order of the day?
A little more faith in Jesus.

(FJS)

Mary Wept An' Marthy Moaned

Mary wept an'-a Marthy moaned,
Mary wept an'-a Marthy moaned,
Mary wept an'-a Marthy moaned,
Round a willow tree.
Round a willow tree.

Who's-a been here since I been gone?
Who's-a been here since I been gone?
Who's a been here since I been gone?
Good Lord done come an' gone.
Good Lord done come an' gone.

I don' wanta live an' die in sin,
I don' wanta live an' die in sin,
I don' wanta live an' die in sin,
Good Lord deliver me.
Good Lord deliver me.

(Grissom)

Moses Smote The Water

Moses smote the water
And the children all crossed over;
O, Moses smote the water
And the sea give way.
O, children, ain't you glad
You in the holy army;
O, children, ain't you glad
The sea give way.

Aaron crossed the ocean
And the children crossed over;
O, Aaron crossed the ocean
And the sea give way.

Mary crossed the ocean
And the children all cross over;
O, Mary crossed the ocean
And the sea give way.

(St. Helena)

Move Along

Let us move along, move along,
Move along to the heavenly home,

Let us move along, move along,
I am bound to meet you there.

We are on the ocean sailing,
And awhile must face the stormy blast,
But if Jesus is our captain,
We will make the port at last.

Yonder see the golden city,
And the lighthouse gleaming on the shore,
Hear the angels sweetly singing,
Soon our journey will be o'er.

There we'll meet our friends in Jesus,
Who are waiting on the golden shore,
With a shout of joy they'll greet us,
When we meet to part no more.

Let us move along, move along,
Move along to the heavenly home,
Let us move along, move along,
I am bound to meet you there.   (FJS)

My Army's Crossing Over

My brother, take care of Satan,
My army's crossing over,
My brother, take care of Satan,
My army's crossing over.

Satan's very busy,
He washes his face in ashes,
He puts on the leader's apron.

Jordan river's rolling,
Cross it, I tell you, cross it,
Cross Jordan's dangerous river.
My brother, take care of Satan,
My army's crossing over,
My brother, take care of Satan,
My army's crossing over.   (ALLEN)

My Father, How Long?

My father, how long,
My father, how long,
My father, how long,
Poor sinner got to suffer here?

And it won't be long,
And it won't be long,

And it won't be long,
Poor sinner to suffer here.

We'll soon be free,
The Lord will call us home;
We'll walk the merry road
Where pleasure never dies;
We'll walk the golden streets
Of the New Jerusalem;
My brothers do sing
The praises of the Lord;
We'll fight for liberty
When the Lord will call us home.   (ALLEN)

My Ship Is On The Ocean

My ship is on the ocean,
        My ship is on the ocean,
My ship is on the ocean,
        Poor sinner, fare you well.

I'm going away to see good old Daniel,
I'm going away to see my Lord.
I'm going to see the weeping Mary,
I'm going away to see my Lord.
Oh! don't you want to live in that bright glory?
Oh! don't you want to go see my Lord?

My ship is on the ocean,
        My ship is on the ocean,
My ship is on the ocean,
        Poor sinner, fare you well.   (FJS)

O, Daniel

You call yourself a church member,
You hold your head so high,
You praise God with your glittering tongue,
But you leave all your heart behind.

O, my Lord delivered Daniel,
O, Daniel, O, Daniel,
O, my Lord delivered Daniel,
O, why not deliver me too?   (ALLEN)

Oh, Let Me Get Up

Oh! just let me get up
        in the house of God,
    Just let me get up
        in the house of God,
    Just let me get up
        in the house of God,
And I'll never turn back no more;

No more, no more,
Why thank God almighty,

No more, no more,
I'll never turn back no more.

Oh! just let me get on
    my long white robe,
Oh! just let me get on
    my starry crown,
Oh! just let me get on
    my golden shoes,
Oh! the music in heaven,
    and it sounds so sweet.

Oh! just let me get up
        in the house of God,
Just let me get up
        in the house of God,
Just let me get up
        in the house of God,
And I'll never turn back no more;

No more, no more,
Why thank God almighty,
No more, no more,
I'll never turn back no more.   (FJS)

Oh, My Good Lord, Show Me The Way

Oh, my good Lord, show me the way,
Oh, my good Lord, show me the way,
Oh, my good Lord, show me the way,
Enter the chariot, travel along.
Old Noah sent out a mourning dove,
Which brought back a token of heavenly love;
Going to serve my God while I have breath,
So I can see my Jesus after death;
When I get to heaven going to put on my shoes,
I'll walk all over heaven and spread the news.

Oh, my good Lord, show me the way,
Oh, my good Lord, show me the way,
Oh, my good Lord, show me the way,
Enter the chariot, travel along.   (BANS)

Oh, Never Me One

When my mother done gone--
When my mother done gone--
Oh, never me one--
Oh, never me one--.
When my mother done gone--
Aye Lord, aye Lord--
Oh, never me one.

My sister done gone,
Aye Lord.
My brother done gone,
Aye lord.
When the world done 'buked me,
Aye Lord.
When I'm thrown with crosses,
Aye Lord.
When they leave me here to trouble,
Aye Lord, aye Lord--
Oh, never me one.

(St. Helena)

Oh, Wasn't That A Wide River?

Oh, wasn't that a wide river,
          River of Jordan, Lord?
Wide river!
There's one more river to cross.

Oh, the river of Jordan is so wide,
I don't know how to get on the other side;
I have some friends before me gone,
By the grace of God I'll follow on;
Shout, shout, Satan's about,
Shut your door and keep him out;
Old Satan is a snake in the grass,
If you don't mind, he'll get you at last.

Oh, wasn't that a wide river,
          River of Jordan, Lord?
Wide river!
There's one more river to cross,
          One more river to cross.

(FJS)

Old Ship Of Zion (1)

What ship is that a-sailing, Hallelujah?
What ship is that a-sailing, Hallelujah?
Do you think that she is able
For to carry us all home?

'Tis the old ship of Zion, Hallelujah,
'Tis the old ship of Zion, Hallelujah,
She has landed many a thousand,
She has landed many a thousand,
And will land so many more.

She is loaded down with angels,
She is loaded down with angels;
King Jesus is the Captain,
And he'll carry us all home.

'Tis the old ship of Zion, Hallelujah,
'Tis the old ship of Zion, Hallelujah,
She has landed many a thousand
And will land as many more.

(FJS)

The Old Ship Of Zion (2)

What ship is that you're enlisted upon?
O, glory hallelujah.
'Tis the old ship of Zion, hallelujah!
'Tis the old ship of Zion, hallelujah!

And who is the captain
        of that ship you're on?
O, glory hallelujah!
My Saviour is the Captain, hallelujah!!   (ALLEN) (Variant)

The Old Ship Of Zion (3)

Don't you see that ship a-sailing,
A-sailing, a-sailing,
Don't you see that ship a-sailing,
Going over to the Promised Land?

I asked my Lord,
        Shall I ever be the one,
        Shall I ever be the one,
        To go sailing, sailing,
        Sailing, sailing,
Going over to the Promised Land?

She sails like she is heavy loaded;
King Jesus is the Captain;
The Holy Ghost is the Pilot.
Don't you see that ship a-sailing,
A-sailing, a-sailing,
Don't you see that ship a-sailing,
Going over to the Promised Land?   (ALLEN) (Variant)

The Ole Ship Maria

'Tis the ole ship Maria,
Don't you want to go?
'Tis the ole ship Maria,
Don't you want to go?
'Tis the ole ship Maria,
Don't you want to go?
O, Lamb of God,
I come, I come.

She's comin' heavy loaded,
Don't you want to go?
O, Lamb of God,
I come, I come.

She's loaded with bright angels,
Don't you want to go?
O, Lamb of God,
I come, I come.

Get oil in your vessel,
Don't you want to go?
O, Lamb of God,
I come, I come.

She never lend nor borrow,
Don't you want to go?
O, Lamb of God, I come.

(St. Helena)

A Praise Chant

From heaven,
O Lord!
Look down,
Right now.
Allright,
O Lord!
Look down,
Little more.

On high,
O Lord!
Save me,
When I die.
When I die,
O Lord!
Take me,
Up home.

(BDWS)

Put John On The Island

Hail, hail,
Put John on the island,
Hail, hail,
Weep-a low Judgement's coming.

You got Jesus, hold Him fast,
The grace of God you shall receive;
Didn't know Christ was into the field,
Till I heard the rumbling of the chariot wheel;
Going down Jordan to pay my fare,
Have a little meeting when I get there;
Going up to heaven, don't want to stop,
Don't want to be no stumbling block.

(Hampton)

Reign, Master Jesus

O reign, O reign,
O reign, my Savior,
Reign, Master Jesus, reign,
O reign salvation, in my soul,
Reign, Master Jesus, reign.

I never shall forget that day,
When Jesus washed my sins away;

I looked at my hands
And my hands looked new,
I looked at my feet
And my feet looked so too;
I never felt such love before,
Saying, "Go in peace and sin no more."

(Hampton)

Rise Up, Shepherd, And Follow

There's a star in the east on Christmas morn,
Rise up, shepherd, and follow;
It'll lead to the place where the Savior's born,
Rise up, shepherd, and follow.

If you take good heed to the angels words
Rise up, shepherd, and follow;
You'll forget your flocks, you'll forget your herds,
Rise up, shepherd, and follow.
Leave your sheep and leave your lambs,
Rise up, shepherd, and follow;
Leave your ewes and leave your rams,
Rise up, shepherd, and follow;
Follow, follow,
Rise up, shepherd, and follow;
Follow the star of Bethlehem,
Rise up, shepherd, and follow.

(Hampton)

Sail, O Believer

Sail, O believer, sail,
Sail over yonder;
Sail, O my brother, sail,
Sail over yonder.

Bow low, Mary bow low, Martha,
For Jesus comes and locks the door,
And carries the keys away.

Sail, sail, over yonder,
And view the promised land,
Weep, O Mary, bow low, Martha.

Sail, sail, my true believer,
Sail, sail, over yonder;
Mary, bow low, Martha, bow low,
For Jesus comes and locks the door,
And carries the keys away.

(ALLEN)

Same Train

Same train carry my mother,
Same train carry my mother,
Same train be back tomorrow,
Same train, same train.

Same train carry my sister,
Same train carry my brother,
Same train be back tomorrow,
Same train, same train.

Same train up in the heaven,
Same train up in the heaven,
Same train be back tomorrow,
Same train, same train.

(CD)

Save Me, Jesus, Save Me Now

I'm goin' to climb up Jacob's ladder,
    Jacob's ladder,
I'm goin' to climb up Jacob's ladder,
    Jacob's ladder,
I'm goin' to climb up Jacob's ladder,
    Jacob's ladder;
Save me, Jesus, save me now.

I'm goin' to set at the welcome table,
    welcome table;
Save me, Jesus, save me now.

I'm goin' to march with the tallest Angel,
    tallest Angel;
Save me, Jesus, save me now.

I'm goin' to see my lovin' mother,
    lovin' mother;
Save me, Jesus, save me now.

I'm goin' to shake right hand, right hand
    with my Jesus;
Save me, Jesus, save me now.

I'm goin' to mount up higher and higher,
    higher and higher;
Save me, Jesus, save me now.

God's goin' to set your sins before you,
    sins before you;
Save me, Jesus, save me now.

(St. Helena)

Save Me, Lord, Save Me

I called to my Father,
    My Father hearkened to me,
And the last word I heard him say was,
    Save me, Lord, save me.
And I wish that heaven was mine,
And I hope that heaven will be mine,
And I wish that heaven was mine,
O, save me, Lord, save me.

I called to my mother,
        My mother hearkened to me;
I called to my sister,
        My sister hearkened to me;
I called to my brother,
        My brother hearkened to me;
And the last word I heard them say was,
        Save me, Lord, save me.
And I wish that heaven was mine,
And I hope that heaven will be mine,
And I wish that heaven was mine,
O, save me, Lord, save me.   (FJS)

Send Them Angels Down

Peter and John stood on the shore,
Send them angels down,
Drop them sins and follow me.
Send them angels down,
My soul, my soul's determined.
My soul, my soul,
Send them angels down.

Esau was a hunter bold,
He sold his birthright for a mess of pottage;
Joshua was the son of Nun,
He asked God almighty to stop the sun;
Sinner man, you better pray,
You can't get to hell with your own bad way;
Never did feel such a love before
The heaven came open and the love came down.

My soul, my soul's determined,
My soul, my soul,
Send them angels down.   (BDWS)

Somebody's Buried In The Graveyard

Somebody's buried in the graveyard,
Somebody's buried in the sea,
Going to get up in the morning shouting,
Going to join Jubilee.
Although you see me coming along so,
To the promised land I'm bound to go;
I have some friends before me gone,
By the grace of God I'll follow on;
Sometimes I'm up, sometimes I'm down,
But still my soul is heavenly bound.   (ANS)

Sometimes I Feel Like I Wanna Go Home

Sometimes I feel like I wanna go home,
Sometimes I feel like I wanna go home,
Sometimes I feel like a motherless child,
As I kneel by the roadside and pray.

Sometimes I feel like a eagle in the air,
Sometimes I feel like a eagle in the air,
Sometimes I feel like I wanna go home,
As I kneel by the roadside and pray.

(Fisher)

Steal Away

Steal away, steal away,
        Steal away to Jesus!
Steal away, steal away home,
I ain't got long to stay here.

My Lord calls me:
        He calls me by the thunder;
The trumpet sounds within-a my soul;
I ain't got long to stay here.

My Lord calls me:
        He calls me by the lightning;
The trumpet sounds within-a my soul;
I ain't got long to stay here.

Green trees are a-bending:
        Poor sinners stand a-trembling;
The trumpet sounds within-a my soul;
        I ain't got long to stay here.

Tombstones are a-bursting:
        Poor sinners are a-trembling;
The trumpet sounds within-a my soul;
        I ain't got long to stay here.
Steal away, steal away,
        Steal away to Jesus!
Steal away, steal away home,
I ain't got long to stay here.

(Hampton)

Steal Away To My Father's Kingdom

Steal away---steal away,
Steal away to my Father's Kingdom.
Steal away.
Down in the valley,
Steal away.
Talkin' to my Jesus,
Steal away.
No mo' trouble,
Steal away.
My Lord with me,
Steal away.
Steal away---steal away,
Steal away to my Father's Kingdom.
Steal away.

Steal away---steal away,
Steal away to my Father's Kingdom.

Steal away.
Down in the valley,
Steal away.
Shoutin', Hallelujah!
Steal away.
Free from hard trials,
Steal away.
Jesus walkin' with me,
Steal away.
Steal away---steal away,
Steal away to my Father's Kingdom.
Steal away.   (Grissom)

Sweet Canaan

Oh, the land I am bound for,
Sweet Canaan's happy land
        I am bound for,
Sweet Canaan's happy land
        I am bound for,
Sweet Canaan's happy land,
Pray give me your right hand.

Oh, my brother, did you come
        for to help me?
Oh, my sister, did you come
        for to help me?
Pray give me your right hand,
Pray give me your right hand.   (FJS)

Swing Down, Chariot

Swing down, chariot and let me ride,
Swing down, chariot and let me ride,
I've got a home on the other side.
Ride, chariot, ride,
Ride, chariot, ride,
I've got a home on the other side.   (Traditional)

Swing Low, Chariot

Swing low, chariot, low in the East,
Let God's people have some peace,
Going to ride the chariot in the morning.

Swing low, chariot, low in the West,
Let God's people have some rest,
Going to ride the chariot in the morning.

Swing low, chariot, low in the North,
Let God's people have a talk,
Going to ride in the chariot in the morning.

Swing low, chariot, low in the South,
Let God's people have a shout,

Going to ride in the chariot in the morning;
Elijah,
Going to ride in the chariot in the morning.   (Hampton)

Swing Low, Sweet Chariot

Swing low, sweet chariot,
      Coming for to carry me home.
Swing low, sweet chariot,
      Coming for to carry me home.

I looked over Jordan,
      and what did I see
Coming for to carry me home?
Coming after me,
Coming for to carry me home.

If you get there
      before I do,
Coming for to carry me home,
Tell all my friends
      I'm coming too
Coming for to carry me home.

The brightest day
      that ever I saw,
Coming for to carry me home,
When Jesus washed
      my sins away,
Coming for to carry me home.

I'm sometimes up
      and sometimes down,
Coming for to carry me home,

But still my soul
      feels heavenly bound.
Coming for to carry me home.

Swing low, sweet chariot,
      Coming for to carry me home,

Swing low, sweet chariot,
      Coming for to carry me home.   (FJS)

Tell 'Em I'm Gone

When you miss me from 'round the fireside,
Tell 'em I'm gone; tell 'em I'm gone.
When you miss me from 'round the fireside,
Tell 'em I'm gone. Tell 'em I'm gone.
Tell 'em Death has severed me.
Way over in the Rock of Ages,
Clef' for me---Clef' for me.

When you miss me from singin' and prayin',
Tell 'em I'm gone; tell 'em I'm gone.
When you miss me from the Sacrament table,
Tell 'em I'm gone. Tell 'em I'm gone.
When you miss me from weepin' an' moanin',
Tell 'em I'm gone; tell 'em I'm gone.
When you miss me from the Amen corner,
Tell 'em I'm gone; tell 'em I'm gone.
When you miss me from the big baptizin',
Tell 'em I'm gone; tell 'em I'm gone.
When you miss me from the big revival,
Tell 'em I'm gone; tell 'em I'm gone.   (Grissom)

That Same Train

That same train's going to be back tomorrow,
That same train--
That same train's going to be back tomorrow,
That same train.

That same train took away my father,
That same train took away my mother,
Stand right still and steady yourself for
That same train;
That same train's going to be back tomorrow,
That same train.

Oh, get your ticket ready for that same train;
Oh, get you in a hurry for that same train;
Oh, get you on board of
That same train,
Oh, death's train going to be back tomorrow,
That same train.   (BDWS)

There's Room Enough

O, brothers, brothers,
Don't stay away! Don't stay away.
O, sinners, sinners,
Don't stay away! Don't stay away.
O, mourners, mourners,
Don't stay away! Don't stay away.

Don't stay away, don't stay away,
For my Lord says there's room enough
    in the heaven for us all;
My Lord says there's room enough,
So don't stay away.   (ANSAS)

This Train

This train is bound for glory, this train!
This train is bound for glory,
This train is bound for glory,
This train is bound for glory, this train.

This train don't haul no gamblers, this train!
This train don't haul no gamblers,
This train don't haul no gamblers,
This train don't haul no gamblers, this train.

This train don't haul no extras, this train!
This train don't haul no extras, this train!
This train don't haul no extras,
This train don't haul no extras, this train.

This train don't haul no sinners, this train!
This train don't haul no sinners, this train!
This train don't haul no sinners,
This train don't haul no sinners, this train.   (Traditional)

To See God's Bleeding Lamb (2)

Want to go to heaven when I die,
When I die, when I die,
Want to go to heaven when I die,
To see God's bleeding Lamb.

Jacob's ladder's deep and long,
Deep and long, deep and long;
See God's angel coming down,
Coming down, coming down:
Coming down in a sheet of blood,
Sheet of blood, sheet of blood;
Sheet of blood all mingled with fire,
Mingled with fire, mingled with fire.

Then you raise your voice up higher,
Voice up higher, voice up higher;
And you join that heavenly choir,
Heavenly choir, heavenly choir,
To see God's bleeding Lamb.
Yes, I want to go to heaven when I die,
When I die, when I die,
To see God's bleeding Lamb.   (BANS)

'Twas On One Sunday Morning

'Twas on one Sunday morning,
Sunday morning, Sunday morning,
'Twas on one Sunday morning
Just about the break of day.

An angel came down from heaven,
Came down from heaven, came down from heaven;
An angel came down from heaven,
And rolled the stone away.
John and Peter came running,
Came running, came running;
John and Peter came running,
And found an empty tomb.

Mary and Martha came weeping,
Came weeping, came weeping;
Mary and Martha came weeping,
And lo! their Lord had gone.   (ANS)

Two Wings

Lord, I want two wings to veil my face,
I want two wings to fly away;
Lord, I want two wings to veil my face,
And I want to wings for two fly away;
Lord, I want two wings to veil my face,
Lord, I want two wings to fly away.

I want two wings to veil my face,
And I want two wings for to fly away.

O, meet me, Jesus, meet me,
Meet me in the air,
And if these two wings fail me,
Jus' give me another pair.
O, I want two wings to veil my face, Lord,
I want two wings to fly away, Lord,
I want two wings to veil my face,
And I want two wings to fly away.

I want two wings to veil my face, Lord,
I want two wings to fly away, Lord,
I want two wings to veil my face,
And I want two wings for to fly away.   (Hayes)

Walk In Jerusalem, Just Like John

Last Sunday morning, last Sunday morning,
        last Sunday morning,
Walk in Jerusalem, just like John,
Walk in Jerusalem, all God's people,
Walk in Jerusalem, tell the angels,
Walk in Jerusalem, just like John.

Train is a-coming, train is a-coming,
Walk in Jerusalem, just like John,
Walk in Jerusalem, all my brethren,
Walk in Jerusalem, all my sisters,
Walk in Jerusalem, just like John.
She is loaded down with angels,
    loaded down with angels,
Walk in Jerusalem, just like John,
Walk in Jerusalem, see my father,
Walk in Jerusalem, see my mother,
Walk in Jerusalem, just like John.   (CD)

Walk Together, Children

Walk together, children,
Don't you get weary,
Walk together, children,
Don't you get weary,
Oh, walk together, children,
Don't you get weary,
There's a great camp meeting
In the Promised Land.

Going to mourn and never tire,
Mourn and never tire,
Mourn and never tire.
There's a great camp meeting
In the Promised Land.
Oh, sing together, children, children,
Don't you get weary,
Sing together, children,
Don't you get weary, children.

Stand together, children, children,
Don't you get weary,
There's a great camp meeting
In that Promised Land;
Oh, walk together,
Keep on a-walking,
There's a great camp meeting
In that Promised Land.   (Fisher)

Want To Go To Heaven When I Die

Want to go to heaven when I die,
Want to go to heaven when I die,
Want to go to heaven when I die;

Good Lord, when I die,
Good Lord, when I die.

Want to see my mother when I die,
Want to see my mother when I die,
Want to see my mother when I die;
Good Lord, when I die,
Good Lord, when I die.

Want to see my father when I die,
Want to see my father when I die,
Want to see my father when I die;
Good Lord, when I die,
Good Lord, when I die.   (Hampton)

When I Die

Who's gonna make up my dyin' bed?
Who's a-gonna make up my dyin' bed?
Who's a-gonna make up my dyin' bed,

When I die, when I die?
Jesus gonna make up my dyin' bed,
Jesus gonna make up my dyin' bed;
Jesus gonna make up my dyin' bed,
When I die.
Who's goin' down in the grave with me?
Who's a-goin' down in the grave with me,
When I die, when I die?
Jesus goin' down in the grave with me,
When I die.

Who's gonna sing that las' song?
Who's a-gonna sing that las' song,
When I die, when I die?
Jesus gonna sing that las' song,
When I die.

Who's gonna pray that las' prayer?
Who's a-gonna pray that las' prayer,
When I die, when I die?
Jesus gonna pray that las' prayer,
When I die.

Who's gonna take my soul to heaven?
Who's a-gonna take my soul to heaven,
When I die, when I die?
Jesus gonna take my soul to heaven,
When I die.

I'm gonna treat everybody right,
I', gonna treat everybody right,
'Til I die, 'til I die.

I'm gonna stay on the battlefield,
I'm gonna stay on the battlefield,
'Til I die, 'til I die.

I'm gonna take a soldier's fare,
I'm gonna take a soldier's fare;
'Til I die, 'til I die.   (Grissom)

When Moses Smote The Water

When Moses smote the water,
    The children all passed over,
When Moses smote the water,
    The sea gave away.

O, children, ain't you glad
    You've left that sinful army?
O, children, ain't you glad
    The sea gave away?

O, Christians, ain't you glad?
O, brothers, ain't you glad?

When Moses smote the water,
  The children all passed over,
When Moses smote the water,
  The sea gave away.   (FJS)

When The Train Comes Along

When the train comes along,
When the train comes along,
I'll meet you at the station
When the train comes along,
When the train comes along.

I may be blind and cannot see,
But I'll meet you at the station
When the train comes along.

I may be lame and cannot walk,
But I'll meet you at the station
When the train comes along.   (ANS)

Who Built The Ark?

Who built the Ark?
Noah, Noah.
Who built the Ark?
Brother Noah built the Ark.
Who built the Ark?
Noah, Noah.
Who built the Ark?
Brother Noah built the Ark.

Way over yonder in the harvest field,
Who built the Ark?
Why, Noah built the Ark?
Angels working with the chariot wheel,
Who built the Ark?
Oh, Noah built the Ark.

Who built the Ark?
Noah, Noah.
Who built the Ark?
Brother Noah built the Ark.
Who built the Ark?
Brother Noah built the Ark.

Look over yonder and what do I see?
Who built the Ark?
Why, Noah built the Ark?
A band of angels a-coming after me.
Who built the Ark?
Oh, Noah built the Ark.   (Fisher)

Who'll Join The Union?

Oh, hallelujah, Oh, hallelujah,
Oh, hallelujah, Lord,
Who'll join the Union?

My lovely brethren, how ye do?
Who'll join the Union?
Oh, does your love continue true?
Who'll join the Union?
Ever since I have been newly born;
Who'll join the Union?
I love to see-a God's work go on;
Who'll join the Union?

If you want to catch that heavenly breeze,
Go down in the valley upon your knees,
Go bend your knees right smooth with the ground,
And pray to the Lord to turn you around.

Say, if you belong to the Union band,
Then here's my heart, and here's my hand,
I love you all both bond and free,
I love you if you don't love me.

Now if you want to know of me,
Just who I am, and a-who I be,

I'm a child of God with my soul set free,
For Christ has bought my liberty.

Oh, hallelujah, Oh, hallelujah,
Who'll join the Union?   (Hampton)

Who Lock The Lion's Jaw

Who lock, who lock the lion,
Who lock, who lock the lion,
Who lock, who lock the lion's jaw?
God lock, God lock the lion's jaw,
Gone to heaven.

The door lock',
God lock the lion's jaw,
Gone to heaven.

The key lost,
God lock' the lion's jaw,
Gone to heaven.   (St. Helena)

Why Don't You Deliver Me?

Oh, my Lord delivered Daniel,
Daniel, Daniel,
My Lord delivered Daniel,
Why don't you deliver me too?

You delivered David from Goliath,
Jonah from the belly of the whale,
Three Hebrew children from the fiery furnace,
You taught my lips to hail.

Birds, they have nests,
Varmints, they have dens,
Everything has a resting place,
Except a poor sinner-man.

Hypocrite, you concubine,
Your home's amongst the swine;
You go to God with your liver and tongue,
But you leave your heart behind.

Lord, you see me lingering,
Backward in the race,
When I lay my body down to die,
Give my soul a hiding place.   (BDWS)

Why Don't You Let God's People Go?

Pharaoh, Pharaoh,
Why don't you let God's people go?
Pharaoh, Old Moses cried,
Why don't you let God's people go?
Moses under that burning bush--
Why don't you let God's people go?
Moses, Moses pull off your shoes,
Land you stand on is holy land,
Take your brother Aaron along with you,
For he will be a prophet under you.

Pharaoh, Pharaoh,
Why don't you let God's people go?   (BDWS)

The Winter

O, the winter, O, the winter,
O, the winter'll soon be over children,
The winter, O, the winter,
O, the winter'll soon be over children,
Yes, my Lord!

'Tis Paul and Silas bound in chains, chains,
And one did weep and the other did pray, pray;
You bend your knees on holy ground, ground,
Ask the Lord, Lord, for to turn you around;
I turn my eyes toward the sky, sky,
And ask the Lord, Lord, for wing to fly;
For you see me going along so, so,
I have my tri-trials here below.   (Allen)

LYRICS OF
JUBILATION AND TRIUMPH _____

Consistent with the biblical tradition of "jubilee" expressed in Leviticus 25 that every fifty years people were to be freed to repossess themselves, debts were to be erased, and mortgaged land returned to its original owners, the enslaved Africans savored and exploited the word "jubilee" perhaps more than any other word besides the word "freedom." Somehow they had learned of the biblical concept of jubilee and had nurtured its extraordinary prospects deep within their bosoms, making the concept the most central in their sacred and ceremonial consciousness. In consequence, the year of the Emancipation proclamation was most often spoken of as the Year of the Jubilee. This assignation was clearly appropriate because, not only did it speak of the emancipation tradition in Old Testament law, but the designation was a reference to the ritualistic celebration inherent in the tradition. The original Hebrew root word "jubal" meant "principle of sound; source of joy; source of moral affections; source of happiness; cry of joy; jubilation; a constant stream; moral prosperity; harmony; melody; music." Moreover, Jubal himself "was the father of all [who] handle the harp and pipe," and some say that he was the inventor of the harp and the mouth organ.[1] The great expectation, therefore, of the enslaved was for a moral re-ordering of this New World. It was a desire for a new stream of harmony, worthy of celebration.

Especially because the life of enslaved Africans in America was pervaded with anguish, the Africans and their descendants savored and celebrated the moments in which they either experienced or envisioned some form of triumph. Many lyrics were composed to capture the feelings of these moments of both personal and collective joy. The songs in this group, in particular, express a resistance to stoicism and pessimism in the face of a cold world. These songs are a celebration of an affirmative psychology and of spiritual resilience. They constitute a ritual of refreshment, invigoration, and exultation.

In many instances, lyrics of jubilation and triumph celebrate the nativity of the Christ child. The birth of Christ is truly good news because a savior, a redeemer, a deliverer, a transformer, an opener of the way, a master of the cross[roads] has come forth. This is a great hour of proclamation, and the good news should be spread.

The enslaved celebrate the free condition of the spirit with the expectation of the same, at some time, for their whole being. When released from the earthly journey, the once enslaved would celebrate the miraculous power of divinity. Moreover, they would celebrate their own partaking of, or fusion with, the omnipotence of the Creative Force. In their emancipated condition, they would have the power to present

_____

1. METAPHYSICAL BIBLE DICTIONARY. Unity Village, Missouri: Unity School of Christianity, 1931, p.372.

themselves with self-esteem, transcending all limitations through a symbolic power to fly that would be realized as an attribute of their souls. In their new manifestation, they would be able to display all their talents. This would be a time of jubilation because deliverance would bring about a great family reunion. Not only would one see the Son of God but also all of one's relatives and tribal members who had been lost and stolen. One would be united as well with those who might have strayed. It would be a time of jubilation because the captives would have triumphed over want and homelessness and over the disharmony in the universe.

Ain't That Good News? (1)

Ain't that good news,
Ain't that good news,
Ain't that good news, oh Lord!
Ain't that good news?

I'm going down to Jordan,
And I don't know for how long,
It's a life-time journey
But I'll soon get there.

The Bible says one thing,
I say the same,
Son of God drawing water,
Out of every vein.

God done made this religion
For to praise His holy name,
The clouds are hanging heavy,
That's sure a sign of rain.

One of these mornings,
And it won't be long,
I'll go away to heaven,
And I'm going in the storm.   (BDWS)

Ain't That Good News? (2)

I've a crown up in the Kingdom,
Ain't that good news!
I've a crown up in the Kingdom,
Ain't that good news!
I'm going to lay down this world,
Going to shoulder up my cross,
Going to take it home to Jesus,
Ain't that good news!

I've a harp up in the Kingdom,
Ain't that good news!
I've a robe up in the Kingdom,
Ain't that good news!
I've slippers in the Kingdom,
Ain't that good news!
I've a Savior in the Kingdom,
Ain't that good news!

I'm going to lay down this world,
Going to shoulder up my cross,
Going to take it home to Jesus,
Ain't that good news!   (ANSAS)

Ain't You Glad You Got Good Religion?

Ain't you glad, ain't you glad you got good religion,
Ain't you glad, ain't you glad you got good religion,

Ain't you glad, ain't you glad you got good religion?
Take my feet out of the miry clay.

O, sinner, you will feel,
O, this old earth rock and reel;
One day, one day about twelve o'clock
O, this old earth's going to reel and rock;
O, sinner, sinner in the mire,
O, on you heaven will rain fire.

Ain't you glad, ain't you glad you got good religion,
Ain't you glad, ain't you glad you got good religion,
Ain't you glad, ain't you glad you got good religion?
Take my feet out of the miry clay.   (ANS)

All My Sins Are Taken Away

All my sins are taken away, taken away,
All my sins are taken away, taken away,
All my sins are taken away,
Glory, glory to His name.

If I had died when I was young,
I would not have this risk to run,
All my sins are taken away, taken away.

If I had ten thousand tongues,
I'd praise my God with every one,
All my sins are taken away, taken away.

The tallest tree in paradise,
Christians call the tree of life,
All my sins are taken away, taken away.

If I had the wings of Noah's dove,
I'd fly away to heaven above,
All my sins are taken away, taken away.

I've been 'buked and I've been scorned,
I've been talked about sure's you're born,
All my sins are taken away, taken away.   (BDWS)

Animals A-Comin'

The animals a-comin',
Yes, Lord!
Yes, Lord!
Yes, Lord!
The animals a-comin' one by one,
Ole cow chewin' on a bun.

The animals a-comin',
Yes, Lord!
Yes, Lord!
Yes, Lord!

The animals a-comin' two by two,
The elephant and the kangaroo.

The animals a-comin',
Yes, Lord!
Yes, Lord!
Yes, Lord!
The animals a-comin' three by three,
The bear and the bug and the bumble bee.
The animals a-comin',
Yes, Lord!
Yes, Lord!
Yes, Lord!
The animals a-comin' four by four,
The ol' hippopotamus stuck in the door.

The animals a-comin',
Yes, Lord!
Yes, Lord!
Yes, Lord!
The animals a-comin' five by five,
Thus the animals did arrive.

Hallelu! Hallelujah to the Lamb!
Hallelu! Hallelujah to the Lamb!

The animals a-comin',
Yes, Lord!
Yes, Lord!
Yes, Lord!
The animals a-comin' six by six,
The hyena laughing at the monkey's tricks.

The animals a-comin',
Yes, Lord!
Yes, Lord!
Yes, Lord!
The animals a-comin' seven by seven,
"Who's that shovin',"
The old fat pig says.

The animals a-comin',
Yes, Lord!
Yes, Lord!
Yes, Lord!
The animals a-comin' eight by eight,
Noah hollered out, "Shut that gate."

The animals a-comin',
Yes, Lord!
Yes, Lord!
Yes, Lord!
The animals a-comin' nine by nine,
Noah hollered out, "Cut that line!"

The animals a-comin' ten by ten,
Ooh,
An' nobody know where they was at,

Till the ol' ark blew its whistle then,
Till the ol' ark bumped on Ararat.

Hallelu, hallelu, hallelujah to the Lamb.   (Schirmer)

Band Of Angels

There was one, there was two, there was three
                                    little angels,
There was four, there was five, there was six
                                    little angels,
There was seven, there was eight, there was nine
                                    little angels,
Ten little angels in the band.
Oh, wasn't that a band!
Sunday morning, Sunday morning, Sunday morning,
Wasn't that a band!
Sunday morning, Sunday morning, Sunday morning, soon.   (CD)

Band Of Music

I love to hear my bass-o,
O, I love to hear my bass-o,
I love to hear my bass-o
In that ol' church above.

O, what a band of music,
O, what a band of music,
O, what a band of music
Go sounding through the land.

I love to hear good singing,
I love to hear good preaching,
I have a robe in glory,
I love to meet my elder
In that ol' church above.
O, what a band of music,
O, what a band of music
Go sounding through the land.   (Calhoun)

Baptizing Hymn

Freely go marching along,
Down into the water,
Freely go marching along
Like Zion's sons and daughters.

Every time I look up to the House of God,
The angels cry out, Glory!
Glory be to God who lives on high!
To save a soul from danger.   (Khrebiel)

Blow Your Gospel Trumpet

Blow your gospel trumpet,
Blow your silver horn, Sister Mary,
When I get to heaven,
Goin' to shout all around God's throne.

Blow your gospel trumpet, O, Mother;
Blow your gospel trumpet, O, Brother;
Blow your gospel trumpet, O, Leader.
When I get to heaven,
Goin' to shout all around God's throne.

(St. Helena)

Brother, Guide Me Home

Brother, guide me home,
And I am glad,
Bright angels bidding me to come;
Brother, guide me home,

And I am glad,
Bright angels bidding me to come.

What a happy time, children,
What a happy time, children,
What a happy time, children,
Let's go to God, children,
Bright angels bidding me to come.

(Allen)

Built A House In Paradise

My brother built a house in Paradise,
My father built a house in Paradise,
Going to build a house,
In Paradise, Paradise;
Built it without a hammer or a nail,
Built it without a hammer or a nail.

(Allen)

Daniel Saw The Stone

Daniel saw the stone,
          Hewn out of the mountain,
Daniel saw the stone,
          Hewn out of the mountain,
Tearing down the kingdom of the world.

Have you seen the stone,
          Hewn out of the mountain,
Have you seen the stone,
          Hewn out of the mountain,
Tearing down the kingdom of the world.

Yes, I know that stone,
          Hewn out of the mountain,

You'd better seek that stone,
          Hewn out of the mountain,
Jesus was the stone,
          Hewn out of the mountain,
Going to preach about that stone,
          Hewn out of the mountain,
O, that holy stone,
          Hewn out of the mountain,
Tearing down the kingdom of this world.   (ANS)

Didn't Old Pharaoh Get Lost?

Isaac, a ransom
While he lay upon an altar bound;
Moses, an infant cast away,
By Pharaoh's daughter found.

Joseph by his false brethren sold,
God raised above them all;
To Hannah child the Lord foretold
How Eli's house should fall.

Didn't old Pharaoh get lost, get lost,
Didn't old Pharaoh get lost, get lost,

In the Red Sea,
True Believer?

The Lord said unto Moses--
"Go unto Pharaoh now,
For I have hardened Pharaoh's heart,
To me he will not bow."

Then Moses and Aaron,
To Pharaoh did go,
"Thus says the God of Israel,
Let my people go."

Old Pharaoh said, "Who is the Lord
That I should him obey?"
"His name it is Jehovah,
For he hears his people pray."

Hark! hear the children murmur,
They cry aloud for bread,
Down came the hidden manna,
The hungry soldiers fed.

Then Moses numbered Israel,
Through all the land abroad,
Saying, "Children, do not murmur,
But hear the word of God."

Then Moses said to Israel,
As they stood along the shore
"Your enemies you see today,
You'll never see no more."

Then down came raging Pharaoh,
That you may plainly see,
Old Pharaoh and his host
Got lost in the Red Sea.
Then men and women and children
To Moses they did flock;
They cried aloud for water,
And Moses smote the rock.

And the Lord spoke to Moses,
From Sinai's smoking top,
Saying, "Moses lead the people,
Till I shall bid you stop."
Didn't old Pharaoh get lost, get lost,
Didn't old Pharaoh get lost, get lost,
In the Red Sea,
True believer?   (BANS)

Do Don't Touch My Garment, Good Lord I'm Going Home

Do don't touch my garment,
Good Lord, Good Lord;
So don't touch my garment,
Good Lord, I'm going home.
Oh, Lord, I'm going home,
To your God and my God;
Good Lord, Good Lord,
To your God and my God.

Do don't touch my slippers,
Good Lord, Good Lord;
Oh, touch me not, little Mary,
Good Lord, Good Lord.

Do don't touch my starry crown,
Good Lord, Good Lord;
Good Lord, I'm going home
To your God and my God.   (BANS)

Down By The River

When Christ the Lord was here below,
About the work He came to do,
Sister Mary wore a golden chain,
And every link bore my Jesus' name;
Pilate called for water to wash his hands,
"I find no fault in this good man."

O fishing Peter led the way,
But nothing was caught till the break of day;
Sister Mary wept and Martha cried,
When Christ the Lord was crucified;
When we meet in the middle of the air,
We hope to meet our friends all there.

Down by the river, down by the riverside,
We will end this warfare,
Down by the river, down by the riverside.   (Hampton)

Free At Last (1)

Free at last, free at last,
I thank God I'm free at last;
Free at last, free at last,
I thank God I'm free at last.

Way down yonder in the graveyard walk,
Me and my Jesus going to meet and talk;
On my knees when the light passed by,
Thought my soul would rise and fly;
Some of these mornings bright and fair,
Going to meet King Jesus in the air.   (ANSAS) (Variant)

Free At Last (2)

Free at last, free at last,
Thank God almighty I'm free at last;
Free at last, free at last,
Thank God almighty I'm free at last.

Oh, I remember the day,
I remember it well,
My dungeon shook
And my chain fell off.

I know my Lord is a man of war,
He fought my battle at hell's dark door;
Satan thought he had me fast,
I broke his chain and got free at last;
Satan's mad and I am glad,
I hope to God to keep him mad.

You can hinder me here, but you can't
          hinder me there,
The Lord in heaven's going to answer my
          prayer;
I went in the valley, but I didn't go to stay,
My soul got happy and I stayed all day;
Oh, this ain't all, I got more besides,
I'm born of God and I've been baptized.   (BDWS)

The General Roll

I'll be there, I'll be there,
Oh, when the roll is called,
          I'll be there.

O hallelujah to the Lamb,
The Lord is on the giving hand;

Old Satan told me not to pray,
He wants my soul at Judgement Day.
I'll be there, I'll be there,
Oh, when the roll is called,
    I'll be there.

      (FJS)

Getting Ready To Die

Getting ready to die,
    Getting ready to die,
Getting ready to die,
    O Zion, Zion.

When I set out I was but young,
But now my race is almost won;
Religion's like a blooming rose,
And none but those that feel it knows;
The Lord is waiting to receive,
If sinners only would believe;
All those who walk in gospel shoes,
This faith in Christ they'll never lose.
Getting ready to die,
    Getting ready to die,
Getting ready to die,
    O Zion, Zion.

      (FJS)

Going Home In The Chariot

Going home in the chariot in the morning,
Going home in the chariot in the morning,
Going home in the chariot in the morning,
Going home in the chariot in the morning.

O, never you mind what Satan say,
He never did teach one sinner to pray;
O, sinner-man, you better pray,
For judgement is coming every day;
O, mourner, mourner, you must believe
And the grace of God you will receive.

      (ANS)

Going To Shout All Over God's Heaven

I've got a robe, you've got a robe,
All of God's children got a robe;
When I get to heaven,
Going to play on my harp,
Going to put on my robe,
Going to shout all over God's heaven.
Heaven, heaven,
Everybody talking about heaven ain't going there.

I've got a crown, you've got a crown,
All of God's children got a crown;
When I get to heaven,
Going to put on my crown,

Going to shout all over God's heaven.
Heaven, heaven,
Everybody talking about heaven ain't going there.

I've got shoes, you've got shoes,
All of God's children got shoes;
When I get to heaven,
Going to put on my shoes,
Going to walk all over God's heaven.
Heaven, heaven,
Everybody talking about heaven ain't going there.

I've got a harp, you've got a harp,
All of God's children got a harp;
When I get to heaven,
Going to play all over God's heaven.
Heaven, heaven,
Everybody talking about heaven ain't going there.

I've got a song, you've got a song,
All of God's children got a song;
When I get to heaven,
Going to sing my new song,
Going to sing all over God's heaven.
Heaven, heaven,
Everybody talking about heaven ain't going there;
Going to shout all over God's heaven.   (Hampton)

Going To Sing All Along The Way

Oh, I'm going to sing,
Going to sing,
Going to sing all along the way,
Oh, I'm going to sing,
Going to sing,
Going to sing all along the way.

We'll raise the Christians' banner,
The motto's new and old,
Repentance and salvation,
Are engravened there in gold.
We'll shout over all our sorrows,
And sing forever more,
With Christ and all his army,
On that celestial shore.   (BANS)

Going To Study War No More

Going to lay down my burden,
Down by the river side,
Down by the river side,
Down by the river side,
Going to lay down my burden,
Down by the river side,
To study war no more!

I'm going to study war no more,
Going to study war no more,
Ain't going to study war no more!

I'm going to put on my long white robe,
Going to put on my starry crown,
Going to study war no more!

Going to lay down my sword and shield,
Down by the river side,
Down by the river side,
Down by the river side,
Going to lay down my sword and shield,
Down by the river side,
To study war no more!

(Fisher)

Go, Mary, And Toll The Bell (1)

Go, Mary and toll the bell,
Come, John, and call the roll,
I thank God.
Who's all them come dressed in white?
They must be the children of the Israelite.
Who's all them come dressed in red?
They must be the children that Moses led.
Who's all them come dressed in blue?
They must be the children just come through.
Who's all them come dressed in black?
They must be the mourners just turned back.
Go, Mary, and toll the bell,
Come, John, and call the roll,
I thank God.

(Hampton)

Go, Mary, And Toll The Bell (2)

Go, Mary, an' toll the bell,
Come, John, an' call the roll,
M-m-m-m-m, I thank God.

Who that yonder under the sun,
Talking 'bout the thing my Jesus done?
Who that yonder under the moon,
Talking 'bout the thing going to happen soon?
Who that yonder under the stars,
Talking 'bout we going to play on the harp?
Who that yonder dressed in green,
Look like the member that been redeem?
Who that yonder dressed in white,
Look like the member of the Israelite?
Who that yonder dressed in red,
Look like the children that Moses led?
Who that yonder dressed in black,
Look like the member that just turned back?
Satan just like a snake in the grass,
But if you don't mind, he get you at las'.

Go, Mary, an' toll the bell,
Come, John, an' call the roll,
M-m-m-m-m, I thank God.

(Calhoun) (Variant)

Good Morning, Everybody

Good morning, everybody,
Good morning, everybody, Lord.
My soul got happy this morning,
My soul got happy this morning, Lord.
I'm rolling in Zion Jubilee.

You may call me "hypocrite member,"
You may call me "hypocrite member," Lord.
But my soul got happy this morning,
But my soul got happy this morning, Lord.
I'm rolling in Zion Jubilee.

I'm going to see my mother,
I'm going to see my mother, Lord.
Going to sit down by my Jesus,
Going to sit down by my Jesus, Lord.
I'm rolling in Zion Jubilee.

(ANS)

Good News

Good news, good news,
Angel bring glad tidings down;
Good news, good news,
I hear from heaven today.

My brother have a robe and I so glad,
Good news;
Good news, my brother have a robe and I so glad,
Good news from heaven today.

O, heaven so high and I so low,
Good news! Good news!
I wonder in my soul if I ever get there,
Good news from heaven today.

(St. Helena)

Good News, Member

Good news, member,
Good news, member,
Don't you mind what Satan says,
Good news, member, good news,
And I heard from heaven today.

My brother has a seat
And I'm so glad,
Good news, member, good news;
Mr. Hawley has a home in Paradise,
Good news, member, good news,
Archangel's bringing baptizing down;

Good news, member, good news,
And I heard from heaven today.

(Allen)

Go Round, Go Round

Go round, go round,
Look at the mornin' star;
Go round, go round,
We got a soul to save.

Hadn't been for Satan
We wouldn't have to pray;
Now Satan broke God holy law,
And we got a soul to save.

When I was a-layin' at hell's dark door,
No one to pity po' me,
Master Jesus came ridin' by
And bought my liberty.

(St. Helena)

Go Tell It On The Mountain

Go tell it on the mountain,
Over the hills and everywhere;
Go tell it on the mountain
That Jesus Christ is born.

While shepherds kept their watching o'er silent
    flocks by night,
Behold throughout the heavens, there shone
    a holy light.
The shepherds feared and trembled when lo!
    above the earth,
Rang out the angel chorus that hailed
    our Savior's birth.
Down in a lonely manger the humble Christ
    was born,
And God sent out salvation that blessed
    Christmas morn.

(ANSAS) (Variant)

Got Religion All Around The World

Christians, hold up your heads!
Christians, hold up your heads!
Christians, hold up your heads!

Neighbor, you bear your load!
Neighbor, you bear your load!
Neighbor, you bear your load!

Sister, you stand the storm!
Sister, you stand the storm!
Sister, you stand the storm!

Got religion all 'round the world,
O, then I'll shout a "Glory!"
O, then I'll shout a "Glory!"
Lord, then I'll shout a "Glory!"
Got religion all 'round the world.   (ANS)

Hail! Hail! Hail!

Children, hail! hail! hail!
I'm going to join the saints above;
Hail! hail! hail! I'm on my journey home.

Oh, look up yonder, what I see,
Bright angels coming after me,
If you get there before I do,
Look out for me--I'm coming too;
I'm on my journey home.

Oh, hallelujah to the Lamb!
I'm on my journey home;
King Jesus died for every man,
I'm on my journey home.
Children hail! hail! hail!
I'm going to join the saints above;
Hail! hail! hail! I'm on my journey home.   (Hampton)

Hallelu, Hallelu

Oh, one day as another,
Hallelu, hallelu!
When the ship is out a-sailing,
Hallelu, hallelu!
Member, walk and never tire,
Hallelu, hallelu!
Member, walk Jordan road,
Hallelu, hallelu!
Member, walk tribulation!
You go home to Wappoo;
Hallelu, hallelu!
Member, seek new repentance,
Hallelu, hallelu!
I go to see my fortune,
Hallelu, hallelu!
I go to see my dying Savior,
Hallelu, hallelu!
You want to die like Jesus.
Hallelu, hallelu!   (Allen)

Hallelujah

Hallelujah! Hallelujah!
I do belong to the band, hallelujah!

I have a sister in that day,
She'll take wings and fly away;

I never shall forget that day
When Jesus washed my sins away;
Looked at my hands and my hands looked new,
Looked at my feet and they looked so, too;

I never felt such love before saying,
"Go in peace and sin no more.

(ANSAS)

Happy Morning

Weep no more, Mother,
Weep no more, Mary,
Jesus rise from the dead,
Happy morning,
Glorious morning,
My saviour rise from the dead.
Doubt no more, Thomas,
Doubt no more, Thomas,
Jesus rise from the dead,
Happy morning,
My savior rise from the dead.

(FJS)

Hear The Angels Singing

Oh, sing all the way,
        Sing all the way,
Sing all the way, my Lord,
Hear the angels singing.
We're marching up to heaven,
It's a happy time,
And Jesus is on the middle line;
The Christians take up too much time;
They're idling on that battle line.

Now all things well
And I don't dread hell,
I'm going up to heaven
Where my Jesus dwells;
For the angels are calling me away
And I must go, I cannot stay.

Now take your Bible,
And read it through,
And every word you'll find is true;
For in that Bible you will see,
That Jesus died for you and me.

Say if my memory serves me right,
We're sure to have a little shout tonight;
For I love to shout, I love to sing,
I love to praise my heavenly King.

(Hampton)

Heaven Is A-Shining

Run, moaner, run,
Heaven is a shining,
Run, moaner, run
I'm going home.

Oh, my Lord, good Lord,
Didn't you say, good Lord,
If I pray, good Lord,
And pray right, good Lord,
When I die, good Lord,
Heaven's my home, good Lord?
Oh, my Lord, good Lord,
Didn't you promise me, good Lord,
A long white robe, good Lord,
And a starry crown, good Lord,
To fit me well, good Lord,
When I die, good Lord?
Oh, my Lord, good Lord,
Didn't you promise me, good Lord,
A seat on high, good Lord,
And golden shoes, good Lord,
If I pray, good Lord,
When I die, good Lord?

(BDWS)

He Is King Of Kings (1)

He is king of kings,
He is Lord of Lords,
Jesus Christ the first and last,
No man works like him.

He built his throne up in the air,
And called his saints from everywhere;
He pitched his tents on Canaan's ground
And broke the Roman kingdom down.

(ANSAS)

He Is King Of Kings (2)

He is King of kings,
He is Lord of lords.
Jesus Christ, the first and the last,
No man works like Him.

He built a platform in the air,
He meets the saints from everywhere;
He pitched a tent on Canaan's ground,
And broke the Roman kingdom down;
I know that my Redeemer lives,
And by his death sweet blessings gives.

He is King of kings,
He is Lord of lords.
Jesus Christ, the first and the last,
No man works like Him.

(Hampton)

He Rose From The Dead

He rose, He rose, He rose,
He rose from the dead;
He rose , He rose, He rose,
He rose from the dead;
He rose, He rose, He rose,
He rose from the dead,
And the Lord shall bear His children home.

The Jews crucified Him,
And nailed Him to the tree;
Joseph begged His body,
And laid it in the tomb;
Down came an angel,
And rolled the stone away;
Mary, she came weeping,
Her Lord for to see,
But Christ had gone to Galilee.
He rose, He rose, He rose,
He rose from the dead;
He rose, He rose, He rose,
He rose from the dead,
And the Lord shall bear His children home.   (FJS)

The Hypocrite And The Concubine

Hypocrite and the concubine,
Living among the swine,
They run to God with lips and tongue,
And leave all the heart behind.

Aunty, did you hear when Jesus rose?
Did you hear when Jesus rose?
Aunty, did you hear when Jesus rose?
He rose and he ascended on high.   (Allen)

I Ain't Going To Die No More

Oh! ain't I glad, Oh! ain't I glad,
Oh, ain't I glad
        I ain't going to die no more.

Going to meet those happy Christians
        sooner in the morning,
Sooner in the morning,
Meet those happy Christians
Sooner in the morning,
I ain't going to die no more.

Going shouting home to glory
        sooner in the morning,
Going to wear the starry crown
        sooner in the morning,
We'll sing our troubles over
        sooner in the morning.

Oh! ain't I glad, Oh! ain't I glad,
Oh, ain't I glad,
       I ain't going to die no more.   (FJS)

I Am Bound For The Promised Land

I am boun' for the Promised Lan',
I am boun' for the Promised Lan',
O, won't you rise and go with me,
I am bound for the Promised Lan'.

When I get to heaven I'll set an' tell,
I am boun' for the Promised Lan',
Just how I shun the gates of hell,
I am boun' for the Promised Lan'.
O, Christians, Christians be enraged,
I am boun' for the Promised Lan',
Old Satan' in an awful rage,
I am boun' for the Promised Lan'.   (St. Helena)

I Am The Truth And The Light

Lazareth is dead, oh, bless God;
Lazareth is dead, oh, bless God;
Lazareth is dead, oh, bless God;
I am the truth and the light.

Run, Mary, run, oh, bless God;
Run and tell Jesus, oh, bless God;
My brother is dead, oh, bless God;
Weep not, Mary, oh, bless God.

How long he's been dead? oh, bless God;
Four days in the grave, oh, bless God;
He's stinking in the grave, oh, bless God;
You'll see him again, oh, bless God;
On the day of the resurrection, oh, bless God.

Lazareth is dead, oh, bless God;
Lazareth is dead, oh, bless God;
Lazareth is dead, oh, bless God;
I am the truth and the light.   (BDWS)

I Got A Letter This Mornin'

I got a letter this mornin',
Aye Lord;
I got a letter this mornin',
Aye Lord.   (St. Helena)

I Got My Religion On The Way

I thank God for I got religion,
I thank God for I got religion,
I thank God for I got religion,
I got my religion on the way.

The baby took the light and gone to heaven,
The baby took the light and gone to heaven,
I got my religion on the way.

I done found the light and going to heaven,
Moaner took the light and gone to heaven,
My mother got the light and gone to heaven,
My father got the light and gone to heaven,

I thank God for I got religion,
I thank God for I got religion,
I thank God for I got religion,
I got my religion on the way.

(BDWS)

I Heard From Heaven Today

Hurry on, my weary soul,
And I heard from heaven today,
Hurry on, my weary soul,
And I heard from heaven today.

My sin is forgiven,
        And my soul set free,
A baby born in Bethlehem,
The trumpet sound
        In the other bright land;
My name is called
        And I must go,
The bell is a-ringing
        In the other bright world.

Hurry on, my weary soul,
And I heard from heaven today,
Hurry on, my weary soul,
And I heard from heaven today.

(ALLEN)

I Know My Jesus Loves Me

I know my Jesus loves me,
O-----, my Lord;
I know my Jesus loves me, good Lord,
Rolling in Zion, Jubalee!

I wonder what the matter with Zion,
O-----, my Lord;
I wonder what the matter with Zion, good Lord,
Rolling in Zion, Jubalee!

My preacher don' preach-a like a used to,

O-----, my Lord;
My preacher don' preach-a like a used to, good Lord,
Rolling in Zion, Jubalee!

My sister don' shout like she used to,
O-----, my Lord;
My mourner don' mourn like he used to,
O-----, my Lord;
My leader don' lead like he used to,
O-----, my Lord;
My deacon don't pray like he used to,
O-----, my Lord;
I wonder what the matter with the members,
O-----, my Lord.

Rock me, chariot, rock me,
O-----, my Lord;
Rock me down about the Jordan, good Lord,
Rolling in Zion, Jubalee!   (Calhoun)

I'll Make Me A Man

The God walked around,
And God looked around on all that He had made.
He looked at His sun,
He looked at His moon,
And his lit'l stars.
He looked on His world with all its living things,
And God said, "I'm lonely still."
God sat down on the side of a hill,
God sat down where He could think,
God sat down by a deep, wide river,
God sat down with His head in His hands,
God thought and thought,
Till He thought, "I'll make me a man."

Up from the bed of the river,
God scooped-a the clay.
And by the bank of the river,
God kneeled Him down.
And there this great God almighty!
Who lit the sun and fixed it in the sky,
Who flung the stars to the most far corners of the night,
Who rounded the earth in the hollow of His hand,
This great God,
This great God like a mammy bending over her babe,
Kneeled down in the dust
Toiling over this-a lump of clay till He shaped it,
He shaped it, till He shaped it in His own image.
Then into it He blew the breath of life,
And man became a living soul.
Amen, Amen, Amen, A--men!   (Hayes)

I'll Be There In The Morning

I'll be there in the morning,
I'll be there in the morning,
I'll be there in the morning,
When the general roll is called.
Yes, I'll be there.

Going to pray with Hezekiah,
Yes, I'll be there;
Going to sing with Jeremiah,
Yes, I'll be there.

When the general roll is called,
Going to sing around the throne,
Going to pray around the throne,
Going to wear a white robe.
Yes, I'll be there.

When the general roll is called,
Going to see my Master Jesus,
Going to wear a starry crown
Going to live forever more.
I'll be there in the morning,
Yes, I'll be there.

(Hampton)

I'm A-Travelin' To The Land

I'm a travelin' to the land--
I'm a travelin' to the land--
I'm a travelin' to the land--
Where I'm bound, where I'm bound.

There's no sickness in the land where I'm bound;
There's no liars in the land where I'm bound;
Milk and honey's in the land where I'm bound;
I've a sister in the land where I'm bound;
I've a mother in the land where I'm bound;
I've a father in the land where I'm bound;
I've a Savior in the land where I'm bound;
Where I'm bound, where I'm bound.

(St. Helena)

I'm Going Down To The River Of Jordan

I'm goin' down to the river of Jordan,
O, yes--
I'm goin' down to the river of Jordan
Some of these days, halleluia!
I'm goin' down to the river of Jordan,
O, yes--
I'm goin' down to the river of Jordan
Some of these days.

I'm goin' to set at the welcome table;
I'm goin' to feast off milk and honey;
I'm goin' to march with the tallest angel,

O, yes--
I'm goin' to march with the tallest angel
Some of these days.   (St. Helena)

I'm Going Over There

I am goin' over there,
In my Father's house;
I am goin' over there,
In my Father's house.
I am goin' over there,
In my Father's house.
There is joy, joy, joy.

Ain't no liars over there,
In my Father's house;
Ain't no liars over there,
In my Father's house;
Ain't no liars there,
In my Father's house.
There is joy, joy, joy.   (St. Helena)

I'm Going To See My Lovin' Father When I Get Home

I'm goin' to see my lovin' Father when I get home,
I'm goin' to see my lovin' Father when I get home,
I'm goin' to see my lovin' Father when i get home,
I'm goin' to see my lovin' Father when I get home.

I'm goin' to tell Him 'bout my trouble when I get home,
I'm goin' to tell Him 'bout my trouble when I get home,
I'm goin' to tell Him 'bout my trouble when I get home,
I'm goin' to tell Him 'bout my trouble when I get home.

No more rain to wet me when I get home,
No more rain to wet me when I get home,
No more rain to wet me when I get home,
No more rain to wet me when I get home.

God heaven, God heaven, God heaven, when I get home,
God heaven, God heaven, God heaven, when I get home,
God heaven, God heaven, God heaven, when I get home,
God heaven, God heaven, God heaven, when I get home.   (St. Helena)

I'm Going To Sing

I'm going to sing when the spirit says sing,
I'm going to sing when the spirit says sing,
And obey the spirit of the Lord.

I'm going to pray when the spirit says pray,
I'm going to pray when the spirit says pray,
And obey the spirit of the Lord.

I'm going to shout when the spirit says shout,
I'm going to shout when the spirit says shout,
And obey the spirit of the Lord.   (ANSAS)

I'm Runnin' On

I'm runnin' on, I'm runnin' on,
I done left this world behind;
I done crossed the separatin' line,
I done left this world behind.
So free, so free--
I done left this world behind;
I done crossed the separatin' line,
An' I've left this world behind.

Ain't you glad? Ain't you glad?
I done left this world behind;
I done crossed the separatin' line,
An' I've left this world behind.

Pressin' on, pressin' on--
I done left this world behind;
I done crossed the separatin' line,
An' I've left this world behind.

Won't turn back, won't turn back--
I done left this world behind;
I done crossed the separatin' line,
An' I've left this world behind.

Good-bye! Good-bye!
I done left this world behind;
I done crossed the separatin' line,
An' I've left this world behind.   (Grissom)

I'm So Glad

I'm so glad, I'm so glad,
I'm so glad there's nobody dying there;
I'll tell you how I found the Lord,
With a hung down head
And aching heart;
I'm so glad there's nobody dying there.

I hope I'll meet my brother there,
That used to join with me in prayer;
I hope I'll meet my preacher there,
That used to join with me in prayer.

I'm so glad, I'm so glad,
I'm so glad there's nobody dying there;
I'm so glad there's nobody dying there.   (FJS)

In The Morning

In the morning,
In the morning by the bright light,
When Gabriel blows his trumpet,
In the morning.

Shout, shout, children shout,
Children, children, follow me,
Shut the door
And keep your mouth.
Halle, halle, halle, hallelujah.

Oh, what sort of shoes do the angels wear?
Golden slippers,
While they're floating through the air.
Halle, halle, halle, hallelujah.
And what sort of clothes do the angels wear?
Long white robes
And golden hair.
Halle, halle, halle, hallelujah.   (BDWS)

In The New Jerusalem

Well, in that new Jerusalem,
        In that new Jerusalem,
That new Jerusalem, my Lord,
In that new Jerusalem,
In that new Jerusalem,
That new Jerusalem, my Lord.

Oh, when-a that moon drips red with blood,
Oh, when-a that moon drips red with blood,
Oh, when-a that moon drips red with blood,
Oh, when-a that moon drips red with blood,
My Lord.

Oh, when the sun drifts away,
Oh, when the sun drifts away in the day,
My Lord.

Well, we're gonna walk, Lord,
In that new Jerusalem,
We're gonna walk them streets,
We're gonna walk them golden streets,
In that new Jerusalem.   (L-G)

I Thank God I'm Free At Last

Free at last, free at last,
I thank God I'm free at last;
Free at last, free at last,
I thank God I'm free at last.

Way down yonder in the graveyard walk,
Me and my Jesus going to have a talk;

On my knees when the light passes by,
Thought my soul would rise and fly;
Some of these mornings bright and fair,
Going to meet my Jesus in the middle of the air.

Free at last, free at last,
I thank God I'm free at last;
Free at last, free at last,
I thank God I'm free at last.   (BANS)

I've A Message From My Lord

I've a message from my Lord,
Hallelujah,
He has said to me today,
I'm a sinner,
And I'm going up to heaven
To join my Lord,
For my race is almost run.

I'm a lover of my Lord,
Hallelujah,
I prays to Him all day
Because I love Him,
And he'll take me in his bosom
To heaven on high.
And my soul will have a resting place.

I'm a warrior for my Lord,
Hallelujah,
I'll fight for him all day
Against them sinners,
I'll surely whip old Satan,
Go to heaven on high,
And rest with my Savior all my days.   (BDWS)

I've Been Toiling At The Mill

I've been toiling at the mill so long,
I've been toiling at the mill so long,
I've been toiling at the mill so long, my Lord,
And about to get to heaven at last.

Oh, Mother, ain't you glad?
Mother, ain't you glad?
Oh, Mother, ain't you glad, my Lord?
And about to get to heaven at last.

Oh, Father, ain't you glad?
Father, ain't you glad?

Oh, Father, ain't you glad, my Lord?
And about to get to heaven at last.   (Hampton)

I Want To Be Ready

I want to be ready, I want to be ready,
I want to be ready,
To walk in Jerusalem just like John.

John said that Jerusalem was four-square,
Walk in Jerusalem just like John;
I hope, good Lord, I'll meet you there,
Walk in Jerusalem just like John.

When Peter was preaching at Pentecost,
Walking in Jerusalem just like John;
O, he was filled with the Holy Ghost,
Walk in Jerusalem just like John.

I want to be ready, I want to be ready,
I want to be ready,
To walk in Jerusalem just like John.   (Hampton)

Jehovah, Hallelujah

Jehovah, hallelujah,
The Lord is providing,
Jehovah, hallelujah,
The Lord is providing.
The foxes have a hole,
And the birdies have a nest,
The Son of Man,
        He don't know where to lay his head.

Jehovah, hallelujah,
The Lord is providing,
Jehovah, hallelujah,
The Lord is providing.   (Allen)

Jesus Ain't Coming Here To Die No More

Virgin Mary had one Son,
The cruel Jews had him hung;
Hallelujah to the Lamb,
Jesus died for every man.

He died for you, He died for me,
He died to set poor sinner free;
He died for the rich, He died for the poor,
He ain't coming here to die no more.

He died for the blind, He died for the lame,
He bore the pain and all the blame.
But he ain't coming here to die no more,
Ain't coming here to die no more.   (Hampton)

Jesus Is Risen From The Dead

In this band we have sweet music,
In this band we have sweet music,
In this band we have sweet music,
Jesus is risen from the dead.

Go, tell Mary and Martha, Go and tell Mary and Martha,
Go and tell Mary and Martha, "Yes, Jesus is risen from the dead."
Go, tell John and Peter, Go and tell John and Peter,
Go and tell John and Peter, "Yes, Jesus is risen from the dead."
Go, tell doubting Thomas, Go and tell doubting Thomas,
Go and tell doubting Thomas, "Yes, Jesus is risen from the dead."

Go, tell Paul and Silas, Go and tell Paul and Silas,
Go and tell Paul and Silas, "Yes, Jesus is risen from the dead."
Go, tell all the apostles, Go and tell all the apostles,
Go and tell all the apostles, "Yes, Jesus is risen from the dead."
Go, tell everybody, Go and tell everybody,
Go and tell everybody, "Yes, Jesus is risen from the dead."   (ANS)

Joshua Fit The Battle Of Jericho

Joshua fit the battle of Jericho,
                              Jericho, Jericho,
Joshua fit the battle of Jericho,
And the walls came tumbling down.

You may talk about your king of Gideon,
You may talk about your man of Saul,
There's none like good old Joshua
At the battle of Jericho.
Up to the walls of Jericho
He marched with spear in hand;
"Go blow them ramhorns," Joshua cried,
"Cause the battle is in my hands."

Then the lamb ram sheep horns began to blow,
Trumpets began to sound,
Joshua commanded the children to shout,
And the walls came tumbling down.

That morning Joshua fit the battle of Jericho,
                              Jericho, Jericho,
Joshua fit the battle of Jericho,
And the walls came tumbling down.   (BANS)

King Emanuel

O, my King Emanuel,
My Emanuel above,
Sing glory to my King Emanuel.

If you walk the golden street,
And you join the golden band,
Sing glory to my King Emanuel.

If you touch one string,
Then the whole heaven rings;
O, the great cherubim,
O the cherubim above;
O, believer, ain't you glad
That your soul is converted?

O, my King Emanuel,
My Emanuel above,
Sing glory to my King Emanuel.   (Allen)

Lean On The Lord's Side

Wait, poor Daniel,
He leaned on the Lord's side,
Daniel rocked the lion's jaw,
Lean on the Lord's side.

The golden chain to ease him down,
The silver spade to dig his grave;
He leaned on the Lord's side,
He leaned on the Lord's side.   (Allen)

Let Us Praise Him

Let us praise Him,
Let us praise Him,
Glory hallelujah!
Let us praise Him,
O praise, O praise,
Glory hallelujah!

I once was lost,
But now I'm found,
Glory hallelujah!
I once was lost
But now I'm found,
Glory hallelujah!

I never shall forget that day,
Glory hallelujah.
When Jesus washed my sins away,
Glory hallelujah,

Let us praise Him,
Let us praise Him,
Glory hallelujah!   (Hampton)

Little Children, Then Won't You Be Glad?

Little children, then won't you be glad,
Little children, then won't you be glad,
That you have been to heaven,
And you're going to go again,

To try on the long white robe, children,
To try on the long white robe?

King Jesus, he was so strong, my Lord,
That he jarred down the walls of hell;
Don't you hear what the chariot says?
The fore wheels run by the grace of God,
And the hind wheels run by faith.
Don't you remember what you promised the Lord?
You promised the Lord you would feed his sheep,
And gather His lambs so well.
Little children, then won't you be glad,
Little children, then won't you be glad,
That you have been to heaven,
And you're going to go again,
To try on the long white robe, children,
To try on the long white robe?   (Allen)

Little David, Play On Your Harp (1)

Little David, play on your harp,
Hallelu, hallelu,
Little David, play on your harp, hallelu.

God told Moses, O Lord!
Go down in Egypt, O Lord!
Tell old Pharaoh, O Lord!
Loose my people, O Lord!

Down in the valley, O Lord!
Didn't go to stay, O Lord!
My soul got happy, O Lord!
I stayed all day, O Lord!

Come down, angels, O Lord!
With ink and pen, O Lord!
And write salvation, O Lord!
To dying men, O Lord!

Little David, play on your harp, hallelu, hallelu,
Little David, play on your harp, hallelu.   (Hampton)

Little David Play On Your Harp (2)

Little David, play on your harp, hallelujah,
Little David, play on your harp, hallelujah,
Little David, play on your harp, hallelu.

One day, one day I was walking along,
Yes, I heard a reason from on high,
Say, "Go in peace,
"And sin no more,
"Your sins are forgiven,
"And your soul set free."
"I pluck your feet

"Out of the miry clay
"And set them on the rock of eternal age;
"Where the wind may blow,
"And the storm may rise
"But the gates of hell
"Shall never prevail."

Little David, play on your harp, hallelujah,
Little David, play on your harp, hallelujah,
Little David, play on your harp, hallelu.   (BDWS)

Lord, Is This Heaven?

Lord, is this heaven,
Oh, Lord, is this heaven,
Lord, is this heaven,
Have I got here at last?

Sit down child, sit down,
Sit down child, sit down,
Sit down child, sit down,
Good Lord, I can't sit down.

What's the matter, child?
What's the matter, child?
What's the matter, child?

Oh, you know what you promised me,
Good Lord, my long white robe,
You know what you promised me.

Run, angel, and get a robe,
Run, angel, and get a robe,
Run, angel, and get a robe,
And let her try it on.
Sit down, child, sit down;
Good Lord, I can't sit down;
What's the matter, child?
Oh, you know what you promised me,
Good Lord, my starry crown;
Run angel and get a crown,
And let her try it on.

Sit down, child, sit down;
Good Lord, I can't sit down;
What the matter, child?
Oh, you know what you promised me,
Good Lord, my golden shoes;
Run, angel, and get the shoes,
And let her try them on.

Sit down, child, sit down;
Good Lord, I can't sit down;
What's the matter, child?
Oh, you know what you promised me,
Good Lord, my angel wings;

Run, angel, and get the wings,
And let her try them on.   (BDWS)

Love And Serve The Lord

If you love God, serve Him,
Hallelujah, Praise ye the Lord!
Come go to glory with me;
If you love God, serve Him,
Hallelujah! Love and serve the Lord.
Come, go to glory with me.

Good morning, brother traveller,
Pray tell me where you're bound.
I'm bound for Canaan's happy land,
And the enchanted ground.

Oh, when I was a sinner,
I liked my way so well;
But when I come to find out,
I was on the road to hell.
I fled to Jesus--Hallelujah!
Oh, Jesus received me, Hallelujah.

The Father, He looked on the Son, and smiled,
The Son, He looked on me;
The Father, redeemed my soul from hell;
And the Son, He set me free.
I shouted Hallelujah! Hallelujah!
I praised my Jesus, Hallelujah!

Oh when we shall all get there,
Upon that-a heavenly shore,
We'll walk about them-a golden streets,
And never part no more.
No rebuking in the churches--Hallelujah!
Every day'll be Sunday--Hallelujah.   (Hampton)

Mary And Martha

Mary and Martha just gone 'long,
Mary and Martha just gone 'long,
Mary and Martha just gone 'long,'
To ring those charming bells;
Crying free grace and dying love,
Free grace and dying love,
Free grace and dying love,
To ring those charming bells.
Oh! way over Jordan, Lord,
        Way over Jordan, Lord,
        Way over Jordan, Lord,
To ring those charming bells.

The preacher and the elder's just gone 'long,
My father and my mother's just gone 'long,

The Methodist and Baptist just gone 'long,
To ring those charming bells.

Mary and Martha just gone 'long,
Mary and Martha just gone 'long,
Mary and Martha just gone 'long,
To ring those charming bells;
Crying free grace and dying love,
Free grace and dying love,
Free grace and dying love,
To ring those charming bells.
Oh! way over Jordan, Lord,
     Way over Jordan, Lord,
     Way over Jordan, Lord,
To ring those charming bells.   (FJS)

Meet You In The Morning

Shine, shine, I'll meet you in the morning,
Shine, shine, I'll meet you in the morning,
Oh! my soul's going to shine, shine.
Oh! my soul's going to shine, shine.

I'm going to sit at the welcome table,
I'm going to sit at the welcome table,
I'm going to tell God about my trial,
I'm going to tell God about my trial,
I'm going to walk all about the city,
I'm going to walk all about the city.

Shine, shine, I'll meet you in the morning,
Shine, shine, I'll meet you in the morning,
Oh! my soul's going to shine, shine.
Oh! my soul's going to shine, shine.   (FJS)

'Most Done Toiling Here

'Most done toiling here, O, bretheren
Lord, I'm 'most done toiling here.

I long to shout, I love to sing,
I love to praise my heavenly King.
I ain't been to heaven, but I been told,
The streets up there are paved with gold.
'Most done toiling here, O, bretheren,
Lord, I'm 'most done toiling here.   (BANS)

My Brother's Died And Gone To Heaven

My brother's died and gone to heaven,
My brother's died and gone to heaven,
My brother's died and gone to heaven,
He's a-shouting hallelujah for me!
My brother's died and gone to heaven,
He's a-shouting hallelujah for me!

For me!
For me!
He's a-shouting hallelujah for me!

Never knowed no harm in that white soul,
But Jesus Lamb can make him whole,
Never knowed no harm in that white soul,
He's a-shouting hallelujah for me!
For me!
For me!
He's a-shouting hallelujah for me!   (Fisher)

My Name's Written On High

Hail! Hail! I belong to the bloodwashed army,
Hail! Hail! My name's written on high,
O, well then!
My name's written on high.

O, hallelujah to the lamb!
King Jesus died for every man.
If you get there before I do,
Look out for me I'm coming too.

O, get back, Satan, let me by,
Going to serve my Jesus till I die.
Go back, all the powers of hell,
Let God's children take the field.
Shout, my sister, you are free,
Christ has bought you liberty.   (ANS)

No Devil In Our Land

I'm so glad, I'm so glad,
There ain't no devil in our land,
I'm so glad, I'm so glad,
There ain't no devil in our land,
Ain't no devil in the heavenly land,
Ain't no devil in our land.

I'm so glad, I'm so glad,
There ain't no sinner in our land,
There ain't no backbiting in our land,
I'm so glad, I'm so glad,
There ain't no liar in our land,
I'm so glad, I'm so glad
Ain't no devil in our land.   (BDWS)

No More Rain To Wet You

No more rain fall to wet you,
Hallelujah, hallelujah,
No more rain fall to wet you,
Hallelujah.

No more sun shine to burn you,
Hallelujah, hallelujah;
No more parting in the kingdom,
Hallelujah, hallelujah;
No more backbiting in the kingdom,
Hallelujah, hallelujah;
Every day shall be Sunday,
Hallelujah, hallelujah.

No more rain fall to wet you,
Hallelujah, hallelujah,
No more rain fall to wet you,
Hallelujah.   (Allen)

Oh! Holy Lord

Oh! holy Lord! Oh! holy Lord!
Oh! holy Lord!
Done with the sin and sorrow.

Oh! rise up children, get your crown,
And by your Savior's side sit down,
What a glorious morning that will be,
Our friends and Jesus we will see,
Done with sin and sorrow.

Oh! shout, you Christians,
You're gaining ground,
We'll shout old Satan's kingdom down;
I soon shall reach that golden shore,
And sing the songs we sang before.
Oh! holy Lord! Oh! holy Lord!
Oh! holy Lord!
Done with sin and sorrow.   (FJS)

Oh, The Heaven Is Shining

Oh, the heaven is shining, shining,
O Lord, the heaven is shining full of love;
Oh, fare you well friends,
I'm going to tell you all,
The heaven is shining full of love;
Going to leave you all mine eyes to close;
The heaven is shining full of love.

Oh, when I build my tent again,
Build it so old Satan can't get in,
The heaven is shining full of love.

Death said, "I come on that heavenly decree,
My warrant's for to summon thee,
And whether thou art prepared or no,
This very day He says you must go."

Oh, ghastly Death, wouldst thou prevail?
Oh, spare me yet another day,

I'm but a flower in my bloom,
Why wilt thou cut-a me down so soon?

Oh, if I had my time again,
I would hate that road that leads to sin;
And to my God a-with earnest pray,
And wrestle until the break of day.
Oh, the heaven is shining, shining,
Lord the heaven is shining full of love.

(Hampton)

Oh, Then My Little Soul's Going To Shine

I'm going to join the great association,
I'm going to join the great association,
I'm going to join the great association,
Then my little soul's going to shine, shine,
Then my little soul's going to shine along.

I'm going to climb up Jacob's ladder,
I'm going to climb up higher and higher,
I'm going to sit down at the welcome table,
I'm going to feast off milk and honey,
I'm going to tell God how-a you starved me,
I'm going to join the big baptizing.

Then my little soul's going to shine, shine,
Then my little soul's going to shine along.

(Hampton)

Oh, When I Get To Heaven

Oh, when I get to heaven,
Going to sit right down,
Tell it, tell it, tell it,

Ask my Lord for a starry crown,
Sitting down side of the Holy Lamb.

Father Abraham,
Sitting down side of the Holy Lamb,
Help me to sing the song,
Help me to move along.

Oh, when I get to heaven,
Going to sit and tell,
Tell it, tell it, tell it,
Three archangels going to ring them bells,
Sitting down side of the Holy Lamb.

Oh, when I get to heaven,
Going to ease, ease,
Me and my God going to do as we please,
Tell it, tell it, tell it,
Sitting down side of the Holy Lamb.

(Hampton)

Oh, Yes

Oh, yes! Oh, yes!
I tell you, bretheren, a mortal fact,
Oh, yes! Oh, yes!
If you want to get to heaven,
Don't ever look back;
Oh, yes, Oh, yes!
I want to know before I go,
Yea, whether you love the Lord or no,
Oh, wait till I put on my robe,
      wait till I put on my robe,
Oh, yes! Oh, yes!

If ever I land on the other shore,
I'll never come here to sing no more;
A golden band all around my waist,
And the palms of victory in my hand,
And the golden slippers onto my feet,
Going to walk up and down them golden streets.

And my lovely bretheren, that ain't all,
I'm not done a talking about my Lord,
And a golden crown placed on my head,
And my long white robe came dazzling down,
Now wait till I get on my gospel shoes,
Going to walk about heaven and carry the news.

I'm anchored in Christ, Christ anchored in me,
All the devils in hell can't pluck me out;
And I wonder what Satan's grumbling about,
He's bound into hell, and he can't get out,
But he shall be loose and have his sway,
Yea at the great resurrection day.

I went down the hillside to make one prayer,
And when I got there, old Satan was there;
And what do you think he said to me?
Said, "Off from here you'd better be."
And what for to do, I did not know,
But I fell on my knees, and I cried, "Oh, Lord!"
Now my Jesus been so good and kind,
Yea, to the withered, halted, and blind;
My Jesus lowered his mercy down,
And snatched me from those doors of hell,
He snatched me from those doors of hell.

I was in the church and praying loud,
And on my knees to my Jesus bowed,
Old Satan told me to my face,
"I'll get you when you leave this place";
Oh, brother, that scared me to my heart
I was afraid to walk when it was dark.
I started home but I did pray,
And I met old Satan on the way;
Old Satan made one grab at me,
But he missed my soul, and I went free.
My sins went lumbering down to hell,

And my soul went leaping up Zion's hill;
I tell you what, brethren, you'd better not laugh,
Old Satan'll run you down his path;
If he runs you, as he ran me,
You'll be glad to fall upon your knee.   (Hampton)

Oh, Yes! Oh, Yes! Wait 'Til I Get On My Robe

I come this night to sing and pray,
Oh, Yes, Oh, yes,
To drive old Satan far away,
Oh, Yes, Oh, yes.

That heavenly home is bright and fair,
But might few can enter there;
I went down in the valley to pray,
I met old Satan on the way;
Oh, if you want to catch the heavenly breeze,
Go down in the valley on your knees and pray;
Oh, what do you think he said to me,
You're too young to pray and too young to die.
Oh, bow your knees upon the ground,
And ask the Lord to turn you 'round.

Oh, yes, Oh, yes,
Wait 'til I get on my robe,
Wait 'til I get on my robe,
Oh, yes, Oh, yes.   (BANS)

Oh, Zion, Hallelujah

Oh, Zion, hallelujah,
Oh, Zion, hallelujah,
Oh, Zion, hallelujah,

Yes, I wonder what Satan's grumbling about,
He's chained in hell and can't get out;
Get you gone Satan and none of your lies,
I made you out of a lie and kept my way.

Don't you hear those horses' feet?
They're rumbling about the golden street.
Oh, when I was a mourner just like you,
I moaned 'til my God set me free;

He plucked my feet out of the miry clay,
And set them on the rocks of eternity.   (BDWS)

Old Satan

Old Satan is one busy ole man;
He rolls them blocks all in my way;
But Jesus is my bosom friend;
He rolls them blocks away.

If I had died when I was young,
Then how my stam'ring tongue would have sung;
But I am ole, and now I stand
A narrow chance to tread that heavenly land.

Ole Satan thought he had a mighty aim;
He missed my soul and caught my sins.
Cry Amen, cry Amen, cry Amen to God!

He took my sins upon his back;
Went muttering and grumbling down to hell.
Cry Amen, cry Amen, cry Amen to God!
Ole Satan's church is here below.
Up to God's free church I hope to go.
Cry Amen, cry Amen, cry Amen to God!   (Brent)

O, My Little Soul

I don't care where you bury my body,
Don't care where you bury my body,
Don't care where you bury my body.

You may bury my body in the east of the garden,
Bury my body in the east of the garden,
Bury my body in the east of the garden.

Great big stars 'way up yonder,
Great big stars 'way up yonder,
Great big stars 'way up yonder.

O, my little soul's going to shine, shine,
All around heaven going to shine, shine.   (ANS)

On To Glory

O, come my brothers and sisters, too,
We're going to join the heavenly crew,
O, hallelu, O, hallelu,
O, hallelujah to the Lord.

To Christ our saviour let us sing,
And make our loud hosannas ring.

Oh, there's Bill Thomas,
I know him well,
He's got to work to keep from hell;
He's got to pray by night and day,
If he wants to go by the narrow way.

There's Chloe Williams,
She makes me mad,
For you see I know she's going on bad;
She told me a lie this afternoon,
And the devil will get her very soon.   (Allen)

O, Shout Away

O, shout, O, shout,
O, shout, away,
And don't you mind,
And glory, glory,
Glory in my soul!

And when it was night I thought it was day,
I thought I'd pray my soul away,
And glory, glory,
Glory in my soul!

Old Satan told me not to pray,
He wants my soul at judgement day;
And everywhere I went to pray,
There something was in my way.
O, shout, O, shout,
O, shout away,
And don't you mind,
And glory, glory,
Glory in my soul!

(Allen)

O Who That Coming Over Yonder?

O, who that coming over yonder, hallelujah,
O, who that coming over yonder,
O, who that coming over yonder,
O, who that coming over yonder, hallelu.
O, don't that look like a sister?
O, don't that look like a brother?
O, who that coming over yonder?
O, don't that look like my Jesus
With the world upon his shoulder?
O, he's going to rule his people,
O, with a robe of iron.

O, who that coming over yonder, hallelujah,
O, who that coming over yonder,
O, who that coming over yonder,
O, who that coming over yonder, hallelu.

(Calhoun)

Peter, Go Ring Them Bells

Oh, Peter, go ring them bells,
     Peter, go ring them bells,
     Peter, go ring them bells,
     I heard from heaven today.

I wonder where my mother is gone,
I wonder where sister Mary's gone,
I wonder where sister Martha's gone,
I wonder where brother Moses' gone,
I wonder where brother Daniel's gone,
He's gone where Elijah has gone.

Oh, Peter, go ring them bells,
Oh, Peter, go ring them bells,
I heard from heaven today,
It's good news, and I thank God,
I heard from heaven today,
Oh, Peter go ring them bells,
I heard from heaven today.   (FJS)

Praise The Lamb

Got glory and honor, praise Jesus,
Glory and honor, praise the Lamb,
Got praise, Amen.

One day as I was walking
Along that lonesome road,
My Savior spoke unto me,
And filled my heart with love.

I do believe without a doubt,
If Jesus comes we'll have a shout;
I know my God is a man of war,
He fought my battle at Jericho's wall;
I love God almighty, indeed I do,
And I hope God almighty's going to love me to.

I took a walk on the mountain top,
And I spied Job's head on a chopping block;
I remember the day, I remember it well,
When Jesus plucked me out of hell,
That ain't all, I got more besides,
I'm born of God and I been baptized.   (BDWS)

Prancing Horses

Brother, and a-hey,
Brother, and a-hey,
Hey, my Lord.

Who's that coming over yonder?
Hey, Lordy
Who's that coming over yonder?
Hey, my Lord
Don't that look like Jesus?
Don't that look like Jesus?
Hey, my Lord.

How you know it's Jesus?
I know Him by His garment,
I know Him by His garment,
Hey, my Lord.

Look, look, look over yonder,
Yonder comes Jeremiah,
He's riding the prancing horses,
Just look at the prancing horses,
Just look at the prancing horses,
They come pawing in the valley,
Ho, my Lord.

(BDWS)

Reign, Oh! Reign

Reign, Oh! reign,
      Oh! reign, my Savior;
Reign, Oh! reign,
      Oh! reign, my Lord.

Takes an humble soul to join us
      in the service of the Lord,
Takes an humble soul to join us
      in the army;
Here's a sinner come to join us
      in the service of the Lord,
Here's a sinner come to join us
      in the army;
Oh! ain't you glad you've joined us
      in the service of the Lord,
Oh! ain't you glad you've joined us
      in the army.

Reign, Oh! reign,
      Oh, reign, my Savior;
Reign, Oh! reign,
      Oh, reign, my Lord.

(FJS)

Remember The Dying Lamb

Go, Mary, go --
Stay, Martha, stay --
Go tell the Lord I'm on my way,
I got my religion in hard times.

Jesus gave me the eagle's wings,
I got my religion in hard times,
Remember the dying Lamb.

I'm going over Jordan,
I'm on my way to Zion,
You call me a false pretender,
You call me a lying member,
I don't care what you call me,
I know my Jesus love me,
Jesus gave me the eagle's wings,
Remember the dying Lamb.

(BDWS)

The Resurrection Morn

O, run, Mary, run,
Hallelu, hallelu!
O, run, Mary, run,
Hallelu, Hallelujah!
It was early in the morning
That she went to the sepulcher,
And the Lord he wasn't there;
But she saw a man a-coming,
And she thought it was the gardener,
But he said "O touch me not,
"For I am not yet ascended,
"But tell to my disciples
"That the Lord he is arisen."

So run, Mary, run,
Hallelu, hallelu,
O run, Mary, run,
Hallelu, hallelujah!   (Allen)

Ride On

Ride on, ride on,
Ride on, King Emanuel.
Don't you want to go to heaven in the morning?

Some of these mornings bright and fair,
Don't you want to go to heaven in the morning?
Take my flight up to the skies,
Don't you want to go to heaven in the morning?

Some of these mornings bright and fair,
Don't you want to go to heaven in the morning?
Take my flight up through the air,
Don't you want to go to heaven in the morning?

You say you're aiming for the skies,
Don't you want to go to heaven in the morning?
Why don't you stop telling lies,
Don't you want to go to heaven in the morning?

Ride on, ride on,
Ride on, King Emanuel.   (Hampton)

Ride On, Conquering King

Oh, I've been tempted,
        I've been tried,
I've been to the river and I've been baptized,
Oh, yes!
I want to get to heaven in the morning, morning.
Oh, ride on, Jesus, ride on,
Ride on, conquering King,
I want to get to heaven in the morning.

If you see my father,
    Just tell him for me,
I've been to the river and I've been baptized;
Oh, yes!
If you see John the Baptist,
    Just tell him for me,
To meet me tomorrow in Galilee,
Oh, yes!
If you see my class leader,
    Just tell him for me,
I've been to the river and I've been baptized,
Oh, ride on, Jesus, ride on,
Ride on, conquering King,
I want to get to heaven in the morning.   (CD)

Ride On, King Jesus

Ride on, King Jesus, ride on--
    No many can ever work like him,
Ride on, King Jesus, ride on.

Why he's the King of Kings,
    And Lord of Lords,
Jesus Christ, the first and last,
    No man can ever work like him.

I will not let you go, my Lord,
Until you come and bless my soul--
    No man can ever work like him.

King Jesus rides on a milk white horse--
    No man can ever work like him,
For Paul and Silas bound in jail,
The Christians prayed both day and night
    No man can ever work like him.

Ride on, King Jesus, ride on--
He's the King of Kings,
    And Lord of Lords--
Ride on, King Jesus, ride on--
No man can ever work like him.   (FJS)

Rise, Shine, For Thy Light Is Coming

O 'rise! Shine! for thy light is coming,
'Rise! Shine! for thy light is coming,
O 'rise! Shine! for thy light is coming,
My Lord says he's coming by and by.
This is the year of Jubilee,
My Lord has set his people free;
I intend to shout and never stop,
Until I reach the mountain-top;
Wet or dry, I intend to try
To serve the Lord until I die.

O 'rise! Shine! for thy light is coming,
'Rise! Shine! for thy light is coming,
O 'rise! Shine! for thy light is coming,
My Lord says he's coming by and by.   (ANS)

Rocking Jerusalem

O, Mary, O, Martha,
O, Mary, ring them bells.
I hear archangels rocking Jerusalem,
I hear archangels ringing them bells.

Church getting higher!
Rocking Jerusalem!
Listen to the lambs!
Ringing them bells.
New Jerusalem!
Rocking Jerusalem!
New Jerusalem!
Ring them bells.   (ANSAS)

Rock Mount Sinai

O, rock, Mount Sinai,
Rock, Mount Sinai,
Rock, Mount Sinai, in that mornin'.
O, when you hear, my coffin soun',
Then you may know my body's boun'.
O, rock, Mount Sinai.

O, come on, Moses, don't you get los',
Smote the water an' come on the cross,
O, rock, Mount Sinai.

O, David, David, is a shepherd boy,
David killed Goliath and shouted for joy.
He killed Goliath, killed Goliath in that morning.
O, rock, Mount Sinai.

When I get to heaven, going to sit right down;
Going to ask my Lord for a starry crown.
O, rock, Mount Sinai.

O, Pilate's wife she dreamt a dream,
When the dream was over she said to Pilate:
O, give me a little water to wash my han',
So they won't be stained with the innocent man.   (Calhoun)

The Rocks And The Mountains

Oh, the rocks and the mountains
        shall flee away,
And you shall have a new
        hiding place that day.

Seeker, seeker,
       Give up your heart to God,
Doubter, doubter,
       Give up your heart to God,
Mourner, mourner,
       Give up your heart to God,
Sinner, sinner,
       Give up your heart to God,
Sister, sister,
       Give up your heart to God,
Mother, mother,
       Give up your heart to God,
Children, children,
       Give up your heart to God,
And you shall have a new
       hiding place that day.
Oh, the rocks and the mountains
       shall flee away,

And you shall have a new
       hiding place that day.   (FJS)

Run, Moaner, Run

Run, moaner, run,
Heaven is shining;
Run, moaner, run,
I'm going home.

Oh, you can fool me,
But you can't fool God,
'Cause God knows the secret of every heart.

Oh, look up yonder,
What I see
A band of angels coming after me.

Oh, ain't them angels
Swift and strong,
They move like lightning in God's storm.

Oh, Daniel's wisdom,
May, I know,
Stiff in faith and spirit sure.

Run, moaner, run,
Heaven is shining;
Run, moaner, run,
I'm going home.   (BDWS)

See Four And Twenty Elders

See four and twenty elders on their knees,
See four and twenty elders on their knees;
They are bowing 'round the altar on their knees,
They are bowing 'round the altar on their knees;

See Gideon's army bowing on their knees,
See Gideon's army bowing on their knees;
See Daniel 'mong the lions on his knees,
See Daniel 'mong the lions on his knees;

And we'll all rise together and review the rising sun,
O, Lord, have mercy if you please.   (Hampton)

Serving My God

Serving my God,
Serving my God,
I been four thousand year' serving my God.
Ain't you mighty glad,
Ain't you mighty glad.
I been four thousand year' serving my God.

Drinking of the wine,
Drinking of the wine,
I been four thousand year' drinking of the wine.
Ain't you mighty glad,

Ain't you mighty glad.
I been four thousand year' serving my God.

Eating of the bread,
Eating of the bread,
I been four thousand year' eating of the bread.
Ain't you mighty glad,
Ain't you mighty glad.
I been four thousand year' eating of the bread.

Ain't you mighty glad,
I been four thousand year' serving my God.   (Calhoun)

Shine, Shine

I don't care where you bury my body,
Don't care where you bury my body,
Don't care where you bury my body,
Oh, my little soul's going to shine, shine,
Oh, my little soul's going to shine, shine.
All around the heaven going to shine, shine,
All around the heaven going to shine, shine.

You may bury my body in the Egypt garden,
Bury my body in the Egypt garden;
I'm going to join the forty-four thousand,
Going to join the forty-four thousand;
Great big stars way up yonder,
Great big stars way up yonder.

O my little soul's going to shine, shine,
O my little soul's going to shine, shine,
All around the heaven going to shine, shine,
All around the heaven going to shine, shine.   (FJS)

Shout For Joy

O, Lord! Shout for joy!
O, Lord! Shout for joy!

Early in the morning-
Shout for joy! Shout for joy!
Feel like shouting-
Shout for joy! Shout for joy!
Feel like praying-
Shout for joy! Shout for joy!
Now I'm getting happy
Shout for joy! Shout for joy!

(ANSAS)

Shout Jerusalem

Shout Jerusalem,
Preach Jerusalem in the morning,
Shout Jerusalem,
Preach Jerusalem in the morning.

Oh, my sister, how you feels,
My brother, how you feels,
My elder, how you feels?
Jerusalem in the morning,
It's feeling every better,
Jerusalem in the morning,
It's feeling every better.

(BDWS)

Sinner Won't Die No More

O, the Lamb done been down here and died,
The Lamb done been down here and died,
O, the Lamb done been down here and died,
Sinner won't die no more.
I wonder what bright angels,
        angels, angels,
I wonder what bright angels,
        angels, angels,
The robes all ready now.

O, see those ships come a-sailing,
        sailing, sailing,
O, see those ships come a-sailing,
The robes all ready now.

(Allen)

Sit Down, Servant, Sit Down

Sit down, servant, sit down!
Sit down, servant, sit down!
Sit down, servant, sit down!
Sit down and rest a while.

I know you're mighty tired so sit down,
Know you're mighty tired so sit down.

I know you're shouting happy so sit down,
Know you're shouting happy so sit down.

Sit down, servant, sit down!
Sit down, servant, sit down!
Sit down, servant, sit down!
Sit down and rest a while.   (ANS)

Slavery's Chain

Slavery's chain done broke at last, broke at last, broke at last,
Slavery's chain done broke at last,
Going to praise God till I die.

Slavery's chain done broke at last, broke at last, broke at last,
Slavery's chain done broke at last,
Going to Praise God till I die.

Slavery's chain done broke at last, broke at last, broke at last,
Slavery's chain done broke at last,
Going to Praise God till I die.   (Traditional)

Study War No More

I'm going to lay down my sword and shield,
Down by the riverside, down by the riverside,
Down by the riverside;
Going to lay down my sword and shield,
Down by the riverside, down by the riverside,
Ain't going to study war no more.

I'm going to put on my long white robe,
Down by the riverside, down by the riverside.
I'm going to talk with the Prince of Peace,
Down by the riverside, down by the riverside,
Down by the riverside,
Ain't going to study war no more.

Ain't going to study war no more,
Ain't going to study war no more.   (ANSAS)

Sunday Morning Band (1)

What kind of band you going to join?
Sunday morning band;
What kind of band you going to join?
Sunday morning band.

Got one, got two, got three little angels,
Got four, got five, got six little angels,
Got seven, got eight, got nine little angels,
Got ten little angels in the band.

The best band that in the land,
Sunday morning band.

Ho, band, Sunday morning,
Ho, band, Sunday morning,
Ho, band, Sunday morning,
Sunday morning band.

(BDWS)

Sunday Morning Band (2)

What band that Sunday morning,
What band that Sunday morning,
Holy band that Sunday morning,
Holy band that Sunday morning,
Sunday morning, Sunday morning band,
Sunday morning, Sunday morning band.

Jordan River's deep and wide,
And none can cross but the sanctified;
Looked over Jordan and what did I see,
A band of angels coming for me;
Born of God I know I am,
I'm purchased by the dying Lamb.

What band that Sunday morning,
What band that Sunday morning,
Holy band that Sunday morning,
Holy band that Sunday morning,
Sunday morning, Sunday morning band,
Sunday morning, Sunday morning band.

(ANS)

Tell My Jesus "Morning"

In the morning when I rise,
Tell my Jesus huddy, oh;
I wash my hands in the morning glory,
Tell my Jesus huddy, oh.

Pray Tony, pray boy, you got the order,
Tell my Jesus huddy, oh;
Morning, Hester, morning, gal,
Tell my Jesus huddy, oh;
Say brother Sammmy you got the order,
Tell my Jesus huddy, oh;
You got the order,
And I got the order,
Tell my Jesus huddy, oh.

(Allen)

Thank God I'm On My Way To Heaven

You may talk about me just as much as you please,
You may spread my name abroad,
But every lie that you tell on me
Just throws me higher into heaven.
Heaven, heaven,
Thank God! I'm on my way to heaven.

I met my sister the other day,
I asked her, "How do you do?"
She says "I'm doing mighty well,
And I thank God too."
Thank God! I'm on my way to heaven,
Thank God! I'm on my way to heaven.
                    (ANS)

There Is A Mighty Shouting

This day, Lord,
There is a mighty shouting in the heaven,
There is a mighty shouting in the heaven,
There is a mighty shouting in the heaven.

Jesus told me,
There is a mighty shouting in the heaven,
Come on brother,
Come on elder,
There is a mighty shouting in the heaven,
There is a mighty shouting in the heaven.   (BDWS)

These Are All My Father's Children

These are my Father's children,
These are my Father's children,
These are my Father's children,
Outshine the sun.

My Father's done with the trouble of the world,
            with the trouble of the world,
            with the trouble of the world,

My father's done with the trouble of the world,
Outside the sun.   (Allen)

Three Long Nights And Three Long Days

Three long nights and three long days,
Jesus walkin' down the lane,
Walk, Mary, down the lane,
Walk, Mary, down the lane.

In the mornin', in the mornin';
Do believe, do believe;
Jesus call you, Jesus call you;
In the heaven, in the heaven;
Get my license, get my license;
In my pocket, in my pocket;
'Fraid of nobody, 'fraid of nobody.   (St. Helena)

Toll The Bell, Angel

When I lay my body down,
    Ay Lord, in the graveyard;
When I lay my body down,
    Ay Lord, in the graveyard;
Think you hear my coffin sound-
My soul be singing under ground-
Ay Lord, singing in the graveyard:

Toll the bell, angel, I just got over;
Toll the bell, angel, I just got over;
Toll the bell, angel, I just got over;
Well, I just got over at last.

"Toll the bell, Angel" © 1923 Etude Music Mazazine Used By Permission of the Publisher Theodore Presser Company.   (R.E. Kennedy)

Towe the Bell

Towe the bell,
    Done got over;
Towe the bell,
    I done got over;
Towe the bell,
    Done got over,
    Done got over at last.

Old Satan's like a snake in the grass,
Always in a Christian's path;
Old Satan shot his ball at me,
He missed my soul and caught my sin;
Old Satan's mad and I am glad,
I trust the Lord I'm going to keep him mad;
Old Satan thought he had me fast,
But I broke his chain and got free at last;
Sister, you better mind how you walk on the cross,
Your foot might slip and your soul get lost.
What makes me praise my Lord so bold,
He washed my sins as white as snow.

Towe the bell,
    Done got over;
Towe the bell,
    I done got over,
    Done got over at last.

(BDWS)

Trying To Cross The Red Sea

Didn't old Pharaoh get lost, get lost?
Didn't old Pharaoh get lost, yes,
Trying to cross the Red Sea?
Creep along, Moses, Moses creep along,
Creep along, Moses, I thank God.

I went down in the valley and I didn't go to stay,
My soul got happy and I stayed all day;
I went down in the valley to offer my prayer,

When I got there old Satan was there
Trying to cross the Red Sea.

Old Satan's mad and I am glad,
He missed that soul he thought he had;
I wonder what old Satan's grumblin' about,
He down in hell and can't get out.   (ANSAS)

View The Land

Oh way over Jordan,
View the land, view the land
Way over Jordan,
Go view the heavenly land.

I'm born of God, I know I am,
And you deny it if you can;
I want to go to heaven when I die,
To shout salvation as I fly.
What kind of shoes are those you wear?
That you can walk upon the air?
The shoes I wear are gospel shoes,
And you can wear them if you choose.

There is a tree in Paradise,
The Christian he calls it the tree of life;
I expect to eat fruit right off that tree,
If busy old Satan will let-a me be.

You say your Jesus set-a you free,
Why don't you let-a your neighbor be?
You say you're aiming for the skies,
Why don't you stop-a telling lies?   (Hampton)

Walk In Jerusalem Just Like John

I want to be ready,
I want to be ready,
I want to be ready,
To walk in Jerusalem just like John.

John said the city was just four square,
And he declared he'd meet me there;
John! Oh, John! what do you say?
That I'll be there in the coming day.
When Peter was preaching at Pentecost
He was endowed with the Holy Ghost.

I want to be ready,
I want to be ready,
I want to be ready,
To walk in Jerusalem just like John.   (BANS)

What Shall I Do?

I'm so glad trouble don't last always,
I'm so glad trouble don't last always,
Hallelujah, I'm so glad trouble don't last always,
O, my Lord, O, my Lord
What shall I do?

Early one morning, Death came knocking at my door,
Early one morning, stole my mother away;
Mother, told me to meet her in Galilee,
Hush! Hush! Hush! The angels calling me;
I'm so glad I got my religion in time,
Goin' to rise and shine, shine like a morning star.   (ANSAS)

What You Going To Name That Pretty Little Baby?

Oh, Mary, what you going to name
That pretty little baby?
Oh, Mary, what you going to name
That pretty little baby?
Glory, glory, glory.

Oh, Mary, what you going to name
That pretty little baby?
Oh, Mary, what you going to name
That pretty little baby?
Glory, glory, glory.   (Traditional)

When I Come To Die

Oh, when I come to die,
I want to be ready,
When I come to die,
Want to walk about Jerusalem just like Job.
When I come to die,
I want to be ready,
When I come to die.

When I get there I will sit down and tell,
Tell about the world I just come from,
Want to walk about Jerusalem just like Job.

Walk about heaven and carry the news,
Tell about the world I just come from,
Want to walk about Jerusalem just like Job.

I'll skip around heaven and carry the news,
Tell about the world I just come from,
Want to walk about Jerusalem just like Job.
Christian, Christian, be engaged,
Old Satan's getting in a mighty rage,
Want to walk about Jerusalem just like Job.   (Hampton)

When I Get In Heaven In My Elbow Chair

When I get in heaven in my elbow chair,
Thank God I get over Jordan,
Then I will rock like angel rock,
Thank God I get over Jordan.

Over Jordan, over Jordan,
Thank God I get over Jordan,
Over Jordan, over Jordan,
Thank God I get over Jordan.

One mornin' by the break of day,
Thank God I get over Jordan,
Heard a voice and saw no one,
Thank God I been over Jordan.

'Twas King Jesus passin' by,
Thank God I get over Jordan,
"Twas King Jesus passin' by,
Thank God I get over Jordan.   (St. Helena)

When Jesus Comes

When Jesus comes,
He'll outshine the sun,
Outshine the sun,
Outshine the sun;
When Jesus comes,
He'll outshine the sun,
Look away beyond the moon.

We'll shout Hallelujah!
When Jesus comes,
When Jesus comes,
When Jesus comes.
We'll shout Hallelujah!
When Jesus comes,
Look away beyond the moon.

We'll sing Hosyannah--
When Jesus comes,
When Jesus comes,
When Jesus comes,
When Jesus comes.
We'll sing Hosyannah--
When Jesus comes,
Look away beyond the moon.

There'll be no more sorrow in
Sweet Beulah Land,
Sweet Beulah Land.
There'll be no more sorrow in
Sweet Beulah land,
Look away beyond the moon.

If you wanta see King Jesus,
Keep prayin' on,
Keep prayin' on,
Keep prayin' on.
If you wanta see King Jesus,
Keep prayin' on,
Look away beyond the moon.

Gonna meet my dear Mother in
Sweet Beulah Land,
Sweet Beulah Land,
Sweet Beulah Land.
Gonna meet my dear Mother in
Sweet Beulah land,
Look away beyond the moon.

Gonna meet my dear Sister in
Sweet Beulah Land,
Sweet Beulah Land,
Sweet Beulah Land.
Gonna meet my dear sister in
Sweet Beulah Land,
Look away beyond the moon.

Gonna meet all my dear frien's in
Sweet Beulah Land,
Sweet Beulah Land,
Sweet Beulah Land.
Gonna meet all my frien's in
Sweet Beulah Land,
Look away beyond the moon.

(Grissom)

When The Saints Come Marchin' In

When the saints come marchin' in,
When the saints come marchin' in,
Lord, I want to be in that number
When the saints come marchin' in.

I have a lovin' brother,
He is gone on before.
An' I promised I would meet him
When they crown Him Lord of all.

When they crown Him Lord of all,
When they crown Him Lord of all,
Lord, I want to be in that number
When they crown Him Lord of all.

I have a lovin' sister.
She is gone on before.
An' I promised I would meet her
When they gather roun' the throne.

When they gather roun' the throne,
When they gather roun' the throne,

Lord, I want to be in that number
When they gather roun' the throne.   (Dixon)

Who Love My Lord

Do tell the world,
I love my Jesus;
Do tell the world,
I love my Lord;
Do tell the world,
I love my Jesus;
Do tell the world,
I love my Lord.

Anybody here what love my Jesus?
Anybody here who love my Lord?
Anybody here what love my Jesus?
Anybody here who love my Lord?

Sinners all here who love my Jesus,
The preachers all here who loves my Lord;
Anybody here like doubting Thomas?
Anybody here who love my Lord?   (BDWS)

Yonder Come Sister Mary

Yonder come sister Mary,
How do you know it is her?
With the palms of victory in her hand,
And the keys of Bethlehem,
And the keys of Bethlehem,
O Lord!
The keys of Bethlehem,
And the keys of Bethlehem,
O Lord!
And the keys of Bethlehem,
O Lord!

Yonder comes brother Joseph,
How do you know it is him?
With the palms of victory in his hand.   (Fisher)

You Publican, You Pharisee

You publican, you pharisee,
You feed among the swine,
You go to God with your lip and tongue,
You leave your heart behind.

Wasn't that a mighty day,
Hallelu--
Hallelu--
Wasn't that a mighty day,
When Jesus Christ was born.   (St. Helena)

Zion, Weep-a Low

Zion, weep-a low, Zion, weep-a low,
                Zion, weep-a low,
Then hallelujah to the Lamb.

My Jesus Christ, a-walking down the road,
Then out of his mouth came a two-edged sword,
Say, what kind of sword's that you're talking about,
I'm talking about that two-edged sword.
Then hallelujah to the Lamb.
Oh, look up yonder, Lord, a-what I see,
There's a long tall angel coming after me,
With-a palms of victory in my hand,
With-a golden crown placed on-a my head.
Then hallelujah to the Lamb.

Zion's been a-weeping all the day,
Say, come, poor sinners, come and pray,
Oh, Satan like that hunting dog,
He hunts those Christians home to God.
Then hallelujah to the Lamb.

Oh, heaven so high, and I so low,
I don't know shall I ever get to heaven or no,
Going to tell my brother before I go,
What a lonesome road I had to go.
Then hallelujah to the Lamb.

Zion, weep-a low, Zion weep-a low,
                Zion weep-a low,
Then hallelujah to the Lamb.   (Hampton)

LYRICS OF
JUDGMENT AND RECKONING _____

The spirituals in this category express little doubt that the world is in disharmony and that the world serves to be corrected. The themes of these lyrics are highly eschatological. The lyrics insist that slavery is not the end of things. The end of things will be the meting out of justice--retribution. Retribution will be brought to this New World order for having set itself against the natural laws of human dignity; for the just order of the universe is generative, not degenerative. The Day of Judgment brings the declaration of human dignity as a human birthright upheld by the laws of the cosmos. The claims will be heard for those who have endured and for those who have succumbed to the humiliation of being used for someone else's benefit while simultaneously having been made an object of that same person's derision and scorn. These spirituals are composed with the conviction that Justice is indeed blind but that it, nevertheless, can see the wrongs.

In the world of traditional Africa, ceremonial ritual was of primary importance in maintaining an essential harmony that had attributes which were not only social but also cosmic. The interference with and disruption of African cultural autonomy has generally prevented this ritual enactment in the enslaved African's new world. The time for the proper reckoning ceremony is well overdue, and because the neglect has deepened the disharmony, the great apocalyptic day of reckoning envisioned by Christianity seems not only requisite but appropriate and clearly justifiable. The disorder has to be extinguished, and the world needs a general purification. And, too, each individual must stand ready to make his own personal and moral account before the bar of judgment.

All Over This World

All over this world,
All over this world,
Yes, all over this world,
All over this world.

Going to the graveyard soon be over,
Soon be over, soon be over,
Going to the graveyard soon be over,
All over this world.

'Buking the gospel soon be over,
Old back-biting soon be over,
All of this sinning soon be over,
Ringing of the church bell soon be over,
Oh, that praying soon be over.

All over this world,
All over this world,
Yes, all over this world,
All over this world.   (BDWS)

Are You Ready?

Are you ready, are you ready,
Ready for the Judgment Day?
Are you ready, are you ready,
Ready for the Judgment Day?

Oh, it's a sad day coming,
Oh, it's a sad day coming by and by,
When the saints and sinners
Be falling right and left.
Are you ready for the Judgment Day?

There's a better day coming,
There's a better day coming,
There's a better day coming by and by,
When we gather with the saints
In sweet heaven above.
To be ready for the Judgment Day.   (BDWS)

At The Bar Of God

O, mourner!
O, mourner, O, mourner,
Look at the people at the bar of God.

O, seeker!
O, seeker, O, seeker,
Look at the people at the bar of God.

O, sinner!
O, sinner, O, sinner,
Look at the people at the bar of God.

Look at the people at the bar of God,
At the bar of God, at the bar of God,
Look at the people at the bar of God.

(ANS)

At The Judgment Bar

At the judgment bar,
At the judgment bar,
At the judgment bar,
At the judgment bar.

(St. Helena)

Babylon's Falling

Pure city, Babylon's falling, to rise no more,
Pure city, Babylon's falling, to rise no more.
Oh, Babylon's falling, falling, falling,
Babylon's falling to rise no more,
Oh, Babylon's falling, falling, falling,
Babylon's falling to rise no more.

Oh, Jesus told you once before,
Babylon's falling to rise no more;
To go in peace and sin no more,
Babylon's falling to rise no more.

If you get there before I do,
Babylon's falling to rise no more;
Tell all my friends I'm coming too,
Babylon's falling to rise no more.

(Hampton)

Calvary

Every time I think about Jesus,
Every time I think about Jesus,
Every time I think about Jesus,
Surely He died on Calvary.
Makes me troubled thinking about dying,
Makes me troubled thinking about dying,
Makes me troubled thinking about dying,
Surely He died on Calvary.

Calvary, Calvary --
Calvary, Calvary --
Surely He died on Calvary.

(BANS)

Can't Hide, Sinner, Can't Hide

Can't hide, sinner, can't hide,
Can't hide, sinner, can't hide,
Can't hide, sinner, can't hide,
Can't hide, sinner, can't hide.

Can't hide, liar, can't hide,
Can't hide, liar, can't hide,
Can't hide, liar, can't hide,
Can't hide, liar, can't hide.

Can't hide, gambler, can't hide,
Can't hide, gambler, can't hide,
Can't hide, gambler, can't hide,
Can't hide, gambler, can't hide.

Can't hide, hypocrite, can't hide,
Can't hide, hypocrite, can't hide,
Can't hide, hypocrite, can't hide,
Can't hide, hypocrite, can't hide.   (St. Helena)

Come Down, Angels

Come down, angels, trouble the water,
Come down, angels, trouble the water,
Come down, angels, trouble the water,
Let God's saints come in,
Oh, let God's saints come in.

I love to shout, I love to sing,
I love to praise my heavenly King;
I think I hear the sinner say,
My savior taught me how to pray;
I hope to meet my brother there,
That used to join with me in prayer;
Didn't Jesus tell you once before,
To go in peace and sin no more.

Come down, angels, trouble the water,
Come down, angels, trouble the water,
Come down, angels, trouble the water,
Let God's saints come in,
Oh, let God's saints come in.   (FJS)

Coming Down The Line

Coming down the line,
My Lord's coming down the line,
My Lord, I saw God almighty,
Coming down the line.

Oh, it looks mighty cloudy,
But it ain't going to rain,
The sun's drawing water from every vein.

There's a star in the east,
There's a star in the west,
Don't you wish you were
That star in your breast?

Oh, Satan wears a crooked shoe,
If you don't mind, he'll slip it on you;

I place my feet right level in the path,
The gates flew open at the springing of the sun.
Oh, some people say my religion ain't true,
Thank God almighty I didn't get it from you;
If religion was something that money could buy,
The rich would live and the poor would die;
Oh, when I get to heaven going to walk right in,
Choose my seat and sit right down.   (BDWS)

The Day Of Judgment

And the moon will turn to blood,
And the moon will turn to blood,
And the moon will turn to blood,
In that day--
O, joy, my soul!
And the moon will turn to blood,
In that day.

And you'll see the stars a-falling,
And the world will be on fire,
And you'll hear the saints a-singing,
And the Lord will say to the sheep
To go to His right hand,
But the goats must go to the left.
And the moon will turn to blood,
And the moon will turn to blood,
And the moon will turn to blood,
In that day,
O, joy, my soul.   (ALLEN)

Didn't It Rain!

O, didn't it rain, children,
Didn't it rain!
Didn't it rain, children,
Didn't it rain!

Didn't it rain, children,
Didn't it rain, children,
Didn't it rain, children,
Didn't it rain!   (Traditional)

Don't Let The Wind Blow Here No More

Don't let the wind, don't let the wind,
Don't let the wind blow here no more;
O, don't let the wind, don't let the wind,
Don't let the wind blow here no more.

When the day of judgment come,
Don't let the wind blow here no more.
All God's children go marchin' home,
Don't let the wind blow here no more.

When the sea gives up the dead,
Don't let the wind blow here no more.
Want a golden crown put on my head,
Don't let the wind blow here no more.   (St. Helena)

From Every Graveyard

Just behold that number,
Just behold that number,
Just behold that number,
From every graveyard.

Going to meet the brothers there,
That used to join in prayer;
Going to meet the sisters there,
That used to join in prayer;
Going to meet the preachers there,
That used to join in prayer;
Going to meet the mourners there,
That used to join in prayer;
Going to meet the Christians there,
That used to join in prayer;
Going up through great tribulation,
From every graveyard.   (FJS)

Gabriel's Trumpet's Going To Blow

Gabriel's trumpet's going to blow,
By and by, by and by,
Yes, Gabriel's trumpet going to blow,
At the end of time.

Oh, get you all ready for to go,
Then my Lord will say to Gabriel,
Go, get you down your silver trumpet;
The first sounding of the trumpet
                              for the righteous.
Go, wake the sleeping nations,
Then, poor sinner, what will you do?
You'll run for the mountains to hide you,
At the end of time.

Gabriel's trumpet's going to blow
By and by, by and by,
Yes, Gabriel's trumpet going to blow,
At the end of time.   (FJS)

God's Going To Straighten Them

We got deacons in the church,
They ain't straight,
Who's going to straighten them?
God's going to straighten them,
He says He's going to straighten them,

God's going to straighten all the people
      in His church.
We got preachers in the church,
We got members in the church,
They ain't straight,
Who's going to straighten them?
God's going to straighten them,
He says He's going to straighten them,
God's going to straighten all the people
      in His church.

                                                (ANSAS)

God's Gonna Set This World On Fire

God's gonna set this world on fire,
One of these days;
God's gonna set this world on fire,
One of these days,
Oh, God's gonna set this world on fire,
One of these days.

I'm gonna drink from the healing cup,
One of these days;
I'm gonna drink from the healing cup,
I'm gonna drink from the healing cup,
I'm gonna drink from the healing cup,
One of these days.

                                        (Traditional)

The Gold Band

Going to march away in the gold band,
In the army by and by;
Going to march away in the gold band,
In the army by and by;
Sinner, what you going to do that day?
Sinner, what you going to do that day:
When the fire's a-rolling behind you,
In the army by and by?

Sister Mary's going to hand down the robe,
In the army, by and by;
Going to hand down the robe and the gold band,
In the army by and by.

                                        (ALLEN)

Got To Go To Judgment

Got to go to judgment, stand your trial,
                      stand your trial,
Got to go to judgment, stand your trial,
                      stand your trial,
Got to go to judgment, stand your trial,
                      stand your trial,
Can't stay away,
O, can't stay away.

Cried all night long, looking for Jesus,
       looking for Jesus,
Cried all night long, looking for Jesus,
       looking for Jesus,
Cried all night long, looking for Jesus,
       looking for Jesus,
Can't stay away,
O, can't stay away.

I prayed so hard looking for Jesus,
       looking for Jesus,
I prayed so hard looking for Jesus,
       looking for Jesus,
I prayed so hard looking for Jesus,
       looking for Jesus,
Can't stay away,
O, can't stay away.   (ANS)

Hallelujah To The Lamb

Hallelujah to the Lamb,
Hallelujah to the Lamb,
Hallelujah to the Lamb of God,
Hallelujah to the Lamb.

Sister Mary had a little Lamb,
Little Lamb,
It was born in Bethlehem,
And every where sister Mary went,
That Lamb would surely go.

When the moon goes down the valley stream,
Valley stream,
When the sun refuses to shine,
When every star shall disappear,
When the moon goes down the valley stream.

Hallelujah to the Lamb,
Hallelujah to the Lamb,
Hallelujah to the Lamb of God,
Hallelujah to the Lamb.   (BDWS)

Hammering Judgment

Don't you hear God talking, hammering?
Don't you hear God talking, hammering?
Don't you hear God talking, hammering?

He's talking to Moses, hammering.
He's talking through thunder, hammering.
Hammering judgment, hammering.
Hammer keep a-ringing, hammering.
God tol' Moses, hammering,
Go down in Egypt, hammering,
To tell ol' Pharaoh, hammering,
To loose his people, hammering,

Ol' Pharaoh had a hard heart, hammering,
An' would not loose them, hammering.

Don't you hear God talking, hammering?
Don't you hear God talking, hammering?
Don't you hear God talking, hammering?   (Calhoun)

Hear Gabriel Blow In That Morn

Didn't you know, pilgrim,
Learn me the way to go along,
Hear Gabriel in that morn.

O, way down yonder 'bout some graveyard,
Says me and my God going to walk and talk,
Says-a God don't talk like a natural man,
But he do talk so you can understand.
Graveyard going to be my dressing room,
Get up body, come away, come deaf, come dumb,
        come cripple, come get up lame,
Tell me little mo' 'bout judgment day.

I receive a letter the other day,
What you reckon that letter say?
Any one sick here an' want to be heale',
Write to Mary at the Gideon tree,
Hear Gabriel blow on that morn.

O God sent Jonah down to preach the word,
Jonah went down and took the ship,
The wind begin to blow and the ship begin to sail.
Say the captain of the vessel got trouble in min'.
Search the ship from bottom to top,
Say he found poor Jonah in the low' mos' deck.
Wake up man, who are you?
I am the man you call Hebrew.
Wake up man lie sleep away.
Jonah lie sleeping in the belly of the whale.
Hear Gabriel blow in that morn.   (Calhoun)

Heaven Bell A-Ring

My Lord, my Lord,
What shall I do?
And a heaven bell a-ring
And praise God.

What shall I do for a hiding place?
I run to the sea, but the sea run dry,
I run to the gate, but the gate shut fast,
No hiding place for sinner there.

Say, you, when you get to heaven,
Say, you, remember me,
Remember me, poor fallen soul;
Say when you get to heaven,

Say your work shall prove,
Your righteous Lord shall prove 'em well,
Your righteous Lord shall find you out,
He casts out none that come by faith.

You look to the Lord with a tender heart,
I wonder where poor Monday there,
For I am bone and set to hell;
We must hark to what the worldly say,
Say Christmas come but once a year,
Say Sunday come but once a week.

My Lord, my Lord,
What shall I do?
And a heaven bell a-ring
And praise God.   (ALLEN)

The Heaven Bells

O, mother, I believe,
                    O, mother, I believe,
O, mother, I believe,
That Christ was crucified!

O, don't you hear the heaven bells
                    a-ringing over me?
                    a-ringing over me?
                    a-ringing over me?
O, don't you hear the heaven bells
                    a-ringing over me?
It sounds like the judgement day!   (ALLEN)

He's Got His Eyes On You

He's got His eyes on you,
He's got His eyes on you;
My Lord's sitting in the Kingdom,
He's got His eyes on you.

I would not be a sinner,
I would not be a gambler,
I would not be a liar,
I tell you the reason why,
'Fraid my Lord might call me,
And I wouldn't be ready to die.   (ANSAS)

Get Yo' Ticket

Get yo' ticket,
Get yo' ticket,
Get yo' ticket, Good Lord.
Get yo' ticket,
Oh! When, when, when,
Oh! When?

Train's a-comin',
Train's a-comin',
Train's a-comin', Good Lord.
Train's a-comin',
Oh! When, when, when,
Oh! When?

Bound for Glory,
Bound for Glory,
Bound for Glory, Good Lord.
Bound for Glory,
Oh! When, when, when,
Oh! When?

I can tell it,
I can tell it,
I can tell it, Good Lord.
I can tell it,
Oh! When, when, when,
Oh! When?

I can read it,
I can read it,
I can read it, Good Lord.
I can read it,
Oh! When, when, when,
Oh! When?

I can live it,
I can live it,
I can live it, Good Lord.
I can live it,
Oh! When, when, when,
Oh! When?

I can sing it,
I can sing it,
I can sing it, Good Lord.
I can sing it,

Oh! When, when, when,
Oh! When?

Judgment's comin',
Judgment's comin',
Judgment's comin', Good Lord.
Judgment's comin',
Oh! When, when, when,
Oh! When?

(Grissom)

Hide-A-Me

When this world is all on fire,
Hide-a-me;
When this world is all on fire,
Hide-a-me.
When this world is all on fire,

Let Thy bosom be my pillow,
Hide me o'er the Rock of Ages,
Safe in Thee.

When the stars in heaven are fallin',
Hide-a-me;
When the stars in heaven are fallin',
Hide-a-me.
When the stars in heaven are fallin',
Let Thy bosom be my pillow,
Hide me o'er the Rock of Ages,
Safe in Thee.

When the trumpet sounds for judgment,
Hide-a-me;
When the trumpet sounds for judgment,
Hide-a-me.
When the trumpet sounds for judgment,
Let Thy bosom be my pillow,
Hide me o'er the Rock of Ages,
Safe in Thee.

When my name is called at judgment,
Hide-a-me;
When my name is called at judgment,
Hide-a-me.
When my name is called at judgment,
Let Thy bosom be my pillow,
Hide me o'er the Rock of Ages,
Safe in Thee.   (Grissom)

Humble Yourself, The Bell Done Rung

Live humble, humble, Lord;
Humble yourself, the bell done rung;
Live humble, humble, Lord;
Humble yourself, the bell done rung.
Glory and honor! Praise King Jesus!
Glory and honor! Praise the Lord!
Glory and honor! Praise King Jesus!
Glory and honor! Praise the Lord!

Oh, my young Christians, I got lots to tell you,
Jesus Christ speaking through the organs of the clay.
("One day, one day, Lord!")
God's going to call them children from a
          distant land.
Tombstones a-cracking, graves a-busting,
Hell and the sea are going to give up the dead.

False pretender wears sheep clothing on his back,
In his heart he's like a raving wolf.
("Judge ye not, brothers")
For ye shall be judged false pretender
            getting in the Christian band.

Watch that sun how steady he runs,
Don't let him catch you with your work undone.
Ever see such s man as God?
He gave up his son to come and die,
Gave up his son to come and die,
Just to save my soul from a burning fire.

See God and you see God,
And you see God in the morning,
He'll come riding on the line of time.
The fire'll be falling, He'll be calling,
"Come to judgment, come."

Live humble, humble, Lord;
Humble yourself, the bell done rung;
Glory and honor! Praise the Lord?
Glory and honor! Praise King Jesus.   (BANS)

I Ain't Going To Trust Nobody

I ain't going to trust nobody,
I ain't going to trust nobody,
I ain't going to trust nobody that day.
I ain't going to trust nobody,
I ain't going to trust nobody,
I ain't going to trust nobody that day,
That day, that day, that day, that day.
I'm going to trust my Jesus that day.

I ain't going to trust my mother,
I ain't going to trust my mother,
I ain't going to trust my mother that day,
That day, that day, that day, that day,
I'm going to trust my Jesus that day.   (BDWS)

I Feel Like My Time Ain't Long

I feel like, I feel like, Lord,
I feel like my time ain't long;
I feel like, I feel like, Lord,
I feel like my time ain't long.
Went to the graveyard the other day,
I looked at the place where my mother lay;
Sometimes I'm up, sometimes I'm down,
And sometimes I'm almost on the ground;
Mind out, my brother, how you step on the cross,
Your foot might slip and your soul get lost.

I feel like, I feel like, Lord,
I feel like my time ain't long;
I feel like, I feel like, Lord,
I feel like my time ain't long.   (BANS)

If I Have My Ticket, Lord

If I have my ticket, Lord, can I ride?
If I have my ticket, Lord, can I ride-a?
If I have my ticket, Lord, can I ride?
Ride away to Heaven in that mornin'.

This is what we Christians ought to do;
Be certain an' sure that we are livin' true.
For by an' by without a doubt,
Jehovah's gonna order His Angels out.

They will clean out the world an' leave no sin,
Now tell me, hypocrite, where you been?
I heard the sound of the Gospel train,
Don't you want to get on? Yes, that's my aim.

I'll stand at the station an' patiently wait
For the train that's comin', an' she's never late.
You must have your ticket stamped bright an' clear,
Train is comin', she's drawin' near.

Hope to be ready when the train do come,
My ticket all right an' my work all done.
She's so long comin' till she worries my mind,
Seems to be late, but she's just on time.

It keeps me always in a move an' a strain,
Tryin' to be ready for the Gospel train.
Ever now an' then, either day or night,
I examine my ticket to see if I'm right.
If the Son grant my ticket the Holy Ghost sign,
Then there is no way to be left behind.

There's a great deal of talk 'bout the Judgment Day,
You have no time to trifle away.
I'll tell you one thing certain an' sho',
Judgment Day's comin' when you don't know.
I hope to be ready when I'm called to go,
If anything's lackin', Lord, let me know.   (Grissom)

I'll Be Sleepin' In My Grave

When He calls me I will answer,
I'll be somewhere sleepin' in my grave;
When He calls me I will answer,
I'll be somewhere sleepin' in my grave.

I'll be sleeping' in my grave,
I'll be sleeping' in my grave,
I'll be somewhere sleepin' in my grave.
I'll be sleeping' in my grave,
I'll be sleeping' in my grave,
I'll be somewhere sleepin' in my grave.

When the Master calls us to Him,
I'll be somewhere sleepin' in my grave;

When the Master calls us to Him,
I'll be somewhere sleepin' in my grave.

In that great day when He calls me,
I'll be somewhere sleepin' in my grave;
In that great day when He call me,
I'll be somewhere sleepin' in my grave.

(Grissom)

In That Day

When you hear the thunder rolling,
In that day, in that day,
O, sinner, why will you die in that day?
When you see the rocks a-rending,
In that day, in that day,
O, sinner, why will you die in that day?

When you feel the earth a-reeling,
In that day, in that day,
O, sinner, why will you die in that day?
When you see the moon a-bleeding,
In that day, in that day,
O, sinner, why will you die in that day?

When you hear the trumpet a-calling,
In that day, in that day,
O, sinner, why will you die in that day?
In that day, in that day.

(Fisher)

In That Great Getting-Up Morning (1)

In that great getting-up morning,
Fare you well! Fare you well!
In that great getting-up morning,
Fare you well! Fare you well!

There's a better day a-coming,
Prayer-makers, pray no more,
Oh, preachers, fold your Bibles,
For the last soul's converted.

The Lord spoke to Gabriel:
Go look behind the alter,
Take down the silver trumpet,
Blow your trumpet, Gabriel.
Lord, how loud shall I blow it?
Blow it right calm and easy,
Do not alarm My people,
Tell them to come to judgment;
Gabriel, blow your trumpet.
Lord, how loud shall I blow it?
Loud as seven peals of thunder!
Wake the sleeping nations.

Then you'll see poor sinners rising;
Then you'll see the world on fire;

See the moon a-bleeding,
See the stars falling,
See the elements melting,
See the forked lighting,
Hear the rumbling thunder;
Earth shall reel and totter.
Then you'll see the Christians rising;
Then you'll see the righteous marching,
See them marching home to heaven.
Then you'll see my Jesus coming
With all His holy angels,
Take the righteous home to heaven,
There they'll live with God for ever.

In that great getting-up morning,
Fare you well! Fare you well!
In that great getting-up morning,
Fare you well! Fare you well!   (FJS)

In That Great Getting-Up Morning (2)

I'm going to tell you about the coming of the Savior;
Fare you well, fare you well.
I'm going to tell you about the coming of the Savior;
Fare you well, fare you well.
There's a better day a-coming,
Fare you well, fare you well.

There's a better day a-coming,
When my Lord speaks to his Father,
Says, Father, I'm tired of bearing,
Tired of bearing for poor sinner,
Oh preachers, fold your Bibles,
Prayer-makers, pray no more
For the last soul's converted.

The Lord spoke to Gabriel.
Say, go look behind the altar,
Take down the silver trumpet,
Go down to the sea-side,
Place one foot on the dry land,
Place the other on the sea,
Raise your hand to heaven,
Declare by your maker,
That time shall be no longer.

Blow your trumpet, Gabriel.
Lord, how long shall I blow it?
Blow it right calm and easy,
Do not alarm my people,
Tell them to come to judgment.

Then you see the coffins bursting,
Then you see the Christians rising,
Then you see the righteous marching,
They are marching home to heaven.
Then look upon Mount Zion,

You see my Jesus coming
With all his holy angels.
Where you running, sinner?
Judgement day is coming.

Gabriel, blow your trumpet,
Lord, how loud shall I blow it?
Loud as seven peals of thunder,
Wake the sleeping nations.
Then you see poor sinners rising,
See the dry bones a-creeping.

Then you see the world on fire,
You see the moon a-bleeding,
See the stars a-falling

See the elements melting,
See the elements melting,
See the forked lighting,
Hear the rumbling thunder.
Earth shall reel and totter,
Hell shall be uncapped,
The dragon shall be loosened.
Fare you well poor sinner.

Then you look up in the heaven,
See your mother in heaven,
While you're doomed to destruction.
When the parting word is given,
The Christian shouts to your ruin.
No mercy'll ever reach you.

Then you'll cry out for cold water,
While the Christian's shouting in glory,
Saying amen to your damnation,
Then you hear the sinner saying,
Down I'm rolling, down I'm rolling,
Then the righteous housed in heaven,
Live with God forever.

In that great getting-up morning,
Fare you well, fare you well.

                                        (Hampton)

It May Be The Las' Time

Oh, it may be,
Oh, it may be,
Oh, it may be,
It may be the las' time-uh
I don' know.

Come on, sinner, come on across,
It may be the las' time-uh,
I don' know.
Come on, sinner, don't step on the Cross,
It may be the las' time,
I don' know.

Look out, sinner, how you step on the Cross,
It may be the las' time-uh,
I don' know.
Yo' foot might slip an' yo' soul get los',
It may be the las' time,
I' don' know.

Sinner man, you better pray,
It may be the las' time-uh,
I don' know.
It won't be long 'til Judgment Day,
It may be the las' time,
I don' know.

The Bible warns you day by day,
It may be the las' time-uh,
I don' know.
That you got to change yo' wicked way,
It may be the las' time,
I don' know.

(Grissom)

I've Done What You Told Me To Do

O, Lord, I've done what you told me to do,
O, Lord, I've done what you told me to do;
O, Gabriel, come on down the line,
O, Gabriel, come on down the line;
O, gambler, you can't get on this train,
O, gambler, you can't get on this train;
O, sister, have you got your ticket signed?
O, sister, have you got your ticket signed?

In that morning, O my Lord,
In that morning, O my Lord,
In that morning when the Lord says "Hurry!"
In that morning, O my Lord.

(ANSAS)

I Want To Die Easy When I Die

I want to die easy
When I die, when I die;
I want to die easy
When I die, when I die.

I want to die easy when I die,
Shout salvation as I fly;
I want to see my mother
When I die, when I die.
I want to see my Jesus
When I die, when I die;
I want to see my Jesus
When I die, when I die.

I want to die easy
When I die, when I die;
I want to die easy
When I die, when I die.

(BANS)

John Done Saw That Number

John done saw that number,
'Way in the middle of the air;
Don't you wanta join that number,
'Way in the middle of the air?

On the right I saw a sight,
'Way in the middle of the air;
A band of Angels dressed in white,
'Way in the middle of the air.

Havin' great tribulations,
'Way in the middle of the air;

Havin' their harps in their han's,
'Way in the middle of the air.

Singin' a new song before the throne,
'Way in the middle of the air;
That Angels in Heaven could not sing,
'Way in the middle of the air.

John done saw that number,
'Way in the middle of the air;
Comin' up from hard trials,
'Way in the middle of the air.

On the left I saw no rest,
'Way in the middle of the air.
I'm gonna talk about God myse'f,
'Way in the middle of the air.

(Grissom)

John Saw The Number No Man Could Number

John saw the number that no man could number,
John saw the number that no man could number,
John saw the number that no man could number,
Comin' up, comin' up on high.
John saw the hundred and forty-thousand,
John saw the hundred and forty-thousand,
John saw the hundred and forty-thousand,
Comin' up, comin' up on high.

Tell John not to call the roll till I get there,
Tell John not to call the roll till I get there,
Tell John not to call the roll till I get there,
Sinner man, you better believe.

(St. Helena)

Jubalee (Or What Is The Matter With The Mourners?)

Jubalee, Jubalee, O, my Lord!
Jubalee, Jubalee, O, my Lord!
Jubalee, Jubalee.

What is the matter with the mourners,
O, my Lord!
The devil's in the Amen corner,
    O, Lord!
What is the matter with old Zion,
O, my Lord!
You better stop Your fooling sinner man,
O, Lord!

Jubalee, Jubalee, O, my Lord!
Jubalee, Jubalee, O, my Lord!
Jubalee, Jubalee.   (BANS)

Judgment Day Is Rolling Round

Judgment, Judgment, Judgment Day is rolling round,
Judgment, Judgment, O how I long to go.
I've a good old mother in the heaven, my Lord,
How I long to go there, too;
There's no back sliding in the heaven, my Lord,
How I long to go there too;
King Jesus sitting in the heaven, my Lord,
How I long to go there, too;
There's a big camp meeting in the heaven, my Lord,
How I long to go there, too;
Judgment, Judgment, Judgment Day is rolling round;
Judgment, Judgment, O how I long to go.   (FJS)

Judgment Day Is Trying Time

Let your light shine,
Let your light shine,
Let your light shine,
Judgment Day is trying time.

Judgment Day is trying time,
I remember the day,
I remember it well,
My dungeon shook
And my chain fell off.

We all got to appear
At the judgment bar
So get you ready
Against Gabriel's call.

You better get ready
Against Gabriel's call
Oh, Gabriel's going to make
That awful call.   (BDWS)

Judgment Will Find You So

Just as you live,
         Just as you die,
And after death,
         Judgment will find you so.
O, brethren, brethren, watch and pray,
         Judgment will find you so,
For Satan's 'round you every day,
         Judgment will find you so.

The tallest tree in paradise,
The Christian calls the tree of life,
Oh! Hallelujah to the Lamb,
The Lord is on the giving hand.

Just as you live,
         Just as you die,
And after death,
         Judgment will find you so.
O, brethren, brethren, watch and pray,
         Judgment will find you so,
For Satan's round you every day,
         Judgment will find you so.   (FJS)

Little Black Train Is A-Comin'

God tol' Hezekiah
In a message from on high:
Go set yo' house in order,
For thou shalt sholy die.
He turned to the wall an' a weepin',
Oh! See the King in tears;
He got his bus'ness fixed all right,
God spared him fifteen years.

Little black train is a-comin',
Get all yo' bus'ness right;
Go set yo' house in order,
For the train may be here tonight.

Go tell that ball room lady,
All filled with worldly pride,
That little black train is-a comin',
Prepare to take a ride.
That little black train and engine
An' a little baggage car,
With idle thoughts and wicked deeds,
Must stop at the judgment bar.

There was a po' young man in darkness,
Cared not for the gospel light,
Suddenly a whistle blew
From a little black train in sight.
"Oh, death will you not spare me?
I'm just in my wicked plight.
Have mercy, Lord, do hear me,

Pray come an' set me right."
But death had fixed his shackles
About his soul so tight,
Just befo' he got his bus'ness fixed,
The train rolled in that night.   (Grissom)

Little David

Little David, play on your harp,
    Hallelu! Hallelu!
Little David, play on your harp,
    Hallelu! Hallelu!
Little David was a shepherd boy,
He killed Goliath and shouted for joy.
Joshua was the son of Nun,
He never would quit till the work was done.
Done told you once, done told you twice,
There're sinners in hell for shooting dice.   (ANS) (Variant)

Meet, O Lord!

Meet, O Lord, on the milk-white horse,
And the anointing vial in his hand;
Drop on, drop on the crown of my head,
And roll me in my Jesus' arms.

In that morning all day,
In that morning all day,

In that morning all day,
When Jesus Christ was born.

The Moon went into the popular tree,
And the stars went into blood,
In that morning all day,
When Jesus Christ was born.   (ALLEN)

My Lord Says He's Going To Rain Down Fire

My Lord, my Lord,
My Lord says He's going to rain down fire;
My Lord, my Lord,
My Lord says He's going to rain down fire.

Pharaoh, Pharaoh,
Pharaoh and his host got drowned;
Gabriel, Gabriel,
Gabriel, blow your silver trumpet;
Peter, Peter,
Peter on the Sea of Galilee,
Take your net and follow me.

Moses, Moses,
Moses smote the Red Sea over;

Moses, Moses,
Moses smote the Red Sea over.

My Lord, my Lord,
My Lord says He's going to rain down fire;
My Lord, my Lord,
My Lord says He's going to rain down fire.   (BANS)

My Lord's Going To Move This Wicked Race

My Lord's going to move this wicked race,
My Lord's going to move this wicked race,
He's going to raise up a nation that shall obey!

Nicodemus he desired to know, desired to know,
        desired to know,
Nicodemus he desired to know
How can a man be born when he is old.
Marvel not man if you want to be wise, if
        you want to be wise, if you want to be wise,
Marvel not man if you want to be wise,
Just believe on Jesus and be baptized!

God called old Moses on the mountaintop, on
        the mountaintop, on the mountaintop,
God called old Moses on the mountaintop,
And He stamped His law on Moses' heart!   (ANSAS)

My Lord's Riding All The Time

O, He sees all you do,
And hears all you say,
My Lord's riding all the time.

When I was down in Egypt's land,
I heard a mighty talking about the promised land,
Come down, come down, my Lord, come down,
And take me up to wear the crown;
O, sinner, you had better pray,
It looks like judgement every day.

O, He sees all you do,
And hears all you say,
My Lord's riding all the time,
My Lord's riding all the time.   (Hampton)

My Lord's Writing All The Time

Come down, come down,
My Lord, come down,
And take me up to wear the crown;
King Jesus rides in the middle of the air,
He's calling sinners from everywhere.

My Lord's writing all the time,
My Lord's writing all the time,
Oh, He sees all you do,
He hears all you say,
My Lord's writing all the time.
When I was down in Egypt's land,
I hard some talk of the promised land,
Christians you had better pray,
For Satan's 'round you every day.

My Lord's writing all the time,
My Lord's writing all the time.   (BANS)

My Lord, What A Mourning

My Lord, what a mourning,
                My Lord, what a mourning,
My Lord, what a mourning,
When the stars begin to fall.

You'll hear the trumpet sound,
To wake the nations underground;
You'll hear the sinner mourn,
To wake the nations underground;
You'll hear the Christian shout,
To wake the nations underground,
Looking to my God's right hand,
When the stars begin to fall.

My Lord, what a mourning,
                My Lord, what a mourning,
My Lord, what a mourning,
When the stars begin to fall.   (FJS)

No Liar Can Stand

Oh-o, juniors, ride all around God's altar,
Oh-o, juniors, no liar can stand,
Oh-o, juniors, ride all around God's altar,
Oh-o, juniors, no liar can stand,
None can stand but the pure in heart;
No liar can stand;
None can stand when God get in anger,
No liar can stand.

None can stand God's zigzag lightning,
No liar can stand;
None can stand God's muttering thunder,
No liar can stand.
None can stand, none can stand.
No liar can stand;
O, sinner you better pray.
No liar can stand.   (BDWS)

O, Didn't It Rain

O, didn't it rain,
O, didn't it rain,
O, didn't it rain,
Some forty nights and forty days,
       forty nights and forty days;
O, my sister, you pray but you pray so slow,
You pray like you ain't going to pray no more,
O, didn't it rain, halleluja!

My preacher, you mourn but you mourn so slow;
My elder, you sing but you sing so slow;
O, didn't it rain, halleluja!

Some call Noah the foolish man
To build his house upon the sand.
O, didn't it rain, halleluja!

I asked my sister had the train gone on,
She said it was gone but it ain't been gone long;
O, didn't it rain, halleluja!

She said if I run and run right fas',
I'll overtake the train at las',
O, didn't it rain.
O, didn't it rain, halleluja!   (Calhoun) (Variant)

O, Gambler, Get Up Off Your Knees

O, gambler, get up off your knees,
O, gambler, get up off your knees,
O, gambler, get up off your knees,
End of that morning, Good Lord,
End of that morning, Good Lord,
End of that morning when the Lord said to hurry.

O, gambler, you can't ride on this train,
O, gambler, you can't ride on this train,
O, gambler, you can't ride on this train,
End of that morning, Good Lord,
End of that morning, Good Lord,
End of that morning when the Lord said to hurry.   (BANS)

Oh! Didn't It Rain

Oh! didn't it rain, Oh! didn't it rain,
Oh! didn't it rain, Oh! didn't it rain,
Some forty days and nights.

They called old Noah a foolish man,
Oh! didn't it rain.
Cause Noah built the ark upon dry land.
Oh! didn't it rain.

When it begun to rain,
Oh! didn't it rain.
Women and children begun to scream.
Oh! didn't it rain.

It rain all day and it rain all night,
Oh! didn't it rain.
It rain 'til mountaintop was out of sight.
Oh! didn't it rain.

God told Noah by the rainbow sign:
Oh! didn't it rain.
No more water but the fire next time.
Oh! didn't it rain.

Judgment Day is coming,
Coming in the Prophet's way.
Some folks say they never prayed a prayer;
They sho' will pray that day.   (Dixon)

Oh, Sinner

Oh, sinner, yo' bed's too short,
Oh, sinner, yo' bed's too short,
Oh, sinner, yo' bed's too short,
Um.......... My Lord.

Oh, sinner, you better pray,
Oh, sinner, you better pray,
Oh, sinner, you better pray,
Um.......... My Lord.

Oh, sinner, yo' time ain't long,
Oh, sinner, yo' time ain't long,
Oh, sinner, yo' time ain't long,
Um......... My Lord.

Ev'rybody's got to die sometime,
Ev'rybody's got to die sometime,
Ev'rybody's got to die sometime,
Um......... My Lord.

I'm goin' home on the mornin' train,
I'm goin' home on the mornin' train,
I'm goin' home on the mornin' train,
Um........ My Lord.   (Grissom)

Oh, Sinner, You'd Better Get Ready

Oh, sinner, you'd better get ready,
Ready, my Lord, ready,
Oh, sinner, you'd better get ready,
For the time is a-coming that sinner must die.

Oh, sinner man, you'd better pray,
Time is a-coming that sinner must die,

For it look-a like judgment every day;
Time is a-coming that sinner must die,
I heard a lumbering in the sky,
That made me think my time was nigh.

I heard of my Jesus a many one say -
Could remove poor sinner's sins away,
Yes, I'd rather pray myself away --
Than to die in hell and burn one day;
Time is a-coming that sinner must die.

I think I heard my mother say,
'Twas a pretty thing to serve the Lord;
Oh, when I get to heaven I'll be able to tell,
Oh, how I shunned that dismal bell.
Oh, sinner, you'd better get ready,
Ready, my Lord, ready,
Oh, sinner, you'd better get ready,
For the time is a-coming that sinner must die.   (Hampton)

Oh Yes, Yonder Comes My Lord

Oh, yes, yonder comes my Lord,
Oh, yes, yonder comes my Lord,
Oh, yes, yonder comes my Lord.

He is coming this way,
With His sword in his hand,
He's going to hew those sinners down.
Right level to the ground.

Oh, yes, yonder comes my Lord,
Oh, yes, yonder comes my Lord,
Oh, yes, yonder comes my Lord.   (Hampton)

O, It's Going To Be A Mighty Day

O, it's going to be a mighty day,
O, it's going to be a mighty day,
O, it's going to be a mighty day,
O, it's going to be a mighty day.

Yes, the book of Revelations to be brought forth
        on that day,
And every leaf unfolded the book of the
        seven seals.
As I went down into Egypt, I camped
        upon the ground,
At the sounding of the trumpet, the Holy
        Ghost came down.
The good old Chariot passing by,
She jarred the earth and shook the sky.
I ain't got time for to stop and talk,
The road is rough and it's hard to walk.   (ANSAS)

O, Rocks Don't Fall On Me

O, rocks, don't fall on me,
O, rocks, don't fall on me
Rocks and mountains, don't fall on me,
I'm praying, O, rocks don't fall on me.

I look over yonder on Jericho's walls,
And see them sinners tremble and fall,
O, in that great judgement day
The sinners will run to the rocks and say,
Rocks and mountains, don't fall on me.

O, every star refuses to shine,
I know that King Jesus will be mind,
The trumpet shall sound,
And the dead shall rise
And go to the mansions in the skies--
Rocks and mountains, don't fall on me.   (BANS)

O, That Sun Going Down

O, that sun going down,
O, that sun going down,
O, that sun going down,
O, that sun going down,
O, that sun going down.

O, yes, yonder come my Lord,
O, yes, yonder come my Lord,
O, yes, yonder come my Lord,
O, yes, yonder come my Lord.

He's coming this-a way
With that sword in his hand;
God's going to hew them sinners down,
O, right level with the groun'
To rise no mo'.

O, yes, yonder come my Lord,
O, yes, yonder come my Lord,
O, yes, yonder come my Lord,
O, yes, yonder come my Lord.   (Calhoun)

Poor Sinner, Fare You Well

Big camp meeting on the praying ground,
Big camp meeting on the praying ground,
Big camp meeting on the praying ground,
Poor sinner, fare you well.

Don't you feel happy on the praying ground?
Don't you feel happy on the praying ground?
Don't you feel happy on the praying ground?
Poor sinner, fare you well.

I got my religion on the praying ground,
I got my religion on the praying ground,
I got my religion on the praying ground,
Poor sinner, fare you well.

I feel a little better on the praying ground,
I feel a little better on the praying ground,
I feel a little better on the praying ground,
Poor sinner, fare you well.

Is a mighty shouting on the praying ground,
Is a mighty groaning on the praying ground,
My soul got happy on the praying ground,
Poor sinner, fare you well.   (BDWS)

Pure Religion

Oh Lord, you must have that pure religion,
You must get your soul converted,
Oh, you must have that pure religion,
Or you can't pass here.

When speaking of each other's faults,
Pray don't forget your own,
We are all of us living in a house of glass,
And we should not throw a stone.

We all have faults and who has none,
The old as well as young,
It may be so for all I know,
You have fifty to my one.

You never should judge a man
Until he's fairly tried,
For if you don't like his company,
You know the world is wide.
Oh Lord, you must have that pure religion,
You must get your soul converted,
Or you can't pass here.   (BDWS)

Remember Me

Do Lord, remember me,
Do Lord, remember me,
Will you remember me whilst the hours roll around?
Do Lord, remember me.
Oh, if you let me die like Samuel died,
Lay down in my grave
And stretch out my arms with free good will,
I'd be happy all-a my days.

Oh, when old Satan's following around,
I'll stand the test,
And be free from sin.
I'll be yours on-a that day.

Do Lord, remember me,
Do Lord, remember me,
Will you remember me whilst the hours roll around?
Do Lord, remember me.   (BDWS)

Satan's Camp A-Fire

Fire, my Savior, fire,
Satan's camp a-fire;
Fire, believer, fire,
Satan's camp a-fire.   (ALLEN)

See The Signs Of The Judgment

See the signs of the judgment,
See the signs of the judgment,
See the sign of the judgment,
The Time is drawing nigh.

Read the book O' Saint Luke,
'Bout the twenty-first chapter,
See the sign of the judgment,
The time is drawing nigh.   (ANSAS)

The Sin-Sick Soul

Brother George's gone to glory,
Take care sin-sick soul,
Brother George's gone to glory,
Take care sin-sick soul.
Brother Stephen's gone to glory,
Take care sin-sick soul.   (ALLEN)

Somebody's Calling My Name

Hush, oh, hush,
Somebody's calling my name,
Hush, oh, hush,
Somebody's calling my name,
Hush, oh, hush,
Somebody's calling my name,
Oh, my Lord,
Oh, my Lord,
What shall I do?

I'm so glad
I got my religion in time,
I'm so glad
I got my religion in time,
Oh, my Lord,
Oh, my Lord,
What shall I do?   (Traditional)

Some Of These Days

I'm gonna tell God how you treat me,
I'm gonna tell God how you treat me,
Some o' these days. Hallelujah!
I'm gonna tell God how you treat me,
I'm gonna tell God how you treat me,
Some of these days.

I'm gonna cross the river of Jordan;
I'm gonna drink o' the healin' waters;
I'm gonna drink and never get thirsty;
I'm gonna eat off the welcome table;
I'm gonna walk and talk with Jesus;
I'm gonna ride in the chariot with Jesus;
I'm gonna shout an' not be weary;
You're gonna wish that you'd-a been ready;
God's gonna set yo' sins befo' you;
God's gonna bring this world to judgment;
Some o' these days. Hallelujah!
Some o' these days.   (Grissom)

So Sad

Got to go to the judgment by myself,
An' I'm so sad;
Got to go to the judgment by myself,
An' I'm so sad;
Got to go to the judgment by myself,
An' I'm so sad.

Journey deep and journey wide,
An' I'm so sad;
Journey deep and journey wide,
An' I'm so sad;
But I got a home on the other side,
An' I'm so sad.

Don't but the one train run this track,
An' I'm so sad;
Don't but the one train run this track,
An' I'm so sad;
O, right straight back to heaven, and right straight back,
An' I'm so sad.

Two white horses standin' 'roun',
An' I'm so sad;
Two white horses standin' 'roun',
An' I'm so sad;
Two take my body to the buryin' groun',
An' I'm so sad.

Three white angel' 'roun' my bed,
An' I'm so sad;
Two white angel' 'roun' my bed,
An' I'm so sad;

Carry the news when I'm dead,
An' I'm so sad.   (Calhoun)

Stars Begin To Fall

I think I hear my brother say,
    Call the nations great and small;
I look there on God's right hand,
    When the stars begin to fall.

Oh, what a mourning, sister,
Oh, what a mourning, brother,

Oh, what a mourning,
When the stars begin to fall.   (ALLEN)

Stars In The Elements

O, the stars in the elements are falling,
And the moon drips away in the blood,
And the ransomed of the Lord are returning home to God.
O, blessed is the name of the Lord!
Don't you hear those Christians a-praying,
While the moon drips away in the blood;
Don't you hear the sinners screaming,
While the moon drips away in the blood;
Don't you hear the sinners crying,
While the moon drips away in the blood?
And the ransomed of the Lord are returning home to God.
O, blessed is the name of the Lord!   (Hampton)

Sweet Turtle Dove, Or Jerusalem Morning

Sweet turtle dove, she sings so sweet,
Muddy the water, so deep,
And we had a little meeting in the morning,
For to hear Gabriel's trumpet sound.
Jerusalem morning,
Jerusalem morning by the light,
Don't you hear Gabriel's trumpet in that morning?

Old sister Hannah, she took her seat,
And she wanted all the members to follow her,
Jerusalem morning,
Jerusalem morning by the light,
Don't you hear Gabriel's trumpet in that morning?   (Hampton)

Tall Angel At The Bar

Weeping Mary,
Tall angel at the bar;
Weeping Mary,
Tall angel at the bar.

Keep your foot up on the treadle,
Tall angel at the bar;
Keep your foot up on the treadle,
Tall angel at the bar.

Weeping Mary gone to heaven,
Mourning Martha gone to heaven,
Doubting Thomas gone to heaven,
Elisha gone to heaven.
I'm going down to Jordan,
Get your ticket ready.
Hear the train a-coming,
She's coming 'round the mountain,
She's blowing for the station,
Get your heart in order.
Tall angel at the bar,
Tall angel at the bar.   (Calhoun)

The Ten Virgins

Five of them were wise
                    when the bridegroom came,
Five of them were wise
                    when the bridegroom came.
O, Zion, O, Zion, O, Zion,
                    when the bridegroom came.

Five of them were foolish
                    when the bridegroom came,
The wise they took oil
                    when the bridegroom came;
The foolish took no oil
                    when the bridegroom came,
The foolish they kept knocking
                    when the bridegroom came,
Depart, I never knew you,
                    said the bridegroom then.
O, Zion, O, Zion, O, Zion,
                    When the bridegroom came.   (FJS)

There's A Handwriting On The Wall

There's a handwriting on the wall,
There's a handwriting on the wall,
Oh, won't you come and read it,
See what it says.

Oh, Daniel,
There's a handwriting on the wall.
Who wrote the letter?
God wrote the letter.
Tell old Nebuchadnezzar he's weighted
        in the balance and found wanting.

There's a handwriting on the wall,
There's a handwriting on the wall,

Oh, won't you come and read it,
See what it says.   (BANS)

There's A Mighty War In Heaven

There's a mighty war in heaven,
I, John, saw,
There's a mighty war in heaven,
I, John, saw,
I, John, saw the holy number.

My Lord's coming in the sky,
I, John, saw,
My Lord's coming in the sky,
I, John, saw,
My Lord's coming in the sky,
I, John, saw.

There's a mighty war in heaven,
I, John, saw,
There's a mighty war in heaven,

I, John, saw,
I, John, saw the holy numbers.   (BDWS)

There's No Hiding Place Down There

There's no hiding place down there,
There's no hiding place down there.

Oh, I went to the rock to hide my face,
The rock cried out, "No hiding place."
There's no hiding place down there.

Oh, the rock cried, "I'm burning, too,"
Oh, the rock cried, "I'm burning, too,"
Oh, the rock cried, "I'm burning, too,"
I want to go to heaven as well as you,
There's no hiding place down there.

Oh, the sinner man, he gambled and fell,
Oh, the sinner man, he gambled and fell,
Oh, the sinner man, he gambled and fell;
He wanted to go to heaven,
But he had to go to hell,
There's no hiding place down there.   (BANS)

Time Is Drawin' Nigh

See the signs of the Judgment, yes,
See the signs of the Judgment, yes,
See the signs of the Judgment, yes, Lord,
Time is drawin' nigh.

God talkin' in the lightenin', yes,
An' He's talkin' in the thunder, yes,
An' the world's all a-wonder, yes,
Time is drawin' nigh.

See the sign of the fig tree, yes,
My Jesus said it would be, yes,
The sign of the Judgment, yes, Lord,
Time is drawin' nigh.

Loose horse in the valley, yes,
Don't you hear him laughin', yes,
He's laughin' like Judgment, yes, Lord,
Time is drawin' nigh.

God told Moses, yes,
Sanctify the people, yes,
An' take to the mountains, yes, Lord,
Time is drawin' nigh.

In the city of Jerusalem, yes,
On the day of Pentecost, yes,
The people received the Holy Ghost, Lord,
Time is drawin' nigh.

Who is that yonder, yes,
Comin' from Eden, yes,
Dyed garments from Bozah, yes, Lord,
Time is drawin' nigh.
It looks like Jesus, yes,
Glorious in His appearance, yes,
Treadin' the wine press, yes, Lord,
Time is drawin' nigh.

Thy Kingdom come, yes,
Thy will be done, yes,
They'll speak in other tongues, yes, Lord,
Time is drawin' nigh.

They will hate one another, yes,
My Jesus said it would be, yes,
They'll take you in council, yes, Lord,
Time is drawin' nigh.

Have you been converted, yes,
Sanctified an' holy, yes,
Baptized with the Holy Ghost, yes, Lord,
Time is drawin' nigh.

I have my ticket, yes,
It takes a holy ticket, yes,
Signed all the way to glory, yes, Lord,
Time is drawin' nigh.

Come on, children, yes,
Let's go to glory, yes,
An' don't get tired, yes, Lord,
Time is drawin' nigh.

(Grissom)

Tomorrow You May Die

Sinner, today you better repent,
Tomorrow you may die;
Sinner, today you better repent,
Tomorrow you may die.

I remember that day,
I remember it well,
Tomorrow you may die,
When my poor soul hung over hell,
Tomorrow you may die.

Sinner, today you better repent,
Tomorrow you may die;
Sinner, today you better repent,
Tomorrow you may die.

I'm born of God,
I know I am,
Tomorrow you may die,
And you dispute it if you can,
Tomorrow you may die.   (Fisher)

Too Late (1)

Too late, too late, sinner,
Too late, too late, sinner,
Carried the key and gone home.
Master Jesus locked the door,
O, Lord! too late;
Master Jesus locked the door,
Carried the key and gone home.

Too late, too late, false pretender,
Too late, too late, back-slider,
Carried the key and gone home.
Master Jesus locked the door,
O, Lord! too late;
Master Jesus locked this door,
Carried the key and gone home.   (BANS)

What A Trying Time

Adam, where are you?
O Adam, where are you?
O Adam, where are you?
O what a trying time!

Lord, I'm in the Garden,
Lord, I'm in the Garden,
Lord, I'm in the Garden,
O what a trying time!

Adam, you ate the apple,
Adam, you ate the apple,

Adam, you ate the apple,
O what a trying time!

Lord, Eve she gave it to me;
Lord, Eve she gave it to me;
Lord, Eve she gave it to me;
O what a trying time!

Adam, it was forbidden,
Adam, it was forbidden,
Adam, it was forbidden,
O what a trying time!

Lord said, "Walk out the Garden,"
Lord said, "Walk out the Garden,"
O what a trying time!   (Fisher)

What You Going To Do When Your Lamp Burns Down

O, poor sinner,
O, now is your time,
O, poor sinner,
O, now is your time,
What you going to do when your lamp burns down?

Find the East, find the West,
Fire going to burn down the wilderness;
They whipped Him up and they whipped Him down,
They whipped that man all over town.
They nailed His hands and they nailed His feet,
The hammer was heard on Jerusalem street,
O, poor sinner,
O, now is your time,
What you going to do when your lamp burns down?   (BANS)

Where Shall I Be When That First Trumpet Soun'?

Where shall I be when that first trumpet soun',
Where shall I be when it soun' so loud,
When it soun' so loud till it wake up the dead,
Where shall I be when it soun'?

Going to try on my robe
When the first trumpet soun';
Going before the bar
When the first trumpet soun';
Going to see my Lord
When the firs' trumpet soun'.   (Calhoun)

Where Shall I Be When That First Trumpet Sounds?

Where shall I be when the first trumpet sounds?
Where shall I be when it sounds so loud?
Sounds so loud till it wake up the dead,
Where shall I be when it sounds?

Moses died in the days of old,
Where shall I be?
Where he was buried has never been told,
Oh, where shall I be?

God gave the people the rainbow sign,
Where shall I be?
No more water but fire next time,
Where shall I be?

Where shall I be when the first trumpet sounds?
Where shall I be when it sounds so loud?
Sounds so loud till it wake up the dead,
Where shall I be when it sounds?   (Hampton)

Yo' Sins Are Gonna Find You Out

You can run a long time
With the cover of the world pulled over yo' face;
You can run a long time,
But yo' sins are gonna find you out.

We have some people in the church,
You have often heard it said,
You cannot live that holy life
'Til you get on yo' dyin' bed.

We have some people in the church
Who love to sing an' pray;
They love to shout an' testify,
But take the Bible away.

Just let me tell you about a liar,
He will not do to trust;
He will tell a lie to make a fuss,
And tell another to make it worse.
I can see that sister shoutin',
She seems to be mighty glad;
But as soon as you preach the Bible true,
You are sure to make her mad.
We have some people in the church,
Believes in having two wives;
An' when you call him to council,
His temper will begin to rise.

We have some preachers in the church,
With a wife an' a sweetheart, too;
They seem to be living satisfied,
But God has a time for you.

Some preachers out a preachin',
Just for the preacher's name;
The gospel they are preachin',
It is a scandal an' a shame.

Preachers in the pulpit preachin',
Seem to talk mighty sweet;
But the reason they don't like holiness,
They want to court every sister they meet.

Some women love other women's husbands
They ought to be loving their own;
If you ain't got one you better get one,
To be ready when the judgment comes.

You say you been converted,
Be sure you have not lied;
They tell me in my Father's house,
They are holy an' sanctified.

(Grissom)

You Better Run To The City Of Refuge

You better run, you better run,
You better run to the city of refuge,
You better run.

There was some he prayed and prevail--
They caught him at Jerusalem and put him in jail--
He stand his trial in the name of the Lord.
For he know he had a buildin' not made with hand.

Daniel sat in the lion's den,
By the hand of wicked men;
Prayed to the Lord and the Lord come down,
And the jaws of the lion they were boun'.

Now you better run, you better run,
You better run to the city of refuge,
You better run.

(St. Helena)

You Can't Find A New Hidin' Place

You can't find a new hidin' place,
You can't find a new hidin' place.

If religion was a thing that money could buy,
The rich would live and the po' would die.
You can't find a new hidin' place.
You can't find a new hidin' place.

But I thank the Lord that it is not so,
The rich and the po' together must go.
You can't find a new hidin' place.
You can't find a new hidin' place.

I run to the rocks and the rocks fall in,
I run to the sea and the sea run dry.
You can't find a new hidin' place.
You can't find a new hidin' place.

(St. Helena)

You'd Better Mind

You'd better mind how you talk,
You'd better mind what you talk about,
For you got to give account in Judgment,
You'd better mind.

You'd better mind how you sing,
You'd better mind what you sing about,
For you got to give account in Judgment,
You'd better mind.

You'd better mind how you shout,
You'd better mind what you shout about,
For you got to give account in Judgment,
You'd better mind.   (ANSAS)

You'd Better Run

You'd better run, run, run-a-run,
You'd better run, run, run-a-run,
You'd better run to the city of refuge,
You'd better run, run, run.

God sent old Jonah to the Ninevah land,
He didn't obey my God's command,
The wind blew the ship from shore to shore,
A whale swallowed Jonah and he wasn't no more.
He had to run, run, run.
He had to run, run, run.

Read about Samson from his birth,
He was the strongest man on earth,
He lived way back in ancient times,
He killed about a thousand Philistines.
He had to run, run, run.
He had to run, run, run.   (ANS)

You May Bury Me In The East

You may bury me in the East,
You may bury me in the West,
But I'll hear that trumpet sound
In that morning.
In that morning, my Lord,
How I long to go for to hear
The trumpet sound in that morning.

Father Gabriel in that day,
He'll take wings and fly away,
For to here the trumpet sound
In that morning.

In that dreadful judgment day,
I'll take wings and fly away.   (Khrehbiel)

Your Low Down Ways

Your low down ways, your low down ways,
God's going to get you about your low down ways,
God's going to get you about your low down ways.

You talk about your elder when he's tryin to
                                    preach the word,
You talk about your neighbor when he's tryin to
                                    praise the Lord,
You talk about your sister when she's on her
                                    knees praying.

Your low down ways, your low down ways,
God's going to get you about your low down ways,
God's going to get you about your low down ways.   (ANS)

You Shall Reap

You shall reap just what you sow,
You shall reap just what you sow,
On the mountain, in the valley,
You shall reap just what you sow.

Brother, sister, sinner,
You shall reap just what you sow,
On the mountains, in the valley,
You shall reap just what you sow.   (ANS)

LYRICS OF
REGENERATION _____

Since American slavery sought to thwart the natural development of the Africans in their movement toward adulthood and sought systematically to distort the African's sense of being in the world, the enslaved Africans were constantly challenged by forces of demoralization. Knowing that they were in the midst of corruption and were confronted with attempts to render them degenerate, the captives created many lyrics that reveal to us how they sought to keep themselves charged with the life-force. Thus the Africans in America sang, for example, of the ritual of baptism as an invigorating and electrifying experience as well as a cleansing experience.

In many traditional African societies, rivers and living water areas were thought of as the habitats of the spirits. These aqueous areas were the connecting points between this world and the next.[1] Thus, by singing of immersing oneself into the ritual waters, the enslaved Africans not only envisioned becoming purified of corruption, as in the Christian sense, but, in the African sense, they also made an essential reconnection with the forces of power and of life. And, too, it is certainly not to be overlooked that through the composing and singing of these lyrics, Christianity, as it had been handed to the captives in a corrupt form, was also being redeemed and regenerated. Moreover, the composers of these songs, in their widest range, utilized any manifestation or testimonial regarding the existence of a spiritual reality or spiritual presence as a means of rekindling the spirit force within themselves and their fellows. Even further, the captives remembered that in the essential African worldview, human life needs the guidance of the spiritual world. Thus, they knew that in order to receive this guidance, they had to involve themselves periodically in the rituals of preparation for renewal.

_____

1. Sterling Stuckey, SLAVE CULTURE. New York: Oxford University Press, 1987, p.34.

All The Way To Calvary

O, I had many, many sins,
But He taken them all away
When He sanctified me.
All the way to Calvary
He went for me.
All the way to Calvary
He went for me.

O, I had so many, many fears,
But He taken them all away
When He sanctified me.

O, I had so many, many doubts,
But He taken them all away
When He sanctified me.
All the way to Calvary
He went for me.   (Calhoun)

Angel Done Changed My Name

Angel done changed my name,
Angel done changed my name,
Done changed my name from natural to grace.

Angel done changed my name,
So glad angel done changed my name,
I know angel done changed my name,
Jesus told me angel done changed my name.

Fare you well,
Fare you well,
Angel done changed my name;
How you know?
Jesus told me;
Angel done changed my name.

Angel done changed my name,
Angel done changed my name,
Done changed my name from natural to grace,
Angel done changed my name.   (BDWS)

Baptizing

Baptizing begin,
        Baptizing begin,
Oh! hallelujah!
Baptizing begin,
Baptizing begin.
Oh halle, oh halle, oh hallelujah!
John came down to the waterside
To examine poor sinners
And see what he'd find.

Oh, Jesus came down to this sinful earth,
For to save God's children
From the pains of hell.

Oh, get your religion and get it now,
For the day is coming
You'll appear at the judgement bar.   (BDWS)

Been Washed In The Blood

Redeemed, redeemed,
Been washed in the blood of the Lamb,
I've been redeemed, redeemed,
Been washed in the blood of the Lamb.

Joshua was the son of Nun,
Asked God almighty to stop the sun,

Stop the sun 'til the battle was won;
Battle was won at the hour of seven.

Trumpets blew and the children shouted,
Oh the wall fell down,
God heard it in heaven.

Watch the sun how it runs,
Never let it catch you,
With your work undone.

Sinner jumped from the bottom of the well,
Swore by God he's just from hell.
Don't say he didn't and I don't say he did
But I say if he did,
He did damn well.   (BDWS)

The Book Of Life

Brother Joe, you ought to know my name,
Hallelujah,
My name is written in the book of life;
If you look in the book you'll find it there.

One morning I was a-walking down,
I saw the berry hanging down, Lord,
I picked the berry and I sucked the juice,
Just as sweet as the honey in the comb,
I wonder when father Jimmy's gone,
My father's gone to the yonder world.

You dig the spring that's never dry,
The more I dig, the water springs,
The water springs that's never dry.   (Allen)

Come Unto Me

Can't you hear what my Lord said,
Can't you hear what my Lord said,
Can't you hear?
Can't you hear what my Lord said,
Come unto me an' be saved.

Oh, if you are a gambler,
Come unto me,
Come unto me,
Come unto me.
Oh, if you are a gambler,
Come unto me.
Come unto me an' be saved.

Oh, if you are a liar,
Come unto me,
Come unto me,
Come unto me.
Oh, if you are a liar,
Come unto me.
Come unto me an' be saved.

Oh, if you are a murderer,
Come unto me,
Come unto me,
Come unto me.
Oh, if you are a murderer,
Come unto me.
Come unto me an' be saved.

Oh, if you are a sinner,
Come unto me,
Come unto me,
Come unto me,
Oh, if you are a sinner,
Come unto me.
Come unto me an' be saved.   (Grissom)

Don't Be Weary, Traveller

Don't be weary, traveller,
Come along home to Jesus;
Don't be weary, traveller, traveller,
Come along home to Jesus.

My head got wet with the midnight dew,
Angels bear me witness too;
Where to go I did not know
Ever since He freed my soul;
I look at the world and the world looks new,
I look at the world and the world looks new.

Don't be weary, traveller,
Come along home to Jesus;

Don't be weary, traveller, traveller,
Come along home to Jesus.   (Allen)

Drive Satan Away

Takes a pure in heart to drive Satan away,
Takes a pure in heart to drive Satan away,
No pretender can't drive Satan away,
No pretender can't drive Satan away.
Drive Satan away, drive Satan away,
Drive Satan a-out of my heart, drive Satan away.

Takes a happy soul to drive Satan away,
Takes a happy soul to drive Satan away,

No unhappy soul can't drive Satan away,
No unhappy soul can't drive Satan away.

No liar can't drive Satan away,
No liar can't drive Satan away.
Can't you help me to drive satan away,
Can't you help me to drive Satan away.
Drive Satan away, drive Satan away,
Drive Satan a-out of my heart, drive Satan away.   (Calhoun)

Dry Bones Going To Rise Again

All them bones,
All them bones,
In the morning,
All them bones,
Dry bones going to rise again.

Some of them bones my mother's bones,
Some of them bones my father's bones,
Dry bones going to rise again.

Sinners go to meeting house to sing and shout,
But the preacher surely will turn them out,
Dry bones going to rise again.

If you want to get a seat in heaven on high,
Don't you steal, don't you 'dulter, and don't you lie,
Dry bones going to rise again.

Got my religion and I got it good and strong,
'Cause God almighty never done me wrong,
Dry bones going to rise again.   (BDWS)

Every Time I Feel The Spirit

Every time I feel the spirit moving in my heart
     I will pray,
Every time I feel the spirit moving in my heart
     I will pray.

Upon the mountain my Lord spoke,
Out of his mouth came fire and smoke;
All around me looks so fine,
Asked my Lord if all was mine;
Jordan river is chilly and cold,
Chills the body but not the soul,

Every time I feel the Spirit moving in my heart
          I will pray.
Every time I feel the Spirit moving in my heart
          I will pray.   (Hampton)

Fare Ye Well

O, fare you well, my brother,
Fare you well by the grace of God,
For I'm going home;
I'm going home, my Lord,
I'm going home.
Master Jesus gave me a little broom,
To sweep my heart clean,

Sweep it clean by the grace of God,
And glory in my soul.   (Allen)

Fix Me, Jesus

Oh, fix me, Jesus, fix me right,
Fix me right, fix me right;
Oh, fix me, Jesus, fix me right,
Fix me so I can stand.

Oh, place my feet on solid ground,
Oh, place my feet on solid ground;
Oh, when I die, you must bury me deep,
Oh, when I die, you must bury me deep;
Oh, dig my grave with a silver spade,
Oh, dig my grave with a silver spade;
And let me down with a golden chain,
And let me down with a golden chain.

Oh, fix me, Jesus, fix me right,
Fix me right, fix me right;
Oh, fix me, Jesus, fix me right,
Fix me so I can stand.   (CD)

The Gift Of God

O, the gift of God is eternal life,
          eternal life,
O, the gift of God is eternal life,
          eternal life,
And the wages of sin is death.
When I was seeking Jesus

And thought he couldn't be found,
The grace of God came into my soul,
And turned me all around.

When first I got converted,
I had no doubts at all,
But I've had so many crosses
That I feel the least of all.
I wonder where's my dear mother,
She's been gone so long;
I think I hear her shouting
Around the throne of God.

Yonder comes my brother
Whom I loved so well,
But by his disobedience
Has made his home in hell.

(ANS) (Variant)

Give Up The World

My brother, won't you give up the world,
My brother, won't you give up the world,
My brother, won't you give up the world,
Hear what my Jesus say?
Pray a little longer, give up the world,
Pray a little longer, give up the world.

Pretender, won't you give up the world,
Backslider, won't you give up the world,
Hypocrite, won't you give up the world,
Hear what my Jesus say?
Pray a little longer, give up the world,
Pray a little longer, give up the world.

(Calhoun)

God's Going To Trouble The Water

Wade in the water, children,
Wade in the water, children,
Wade in the water, children,
God's going to trouble the water.

See that host all dressed in white,
The leader looks like the Israelite;
See that band all dressed in red,
Looks like the band that Moses led.

Wade in the water, children,
Wade in the water, children,
Wade in the water, children,
God's going to trouble the water.

(BANS)

Going to Heaven

The book of revelation God to us revealed,
Mysteries of salvation,

The book of seven seals.
Going to heaven, going to Heaven,
Going to heaven to see that bleeding Lamb.

John saw the heavens open,
The Conqueror riding down,
He looked and saw white horses;
And rider following on.
If you want to know the Conqueror,
He is the word of God,
His eyes are like a burning throne,
He is the word of God.
Hosanna to the Prince of Life,
Who clothed Himself in clay,
And entered the iron gate of death,
And bore the ties away.
See how the conqueror mounts aloft.
And to his Father flies.
With scars of honor on His flesh,
And trails in His eyes.   (Hampton)

Going To Toll In My Jesus' Arms

Going to roll in my Jesus' arms,
Going to roll in my Jesus' arms,
On the other side of Jordan.

I really do remember when wandering in my sins,
The Lord has spoken to me.
He has taken my spirit in.
Yes!
Going to roll in my Jesus' arms.

I used to have some playmates
To walk and talk with me,
But now I'm on the bed of affliction
They turn their backs on me.
Yes!
Going to roll in my Jesus' arms.

When we get to the New Jerusalem
And with those angels blest,
Going to talk about all of my troubles,
Going to roll on my Jesus' breast.
Yes!
Going to roll in my Jesus' arms.

You talk about your playmates,
You talk about your friends,
But when you lose your mother,
You lost your onliest friend.
Yes!
Going to roll in my Jesus' arms.
Going to roll in my Jesus' arms,
Going to roll in my Jesus' arms,
On the other side of Jordan.   (Calhoun)

The Good Old Way

As I went down in the valley to pray,
Studying about that good old way,
When you shall wear the starry crown,
Good Lord, show me the way.

O mourner, let's go down,
Let's go down, let's go down,

O mourner, let's go down,
Down in the valley to pray.

(Allen)

Got My Letter

Got my letter, got my letter,
Got my letter, got my letter,
Got my letter going to hail the train.
Fisherman Peter out on the sea,
Stop your fishing, come and follow me;
I got my religion from out the sun,
I clapped my hands and began to run;
You can weep like a willow, you can mourn like
    a dove,
But you can't get to heaven without Christian
    love.

(ANSAS)

Hallelujah!

Hallelujah! and a hallelujah!
Hallelujah, Lord!
I been down into the sea.

O, I've been to the sea,
And I done been tired,
I've been to the sea,
And I've been baptized.

Christians, can't you rise and tell,
The glories of Immanuel?
If you don't believe I've been redeemed,
Just watch my face for the gospel gleam.

I'm born of God I know I am;
I'm purchased by the dying Lamb.

Hallelujah! and a hallelujah!
Hallelujah, Lord!
I been down into the sea.

(BANS)

He's The Lord Of Lords

Why, He's the Lord of Lords,
And the King of Kings,

Why Jesus Christ is the first and the last,
No one can work like Him.

I will not let you go my Lord,
Until you come and bless my soul;
For Paul and Silas bound in jail,
The Christians prayed both night and day.
I wish those mourners would believe
That Jesus is ready to receive.

Why, He's the Lord of lords
And the King of kings,
Why Jesus Christ is the first and the last,
No one can work like Him.   (Hampton)

Holy Is My God

Holy, holy, holy is my God!
Holy, holy, I'm a new born again.

Paul and Silas boun' in jail,
I'm a new born again,
I been a long time talking about trying for to pray.

One did sing while the other prayed,
I'm a new born again.
Fisherman Peter 'round the sea,
I'm a new born again.
Drop your net and follow me,
I'm a new born again.

Holy, holy, holy is my God!
Holy, holy, I'm a new born again.   (Calhoun)

How Can I Pray?

How can I pray, how can I pray,
How can I pray when my heart is burdened down?

Crown me, O, Lord,
Crown me, O, Lord,
Crown me, O, Lord,
Crown me, O, Lord,
When my heart is burdened down.

Down on my knees,
Down on my knees,
Down on my knees,
Down on my knees,
When my heart is burdened down.

Oh, Devil's in the way,
Oh, Devil's in the way,
Oh, Devil's in the way,
Oh, Devil's in the way,
When my heart is burdened down.

Pray all night sometime,
Pray all night sometime,
Pray all night sometime,
Pray all night sometime,
When my heart is burdened down.

King Jesus is my friend,
King Jesus is my friend,
King Jesus is my friend,
King Jesus is my friend,
When my heart is burdened down.

(St. Helena)

Humble

Humble, humble, humble,
Humble, humble, humble,
Down in your soul you better get you humble,
Humble, humble, humble,
Humble in my soul,
Oh, in my soul.

Stop and let me tell you about Chapter One:
The Lord God's work has just begun;
Stop and let me tell you about Chapter Two:
The Lord let them mourners through;
Stop and let me tell you about Chapter Three:
The Lord, he set them prisoners free;
Stop and let me tell you about Chapter Four:
The Lord God visit among the poor.

God sent Jonah to Ninevah land,
Jonah disobey his Lord's command,
God cause a mighty big wind to blow,
Tossed that ship from sho' to sho';
The ship kept a-rocking from side to side,
The captain and the mate got worried in mind.
Captain said, "This has got to stop.
"Go search the ship from bottom to top."
They found ol' Jonah fast asleep,
The throwed ol' Jonah in the briny deep.
A whale come along and swallowed him whole,
And spit ol' Jonah on the Ninevah sho'!

Boom, boom, boom,
Humble, humble, humble,
Down in your soul you better get humble,
Oh, in my soul.

(Schirmer)

I Am The True Vine

I am the true vine, I am the true vine,
I am the true vine,
My Father is the husbandman.

I am in Him, and He's in me,
Every day he comforts me;

I know my Lord has set me free,
I'm in Him and He's in me;
I know my Lord is kind and true,
For he loves me and He loves you.

(ANSAS)

I Believe I'll Go Back Home

I believe I'll go back home,
I believe I'll go back home,
I believe I'll go back home,
An' acknowledge I done wrong.

When I was in my Father's house,
I was well supplied;
I made a mistake in doin' well,
An' now I'm dissatisfied.

When I was in my Father's house,
I had peace all the time;
But when I left home an' went astray,
I had to feed the swine.

When the Prodigal son first left home,
He was feelin' happy an' gay;
But he soon found out a riotous life
Was more than he could pay.

When I was in my Father's house,
I had bread enough to spare;
But now I am naked an' hungry, too,
An' I'm ashamed to go back there.

When I left home I was in royal robes,
An' sumptuously fed;
But I soon got ragged an' hungry, too,
An' come back home so sad.

When I get home I'll confess my sins,
And Father's love embrace;
I'm no more worthy to be called thy son,
I'll seek a servant's place.

When his Father saw him comin',
He met him with a smile;
"He threw his arms around him...
"Here comes my lovin' child!"
He spake unto his servants--
"Go kill the fatted calf;
An' call my friends an neighbors,
My son has come at last."

His oldest son got jealous,
And he began to say:
"You did more for my brother,
Who left and went away."
He spake unto his eldest son--
It was an humble mind--

"Son, you have always been with me,
An' all I have is thine."

They met together rejoicing,
I imagine it was fine;
The old man he got happy,
An' he was satisfied in mind.   (Grissom)

If You Want To See Jesus

If you want to see Jesus,
Go in the wilderness,
Go in the wilderness,
Go in the wilderness;
If you want to see Jesus,
Go in the wilderness
Leaning on the Lord.

Oh, brother how do you feel,
When you come out the wilderness?
I felt so happy
When I come out the wilderness,
I heard the angels singing,
When I come out the wilderness,
I heard the harps a-harping,
When I come out the wilderness.

I heard the angels moaning,
When I come out the wilderness,
I gave the devil a battle,
When I come out the wilderness,
Leaning on the Lord.   (Hampton)

I Got A New Name

I got a new name over in Zion,
I got a new name over in Zion,
I got a new name over in Zion,
Well, it's mine, mine, mine,
I declare it's mine.

I got a mother over in Zion,
I got a mother over in Zion,
I got a mother over in Zion,
Well, she's mine, mine, mine,
I declare she's mine.

I got a father over in Zion,
I got a father over in Zion,
Well, he's mine, mine, mine,
I declare he's mine.

I got a new name over in Zion,
I got a new name over in Zion,
I got a new name over in Zion,

Well, it's mine, mine, mine,
I declare it's mine.   (L-G)

I Have A Leader Over There

I have a leader over there,
I have a leader over there,
I have a leader over there.

Play on your harp, little David,
Play on your harp, little David,
Play on your harp, little David.

I have a Savior over there,
I have a Savior over there,
I have a Savior over there.

I'm going over there,
I'm going over there,
I'm going over there.

In the Kingdom of my Lord,
Trumpet of God going to sound,
Remember, if you die in Christ you going to shine,
In the Resurrection morning you got to shine.   (St. Helena)

I'm Going To Wait Till The Holy Ghost Come

I'm goin' to wait,
I'm goin' to wait,
I'm goin' to wait till the Holy Ghost come,
O, my Lord, have mercy now.
I'm goin' to sing,
I'm goin' to sing,
I'm goin' to sing till the Holy Ghost come,
O, my Lord, have mercy now.

I'm goin' to watch,
I'm goin' to watch,
I'm goin' to watch till the Holy Ghost come,
O, my Lord, have mercy now.

I'm goin' to pray,
I'm goin' to pray,
I'm goin' to pray till the Holy Ghost come,
O, my lord, have mercy now.   (St. Helena)

I'm So Glad

I'm so glad, I'm so glad,
I'm so glad I've been in the grave and rose again.

I'll tell you how I found the Lord,
With a hung down head and aching heart;
My soul is bound for that bright land,

And there I'll meet that happy band;
I'll go to heaven and take my seat
And cast my crown at Jesus' feet.   (ANS)

In The River Of Jordan

In the river of Jordan, John baptized;
        How I long to be baptized;
In the river of Jordan, John baptized
        To the dying Lamb.

Pray on, pray on, ye mourning souls;
Pray on, pray on, unto the dying Lamb.

We baptize all that come by faith,
        How I long to be baptized.
Here's another one come to be baptized,
        How I long to be baptized.

Pray on, pray on, ye mourning souls,
Pray on, pray on, unto the dying Lamb.   (FJS)

I've Been Redeemed

I've been redeemed, I've been redeemed,
I've been redeemed, I've been redeemed,
Been washed in the blood of the Lamb,
Been washed in the blood of the Lamb,
That flows from Calvary.

There is a fountain filled with blood,
Drawn from Immanuel's veins;
And sinners plunged beneath that flood,
Lose all their guilt and stains.
The dying thief rejoiced to see,
That fountain in his day;
And there may I though vile as he,
Wash all my sins away.

I've been redeemed, I've been redeemed,
I've been redeemed, I've been redeemed,
Been washed in the blood of the Lamb,
Been washed in the blood of the Lamb,
That flows from Calvary.   (FJS)

I've Just Come From The Fountain

I've just come from the fountain,
        I've just come from the fountain, Lord!
I've just come from the fountain,
        His name so sweet.

Been drinking from the fountain,
Been drinking from the fountain, Lord!
His name so sweet.

I found free grace at the fountain,
     I found free grace at the fountain,
My soul's set free at the fountain,
     My soul's set free at the fountain.

O, brothers, I love Jesus.
O, preachers, I love Jesus.

O, sinners, I love Jesus.
His name so sweet.   (FJS)

I Wanta Live So God Can Use Me

I wanta live so God can use me,
Victorious, in this lan';
I wanta live so God can use me,
Victorious, in this lan'.

I wanta walk so God can use me,
Victorious, in this lan';
I wanta walk so God can use me,
Victorious, in this lan'.

I wanta pray so God can use me,
Victorious, in this lan';
I wanta pray so God can use me,
Victorious, in this lan'.

I wanta sing so God can use me,
Victorious, in this lan';
I wanta sing so God can use me,
Victorious, in this lan'.

I wanta work so God can use me,
Victorious, in this lan';
I wanta work so God can use me,
Victorious, in this lan'.

I wanta preach so God can use me,
Victorious, in this lan';
I wanta preach so God can use me,
Victorious,in this lan'.

Treat my sisters so God can use me,
Victorious, in this lan';
Treat my sisters so God can use me,
Victorious, in this lan'.

Treat my brothers so God can use me,
Victorious, in this lan';
Treat my brothers so God can use me,
Victorious, in this lan'.

Treat my children so God can use me,
Victorious, in this lan';

Treat my children so God can use me,
Victorious, in this lan'.

Treat my neighbors so God can use me,
Victorious, in this lan';

Treat my neighbors so God can use me
Victorious, in this lan'.   (Grissom)

I Wants To Climb Up Jacob's Ladder

I wants to climb up Jacob's ladder,
Up Jacob's ladder, up Jacob's ladder;
I wants to climb up Jacob's ladder,
But I can't until I make my peace with the Lord;
I will praise ye the Lord,
I will praise Him till I die,
I will praise Him till I die,
In the new Jerusalem.

I wants to pray like paul and Silas,
But I can't until I make my peace with the Lord;
I will praise ye the Lord,
I will praise Him till I die,
In the new Jerusalem,
I will praise Him till I die.

I wants to sing in Heaven with the angel,
But I can't until I make peace with the Lord;
I wants to climb up higher and higher,
But I can't until I make peace with the Lord;
I will praise ye the Lord,
I will praise Him till I die,
In the new Jerusalem,
I will praise Him till I die.   (St. Helena)

I Want To Die Lie Lazarus

I want to die like-a Lazarus died,
Die like-a Lazarus died;
I want to die like-a Lazarus died,
Like-a Lazarus died,
Like-a Lazarus died.   (Allen)

I Want To See Jesus In The Morning

In the morning,
O, in the morning,
I want to see Jesus in the morning.

I want to see my Jesus at the breaking of the day,
I want to see my Jesus at the rising of the sun;
I want to see my Jesus in the morning,
I want to see my Jesus when the sinner man runs;
I want to see my Jesus in the morning.

I want to see my Jesus when the tombstone busted,
I want to see my Jesus in the morning;
I want to see my Jesus when this world's on fire,
I want to see my Jesus in the morning;

I want to see my Jesus when the dead be rising,
I want to see my Jesus in the morning.   (BDWS)

I Will Pray

Every time I feel the Spirit moving in my heart, I will pray.
When you hear me pray, my Jesus,
When you see me on my knees,
When you hear me calling, Jesus,
Hear me, Jesus, if you please.

Jesus died for every sinner,
Jesus died for you and me,
Jesus died for Jew and Gentile,
Jesus died upon the tree.

Jesus Christ, the son of David,
Jesus Christ, the Lord of all,
Jesus Christ, the King of heaven,
Jesus, hear me when I call.   (ANS)

Jacob's Ladder Long And Tall

Jacob's ladder long an' tall,
Jacob's ladder long an' tall,
Jacob's ladder long an' tall,
If you ain't got grace, you boun' to fall.

Carried my Lord away,
Laid Him away,
Stole Him away.
Going to show where to find Him.

Sinful Peter, sinful Paul,
Sinful Peter, sinful Paul,
Sinful Peter, sinful Paul,
If you ain't got grace, you boun' to fall.

Carried my Lord away,
Laid Him away,
Stole Him away.
Going to show where to find Him.   (Calhoun)

Jesus Blood Done Make Me Whole

Jesus blood done make me whole,
Jesus blood done make me whole,
Since I touched the hem of His garment,
Jesus blood done make me whole.

I don't feel like I used to feel,
I don't feel like I used to feel,
Since I touched the hem of His garment,
I don't feel like I used to feel.

I don't mourn like I used to mourn;
I don't walk like I used to walk,
I don't talk like I used to talk,
I don't sing like I used to sing.

Jesus blood done make me whole,
Jesus blood done make me whole,

Since I touched the hem of His garment,
Jesus blood done make me whole.   (St. Helena)

Jordan's Mills

Jordan's mill's a-grinding, Jordan's a-hay;
Jordan's mill's a-grinding, Jordan's a-hay.

Built without nail or hammer.
Runs without wind or water.

Jordan's mill's a-grinding, Jordan's a-hay;
Jordan's mill's a-grinding; Jordan's a-hay.   (Allen)

Just Now

Sanctify me, sanctify me,
Sanctify me, sanctify me,
Sanctify me, just now;
Just now, just now,
Sanctify me, just now.   (Allen)

Keep The Ark A-Moving

Let's keep the ark a-moving,
Let's keep the ark a-moving,
Let's keep the ark a-moving,
For to hear what Jesus says.
My brother says go on, go on, go on,
My mother says go on, go on, go on,
That upright says go on, go on, go on,
The elder says, says go on, go on, go on,
Old Nora says, says go on, go on, go on,
For to hear what Jesus says.   (BDWS)

King Jesus Sitting On The Water Side

Do Lord, come show me the way,
Do Lord, come show me the way,

Do Lord, come show me the way,
King Jesus sitting on the waterside.

Old sheep, you know the way,
Old sheep, you know the way,
Young lamb, come learn the way,
Young lamb, come learn the way,
King Jesus sitting on the waterside.

Oh, how long before we'll go,
How long before we'll go,

How long before we'll go,
King Jesus sitting on the water side.

When I know I'll show you the way,
When I know I'll show you the way,

When I know I'll show you the way,
King Jesus sitting on the waterside.   (BDWS)

Lead Me To The Rock

Lead me, lead me, my Lord,
Lead me to the Rock that is higher than I.

The man who loves to serve the Lord,
Will surely get his just reward;
As I go down the stream of time,
I leave this sinful world behind;
Old Satan's mad and I am glad,
He missed the soul be thought he had.

O, lead me, lead me, my Lord,
Lead me to the Rock that is higher than I.   (ANS)

Let Us Go Down To Jordan

Then, let us go down to Jordan,
Let us go down to Jordan,
Let us go down to Jordan,
Religion is so sweet.

You must believe to be baptized,
Be baptized, be baptized,
You must believe to be baptized,
Religion is so sweet.

You must repeat and be baptized,
I'm going down to Jordan to get baptized,
Waters of Jordan are chilly and cold
Religion is so sweet.

I been down to Jordan and I been baptized,
I been baptized in Jesus' name,
I been tried by the water and didn't get lost,

I been tried by the fire and didn't get burnt,
Religion is so sweet.

(BDWS)

Little Children You Better Believe

Little children, you better believe,
I'm most done waggling with the crosses;
Little children, you better believe,
I'll get home to heaven by and by.

My knee bones is-a aching,
My body is racking with pain,

If you don't believe I'm a child of God,
Meet me on the other shore.

Yonder comes my mother,
She walks like she don't mind crosses,
But hard crosses is her name,
Still she's marching along.

My old grey headed father
Is not fitting to die,
Is not fitting to die,
Or either face the crossing.

All you see me lingering,
Lay me down to die,
Lay my body down to die,
My soul's got a resting place.

If you want to be a soldier,
You must stand a soldier's fare,
If you can't stand the trials,
You can't enter there.

(BDWS)

Little Wheel Turning In My Heart

There's a little wheel turning in my heart,
There's a little wheel turning in my heart,
In my heart, in my heart,
There's a little wheel turning in my heart.
O, I feel so very happy in my heart,
In my heart, in my heart,
O, I feel so very happy in my heart.

O, I don't feel no ways tired in my heart,
In my heart, in my heart,
O, I don't feel no ways tired in my heart.

O, I feel like shouting in my heart,
In my heart, in my heart,
O, I feel like shouting in my heart.

I've a double determination in my heart,
In my heart, in my heart,
I've a double determination in my heart.   (Hampton)

Look What A Wonder Jesus Done

Look what a wonder Jesus done,
    Sinner believe--
Look what a wonder Jesus done,
    Sinner believe--
Look what a wonder Jesus done,
    Sinner believe--
King Jesus had died for me.

King Jesus make the cripple walk,
    Sinner believe--
King Jesus had died for me.

King Jesus gave the blind the sight,
    Sinner believe--
King Jesus had died for me.

King Jesus make the dumb man speak,
    Sinner believe--
King Jesus had died for me.

Look what a wonder Jesus done,
    Sinner believe,
Look what a wonder Jesus done,
    Sinner believe,
King Jesus had died for me.   (ANS)

The Lord's Been Here

The Lord's been here and blessed my soul,
The Lord's been here and blessed my soul,
O glory,
The Lord's been here and blessed my soul,
The Lord's been here and blessed my soul.
I ain't going to lay any religion down,
I ain't going to lay any religion down,
O glory,
I ain't going to lay any religion down,
I ain't going to lay any religion down.

Going to shoulder up my cross,
Going to shoulder up my cross,
O glory,
Going to shoulder up my cross,
Going to shoulder up my cross.   (ANS)

My Good Lord's Been Here

My good Lord's been here,
    Been here, been here,

My good Lord's been here,
And he's blessed my soul and gone.

O, brothers, where were you?
O, sisters, where were you?
O, Christians, where were you?
O, mourners, where were you?
When my good Lord was here?

My good Lord's been here,
    Been here, been here,
My good Lord's been here,
And he's blessed my soul and gone.   (FJS) (Variant)

My Head Wet With The Midnight Dew

My head wet with the midnight dew,
My head wet with the midnight dew,
My head wet with the midnight dew,
My head wet with the midnight dew.   (St. Helena)

My Sins Been Taken Away

My Lord's done just what He said,
Some these days it won't be long,
All my sins been taken away.

My Lord's done jus what He said,
Healed the sick and raised the dead,
All my sins been taken away,
Glory! Glory! I am saved;
All my sins been taken away, taken away.

Some these days it won't be long,
Goin' home to sing my song,
All my sins been taken away,
Glory! Glory! I am saved;
All my sins been taken away, taken away.   (ANSAS)

New Born Again

I found free grace and dying love,
I'm new born again,
I know my Lord has set me free,
I'm new born again;
My Savior died for you and me,
I'm new born again.

Been a long time talking about my trials here below,
Free grace, free grace, free grace.
Sinner, free grace, I'm been born again,
So glad! So glad! I'm new born again,
Been a long time talking about my trials here below.   (ANS)

No, I Ain't Ashamed

No, I ain't ashamed,
Oh, no, I ain't ashamed,
No, I ain't ashamed,
God, no, I ain't ashamed
To go down in the valley to pray.
Oh, did not conscience tell you,
Oh, did not conscience tell you,
Oh, did not conscience tell you,
Go down in the valley to pray?

Oh, didn't that preacher tell you,
Oh, didn't that preacher tell you,
Oh, didn't that preacher tell you,
Go down in the valley to pray?

Oh, didn't my Jesus tell you,
Oh, didn't my Jesus tell you,
Oh, didn't my Jesus tell you,
Go down in the valley to pray?   (BDWS)

O, Lamb, Beautiful Lamb

O, Lamb, beautiful Lamb!
I'm going to serve God till I die;
O, Lamb, beautiful Lamb!
I'm going to serve God till I die.

Down on my knees when the light passed by,
Thought my soul would rise and fly;
Never felt such love before,
Go in peace and sin no more.

Never felt such love before,
Made me run from door to door;
Looked at my hands and they looked new,
Looked at my feet and they did too.   (ANS)

The Old Sheep Know the Road

Oh, the old sheep know the road,
The old sheep know the road,
The old sheep know the road,
The young lambs must find the way.

Oh, sooner in the morning when I rise,
With crosses and trials on every side;
My brother ain't you got your accounts all sealed,
You'd better go get them before you leave this field.

Oh, shout my sister, for you are free,
For Christ has bought you liberty;
I really do believe without one doubt,
That the Christian has a mighty right to shout.

My brother, better mind how you walk on the cross,
For your foot might slip and your soul get lost;
Better mind that sun and see how she runs,
And mind, don't let her catch you with your work undone.
Oh, the old sheep know the road,
The old sheep know the road,
The old sheep know the road,
The young lambs must find the way.   (Hampton)

O, Lord, These Bones Of Mine

O, Lord, these bones of mine,
O, Lord, these bones of mine,
O, Lord, these bones of mine,
Comin' together in the mornin'.

Some join the church to sing and shout,
Comin' together in the mornin',
Befo' six months they all turned out,
Comin' together in the mornin'.

I look at me hand and me hand look new,
Comin' together in the mornin',
I look at my foot and it look so too,
Comin' together in the mornin'.   (St. Helena)

O, Make Me Holy

O, make me holy, holy,
I do love, I do love,
O, make me holy, holy,
I do love the Lord.

Did you ever see such love before,
King Jesus preaching to the poor;
I'm born of God I know I am,
I'm purchased by the dying Lamb;
Down on my knees when the light passed by,
I thought my soul would rise and fly.

O, make me holy, holy,
I do love, I do love,
O, make me holy, holy,
I do love the Lord.   (ANS)

Open The Window, Noah

Open the window, Noah!
Open the window, Noah,
Open the window, Noah,
Open the window,
Let the dove come in.

The little dove flew in the window and mourned,
Open the window,
Let the dove come in.

The little dove brought back the olive leaf,
Open the window,
Let the dove come in.

Open the window, Noah!
Open the window, Noah,
Open the window, Noah,
Open the window,
Let the dove come in.   (ANS)

O Redeemed

O redeemed, redeemed,
I'm washed in the blood of the Lamb.

Although you see me going along so,
    I'm washed in the blood of the Lamb,
I have my trials here below.

When I was a mourner just like you,
    I'm washed in the blood of the Lamb,
I mourned and prayed till I got through.

Religion's like a blooming rose,
    I'm washed in the blood of the Lamb,
As none but those that feel it knows.

O redeemed, redeemed,
I'm washed in the blood of the Lamb.   (FJS)

The Poor Heathens Are Dyin'

The po' heathens are dyin',
The po' heathens are dyin',
The po' heathens are dyin',
The po' heathens are dyin', dyin'.

Oh, send them some teachers, teachers, teachers, teachers,
Oh, send them some Bibles, Bibles, Bibles, Bibles,
Oh, send them some preachers, preachers, preachers, preachers.

Oh, Lord, have mercy,
Oh, Lord, have mercy,
Oh, Lord, have mercy,
Mercy, mercy, mercy, mercy.   (St. Helena)

Pray On (1)

Pray on, Pray on,
They light us over;

Pray on, pray on,
The union's break of day.

My sister, you come to see baptizing,
In the union break of day;
My 'loved sister, you come to see baptizing,
In the union break of day.   (Allen)

Pray On (2)

In the river of Jordan John baptized,
How I long to be baptized,
In the river of Jordan John baptized,
Unto the dying Lamb.

We baptize all that come by faith,
How I long to be baptized,
We baptize all that come by faith
Unto the dying Lamb.

Here's another one come to be baptized,
How I long to be baptized,
We baptize all that come by faith
Unto the dying Lamb.
Pray on! Pray on!
Pray on! you mourning souls,
Pray on! Pray on!
Unto the dying Lamb.   (ANS)

Ring Jerusalem

Jerusalem, my happy home,
Ain't got nothing at all to do
But ring Jerusalem.

I went to the river
And been baptized,
I'm going to sing and pray myself away;
Oh, Satan's mad, and I'm glad,
I hope to God to keep him mad-o;
Old Satan shot his ball at me,
He missed my soul, and caught my feet.

When I get to heaven,
My feet going to touch, and my tongue going to tell;
One day, one day, I heard a reason from on high,
It made me laugh, and it made me cry;
I wonder what Satan's grumbling about,
He's chained in hell, and can't come out.

Jerusalem, my happy home,
Ain't got nothing at all to do
But ring Jerusalem.   (BDWS)

Roll Him Out Again

Oh, the devil was a busy ole man,
He put the stumbling block in my way,
Jesus sent the good ole soul
To roll him out again.

Oh, Thomas was a busy ole man,
He put the stumbling block in my way,
Jesus sent the good ole soul
To roll him out again.

Oh, Herod was a mean ole man,
He put the stumbling block in my way,
Jesus sent the good ole soul
To roll him out again.   (St. Helena)

Run, Mourner, Run

There's singing here, there's singing there,
I believe down in my soul there's singing
     everywhere;
There's preaching here, there's preaching there,
I believe down in my soul there's preaching
     everywhere;
There's praying here, there's praying there,
I believe down in my soul there's praying
     everwhere.

Run, mourner, run!
Lo! Says the bible,
Run, mourner, run,
Lo! Singing is the way,
Lo! preaching is the way,
Lo! praying is the way.   (ANSAS)

The Sea Gwine Deliver Up Dry Bones

The sea gwine deliver up dry bones,
Oh, Lord--
The sea gwine deliver up dry bones,
Oh, Lord.

Is a dreadful mornin',
Oh, Lord--
Is a dreadful mornin',
Oh, Lord.

When Gabriel blows his trumpet,
Oh, Lord--

When Gabriel blows his trumpet,
Oh, Lord.

When the grave gwine deliver up the dry bones,
Oh, Lord--

When the grave gwine deliver up the dry bones,
Oh, Lord.   (St. Helena)

Seek And Ye Shall Find

Seek, and ye shall find;
Knock, and the door shall be opened;
Ask and it shall be given,
And the Love came trickling down.

My brother, the Lord has been here,
My brother, the Lord has been here,
My sister, the Lord has been here,
My sister, the Lord has been here,
And the Love came trickling down.   (Hampton)

Send One Angel Down

Oh-o Lord, send one angel down,
Oh-o Lord, send one angel down,
Oh-o Lord, send one angel down,
Send him in a hurry,
Send him in a hurry.

Oh-o Lord, this is the needed time,
Oh-o Lord, this is the needed time,
Send him in a hurry.
Oh-o Lord, I'm in trouble now,
Oh-o Lord, I'm in trouble now,
Send him in a hurry.

Oh-o Lord, I'll need a little more faith,
Oh-o Lord, I'll need a little more faith,
Send him in a hurry.

Oh-o Lord, send one angel down,
Oh-o Lord, send one angel down.   (BDWS)

Show Me The Way (1)

Brother, have you come to show me the way?
Brother, have you come to show me the way?
Show me the way how to watch and pray.

Sister, have you come to show me the way?
Sister, have you come to show me the way?
Show me the way how to watch and pray.

Yes, my good Lord, show me the way.
Yes, my good Lord, show me the way.
Show me the way how to watch and pray.   (FJS)

Show Me The Way (2)

O, my good Lord, show me the way,
O, my good Lord, show me the way;
Enter the chariot, travel along.
Enter the chariot, travel along.

Noah sent out a mourning dove,
Which brought back a token of heavenly love;
Going to serve my Lord while I have breath,
So I can see him after death;
When I get to heaven and get on my shoes,
Going to fly about heaven and tell the news.

O, my good Lord, show me the way,
O, my good Lord, show me the way;
Enter the chariot, travel along.
Enter the chariot, travel along.   (ANS)

Some Of These Days

I'm going down to the river of Jordan,
O, yes, I'm going down to the river of Jordan
    Some of these days, hallelujah!
I'm going down to the river of Jordan,
I'm going down to the river of Jordan
    Some of these days.

I'm going down to the big baptizing,
I'm going down to the big baptizing
    Some of these days.
I'm going to drink at the crystal foundation,
I'm going to drink at the crystal foundation
    Some of these days.
I'm going to sit down by my Jesus,
I'm going to sit down by my Jesus
    Some of these days.   (ANSAS)

Steady, Jesus Is Listening

Steady, Jesus is listening,
Steady, Jesus is listening,
Steady, Jesus is listening,
You must be born again.

Stop, poor sinner, don't you run,
Just let me tell you what the lightning's done.
Lightning flashed and thunder rolled,
Made me think about my poor soul.

Steady, Jesus is listening,
Steady, Jesus is listening,
Steady, Jesus is listening,
You must be born again.   (ANS)

Sweet Water Rollin'

Sweet water rollin',
Sweet water rollin'.
Rollin' from the fountain,
Sweet water, roll.

(St. Helena)

This Is The Way I Pray

This is the way I pray in my home,
This is the way I pray in my home,
This is the way I pray in my home,
I pray like this:
"Lord, have mercy."

This is the way I sing in my home,
This is the way I sing in my home,
This is the way I sing in my home,
I sing like this:
"Praise his name."

This is the way I moan in my home,
This is the way I moan in my home,
This is the way I moan in my home,
I moan just like this:
"Mmmmmmmmmmmmmmmmmm."

This is the way I pray in my home,
This is the way I pray in my home,
This is the way I pray in my home,
I pray just like this:
"Lord, have mercy."

(Traditional)

Walking In God's Commandments

Halleluja, halleluja,
Halleluja, my God,
Walking in God's commandments,
Hallelu.

Old satan was a liar and conjurer, too;
Walking in God's commandments.
Hallelu.
He made him out a liar and he kept on the way,
Walking in God's commandments,
Hallelu.

One day, one day was walking 'long,
Walking in God's commandments,
Hallelu.
With a hung down head an' a aching heart.
Walking in God's commandments.
Hallelu.
Halleluja, halleluja.

(Calhoun)

Walking In the Light

We are walking in the light,
We are walking in the light,
We are walking in the light of God.

Hallelujah to the Lamb,
Jesus died for every man,
The rich would live and the poor would die,
The rich and poor together must go.
We are walking in the light,
We are walking in the light,
We are walking in the light of God.   (Hampton)

'Way In The Kingdom

There's plenty-uh room, plenty-uh room,
'Way in the Kingdom;
There's plenty-uh good room where my Jesus is,
'Way in the Kingdom.
Mary had a link an' chain,
'Way in the Kingdom;
An' every link was-a Jesus name,
'Way in the Kingdom.
There's plenty-uh room, plenty-uh room,
'Way in the Kingdom;
There's plenty-uh good room where my Jesus is,
'Way in the Kingdom.

Jesus done jus' what he said,
'Way in the Kingdom;
Healed the sick an'-a raised the dead,
'Way in the Kingdom.
There's plenty-uh room, plenty-uh room,
'Way in the Kingdom;
There's plenty-uh good room where my Jesus is,
'Way in the Kingdom.

One day 'bout twelve o'clock,
'Way in the Kingdom;
He place-uh my feet on the solid rock,
'Way in the Kingdom.
There's plenty-uh good room where my Jesus is,
'Way in the Kingdom.

I never shall forget that day,
'Way in the Kingdom;
That Jesus washed-uh my sins away,
'Way in the Kingdom.
There's plenty-uh room, plenty-uh room,
'Way in the Kingdom;
There's plenty-uh good room where my Jesus is,
'Way in the Kingdom.   (Grissom)

Weeping Mary

If there's anybody here like weeping Mary,
If there's anybody here like praying Samuel,
If there's anybody here like doubting Thomas,
Call upon your Jesus,
And He'll draw nigh.
O, glory, glory hallelujah,
Glory be to God who rules on high.

(Krehbiel)

When I'm Gone

It'll be Lord, Lord, Lord,
When I'm gone;
It'll be Lord, Lord, Lord,
When I'm gone.
It'll be Lord, Lord, Lord,
It'll be Lord, Lord, Lord,
It'll be Lord, Lord, Lord,
When I'm gone.

I'm gonna fly from mansion to mansion,
When I'm gone;
I'm gonna fly from mansion to mansion,
When I'm gone.
I'm gonna fly from mansion to mansion,
Gonna fly from mansion to mansion,
Gonna fly from mansion to mansion,
When I'm gone.

I'll be done with 'bukes an' 'buses,
When I'm gone;
I'll be done with 'bukes an' 'buses,
When I'm gone.
I'll be done with 'bukes an' 'buses,
Be done with 'bukes an' 'buses,
Be done with 'bukes an' 'buses,
When I'm gone.

I'll be done with troubles an' trials,
When I'm gone;
I'll be done with troubles an' trials,
When I'm gone.
I'll be done with troubles an' trials,
Be done with troubles an' trials,
Be done with troubles an' trials,
When I'm gone.

I'm gonna walk an' talk with Jesus,
When I'm gone;
I'm gonna walk an' talk with Jesus,
When I'm gone.
I'm gonna walk an' talk with Jesus,
Gonna walk an' talk with Jesus,
Gonna walk an' talk with Jesus,
When I'm gone.

I'm gonna set down at the welcome table,
When I'm gone;
I'm gonna set down at the welcome table,
When I'm gone.
I'm gonna set down at the welcome table,
Gonna set down at the welcome table,
Gonna set down at the welcome table,
When I'm gone.

I'm gonna drink an' never get thirsty,
When I'm gone;
I'm gonna drink an' never get thirsty,
When I'm gone.
I'm gonna drink an' never get thirsty,
Gonna drink an' never get thirsty,
Gonna drink an' never get thirsty,
When I'm gone.   (Grissom)

The White Marble Stone

Sister Dolly lights the lamp.
And the lamp lights the road,
And I wish I had been there,
For to hear Jordan roll.
O, the city lights the lamp,
The white man he will sold,
And I wish I had been there,
For to hear Jordan roll.

O, the white marble stone,
And the white marble stone,

And I wish I had been there,
For to hear Jordan roll.   (Allen)

Why Don't You Come Along?

Hey, hey, hey, hey,
Why don't you come along?
Hey, hey, hey, hey,
Why don't you come along?

Sinner man, you better pray.
Going to hell your own bad way;

Since the Lord threw Satan out of heaven,
Sinner going to hell rolling, seven and eleven.

I've got religion and I've got it strong,
Going to heaven and I'm going in the storm;
Lord made heaven to give us wings,
Satan made heaven so you'd dance, I sing.

Hey, hey, hey, hey,
Why don't you come along?

Hey, hey, hey, hey,
Why don't you come along?

(BDWS)

You Go I'll Go With You

You go, I'll go with you,
Open your mouth, I'll speak for you,
Lord, if I go, tell me what to say,
They won't believe in me.

Lord, I give myself away,
'Tis all that I can do,
If thou withdraw Thyself from me,
Oh! whither shall I go?

The arcangels don' droop their wings,
Went on Zion hill to sing,
Now, you go, I'll go with you,
Open your mouth, I'll speak for you,
Lord, if I go tell me what to say,
They won't believe in me.

(St. Helena)

You Must Be Pure And Holy

When I was wicked and prone to sin,
My Lord, bretheren, ah, my Lord!
I thought that I couldn't be born again,
My Lord, bretheren, ah, my Lord!
You must be pure and holy,
You must be pure and holy,
You must be pure and holy,
To see God feed his lambs.

I'll run all around the cross and cry,
Or give me Jesus, or I die;
The Devil is a liar and conjurer too,
If you don't look out he'll conjure you;
O, run up, sonny, and get your crown
And by your Father sit you down.

I was pretty young when I begun,
But, now my work is almost done;
The devil's mad and I am glad,
He lost this soul he thought he had.

Go 'way, Satan, I don't mind you,
You wonder, too, that you can't go through,
A lily white stone came rolling down,
It rolled like thunder through the town.

You must be pure and holy,
You must be pure and holy,
You must be pure and holy,
To see God feed his lambs.

(Allen)

LYRICS OF
SPIRITUAL PROGRESS _____

Spiritual progress was an essential sphere of concern in the traditional African world. The traditional African cultural mind had a preoccupation with mastery of spiritual laws, a mastery that it understood would be achieved by degrees. The soul was always on a migratory expedition back to the Potent Source of the cosmos. As the Afro-Americans began to adopt Christianity as a part of their worldview, and attempted to reconstruct their worldview through Christianity, they necessarily made use of many of the Christian laws of spiritual progress. Biblical references such as Jacob's ladder become very appropriate for speaking of spiritual progress as a movement by degrees. Climbing signifies the nature of human experience and existence. Sometimes one seems to be moving steadfastly forward with tremendous momentum. At other times, one seems to be standing still, caught for an extended period on the same round, or one seems to be moving backwards. Sometimes the way is clear; sometimes it is cloudy. The spiritual journey may be lonely; yet it has no ultimate meaning without giving consideration to the larger sphere of humanity. Images of obstacles, like the river, as well as signposts, like the pearly gates, serve as markers of the way.

Surely, the world itself provides enough obstacles, but sometimes the obstacle preventing spiritual progress may be the self. Outside encouragement is helpful, but personal motivation is also seen as essential for maintaining the necessary stamina one needs in order to keep progressing. Spiritual progress begins with humility, faith and steadfastness, and honest confession. Thus, some of the lyrics of spiritual progress remind us that the first mandate of salvation is the uprightness of the inner self, as indicated in the saying, for example, "It's me, it's me, it's me, O, Lord, standing in the need of prayer." One's spiritual well-being is seen as the essential mark of one's nobility and of one's power to endure and transcend.

Ain't I Glad I've Got Out The Wilderness

O, ain't I glad I've got out the wilderness,
Got out the wilderness, got out the wilderness,
Ain't I glad I've got out the wilderness,
Leaning on the Lord.

Come leaning on the Lord,
Come leaning on the Lord,
Come leaning on the Lamb of God,
That takes away the sin of the world.

O, come along mourner, run out the wilderness,
Run out the wilderness, run out the wilderness,
Come out the wilderness,
Leaning on the Lord.

O, you're a long time mourner, coming out the wilderness,
Coming out the wilderness, coming out the wilderness,
Long time mourner coming out the wilderness,
Leaning on the Lord.   (ANSAS)

Amazing Grace

Amazing grace how sweet the soun',
                    sweet the soun',
Amazing grace how sweet the soun',
                    sweet the soun',
Amazing grace how sweet the soun',
That saved a wretch like me.
When I was seeking Jesus,
Some said he couldn't be foun',
But he filled my heart with gladness,
An' he turned me all aroun'.

I once was los' but now I'm foun',
                    now I'm foun',
I once was los' but now I'm foun',
                    now I'm foun',
I once was los' but now I'm foun',
Was blind but now I see.
When I was seeking Jesus,
Some said He couldn't be foun',
But he filled my heart with gladness,
An' He turned me all aroun'.
Don't you know He is a rock in a weary lan',
                         in a weary lan',
Don't you know He is a rock in a weary lan',
                         in a weary lan',
Don't you know He is a rock in a weary lan',
Shelter in the time of storm.

I believe He is a rock in a weary lan',
My Jesus is a rock in a weary lan',
My God He is a rock in a weary lan',
God knows He is a rock in a weary lan',
Shelter in the time of storm.   (Calhoun)

Archangel, Open The Door

I ask all them brothers around,
Brother, why can't you pray for me?
I ask all them sisters around,
Sisters, why can't you pray for me?

I'm going to my heaven,
I'm going home,
Archangel, open the door;
Brother, take off your knapsack, I'm going home,
Archangel, open the door.   (Allen)

Bound For Canaan Land

Where're you bound?
Bound for Canaan land
Where're you bound?
Bound for Canaan land.

Oh, you must not lie,
You must not steal,
You must not take God's name in vain;
I'm bound for Canaan land.

Your horse is white, your garment bright,
You look like a man of war;
Raise up your head with courage bold,
For your race is almost run.

How you know?
How you know?
Jesus told me.

Although you see me going so,
I'm bound for Canaan land;
I have hard trials here below,
I'm bound for Canaan land.

Where're you bound?
Bound for Canaan land
Where're you bound?
Bound for Canaan land.   (BDWS)

Bound To Go

I build my house upon the rock,
O yes, Lord!
No wind, no storm can blow it down,
O yes, Lord!
March on, member,
Bound to go,
Been to the ferry,

Bound to go;
Brother, fare you well.

I build my house on shifting sand,
The first wind come and blew it down.
I am not like the foolish man,
He builds his house upon the sand.

One morning I was walking along,
I saw the berries a-hanging down,
I pick the berries and I suck the juice,
He sweeter than the honeycomb;
I took them, brother, two-by-two,
I took them sister, three-by-three.

I build my house upon a rock,
O yes, Lord!
No wind nor storm shall blow it down,
O yes, Lord!
March on, member,
Bound to go;
March on, member,
Bound to go;
March on, member,
Bound to go;
Bid them fare you well.   (Allen)

Children Do Linger

O, member, will you linger?
See the children do linger here,
I'll go to glory with you,
O, Jesus is our Captain,
He leads us on to glory.

We'll meet at Zion's gateway,
We'll talk this story over;
We'll enter into glory,
When we're done with this world of trials,
When we've done with all our crosses.

O, brother, will you meet us?
When the ship is out a-sailing,
O Jesus got the healing;
Father, gather in your children,
O gather them for Zion.

'Twas a beauteous Sunday morning,
When He rose from the dead,
He will bring you milk and honey.

O, member, will you linger?
See the children do linger here;
I'll go to glory with you,
O, Jesus is our Captain,
He leads us on to glory.   (Allen)

Come, Come, Come And Go With Me

Come, come, come and go with me,
Come, come, come and go with me,
Come, come, come and go with me,
Oh, hallelujah, Amen.

If you are a Christian come and go with me,
Oh, hallelujah, Amen.
If you are a warrior come and go with me,
Oh, hallelujah, Amen.

If you are a true believer come and go with me,
Oh, hallelujah, Amen.

Christ told the blind man, go to the river and bathe,
Oh, hallelujah, Amen.

Christ told Nichodemus, you must be born again.
Oh, hallelujah, Amen.   (St. Helena)

Come Go With Me

Ole Satan is a busy ole man,
He rolls stones in my way;
Master Jesus is my bosom friend,
He rolls them out of my way.

O, come go with me,
O, come go with me,
O, come go with me,
A-walking in the heaven I roam.

I did not come here myself, my Lord,
It was my Lord who brought me here;
And I really do believe I'm a child of God,
A-walking in the heaven I roam.

O, come go with me,
O, come go with me,
O, come go with me,
A-walking in the heaven I roam.   (Allen)

Come, Let Us All Go Down

By and by we'll all go down,
All go down, all go down,
By and by we'll all go down,
Down in the valley to pray.

As I went down in the valley to pray,
Studying about that good old way;
You shall wear the starry crown,
Good Lord, show me the way.
I think I hear the sinner say,

Come, let's go in the valley to pray;
You shall wear the starry crown,
Good Lord, show me the way.

By and by we'll all go down,
All go down, all go down,
By and by we'll all go down,
Down in the valley to pray.   (FJS)

Coming Here Tonight

Brother, I never know I comin' here tonight,
Yes, my Lord, I come.

Brother, I never know I comin' here tonight.
Yes, my Lord, my Lord, I come.
I come to my Father's will--
Yes, my Lord, I come.
My Father's will it must be done--
Yes, my Lord, I come.
I come to save the sinful race--
Yes, my Lord, I come.   (St. Helena)

Did You Hear My Jesus?

If you want to get to heaven,
        Come along, come along,
If you want to get to heaven,
        Come along, come along;

Did you hear my Jesus when He called you?
Did you hear my Jesus when He called you?
Did you hear my Jesus when He called you
For to try on your long white robe?

Oh, the heaven gates re-open,
Come along, come along;
Oh, my mother's in the Kingdom,
Come along, come along;
I am going to meet her yonder,
Come along, come along;

If you want to wear the slippers,
Come along, come along;
If you want to live forever,
Come along, come along;
Did you hear my Jesus calling,
"Come along, come along."   (Hampton)

Done Made My Vow To The Lord

Done made my vow to the Lord and I never
        will turn back,
I will go,
I shall go to see what the end will be.

Done opened up my mouth to the Lord and I never
    will turn back,
I will go,
I shall go to see what the end will be.

Sometimes I'm up, sometimes I'm down,
But still my soul is heavenly bound;
I'll pray and pray and never stop,
Until I reach the mountain top;
If you get there before I do,
Tell all my friends I'm coming too.

Done made my vows to the Lord and I never
    will turn back.
                                            (ANSAS)

Don't You Have Everybody For Your Friend

Don't you have everybody for your friend,
Don't you have everybody for your friend,

They will make you fold your arms and cry Lord how long,
Don't you have everybody for your friend.

I tell you what your friend will do,
They will sit and eat and drink with you,
But when your trouble come,
Your friend begin to run.

Meet your brother in the mornin',
Ask him how he do,
You meet him again in the evenin',
He done tell a lie on you.

Don't you forsake your mother,
I tell you what you must do,
When your father forsake you,
Your mother will stand by you.
                                       (St. Helena)

The Downward Road Is Crowded

O, the downward road is crowded, crowded, crowded,
O, the downward road is crowded with unbelievin' souls,
O, the downward road is crowded with unbelievin' souls.

The wind blows East, and the wind blows West,
It blows like the judgement day,
And every po' soul that never did pray,
Will be glad to pray that day.

Some people say they believe in Him,
And then won't do what he says;
You can't ride the empty air
And get to heaven that day.
                              (ANSAS) (Variant)

Dry Bones

God called Ezekiel by his word,
"Go down and prophesy!"
"Yes, Lord!"
Ezekiel prophesied by the power of God,
Commanded the bones to rise.

They gonna walk aroun', dry bones,
They gonna walk aroun', with the dry bones,
They gonna walk aroun', dry bones,
Why don't you rise and hear the word of the Lord?
"Tell me, how did the bones get together with the long bones?
Prophesy?"

Ah, well, the toe bone connected with the foot bone,
The foot bone connected with the ankle bone,
The ankle bone connected with the leg bone,
The leg bone connected with the knee bone,
The knee bone connected with the thigh bone,
Rise an' hear the word of the Lord!   (Dixon)

Everybody Wants To Know Just How I Die

Everybody wants to know just how I die,
          how I die, how I die.
Everybody wants to know just how I die.
Everybody wants to know just how I die.
I'm going to read my testimony on my bed,
On my bed, on my bed;
I'm going to read my testimony on my bed,
On my bed, on my bed,
Everybody wants to know how I die.

I'm going to have it written in my forehead,
          in my forehead, in my forehead;
I'm going to have it written in my forehead,
Everybody wants to know how I die.   (St. Helena)

Father Abraham

Father Abraham,
Sitting down side of the Lamb,
Father Abraham,
Sitting down side of the Lamb.
Walking in the mansion now,
Sitting down side of the Lamb,
Oh, walking in the mansion now,
Sitting down side of the Lamb.
Oh, brother, you better mind
How you walk on the cross,
Your foot might slip
And your soul get lost.
Sitting down side of the Lamb.

Father Abraham,
Sitting down side of the Lamb,
Father Abraham,
Sitting down side of the Lamb.
Talking in the mansion now,
Oh, talking in the mansion now,
Oh, talking in the mansion now;
Oh, brother, you better mind
How you talk in the mansion,
Your tongue might slip
And your soul get lost.
Sitting down side of the Lamb.   (BDWS)

General Roll Call

O come, my brethren, one and all,
When the general roll is called I'll be there;
O let's get ready when Gabriel calls,
When the general roll is called I'll be there.

I'll be there, I'll be there, I'll be there,
I'll be there,
When the general roll is called I'll be there.   (Hampton)

Glory And Honor

Live humble, humble,
Humble yourselves, the bell done rung,
Live humble, humble,
Humble yourselves, the bell done rung;
Talk the glory and honor,
Praise Jesus,
Talk the glory and honor,
Praise the Lamb!

Oh, my young Christians,
I got lots for to tell you all,
Jesus Christ, speaking through the organ of the call,
Judge ye not, for ye shall be judged,
False pretenders getting in the Christian band.

False pretender wears sheep's clothing on his back,
In his heart's like a raving wolf,
One day, one day
When God's going to call them children
From the distant land,
Tombstones cracking, graves busting,
Hell and the seas going to give up their dead.

Live humble, humble,
Humble yourselves, the bell done rung.   (Hampton)

Go Down In the Valley And Pray

Brother, didn't conscience come and tell you,
Brother, didn't conscience come and tell you,
Brother, didn't conscience come and tell you,
To go down in the valley and pray?

Sister, didn't conscience come and tell you,
Sister, didn't conscience come and tell you,
Sister, didn't conscience come and tell you,
To go down in the valley and pray?

Mourner, didn't conscience come and tell you,
Mourner, didn't conscience come and tell you,
Mourner, didn't conscience come and tell you,
To go down in the valley and pray?

No, I ain't ashamed,
No, I ain't ashamed to honor my Lord,
No, I ain't ashamed to honor my Lord,
No, I ain't ashamed to go down in the valley and pray.   (ANS)

Going To Follow

Titty Mary, you know I'm going to follow,
I'm going to follow,
Brother William, you know I'm going to follow,
I'm going to follow,
For to do my Father's will.

'Tis well and good I'm a-coming here tonight,
I'm a-coming here tonight,
I'm a-coming here tonight,
'Tis well and good I'm a-coming here tonight,
For to do my Father's will.   (Allen)

Going To Quit All Of My Worldly Ways

Going to quit all of my worldly ways,
Quit all of my worldly ways,
Quit all of my worldly ways,
Join the social band.

Left my mother grieving, grieving,
Left my mother grieving,
Grieving upon my soul;
Left my sister grieving, grieving,
Grieving upon my soul;
Left my brother grieving, grieving,
Grieving upon my soul.   (Calhoun)

Good Lord, I Done Done

Good Lord, I done done,
Good Lord, I done done,

Good Lord, I done done,
I done done what you told me to do.

You told me to pray and I done that too,
I prayed and prayed till I come through;
You told me to mourn and I done that too,
I mourned and mourned till I come through;
You told me to shout and I done that too,
I shout and shout till I come through.   (ANSAS)

Good Lord, Shall I Ever Be The One?

Good Lord, shall I ever be the one?
Good Lord, shall I ever be the one?
Good Lord, shall I ever be the one,
To get over in the Promised Land?

God placed Adam in the garden,
'Twas about the cool of the day,
Called for old Adam,
And he tried to run away.

The Lord walked in the garden,
'Twas about the cool of the day,
Called for old Adam,
And Adam said "Hear me, Lord."

Good Lord, shall I ever be the one?
Good Lord, shall I ever be the one?
Good Lord, shall I ever be the one,
To get over in the Promised Land?   (Hampton)

Go Tell It On The Mountain

When I was a seeker,
I sought both night and day,
I asked the Lord to help me,
And He showed me the way.

He made me a watchman
Upon a city wall,
And if I am a Christian,
I am the least of all.

Go tell it on the mountain
Over the hills and everywhere;
Go tell it on the mountain,
That Jesus Christ is born.   (Hampton)

Hail The Crown

Some come crippled,
And some come lame,
Hail the Crown of the Lord of All!

Some come seeking,
And some come praying,
Hail the Crown of the Lord of All!

Hallelujah! Hallelujah!
Lord of All!
Hallelu, Hallelujah, Hallelu!

Some come crippled,
And some come lame,
Hail the Crown of All!   (Fisher)

Hard Trials

Ain't that hard trials,
Tribulation's very great,
Ain't that hard trials,
I'm bound to leave this world.

Some say John the Baptist
Wasn't nothing but a Jew,
But the Holy Bible tells us
Saint John was a preacher too.

Some times I go to meeting,
Some times I stay at home;
Some times I get contrary,
Lord, and I don't do not a one.

One day as I was walking,
Along that lonesome road,
My Saviour spoke unto me
And filled my heart with love.   (BDWS)

Hear Me Praying

Lord, oh, hear me praying,
Lord, oh, hear me praying,
Lord, oh, hear me praying;
I want to be more holy every day, oh, every day.

Like Peter when you said to him,
          Feed my sheep,
          Feed my lambs.
Like Peter when you said to him,
          Feed my sheep,
          Feed my lambs.
Like Peter when you said to him,
          I build my church,
          Upon this rock.
Like Peter when you said to him,
          The gates of hell
          Will never shock.
Like the Baptist when you said,
          I am a voice
          Crying everyday,

Like the Baptist when you said,
  In the wilderness
   Prepare the way.   (ANS)

Heaven-Bound Soldier

Hold out your light,
  You heaven-bound soldier,
Hold out your light,
  You heaven-bound soldier,
Hold out your light,
  You heaven-bound soldier,
Let your light shine around the world.

O, deacon can't you hold out your light,
O, preacher can't you hold out your light,
Let your light shine around the world.   (BANS)

Heaven Goin' To Be My Home

I am trampin', I am trampin',
Heaven goin' to be my home;
I am trampin', I am trampin',
Heaven goin' to be my home.

'Tain't but one thing grieve my mind,
Heaven goin' to be my home,
Christian going to heaven,
Left the sinner behind,
Heaven goin' to be my home.

'Tain't but one thing I desire,
Heaven goin' to be my home,
I wants to go to heaven in a chariot of fire,
Heaven goin' to be my home.

'Tain't but one thing I desire,
Heaven goin' to be my home;

I want to sing in the heavenly choir,
Heaven goin' to be my home.   (St. Helena)

I Ain't Going To Grief My Lord No More

I ain't going to grief my Lord no mo'
  for the Bible tell me so,
I ain't going to grief my Lord no mo'.

The tallest tree in Paradise,
The Christians call the tree of life;
I ain't going to grief my Lord no mo'
  for the Bible tell me so.

O, Paul and Silas bound in jail,
The one did sing while the other prayed.

I wants to go to heaven and I wants to go right,
I wants to go to heaven all dressed in white.

O, look up yonder what I see,
Bright angels coming after me.

If you get there before I do,
Look out for me I'm coming, too.

O, my name done written, done written down fine,
O, my name done written, in David's line.   (St.Helena)

I Am Going To Join In This Army

I am going to join in this army of my Lord,
I am going to join in this army.

Takes a humble soul to join,
Takes a humble soul to join;
All Christians can join,
All Christians can join;
Preacher, help us to join,
Preacher, help us to join.

In this army of my Lord,
In this army of my Lord.   (Hampton)

I Done Done What You Told Me To Do

So glad I done done,
So glad I done done,
So glad I done done,
So glad I done done,
What you told me to do.

Told me to pray,
And I done prayed,
Told me to pray,
And I done prayed.

So glad I done done,
So glad I done done,
So glad I done done,
So glad I done done,
What you told me to do.   (BANS)

I Feel Like Dying In This Army

I feel like dying in the service of my Lord,
I feel like dying in the service of my Lord,
I feel like dying in the service of my Lord,
I feel like dying in this army.

Oh, stop ye sinner, don't you run no more,
Oh, let me tell you what the lightning done,
Oh, the lightning killed Job's servant son,
I feel like dying in this army.

Oh, let me tell you what my Jesus done,
He brought me home before the setting of the sun,
Oh, stop ye turn-back, don't you run no more,
Oh, you better get ready for the judgment day,
Because on that day Satan'll have his way;
I feel like dying in this army.   (BDWS)

I Heard A Voice Couldn't Tell Where

I been in some strange land
        so far from home,
I been in some strange land,
I heard a voice couldn't tell where,
I heard a voice couldn't tell where,
I heard a voice couldn't tell where.

One day I was a-walking along,
I heard a voice couldn't tell where,
I heard a reason from on high,
Go in peace and sin no more,
Your sins are forgiven and your soul set free.
I heard a voice couldn't tell where.   (BDWS)

I Heard The Preaching Of The Word Of God

I heard the preaching of the Elder,
Preaching the word, preaching the word;
I heard the preaching of the Elder,
Preaching the word of God.

How long did it rain?
Can anyone tell?
For forty days and nights it fell.

How long was Jonah in the belly of the whale?
'Twas three whole days and nights he sailed.

When I was a mourner I mourned till I got through,
My knees got acquainted with the hillside too.

I heard the preaching of the Elder,
Preaching the word, preaching the word;
I heard the Preaching of the Elder,
Preaching the word, preaching the word.   (BANS)

I Know The Lord's Laid His Hands On Me

O, I know the Lord, I know the Lord,
I know the Lord's laid His hands on me.

Did ever you see the like before?
Jesus preaching to the poor;
O, wasn't that a happy day,
Jesus washed my sins away;
Some seek the Lord and don't seek Him right,
Fool all day and pray all night;
My Lord's done just what He said,
Healed the sick and raised the dead.

O, I know the Lord, I know the Lord,
I know the Lord's laid His hands on me.   (Hampton)

I'm Going To Join The Band

I'm going to join the band, Hallelujah!
Can't you sing it?
I'm going to join the band,
O Lord,
I'm going to join the band.

The more come in with a free good will,
Make the band seem sweeter still,
Come children! Join the band!
Sing to Jesus!

Jordan's stream is so chilly and cold,
If you don't mind it'll chill your soul,
Cold Jordan! Chilly waters!
Watch it, Christians!

Watch that sun how steady she runs,
Don't let her catch you with your work undone,
Watch that sun! Steady traveler!
Work, children!

Joshua prayed for to stop the sun,
The sun did stop till the battle was won,
Going to heaven! With Joshua!
And David!

Going to hang my harp on the willow tree,
It'll sound way over in Galilee,
O, the willow! And the children!
Couldn't sing!   (ANSAS)

I'm So Glad

I'm so glad the angels brought the tidings down,
I'm so glad, I'm hunting for a home,
Oh, hunting for a home.

You'll not get lost in the wilderness,
With the love of Jesus in your breast;
Oh, Christians, you had better pray,
For Satan's round you every day;
A little longer here below,
And then to glory we will go;
The angels sang in Bethlehem,
Peace on earth, good will to men.

I'm so glad the angels brought the tidings down,
I'm so glad, I'm hunting for a home,
O, hunting for a home.   (FJS)

I Never Felt Such Love In My Soul Before

I never felt such love in my soul before,
I never felt such love in my soul before,
All the days of my life ever since I've been born,
I never felt such love in my soul before.

I never heard a man speak like this man before,
I never heard a man speak like this man before,
All the days of my life ever since I've been born,
I never heard a man speak like this man before.   (ANS)

In This Field

Lordy, won't you he'p me?
Lordy, won't you he'p me?
Lordy, won't you he'p me
In this field?

Troubles is so hard,
Troubles is so hard,
Troubles is so hard
In this field.

There's mo' than me, Lord,
There's mo' than me, Lord,
There's mo' than me, Lord
In this field.

There's mo' to do, Lord,
There's mo' to do, Lord,
There's mo' to do, Lord
In this field.

There's mo' to be won,
There's mo' to be won,
There's mo' to be won
In this field.   (Grissom)

I Saw The Beam In My Sister's Eye

I saw the beam in my sister's eye,
Couldn't see the beam in mine;
You'd better leave your sister's door,
Go keep your own door clean.

And I had a mighty battle like Jacob and the angel,
Jacob, time of old;
I didn't intend to let him go
Till Jesus blessed my soul.

And bless'ed me, and bless'ed me,
And bless'ed all my soul;
I didn't intend to let him go
Till Jesus bless'ed my soul.   (Allen)

I've Been Trying To Live Humble

Humble, humble,
I've been trying to live humble, humble;
Ever since my soul's been converted,
I've been trying to live humble, humble.

My sister, humble up and humble down,
My brother, humble through and humble 'round;
Humble, humble,
I've been trying to live humble, humble;
Ever since my soul's been converted,
I've been trying to live humble, humble.   (CD)

I Want God's Heaven To Be Mine

Yes, I want God's heaven to be mine,
To be mine, to be mine;
Yes, I want God's heaven to be mine,
Save me, Lord, save me.

I hail to my mother,
My mother hails to me,
And the last word I heard her say,
Save me, Lord, save me.

I hail to my leader,
My leader hails to me,
And the last word I heard him say,
Save me, Lord, save me.

Yes, I want God's heaven to be mine,
To be mine, to be mine;
Yes, I want God's heaven to be mine,
Save me, Lord, save me.   (BANS)

Jacob's Ladder

I want to climb up Jacob's ladder,
Jacob's ladder, O, Jacob's ladder,
I want to climb up Jacob's ladder,

But I can't climb it
Till I make my peace with the Lord.

O, praise ye the Lord,
I'll praise Him till I die,
I'll praise Him till I die,
And sing Jerusalem.   (Allen)

Jesus, Won't You Come By and By?

You ride that horse,
You call him Macadoni,
Jesus, won't you come by and by?
You ride him in the morning,
And you ride in the evening,
Jesus, won't you come by and by?
The Lord knows the world's going to end up,
Jesus, won't you come by and by?   (Allen)

John The Bunyan

John the Bunyan, O Lord,
John the Bunyan, O Lord,
John the Bunyan,
John the Bunyan,
John the Bunyan, O Lord.
Going away to leave you, O Lord,
Got to go to judgment, O Lord,
Sorry to tell you, O Lord,
It's a life time journey, O Lord,
John the Bunyan, O Lord,
Train's a-coming, O Lord,
Got my ticket, O Lord,
Train going to leave you, O Lord,
Preaching in the wilderness, O Lord.   (Calhoun)

Keep A-Inching Along

Keep a-inching along, keep a-inching along,
Master Jesus is coming by and by;
Keep a-inching along, keep a-inching along,
Master Jesus is coming by and by.

O, I died one time,
Going to die no more;
O, you in the word,
And the word in you;
How can I die when I'm in the word?

Keep a-inching along, keep a-inching along,
Master Jesus is coming by and by;
Keep a-inching along, keep a-inching along,
Master Jesus is coming by and by.   (Hampton)

Keep In The Middle Of The Road

Keep in the middle of the road,
Keep in the middle of the road,
Keep in the middle of the road.
I hear them angels callin' loud,
Keep in the middle of the road,
Keep in the middle of the road,
Keep in the middle of the road.
They's a-waitin' there in a great big crowd,
They's a-waitin' there in the middle of the road.
I can see them standing 'round the big white gate,
Keep in the middle of the road,
We must travel along before it gets too late,
For it ain't no use to sit down and wait.

Then, children, keep in the middle of the road,
Children, keep in the middle of the road,
Just keep in the middle of the road
To the right;
Don't you look to the left.

Keep in the middle of the road,
Ain't got time for to stop and talk
'Cause the road is rough and it's hard to walk.
I fix my eye on the golden stair,
And I'll keep a-going till I get there,
'Cause my head is bound for that crown to wear.

This world is full of sinful things,
Keep in the middle of the road,
When you get tired put on your wings,
Keep in the middle of the road,
When you lay down in that road to die,
And you watch them angels in the sky,
Put on your wings
Then get up and fly,
But keep in the middle of the road.   (Schirmer)

Lamb's Blood Done Washed Me Clean

Let me tell you about Lord, Lord, Lord,
I ain't going to live in my sins no longer;
And Lord, Lord, Lord,
Lamb's blood done washed me clean.

Old Satan's mad and I'm glad,
Lamb's blood done washed me clean,
I trust the Lord I'm going to keep him mad,
Lamb's blood done washed me clean.

Old Satan thought he had me fast,
I broke his chain and got free at last;
You knock me down I rise again,
I fight you with my sword and shield;
You hinder me here, but you can't hinder me there,
The Lord in heaven's going to answer my prayer.   (BDWS)

Let The Church Roll On

Let the church roll on, my Lord,
Let the church roll on, my Lord,
You can put the devil out, my Lord,
Let the church roll on.

If there's preachers in the church, my Lord,
An' they're not livin' right, my Lord;
Jus' turn the preachers out, my Lord,
An' let the church roll on.

If there's members in the church, my Lord,
An' they're not livin' right, my Lord;

You can put the members out, my Lord,
An' let the church roll on.

If there's liars in the church, my Lord,
An' they're not livin' right, my Lord;
You can put the liars out, my Lord,
An' let the church roll on.

If there's sinners in the church, my Lord,
An' they're not living right, my Lord,
Jus' put the sinners out, my Lord,
An' let the church roll on.   (Grissom)

Let The Heaven Light Shine On Me

Let the heaven light shine on me,
Let the heaven light shine on me,
For low is the way to the upper bright world,
Let the heaven light shine on me.

Oh, brother, you must bow so low,
Oh, sister, you must bow so low,
Oh, preacher, you must bow so low,
Class leader, you must bow so low,
Oh, elder, you must bow so low,
For low is the way to the upper bright world.

Let the heaven light shine on me,
Let the heaven light shine on me,
For low is the way to the upper bright world,
Let the heaven light shine on me.   (Hampton)

Live Humble

Live humble, humble,
Humble yourselves, the bell done rung,
Live humble, the bell done rung.

Glory and honor! Praise King Jesus!
Glory and honor! Praise the Lord.

Watch that sun, how steady it runs,
Don't let him catch you with your work undone.
Ever see such a man as God?
He gave up his Son for to come and die.
Gave up his Son for to come and die,
Just to save my soul from burning fire.
See God'n' you see God'n' you see God in the morning,
He'll come riding down the line of time;
The fire'll be falling, He'll be calling,
"Come to judgement come."   (ANSAS)

The Lonesome Valley

My brother, want to get religion?
Go down in the lonesome valley,
Go down in the lonesome valley;
My brother, want to get religion?
Go down in the lonesome valley.
Go down in the lonesome valley,
Go down in the lonesome valley, my Lord,
Go down in the lonesome valley,
To meet my Jesus there.

O, feed on milk and honey,
O, John he writes the letters,
And Mary and Martha read them;
Go down in the lonesome valley,
Go down in the lonesome valley,
My brother, want to get religion?
Go down in the lonesome valley,
To meet my Jesus there.   (Allen)

Lord, I Want To Be A Christian

Lord, I want to be a Christian,
In-a my heart, in-a my heart,
Lord, I want to be a Christian,
In-a my heart, in-a my heart.

Lord, I want to be more loving,
In-a my heart, in-a my heart;
Lord, I want to be more holy,
In-a my heart, in-a my heart;
Lord, I don't want to be like Judas,
In-a my heart, in-a my heart;
Lord, I want to be like Jesus,
In-a my heart, in-a my heart.   (Hampton)

Lord, Make Me More Patient

Lord, make me more patient,
Lord, make me more patient,
Lord, make me more patient,
Until we meet again!

Lord, make me more holy,
Lord, make me more loving,
Lord, make me more peaceful,
Until we meet again.

(Allen)

Michael Row The Boat Ashore

Michael, row the boat ashore,
Hallelujah!
Michael's boat's a gospel boat,
Hallelujah!
I wonder where my mother's there,
Hallelujah!
See my mother on the rock going home,
Hallelujah!
On the rock going home in Jesus' name,
Hallelujah!
Michael's boat's a music boat,
Hallelujah!
Gabriel blows the trumpet horn,
Hallelujah!
O, you mind your boasting talk,
Hallelujah!
Boasting talk will sink your soul,
Hallelujah!
Brother, lend a helping hand,
Hallelujah!
Jordan's stream is wide and deep,
Hallelujah!
Jesus stand on the other side,
Hallelujah!
I wonder if my master's there,
Hallelujah!
My Father's gone to an unknown land,
Hallelujah!
O, the Lord plants his garden there,
Hallelujah!
He raises the fruit for you to eat,
Hallelujah!
He that eats shall never die,
Hallelujah!
When the river overflows,
Hallelujah!
O, poor sinner, how's your land?
The river runs and darkness is coming,
Hallelujah!
Sinner, row to save your soul.
Michael, haul the boat ashore,
Then you'll hear the horn they blow,
Then you'll hear the trumpet sound,

Trumpet sound the world around;
Trumpet sound for rich and poor,
Trumpet sound the jubilee,
Trumpet sound for you and me.   (Allen)

Mount Zion

On my journey, now,
On my journey, now,
Mount Zion,
Well, I wouldn't take nothin'
For my journey now,
Mount Zion.

One day, one day,
I was walking along,
Well, the elements opened
And love came down.

You can talk about me
Just as much as you please,
Well, I'll talk about you
When I get on my knees.   (L-G)

My Soul's Been Anchored In The Lord

O, my soul's been anchored in the Lord,
              Ain't you glad!
My soul's been anchored in the Lord,
              Can't you sing it!
My soul's been anchored in the Lord,
              Tell it children!
Where've you been, poor sinner?
              O, I'm happy!
O, where've you been so long?
              Found my Jesus!
Been working out of the sight of man,
              On my knees!

You may talk about me just as much as you please,
              You can't hurt me!
You may spread my name abroad;
              For I'm sheltered!
I'll pray for you when I get on my knees,
              In my Jesus!

See my father in the gospel,
              Left my burden!
Come wagging up the hill so slow,
              At the river!
He's crying now as he cried before,
              In the valley!

O, my soul's been anchored in the Lord,
My soul's been anchored in the Lord.   (ANS) (Variant)

My Soul Wants Something That's New

My soul wants something that's new,
My soul wants something that's new,
My soul wants something that's new,
My soul wants something that's new.

And am I born to die,
To lay this body down,
And shall I fear to own His cause,
Or blush to speak His name.

Am I a soldier of the cross,
A follower of the Lamb.
And shall I fear to own His cause,
Or blush to speak his name?

(Calhoun) (Variant)

No Condemnation In My Soul

I feel all right, no condemnation--
Feel all right, no condemnation--
Well, I feel all right, no condemnation--
No condemnation in my soul.

I been born of God, no condemnation--
Born of God, no condemnation--
I been born of God, no condemnation--
No condemnation in my soul.
I been baptized, no condemnation--
Been baptized, no condemnation--
Well, I been baptized, no condemnation--
No condemnation in my soul.

I been sanctified, no condemnation--
Sanctified, no condemnation--
I been sanctified, no condemnation--
No condemnation in my soul.
Got the Holy Ghost, no condemnation--
Holy Ghost, no condemnation--
Got the Holy Ghost, no condemnation--
No condemnation in my soul.

When I see my Lord, no condemnation--
See my Lord, no condemnation--
When I see my Lord, no condemnation--
No condemnation in my soul.

(Grissom)

No More, My Brother

No mo', my dear brother,
No mo', Lord,
I will never turn back no mo'.

No mo', my lovin' mother,
No mo', my Lord,
I will never turn back no mo'.

No mo' when I cross old Jordan,
No mo', my Lord,
I will never turn back no mo'.

No mo' rain goin' to wet me,
No mo', my Lord,
I will never turn back no mo'.

No mo' sun goin' to burn me,
No mo', my Lord,
I will never turn back no mo'.   (St. Helena)

Oh, Hear Me Praying

Lord, oh hear me praying, Lord,
Oh, hear me praying, Lord,
Oh, hear me praying,
I want to be more holy every day.

Oh, I want to be more holy every day,
Like Peter when you said to him
Feed my sheep, feed my lambs;
Like Peter when you said to him,
I build my church upon this rock,
Oh, the gates of hell will never shock;
Like Jesus when he said to me,
I am the voice,
Everyday come out the wilderness
To prepare the way.

Lord, oh hear me praying, Lord,
Oh, hear me praying, Lord,
Oh, hear me praying,
I want to be more holy every day.   (BANS)

Oh, Jerusalem!

Oh, Jerusalem!
Oh, my Lord! I'm walking the road,
Oh, Jerusalem, walking the road,
Oh, my Lord!
Oh, my Lord!

Mind my sister how you walk on the cross,
Your foot might slip and your soul get lost!
My Lord God Almighty came stepping down,
Came stepping down on a sea of glass!
Sea of glass all mingled with fire,
Goodbye, my brother,
I'm going on higher!

Oh, Jerusalem!
Oh, my Lord! I'm walking the road;
Oh, my Lord, walking the road.   (Hampton)

Oh! Let Me Up

Oh! just let me up in the house of God,
Just let me up in the house of God,
Just let me up in the house of God,
And I'll never turn back no more,
No more, no more,
       Why thank God almighty,
No more, no more,
       I'll never turn back no more.

Oh! just let me get on my long white robe,
Oh! just let me get on my starry crown,
Oh! just let me get on my golden shoes,
Oh! the music in the heaven,
       It sounds so sweet.

Oh! just let me up in the house of God,
Just let me up in the house of God,
Just let me up in the house of God,
And I'll never turn back no more.   (FJS)

Oh! Sinner Man

Oh! sinner, Oh! sinner man,
Oh! sinner, Oh! which way are you going?

Oh! come back, sinner,
              And don't go there,
Which way are you going?
              For hell is deep and dark despair,
Oh! which way are you going?

Though days be dark, and nights be long,
We'll shout and sing till we get home;
'Twas just about the break of day,
My sins forgiven and soul set free.

Oh! sinner, Oh! sinner man,
Oh! sinner, Oh! which way are you going?   (FJS)

Oh, Sister, Get Your Ticket Right

Oh, sister, get your ticket right,
Oh, yes--
For to enter into rest,
Oh, yes--
Oh, get your ticket, get it right,
Oh, yes--
Oh, get your ticket right,
Oh, yes--.   (St. Helena)

The Old Ark's A-Moving And I'm Going Home

O, the old ark's moving, moving, moving,
The old ark's moving
And I'm going home.

See that sister all dressed so fine?
She ain't got Jesus on her mind.
See that brother dressed so gay?
O, death's going to come carry him away.

See that sister there coming so slow?
She wants to get to heaven before the heaven door closes.
'Tain't but one thing on my mind.
My sister's gone to heaven and left me behind.

O, the old ark's moving, moving, moving,
The old ark's moving,
And I'm going home.

The old ark she rocked,
The old ark she landed on the mountain top.

O, the old ark's moving, moving, moving,
The old ark's moving,
And I'm going home.   (BANS)

Old Zion's Children Marching Along

Old Zion's children marching along,
        marching along, marching along;
Old Zion's children marching along,
        marching along, marching along,
Talking about the welcome day.

I hailed my mother in the morning,
        marching along, marching along,
Talking about the welcome day.

I hailed my brother in the morning,
        marching along, marching along,
Talking about the welcome day.
O, don't you want to live up yonder,
O, don't you want to live up yonder,
Talking about the welcome day.   (ANSAS)

Prayer Is The Key Of Heaven

Prayer is the key of heaven,
Prayer is the key of heaven,
Prayer is the key of heaven,
Faith unlocks the door;
        I know that.

I think it was about twelve o'clock,
When Jesus led me to the rock;
I remember the day, I know the time,
Jesus freed this soul of mine;
My head got wet with the midnight dew,
The morning star was witness too.

Prayer is the key to heaven,
Prayer is the key to heaven,
Prayer is the key to heaven,
Faith unlocks the door;
I know that.   (Hampton)

Praying In The Land

Praying in the lan',
Praying in the lan',
Praying in the lan',
I'm a long way from home,
Praying in the lan',
Baby of Bethlehem.

O, sister, don't you want to go to heaven,
O, sister, don't you want to go to heaven,
O, sister, don't you want to go to heaven?
Baby of Bethlehem.

Singing in the lan',
Preaching in the lan',
Mourning in the lan',
Shouting in the lan',
Weeping in the lan',
O, mother, don't you want to go to heaven?   (Calhoun)

Pray Is The Key To The Kingdom

Pray is the key to the kingdom,
And the world can do me no harm;
Pray is the key to the kingdom,
And the world can do me no harm.

Pray is the key to the kingdom,
And faith unlocks the do',
If that so be to the kingdom,
I got a key everywhere I go.

Took Brother Paul and Silas,
And placed 'em in jail below;
But the angel came from heaven,
And unlock the jailer's do'.

Took Brother John on Patmos,
And placed him in a kettle of oil,
But the angel came from heaven,
And tol' him that the oil wouldn't boil.   (St. Helena)

Prepare Us

Prepare me, prepare me, Lord,
Prepare me,
      When death shall shake this frame;
As I go down the stream of time,
      When death shall shake this frame;
I'll leave this sinful world behind;
      When death shall shake this frame.

The many that loves to serve the Lord,
He will receive his just reward.
Am I a soldier of the cross,
Or must I count this soul as lost?
My soul is bound for that bright land,
And there I'll meet that happy band.

Prepare me, prepare me, Lord,
Prepare me,
      When death shall shake this frame;
As I go down the stream of time,
      When death shall shake this frame;
I'll leave this sinful world behind;
      When death shall shake this frame.   (FJS)

Roll, Jordan, Roll

My brother sitting on the tree of life,
And he heard when Jordan roll;
Roll, Jordan, roll,
Roll, Jordan, roll!
O, march the angel march,
O, march the angel march;
O, my soul arise in Heaven, Lord,
For to hear when Jordan roll.

Little children, learn to fear the Lord,
And let your days be long;
Roll, Jordan, roll,
Roll, Jordan, roll!

O, let no false nor spiteful word
Be found upon your tongue;
Roll, Jordan, roll,
Roll, Jordan, roll!   (Allen)

Roll The Old Chariot Along

Oh, roll the old chariot along,
Roll the old chariot along,

Roll the old chariot along,
If you don't hang on behind.

We are travelling from mansions to mansions,
        to mansions;
We are travelling from mansions to mansions,
        to mansions;
We are travelling from mansions to mansions,
        to mansions;
If you don't hang on behind.

Going to join with the hundred and forty-four thousand,
If you don't hang on behind;
If my father will go,
He shall wear a starry crown.

We are travelling from mansions to mansions,
        to mansions;
If you don't hang on behind.   (Hampton)

Sabbath Has No End

Going to walk about Zion,
        I really do believe;
Walk about Zion,
        I really do believe;
Walk about Zion,
        I really do believe;
Sabbath has no end.

I did view one angel
        In the angel's stand;
Let's mark him right down the forehead,
With the harp there in his hand.

Going to follow King Jesus,
        I really do believe;
I love God certain,
        I really do believe;
My sister's got religion,
        I really do believe;
Will sit down in the Kingdom,
        I really do believe;
Religion is a fortune,
        I really do believe.   (Allen)

Sister Hannah

Tell me, sinner, and tell me true,
Where have you been so long gone?

I been a-seeking for the Devil
An' he couldn't be foun',
Now my soul has gone on to glory,
Rolling and rocking them in His arms,
Rolling and rocking them in His arms,
Rolling and rocking them in His arms.

Tell me, sister Hannah, and tell me true,
Where have you been so long gone?
I been a-seeking for my Jesus
An' He has been found.
Now my soul has gone on to glory.

Tell it, my sister, confess your fault,
Hide nothing from the Lord.   (Calhoun)

Somebody's Knocking At Your Door

Somebody's knocking at your door,
Somebody's knocking at your door;
O, sinner, why don't you answer?
Somebody's knocking at your door.

Knocks like Jesus,
Knocks like Jesus;
Can't you hear Him?
Can't you hear Him?
Answer Jesus,
Answer Jesus,
Jesus calls you,
Jesus calls you;
Can't you trust Him?
Can't you trust Him?   (Hampton)

Some Will Love You And Some Will Hate You

Some will love you,
Some will hate you,
Trust in God and do the right,
Oh, do the right, do the right,
Trust in God and do the right.   (St. Helena)

Takes A Little Bit Of Man To Rock Dan

Takes a little bit of man to rock Dan,
Takes a little bit of man to rock Dan,
Takes a little bit of man to rock Dan,
O, my Lord, to rock Dan.

They told me to rock, an' I rock Dan,
O, my Lord, to rock Dan;
Said: Now I'm going to rock, to rock Dan,
O, my Lord, to rock Dan.
There's more than one way to rock Dan,
O, my Lord, to rock Dan;
Then show me how to rock Dan,
O, my Lord, to rock Dan;
That's the humble way to rock Dan,
O, my Lord, to rock Dan;
Everybody can't rock, to rock Dan,
O, my Lord, to rock Dan;
O, help me to rock, to rock Dan,

O, my Lord, to rock Dan;
Sister, help me to rock, to rock Dan,
O, my Lord, to rock Dan.

(Calhoun)

Tell Jesus

Tell Jesus, done done all I can,
Tell Jesus, done done all I can,
Tell Jesus, done done all I can,
I can't do no more.

I went up on the mountains,
I didn't go there for to stay;
But when my soul got happy,
Then I stayed all day.

I could not live a sinner,
I tell you the reason why,
Be afraid my Lord would call me,
And I wouldn't be ready to die.

If you do not like your neighbor,
Don't carry his name abroad;
But take it in your forehead,
And carry it to the Lord.

Tell Jesus, done done all I can,
Tell Jesus, done done all I can,
Tell Jesus, done done all I can,
I can't do no more.

(Hampton)

That Lonesome Valley

Oh, you got to walk-a that lonesome Valley,
You got to go there by yo'se'f;
No one here to go there with you,
You got to go there by yo'se'f.

When you walk-a that lonesome Valley,
You got to walk it by yo'se'f;
No one here may walk it with you,
You got to walk it by yo'se'f.

When you reach the river Jordan,
You got to cross it by yo'se'f;
No one here may cross it with you,
You got to cross it by yo'se'f.
When you face that Judgment mornin',
You got to face it by yo'se'f;
No one here to face it for you,
You got to face it by yo'se'f.

Loud and strong yo' Master callin',
You got to answer by yo'se'f;
No one here to answer for you,
You got to answer by yo'se'f.

You got to stand yo' trial in Judgment,
You got to stand it by yo'se'f;
No one here to stand it for you,
You got to stand it by yo'se'f.

Jordan's stream is strong and chilly,
You got to wade it by yo'se'f;
No one here to wade it for you,
You got to wade it by yo'se'f.

When my dear Lord was hangin' bleedin',
He had to hang there by His-se'f;
No one there could hang there for Him,
He had to hang there by His-se'f.

You got to join that Christian Army,
You got to join it by yo'se'f;
No one here to join it for you,
You got to join it by yo'se'f.

You got to live a life of service,
You got to live it by yo'se'f;
No one here to live it for you,
You got to live it by yo'se'f.   (Grissom)

That Suits Me

Come on, elder, let's go roun' the wall,
That suits me,
Come on, let's go roun' the wall,
That suits me.
Come on, let's go roun' the wall,
Don't want to stumble, don't want to fall.
That suits me.

Can't no liar go roun' the wall,
He's going to stumble, he's going to fall,
That suits me.

Stop right still and steady yourself,
God's going to move that arm Himself,
That suits me.

When I die, Lord, I want to die right,
Want to go to heaven all dressed in white,
That suits me.   (Calhoun)

These Are My Father's Children

These are my Father's children,
These are my Father's children,
These are my Father's children,
All in one band.

And I soon shall be done
with the troubles of the world,
Troubles of the world,
Troubles of the world,
And I soon shall be done
with the troubles of the world,
Going home to live with God.

My brother's done with the troubles of the world,
My sister's done with the troubles of the world,
These are my Father's children,
These are my Father's children,
All in one band,
Going home to live with God.   (FJS)

Turn, Sinner

Turn, sinner, turn,
Turn, sinner, turn,
While your maker asks you to turn,
Oh, turn, sinner, turn,
May the Lord help you to turn.
Oh, turn, why will you die?

Pray, sinner, pray,
Pray, sinner, pray,
While your maker asks you to pray;
Bow, sinner, bow,
Bow, sinner, bow,
While your maker asks you to bow;
Groan, sinner, groan,
Groan, sinner, groan,
While your maker asks you to groan.   (BDWS)

Turn, Sinner, Turn O!

Turn, sinner, turn today,
Turn, sinner, turn O!
Turn, sinner, turn today,
Turn, sinner, turn O!

Turn, O sinner, the world's a-going,
Turn, sinner, turn O!
Turn, O sinner, the world's a-going,
Turn, sinner, turn O!

Wait not for tomorrow's sun,
Tomorrow's sun will sure to shine,
The sun may shine, but on your grave;
Hark! I hear the sinners say,
If you get to heaven,
I'll get there too;
O, sinner, you make a mistake,
While the lamp holds out to burn,
The wild sinner may return.

Turn, sinner, turn today,
Turn, sinner, turn O!
Turn, sinner, turn today,
Turn, sinner, turn O!

(Allen)

Wait, Mr. Mackright

Wait, Mister Mackright,
Ain't you heard what Satan said?
Satan filled me full of music,
And told me not to pray.
Mister Mackright, cry holy,
O, Lord, cry holy.

(Allen)

Wake Up, Jacob

Wake up, Jacob,
Day is breaking,
I'm on my way;
O, wake up, Jacob,
Day is breaking,
I'm on my way;
I want to go to heaven
When I die,
Do love the Lord!
O! Lord.

Got some friends on the other shore,
Do love the Lord!
I want to see them more and more,
Do love the Lord!
Wake up, Jacob,
Day is breaking,
I'm on my way;
I want to go to heaven
When I die,
Do love the Lord!

(Allen)

Wasn't That A Witness For My Lord

Wasn't that a witness for my Lord,
Wasn't that a witness for my Lord.
Read about Samson from his birth,
Stronges' man ever live' on earth.
Read way back in the ancient time,
He killed five thousand of the Philistine.

Samson's strength went wandering about,
Samson's strength was never foun out,
Till Samson's wife fell down on her knees,
Saying -- "Tell me where your strength lie', if you please."
Wasn't that a witness for my Lord,
Wasn't that a witness for my Lord.

Samson's wife she talk so fair,
He said -- "If you cut off my hear
And shave my head jus' as clean as yo' han'.
My strength will become as a natural man."
Wasn't that a witness for my Lord,
Wasn't that a witness for my Lord.

Read about Adam out of the dus',
God created man the firs'.
He made a woman, an' he name' her Eve,
He told her not to eat the forbidden fruit;
Then the disciples told her t'would make her wise,
Then she suffere' until she died.
Wasn't that a witness for my Lord,
Wasn't that a witness for my Lord.

Nicodemus of the human sight,
Went to my Lord Jesus by the night.
The Lord said -- "If thou will be wise,
Repent an' believe an' be baptise'."
Wasn't that a witness for my Lord,
Wasn't that a witness for my Lord.   (Calhoun)

We'll March Down Jordan

We'll march down, march down,
Oh, we'll march down Jordan, hallelu;
Oh, bow, sinner, bow,
Get your religion now,
We'll march down Jordan, hallelu.

Bow, turn-back, bow,
Why don't you come along?
We'll march down Jordan, hallelu.

Religion ain't to buy,
You can get it if you try.
We'll march down Jordan, hallelu.

If that turn-back wants to go,
Why don't he come along?
We'll march down Jordan, hallelu.   (BDWS)

We Shall Walk Through The Valley

We shall walk through the valley
and the shadow of death,
We shall walk through the valley in peace,
If Jesus himself shall be our leader,
We shall walk through the valley in peace.

We shall meet those Christians there,
Meet them there;
There will be no sorrow there,
If Jesus himself shall be our leader,
We shall walk through the valley in peace.   (FJS)

What You Going To Do When the Lamp Burns Down?

Oh, poor sinner, now is your time,
Oh, poor sinner,
What you going to do when the lamp burns down?

Oh, the lamp burned down and you can't see,
Oh, the lamp burned down and you can't see,
What you going to do when the lamp burns down?

Ezekiel saw that wheel of time,
And every spoke was of humankind.
What you going to do when the lamb burns down?

God made man and he made him out of clay,
And put him on the earth, but not to stay,
What you going to do when the lamp burns down?

They cast old Daniel in the lion's den,
And Jesus locked the lion's jaw,
What you going to do when the lamp burns down?

Old Satan's mad and I am glad,
He missed one soul he thought he had,
What you going to do when the lamp burns down?

Old Satan's a liar and a conjurer too,
If you don't mind he'll slip it on you,
What you going to do when the lamp burns down?

Oh, poor sinner, now is your time,
Oh, poor sinner, now is your time,
What you going to do when the lamp burns down?   (Hampton)

When The Lord Called Moses

When the Lord called Moses,
Moses refused to answer;
But the third time the Lord called Moses,
Moses say, "Here I'se, Lord!"
Moses say, "Here I'se, Lord!"

When his head was aching in the fever,
Moses say, "Here I'se, Lord!"
When his head was aching with the fever,
And his soul a-making ready for to go.

When the Lord called Moses,
Moses refused to answer;
But the third time the Lord called Moses,
Moses say, "Here I'se, Lord!"
Moses say, "Here I'se, Lord!"
Been a long time a-wagging of my crosses,
But I'se going to heaven when I die,
When I die.   (Fisher)

You Mus' Come In By And Through The Lamb

My God is so high,
You can't get over Him;
He's so low--
You can't get under Him;
He' so wide
That you can't get around Him.
You mus' come in by an' through the Lamb.

One day as I was walkin' along the heavenly road,
My Savior spoke unto me,
An' He filled my heart with love.

Oh, He's so high,
You can't get over Him;
He's so low,
You can't get under Him;
He's so wide
That you can't get aroun' Him,
You mus' come in by an' through the Lamb!
I tell you fellow members,
Things happen mighty strange,
The Lord was good to Israel,
An' His ways don't ever change.

Oh, He's so high,
You can't get over Him;
He's so low,
You can't get under Him;
He's so wide
That you can't get aroun' Him,
You mus' come in by an' through the Lamb!   (Hayes)

You Must Have That True Religion

You must have that true religion,
You must have your soul converted,
You must have that true religion,
You can't cross there,
O, yes, you can't cross there.

Where You going Poor sinner?
Where You going poor liar?
Where you going poor gambler?
Where you going back-slider?

Where you going, I say,
I'm going to the river of Jordan,
You can't cross there
O, yes, you can't cross there.

You must have that true religion,
You must have your soul converted,
You must have that true religion,
You can't cross there,
O, yes, you can't cross there.   (BANS)

You're My Brother So Give Me Your Hand

It makes no difference what church you may belong to,
While traveling through this barren land,
But listen, if you're working for Christ my Redeemer,
You're my brother so give me your hand.

We may not belong to the same denomination,
While traveling through this barren land,
But if you take my hand and lead me home to my Lord,
You're my brother so give me your hand.   (ANS)

LYRICS OF
TRANSCENDENCE _____

All song is, in essence, a form of transcendence, an act of responding to human situations. While song allows for the synthesizing of experience, it can also give psychological distance and perspective, preventing one from becoming completely overtaken by the reality of harsh experience itself. The Afro-Americans in bondage composed many lyrics that have transcendence as a very explicit theme. These composers felt the human need to express themselves beyond their apparent limitations and restrictions, as well as beyond historical time.

When one is greatly bombarded by the concrete or finite, one must necessarily create a realm of existence in the abstract or in the infinite in order to endure that existence. In the abstract or transcendent world, which in the traditional African mind is no less real than the concrete world (owing to the African preoccupation with spiritual phenomena), one could find the affirmation and inspiration needed to confront the world. However, the enslaved Africans did not always have the strength to confront constantly the world in which they lived. Often they had to stand above or beyond life and view it through other eyes. They had often, then, to use the eyes of the soul because the soul could measure and perceive by criteria not bound by human definition. Through the eyes of the soul the enslaved could apprehend the vanity of earthly phenomena. Therefore they could move toward emphasizing the oneness of all being and not be mesmerized by what was happening to the various finite parts of their existence. By emphasizing that which is not held by physical boundaries and limitations, the enslaved Africans were able to merge the future with the present and sometimes create for themselves a sense of inner peace regarding their pilgrimage through their peculiar American wilderness. As James Cone has said, in many instances the enslaved Africans could "live as if the future had already come."[1]

_____

1. James Cone, THE SPIRITUALS AND THE BLUES. Seabury Press, 1972, p.95.

The Angels In Heaven Going To Write My Name

O, write my name,
O, write my name;
O, write my name,
The angels in heaven going to write my name.

Write my name when You get home,
Yes, write my name with a golden pen;
Write my name in the Book of Life,
Yes, write my name in the dripping blood.

O, write my name,
O, write my name;
O, write my name,
The angels in heaven going to write my name.   (BANS)

Anyhow, My Lord

Anyhow, anyhow, anyhow, my Lord.
At the cross you mus' bow,
I'm goin' to heaven anyhow.

If your father talk about you,
And scandalize your name,
At the cross you mus' bow,
I'm goin' to heaven anyhow.

If your mother talk about you,
And scandalize your name;
If your brother talk about you,
And scandalize your name;
If your sister talk about you,
And scandalize your name,
At the cross you mus' bow,
I'm goin' to heaven anyhow.   (St. Helena)

The Bell Done Rung

I know that the bell done rung,
I know that the bell done rung,
I know that the bell done rung,
On the other side of Jordan.

I know my God is a man of war,
He fought my battle at Jericho's wall,
Oh, let me tell you,
Joshua being the son of Nun,
God being with him
'Til the work was done.
Oh, steady Christian,
Oh, steady yourself,
And let me tell you,
About God himself.

I know that the bell done rung,
I know that the bell done rung,
I know that the bell done rung,
On the other side of Jordan.

(BDWS) (Variant)

The Blood Done Signed My Name

Oh, the blood, Oh, the blood,
Oh, the blood done signed my name,
Oh, the blood, Oh, the blood,
Oh, the blood done signed my name;
Thank God, the blood done signed my name!

Got a witness, got a witness,
Oh, the blood done signed my name;
How you know it? How you know it?
Oh, the blood done signed my name;
Jesus told me, Jesus told me,
Oh, the blood done signed my name;
Thank God, the blood done signed my name!

(CD)

Children, Did You Hear When Jesus Rose?

Children, did you hear when Jesus rose,
Did you hear when Jesus rose;
Children, did you hear when Jesus rose,
He rose an' ascended on high!

Mary set her table
In spite of all her foes;
King Jesus sat at the center place
An' cups did overflow.

The Father looked at his Son an' smiled,
The Son did look at-a Him;
The Father saved my soul from hell
An' the Son freed me from sin.

(Dixon)

Come And Go With Me

This old world is not my home,
This old world is not my home,
This old world is not my home,
Oh, Christian, come and go with me.

Yes, I seek my home in heaven,
Yes, I seek my home in heaven,
Oh, moaner, come and go with me.

My home is in the new Jerusalem,
My home is in the new Jerusalem,
Oh, sinner, come and go with me.

Yes, my home is over Jordan,
Yes, my home is over Jordan,
Oh, sister, come and go with me.   (BDWS) (Variant)

Cross Me Over

Cross me over,
Cross me over, my Lord,
Going to cross Jordan in that morning.

Oh, Christian, like some gloomy cloud,
Gather thick and thunder loud,
I'm going to cross Jordan in the morning.

Religion is not to buy,
You can get it if you try,
I'm going to cross Jordan in the morning.

Oh, won't that be a happy time,
Eating of the honey and drinking of the vine,
I'm going to cross Jordan in that morning.

Oh, stand right still and steady yourself,
Let me tell about God Himself,
I'm going to cross Jordan in that morning.

Oh, how He traveled here below,
Healed the sick and raised the dead,
I'm going to cross Jordan in that morning.

That ain't all I got more beside,
Been born of God and I got baptized,
I'm going to cross Jordan in that morning.

Oh, shout, oh shout, ain't you glad,
You going to cross the sea of glass?
I'm going to cross Jordan in that morning.

Cross me over,
Cross me over, my Lord,
Going to cross Jordan in that morning.   (BDWS)

Death Came To My House, He Didn't Stay Long

Hallelu, hallelu, O, my Lord,
I'm going to see my mother again,
Hallelu, hallelu, O, my Lord,
I'm going to see my mother again.

Death came to my house, he didn't stay long,
I looked on the bed and my mother was gone,
I'm going to see my mother again.
Death came to my house, he didn't stay long,
I looked on the bed and my father was gone,
I'm going to see my father again.

Hallelu, hallelu, O, my Lord,
Hallelu, hallelu, O, my Lord.   (BANS)

Death's Going To Lay His Cold Hands On Me (1)

O, sinner, sinner, you better pray,
Or your soul will get lost at the judgment day;
Some of these mornings bright and fair,
I'll take my wings and cleave the air.
Death's going to lay his cold icy hands on me.
Crying, O, my Lord,
Crying, O, my Lord,
Crying, O, my Lord!
Death's going to lay his cold icy hands on me.

Yes, I'm so glad I've been redeemed,
I'm ready to cross old Jordan's stream,
Death's going to lay his cold icy hands on me.   (BANS) (Variant)

Death's Going To Lay His Cold Icy Hands On Me (2)

Oh, death, throw thy sting away,
Death's going to lay his cold icy hands on me.

One day, one day I was walking along,
I heard a reason from on high,
Death's going to lay his cold icy hands on me.

I remember the day and I remember it well,
My dungeon shook and my chain fell off,
Death's going to lay his cold icy hands on me.

I wrestled with death and threw him in the grave,
And my soul said to Satan you better behave,
Death's going to lay his cold icy hands on me.

Oh, death, throw thy sting away,
Death's going to lay his cold icy hands on me.   (BDWS)

Don't You Wish You Were In Heaven

Don't you wish you were in heaven today,
Don't you wish you were in heaven today,
Don't you wish you were in heaven today,
Don't you wish you were in heaven today,
For to answer your name?
Somebody's calling my name,
Somebody's calling my name,
He's calling me home today.

Yes, He's calling like the angel calls,
Bright angel standing in the gate,
He's standing with a sword in this hand,
He's standing for to cut me down.

Don't you wish you were in heaven today,
Don't you wish you were in heaven today,
Don't you wish you were in heaven today,
Don't you wish you were in heaven today,
For to answer your name?   (BDWS)

Dum-A-Lum

I was way down a-yonder a-by my self,
I was hunting a-for some bosom a-friend.
Away down yonder a-by my self-o
A-hunting for some a-bosom friend-o,
Dum a la dum a lum a dum a lum.

An angel of the Lord done change my name,
      my brother,
An' I don't know where my leader's gone;

Good Lord, my Jesus done died one time,
      my brother,
An' he never 'tends to die no mo'.

'Twas a Mary and a Martha an' a James
      and a John,
An' all of them prophets are dead an' gone.
'Twas like a flower a-in a-bloom
That made Jericho for to fall so soon.

Good Lord, my Jesus done died one time,
      my brother,
An' he never tends to die no mo'.   (Calhoun)

Eagle's Wings

Lord, I wish I had an eagle's wings,
O, Lord, I wish I had an eagle's wings,
O, Lord, I wish I had an eagle's wings,
O, Lord, I wish I had an eagle's wings.

I would fly all the way to Paradise,
O, Lord, I would fly all the way to Paradise,
O, Lord, I would fly all the way to Paradise,
O, Lord, I would fly all the way to Paradise.

O, the thunder is a-rollin' over my head,
O, Lord, the thunder is a-rollin' over my head,
O, Lord, the thunder is a-rollin' over my head,
O, Lord, the thunder is a-rollin' over my head.

And the lightenin' is flashin' in my face;
There is no hidin' place for sinner to hide;
O, I run to the rocks to hide me face;
O, I run to the sea an' the sea run dry.

Lord, I wish I had an eagle's wings,
O, Lord, I wish I had an eagle's wings,

O, Lord, I wish I had an eagle's wings,
O, Lord, I wish I had an eagle's wings.   (St. Helena)

Every Little Step Goes Higher

Every little step goes higher, higher, higher,
Every little step goes higher, higher, higher,
Every little step goes higher, higher, higher,
Save me, Jesus, save me now.

Do you think I'll make a soldier?
Do you think I'll make a soldier?
I'm a-going to climb Jacob's ladder,
I'm a-going to climb Jacob's ladder;
I'm a-going to shake right hands with Jesus,
I'm a-going to shake right hands with Jesus.
Every little step goes higher, higher, higher,
Every little step goes higher, higher, higher,
Every little step goes higher, higher, higher,
Save me, Jesus, save me now.   (CD)

Ezekiel Saw The Wheel (1)

Wheel, oh, wheel,
Wheel in the middle of a wheel;
Wheel, oh, wheel,
Wheel in the middle of a wheel.

Ezekiel saw the wheel of time,
Every spoke was humankind;
Way up on the mountain top,
My Lord spoke and the chariot stopped.
Ezekiel saw the wheel,
Way up in the middle of the air;
Ezekiel saw the wheel,
Way up in the middle of the air.

The big wheel runs by faith,
The little wheel runs by the grace of God;
Wheel in a wheel,
Way in the middle of the air.   (BANS)

Ezekiel Saw The Wheel (2)

Ezekiel saw the wheel,
Away up in the middle of the air,
Ezekiel saw the wheel,
Away up in the middle of the air;
And the little wheel runs by faith,
And the big wheel runs by the grace of God,
'Tis a wheel in a wheel,
Away up in the middle of the air.

Some go to church for to sing and shout,
Before six months they are all turned out;

Let me tell you what a hypocrit'll do,
He'll talk about me and he'll talk about you;
One of these days about twelve o'clock,
This old world's going to reel and rock.

Ezekiel saw the wheel,
Away up in the middle of the air.   (Hampton)

Ezekiel's Wheel

'Zekiel's wheel--Oh, my soul!
E-zekiel's wheel--Oh, my soul!
Uh 'Zekiel's wheel--Oh, my soul!
Let's take a ride on Ezekiel's wheel.

There's 'ligion in the wheel,
Oh, my soul!
There's 'ligion in the wheel,
Oh, my soul!
'Ligion in the wheel,
Oh, my soul!
Let's take ride on Ezekiel's wheel.
There's moanin' in the wheel,
Oh, my soul!
There's prayin' in the wheel,
Oh, my soul!
There's shoutin' in the wheel,
Oh, my soul!
There's cryin' in the wheel,
Oh, my soul!
There's laughin' in the wheel,
Oh, my soul!
Let's take a ride on Ezekiel's wheel.   (Grissom)

Going Away To See My Lord

Going away to see my Savior,
I'm going away to see my Lord;
Going away to see my Savior,
I'm going away to see my Lord.

My sister's mighty happy for to see my Jesus,
My sister's mighty happy on Joshua's wall;
My sister's mighty happy for to see my Jesus,
My sister's mighty happy on Joshua's wall.

If I get on the other side of Judgment,
I ain't coming here to sin no more;
Feet going to touch and my tongue's going to tell,
The wonders of King 'Manuel.

My brother's mighty happy for to see my Jesus,
My brother's mighty happy on Joshua's wall;
My brother's mighty happy for to see my Jesus,
My brother's mighty happy on Joshua's wall.   (BDWS)

Going To Ride Up In The Chariot Soon In The Morning

Going to ride up in the chariot,
Soon in the morning,
Ride up in the chariot,
Soon in the morning,
Ride up in the chariot,
Soon in the morning;
And I hope I'll join the band,
Oh, Lord, have mercy on me.

Going to meet my brother there, yes,
Going to chatter with the angels, yes,
Going to meet my Master Jesus, yes,
Going to walk and talk with Jesus, yes,
Soon in the morning.   (BANS)

Going Up

Oh, yes, I'm going up, going up,
        Going all the way, Lord,
Going up, going up to see the heavenly land,
Oh, yes, I'm going up, going up,
        Going all the way, Lord,
Going up, going up to see the heavenly land.

Oh, saints and sinner's will-a you go,
                See the heavenly land,
I'm a-going up to heaven for to see my robe,
                See the heavenly land,
Going to see my robe and try it on,
                See the heavenly land,
It's brighter than that glittering sun,
                See the heavenly land.

I'm a-going to keep a-climbing high,
Till I meet those angels in the sky;
Those pretty angels I shall see,
Why don't the devil let-a me be.

I tell you what I like the best,
It is them a-shouting Methodists;
We shout so loud the devil looks,
And he gets away with his cloven foot.
Oh, yes, I'm going up, going up,
                Going all the way, Lord,
Going up, going up to see the heavenly land.   (Hampton)

Hand Me Down My Silver Trumpet

Hand me down my silver trumpet, Gabriel,
Hand it down;
Hand me down my silver trumpet, Gabriel,
Hand it down
Hand me down my silver trumpet,

Hand me down my silver trumpet,
All my sins been washed away.   (Traditional)

Hold Out Your Light

Hold out your light you heaven bound soldier,
Hold out your light you heaven bound soldier,
Hold out your light you heaven bound soldier,
Let your light shine aroun' the world.

O, deacon, can you hold out your light,
O, deacon, can you hold out your light,
O, deacon, can you hold out your light,
Let your light shine aroun' the world.

O, preacher, can you hold out your light,
Class leader, can you hold out your light,
Class leader, can you hold out your light,
Let your light shine around the world.   (Calhoun)

How You Do Believer?

How you do, believer, how you do today?
Thank God I get over Jordan--
How you do, believer, how you do today?
Thank God I get over Jordan.

How you do, mourner, how you do today?
Thank God I get over Jordan--
How you do, mourner, how you do today?
Thank God I get over Jordan.

How you do sinners, how you do today?
Thank God I get over Jordan--

How you do sinners, how you do today?
Thank God I get over Jordan.

Go your way sinner and sin no more,
Thank God I get over Jordan--
Go your way sinner and sin no more,
Thank God I get over Jordan.

Over Jordan, over Jordan,
Thank God I get over Jordan.   (St. Helena)

I Done Been Home

I done been home,
I done tri' on my robe,
Children, I done been home,
An' if it fit me going to wear it on.
Children, I done been home.

O, here's your robe,
Come and try it on;
If it fit you may wear it on.
Children, I done been home.

O, I done been home,
An' I want to go again,
Children, I done been home,
An' I want to go again.

Children, I done been home,
Children, i done been home,
Children, I done been home,
Children, I done been home.   (Calhoun)

I Found Jesus Over In Zion

I found Jesus over in Zion,
An' He's mine, mine, mine, mine, mine;
I found Jesus over in Zion,
An' He's mine, mine, mine, mine, mine.

I found the Holy Ghost over in Zion,
An' He's mine, mine, mine, mine, mine;
I found the Holy Ghost over in Zion,
An' He's mine, mine, mine, mine, mine.

I got sanctified over in Zion,
An' it's mine, mine, mine, mine, mine;
I got sanctified over in Zion,
And it's mine, mine, mine, mine, mine.

I got baptized over in Zion,
An' I'm saved, saved, saved, saved, saved;
I got baptized over in Zion,
An' I'm saved, saved, saved, saved, saved.

He's my Savior, He's my Savior--
Oh, He's mine, mine, mine, mine, mine;
He's my Savior, He's my savior--
Yes, He's mine, mine, mine, mine, mine.   (Grissom)

I Got A Hidin' Place

I got a hidin' place--
In the Word of God,
I got a hidin' place.

The ship she stop
In the middle of the sea,
Jonah cried out--
Lord have mercy, is it me?
Throw me overboa'd.
I got a hidin' place.
I got a hidin' place

In the Word of God,
I got a hidin' place.

Wonder what's the matter
That the ship won't go;
There's too many liars
Gettin' on boa'd.
Throw 'em overboa'd.
I got a hidin' place,
Throw 'em overboa'd,
I got a hidin' place--
In the Word of God,
I got a hidin' place.

Wonder what's the matter
That the ship won't go:
There's too many hypocrites
Gettin' on boa'd.
Well you can't hide now,
I got a hidin' place.
I got a hidin' place--
In the Word of God,
I got a hidin' place.
Tell that watchman
That he can't hide;
If he hasn't got the Holy Ghost
He can't ride.
Get the Holy Ghost.
I got a hidin' place,
Get the Holy Ghost,
I got a hidin' place.
I got a hidin' place--
In the Word of God,
I got a hidin' place.

There's too many people
Like Jonah today;
God sends 'em out
An' they will not obey.
Won't you help me, Lord?
I got a hidin' place,
Won't you help me, Lord?
I got a hidin' place.
I got a hidin' place--
In the Word of God,
I got a hidin' place.

If you wanta go to heaven,
Like anybody else;
Treat yo neighbor
Like you treat yo'self.
Treat yo' neighbor right.
I got a hidin' place,
Treat yo' neighbor right,
I got a hidin' place.
I got a hidin' place--
Roun' the throne of God,
I got a hidin' place.

Well, when I get to heaven
Gonna sing an' shout;
There's nobody there
Gonna put me out.
Well in Canaan land,
I got a hidin' place.
I got a hidin' place--
Roun' the throne of God,
I got a hidin' place.

(Grissom)

I Got A Key To The Kingdom

I got a Key to the Kingdom,
I got a Key. Oh, yes, I have-a now.
I got a Key to the Kingdom,
An' the worl' can't do me no harm.

Oh, If you know you're livin' right,
Servin' God both night an' day;
An' when you go down on yo' knees,
God will hear ev'ry word you say.

Oh! When you know you're livin' right,
An' you're doing nobody no wrong;
Jus' call up Central in Heaven,
Tell Jesus to come to the phone.

Oh! Get yo' trumpet, Gabriel,
An' come down on the sea;
Now don't you sound yo' trumpet
'Til you get orders from me.

Now when I get to Heaven,
I want you to be there, too;
An' when I holler, Hallelujah!
I want you to holler, too.

They took ole Paul an' Silas,
An' put 'em in a jail below;
The angel come down from Heaven,
An' they unlocked the do'.

Prayer is the Key to the Kingdom,
An' Faith unlocks the do'. Oh! Yes,
If you got a Key to the Heaven,
You can pray ev'rywhere you go.

(Grissom)

I'm An Everyday Witness

I'm a witness for my Lord,
I'm a witness for my Lord,
I'm a witness for my Lord,
I'm a ever'day witness for my Lord.

I'm a Monday witness for my Lord,
I'm a Monday witness for my Lord,
I'm a Monday witness for my Lord,
I'm a ever'day witness for my Lord.

I'm a Tuesday witness for my Lord,
I'm a Tuesday witness for my Lord,
I'm a Tuesday witness for my Lord,
I'm a ever'day witness for my Lord.

I'm a Wednesday witness for my Lord,
I'm a Wednesday witness for my Lord,
I'm a Wednesday witness for my Lord,
I'm a ever'day witness for my Lord.
I'm a Thursday witness for my Lord,
I'm a Thursday witness for my Lord,
I'm a Thursday witness for my Lord,
I'm a ever'day witness for my Lord.

I'm a Friday witness for my Lord,
I'm a Friday witness for my Lord,
I'm a Friday witness for my Lord,
I'm a ever'day witness for my Lord.

I'm a Saturday witness for my Lord,
I'm a Saturday witness for my Lord,
I'm a Saturday witness for my Lord,
I'm a ever'day witness for my Lord.   (Grissom)

I Mean To Lift Up The Standard For My King

I mean to lift up a standard for my King,
All over this world I mean to sing.

When Daniel was called by wicked men,
They cast po' Daniel in the lion's den;
Daniel went down feelin' no fear,
Because he knew his God was near.
I mean to lift up a standard for my King,
All over this world I mean to sing.

When Daniel found out a writin' was signed,
He went to his room in his own set time;
He fell on his knees an' begin to pray,
An' in this spirit I heard him say:
I mean to lift up a standard for my King,
All over this world I mean to sing.

When the King had signed that wicked decree,
Daniel was found on his knees;
"I'm goin' to pray three times a day,
An look to Jesus to open the way."
I mean to lift up a standard for my King,
All over this world I mean to sing.

The King was in trouble all night long,
He felt that he treated po' Daniel wrong;

He went down early next mornin' to see,
"King, the God I serve has delivered me."
I mean to lift up a standard for my King,
All over this world I mean to sing.

(Grissom)

I'm Just Going Over There

I'm just going over Jordan,
I'm just going over there,
I'm going home to see my brother,
I'm just going over there.

I'm just going over Jordan,
I'm just going over there,
I'm going home to see my mother,
I'm just going over there.

I'm just going over Jordan,
I'm just going over there,
I'm going home to see my Jesus,
I'm just going over there.

(ANSAS)

I've Got A Home In The Rock, Don't You See?

I've got a home in the rock,
          don't you see?
I've got a home in the rock,
          don't you see?
Just between the earth and skies,
I behold my Savior's side,
I've got a home in the rock,
          don't you see?
Swing low, chariot, in the east,
          don't you see?
Swing low, chariot, in the east,
          don't you see?
Let God's people have some peace,
I've got a home in the rock,
          don't you see?

Swing low, chariot, in the west,
          don't you see?
Swing low, chariot, in the west,
          don't you see?
Let God's people have some rest,
I've got a home in the rock,
          don't you see?

Come along, Moses, don't get lost,
          don't you see?
Come along, Moses, don't get lost,
          don't you see?
Stretch your rod and come across;
I've got a home in the rock,
          don't you see?

Heard a mighty rumbling in the ground,
                don't you see.
Heard a mighty rumbling in the ground,
                don't you see?
Must be Satan passing 'round;
I've got a home in the rock,
                don't you see?   (CD)

I Wish I Have Had An Eagle's Wings

Oh, I wish I have had an eagle's wings,
Oh, I wish I have had an eagle's wings;
I would fly all the way to paradise,
I would fly all the way to paradise.

Oh, I wish I have had an eagle's wings,
Oh, I wish I have had an eagle's wings;
Oh, the lightning is flashing in my face,
Oh, the lightning is flashing in my face.

Oh, I wish I have had an eagle's wings,
Oh, I wish I have had an eagle's wings;
Oh, the thunder is rolling over my head,
Oh, the thunder is rolling over my head.

Oh, I wish I have had an eagle's wings,
Oh, I wish I have had an eagle's wings;

I would fly all the way to paradise,
I would fly all the way to paradise.   (CD)

I Won't Die No More

Singing way in the heaven,
I won't die no more,
Singing way in the heaven,
I won't die no more.

One more favor I ask of you,
Bring those children in the fear of God;
There's golden slippers in the heaven for me;
Starry crown in the heaven for me,
Golden girdle in the heaven for me.

Steady, Christian, steady yourself,
Let me tell you about God Himself;
How he traveled here below,
Healed the sick and raised the dead,
Cast out devils in His name,
Turned out all those hypocrites.

Singing way in the heaven,
I won't die no more,
Singing way in the heaven,
I won't die no more.   (BDWS)

Jacob's Ladder

We are climbing Jacob's ladder,
We are climbing Jacob's ladder,
We are climbing Jacob's ladder,
Soldier of the cross.

Every round goes higher and higher,
Soldier of the cross.

Sinner, do you love my Jesus?
Soldier of the cross.
If you love Him, why not serve Him?
Soldier of the cross.

Do you think I'd make a soldier?
Soldier of the cross.

We are climbing higher and higher,
Soldier of the cross.   (Hampton)

Just Like John

When I come to die,
I want to be ready,
When I come to die,
Going to walk Jerusalem just like John.

Walk Jerusalem in the morning,
I'm going to walk Jerusalem in the morning;
Walk Jerusalem when the world's on fire,
I'm going to walk Jerusalem just like John;
Walk Jerusalem when the tombstones busted,
Walk Jerusalem just like John.

When I come to die,
I want to be ready,
When I come to die,
Going to walk Jerusalem just like John.   (BDWS)

Keep Me From Sinking Down

Oh, Lord, O, my Lord!
                        Oh, my good Lord!
Keep me from sinking down.

I tell you what I mean to do
I mean to go to heaven, too;
I look up yonder and what do I see:
I see the angels beckoning to me.
When I was a mourner just like you:
I mourned and mourned till I got through;
I bless the Lord I'm gwine to die:
I'm gwine to judgement by and by.

Oh, Lord, O, my Lord!
                    Oh, my good Lord!
Keep me from sinking down.   (FJS)

Lay This Body Down

O, graveyard, O, graveyard,
I'm walking through the graveyard;
Lay this body down.

I know moonlight, I know starlight,
I'm walking through the starlight;
Lay this body down

I walk in the moonlight, I walk in the starlight,
I lay this body down;
I know the graveyard, I know the graveyard,
When I lay this body down.

I lay in the graveyard and stretch out my arms;
I go to the judgement in the evening of the day,
And my soul and your soul will meet in the day,
When we lay this body down.   (Allen)

Let The Church Roll On

Let the church roll on, Lord,
Let the church roll on, Lordy,
Let the church roll on.
Lord, Lord, Lord, let the church roll on.

If my brother has a fault,
Bring him before the church,

If the council turns him out,
Let the church roll on.

If the liar has a fault,
Bring him before the deacon,
If the deacon turns him out,
Let the church roll on.

If that turn-back has a fault,
Bring him before the elder,
If the elder turns him out,
Let the church roll on.   (BDWS)

Let Us Break Bread Together

Let us break bread together on our knees;
Let us break bread together on our knees;
When I fall on my knees, with my face to the rising sun,
O Lord, have mercy on me.

Let us drink wine together on our knees;
Let us drink wine together on our knees;
When I fall on my knees, with my face to the rising sun,
O Lord, have mercy on me.

Let us praise God together on our knees;
Let us praise God together on our knees;
When I fall on my knees, with my face to the rising sun,
O Lord, have mercy on me.   (Dixon)

Lit'l David, Play On Your Harp

Lit' David, play on yo' harp,
Hallelu, Hallelujah,
Lit'l David, play on yo' harp,
Hallelu.
David had a harp,
Had ten strings,
Touch one string,
An' the whole heaven ring.

David, play on yo' harp,
Hallelu, Hallelujah,
Lit'l David, play on yo' harp,
Hallelu.

I say to David,
"Come play me a piece."
David said to me,
How can I play, when I'm in a strange land?"

David, play on yo' harp,
Hallelu, Hallelujah,
Lit'l David, play on yo' harp,
Hallelu.
David, play on yo' harp,
Hallelu, Hallelujah,
Lit'l David, play on yo' harp,
Hallelu!   (Hayes)

Lord, I Want Two Wings

Lord, I want two wings to veil my face,
Lord, I want two wings to fly away;
Lord, I want two wings to veil my face,
Lord, I want two wings to fly away.

Jesus on the mountain
Preachin' to the po',
Never heard such a sermon
In all my life befo'.

Did not come in the mornin',
Neither in the heat of the day;
But He always come in the evenin',
An' washed my sins away.

When you are in trouble,
Journeyin' on yo' way;
Jus' put yo' trust in Jesus,
An' don't forget to pray.

Get up in the mornin',
Get up out-a yo' bed;
You should not eat one mouthful
Until yo' prayers are said.

I went down in the valley,
Hands across my breast;
Thought I heard King Jesus say--
Come unto me an' rest.

Yonder comes my mother--
Where you been so long?
Well, I been down in the valley,
My soul's done anchored an' gone.

Yonder comes that Angel--
What might be yo' name?
My name is great Jehovah,
Well, you must be born again.   (Grissom)

Lord, Remember Me

Oh, Death he is a little man,
And he goes from door to door,
He kill some souls and he wounded some,
And he left some souls to pray.

Oh, Lord, remember me,
Do, Lord, remember me,
Remember me as the year rolls 'round,
Lord, remember me.

I want to die like Jesus died,
And he died with a free good will;
I lay out in the grave and I stretch out my arms,
Do, Lord, remember me.

Oh, Lord, remember me,
Do, Lord, remember me,

Remember me as the year rolls 'round,
Lord, remember me.   (Allen)

My Father Took A Light

My father took a light and went to heaven,
My father took a light and went to heaven,
My father took a light and went to heaven,
And I'se-a got to linger till I die.

Father, how long has I got to linger,
Oh, how long has I got to linger,
Oh, how long has I got to linger?
Well, I got to linger till I die.

My sister took a light and went to heaven,
My sister took a light and went to heaven,
My sister took a light and went to heaven,
And I'se-a got to linger till I die.

Sister, how long has I got to linger,
Oh, how long has I got to linger,
Oh, how long has I got to linger?
Well, I got to linger till i die.
Oh, how long must I linger in the tomb!   (Fisher)

My Soul's Been Anchored In The Lord

In the Lord, in the Lord,
My soul's been anchored in the Lord;
In the Lord, in the Lord,
My soul's been anchored in the Lord.

Before I'd stay in hell one day,
I'd sing and pray myself away;
I'm going to pray and never stop,
Until I reach the mountain top.

In the Lord, in the Lord,
My soul's been anchored in the Lord;
In the Lord, in the Lord,
My soul's been anchored in the Lord.   (BANS)

Oh, Let Me Shine

Oh, let me shine,
Oh, let me shine,
Oh, let me shine,
Shine like the mornin' star.

Shine like Peter, let me shine,
Shine like Moses, let me shine;
If you can shine,
Oh, let me shine,
Move out the way
And let me shine,
Shine like the mornin' star.   (St. Helena)

O Lord, Write My Name

O, Lord, write my name,
O, Lord, write my name,
O, Lord, write my name,
The angel in the heaven going to write my name.

Better min', sister, how you walk on the cross,
If your right foot slip,
Your soul will be lost.
Come on brother with your up and down,
Christ going to meet you on the half way groun'.

Joshua was the son of Nun,
God was with him till the work was done.
God in the garden an' begin to look out,
The ram horn blow and the children did shout.

O, Lord, write my name,
O, Lord, write my name,
O, Lord, write my name,
The angel in heaven going to write my name.   (Calhoun)

O, Watch The Stars

O, watch the stars,
See how they run;
O, watch the stars,
See how they run
Down at the setting of the sun,
O, watch the stars,
See how they run.

Just watch the stars, see how they run,
The stars run down at the setting of the sun,
Just watch the stars, see how they run.

Oh, God's little army goin' to shine,
The stars run down at the setting of the sun,
O, watch the stars see how they run.   (St. Helena)

O Yes! Oh Yes!

I come this night for to sing and pray,
Oh, yes! Oh, yes!
To drive old Satan far away,
Oh, yes! Oh, yes!

Oh, wait till I get on my robe,
Wait till I get on my robe,
Wait till I get on my robe,
Oh, yes! Oh, yes!

That heavenly home is bright and fair,
But very few can enter there;
Oh, wait till I get on my robe,
Oh, yes! Oh, yes!

As I went down in the valley to pray,
I met old Satan on the way,
And what do you think he said to me?
"You're too young to pray and too young to die."

If you want to catch that heavenly breeze,
Go down in the valley on your knees,
Go, bow your knees upon the ground,
And ask your Lord to turn you 'round.

Oh, wait till I get on my robe,
Wait till I get on my robe,
Wait till I get on my robe,
Oh, yes! Oh, yes!   (FJS)

Plenty Good Room

Plenty good room, plenty good room,
Good room in my Father's kingdom,
Plenty good room, plenty good room,
A-jes' choose yo' seat an' set down.

Oh, plenty good room, plenty good room,
Good room in my Father's kingdom,
Plenty good room, plenty good room,
A-jes' choose yo' seat an' set down.

I would not be a sinner,
I tell you the reason why,
'Cause if my Lord should call on me,
I wouldn't be ready to die.

Plenty good room, plenty good room,
Good room in my Father's kingdom,
Plenty good room, plenty good room,
A-jes' choose yo' seat an' set down.   (Hayes)

Prepare Me One Body

Prepare me one body,
I'll go down, I'll go down,
Prepare me one body like man;
I'll go down an' die.

The man of sorrows, sinner, see;
I'll go down, I'll go down,

He died for you an' He died for me;
I'll go down an' die.

Prepare me, Lord, one body!
Prepare me one body like man!
I'll go down an' die!   (Hayes)

Redeemed, Redeemed

O redeem', redeem',
Been washed in the blood of the Lamb.

Matthew cried out, Lord is it I?
Mark cried out, Lord is it I?
Luke cried out, Lord is it I?
John cried out, Lord is it I?
He tol' John to watch an see,
Him that suppeth in the dish with me.

Joshua was the son of Nun,
God was with him till the work was done.
Got in the window an' begun to look out,
The ram horn blowed and the children did shout.

They boun' my Lord with the purple cord,
An' led Him away to the judgment hall.
"I caught that fellow," I hear' them say.
An' they whipped Him till the break of day.

As Jesus was eatin' his last Passover,
Judas rested upon His shoulder--
He spoke one word which seem' to fright,
Saying -- "One of you shall betray him this night."

Judas went to the highmos' priest,
Said the man he wanted was at the feast,
"When I meet Him you'll know Him by this,
I'll walk up and give Him a kiss."

Some go to church an' cannot keep still,
Because they have not done God's will.
Ol' man Adam has never been out.
When guilty comdemn' they'll get up an' shout.

Some go to church and they put on pretense
Until the day of grace is spent.
If they haven't been changed you'll know it well,
When Gabriel blow, they will go to hell.

Sunday come' they'll have Christian faith.
Monday come they'll lose their grace;
The Devil get in they will role up their sleeve,
Religion come' out and begin to leave.

Isiah spoke of the coming Messi'
Befo' he lef' this word on high.
Matthew's gospel loudly crie'
Saying -- "Jesus is born an' He sholy mus' die."   (Calhoun)

Ride On, Moses

I've been travelling all day,
Ride on, Moses,
To hear the good folk sing and pray.

I want to go home in the morning,
They prayed so long I could not wait,
Ride on, Moses.

I know the Lord would pass that way,
I want to go home in the morning,
Ride on, ride on, ride on, Moses.

Ride on, King Emanuel,
I want to go home in the morning,
I want to go home in the morning.

Ride The Chariot

Ride the chariot in the morning, Lord,
Ride the chariot in the morning, Lord,
Ride the chariot in the morning, Lord,
I'm gonna ride the chariot in the morning, Lord.

I'm gettin' ready for the judgment day,
My Lord, my Lord,
I'm gettin' ready for the judgment day,
My Lord, my Lord.

Are yo ready, my brother?
Are you ready for the journey?
Are you ready my sister?
Are you ready for the journey?
Do you want to see your Jesus?
Do you want to see your Jesus?

Oh, yes, I'm waitin' for the chariot
'Cause I'm ready to go.

I never can forget that day
When all my sins were taken away;
I'll serve my Lord till judgment day,
Ride the chariot to see my Lord,
Ride the chariot in the morning, Lord.

Rise And Shine

Oh, brethren, rise and shine,
And give God the glory, glory.
Rise and shine,
And give God the glory, glory,
Rise and shine,
And give God the glory,
For the year of Jubilee.

Don't you want to be a soldier, soldier, soldier,
Don't you want to be a soldier, soldier, soldier?
Do you think I will make a soldier?
Yes, I think you will make a soldier,
For the year of Jubilee!
Oh, brethren, rise and shine,
And give God the glory, glory.
Rise and shine,
And give God the glory, glory,
Rise and shine,

And give God the glory,
For the year of Jubilee.   (FJS)

Rise, Mourners, Rise

Rise, mourners, rise,
O, can't you rise and tell
                    What the Lord has done for you?

Rise, sinners, rise
O, can't you rise and tell
                    What the Lord has done for you?

Yes, he's taken my feet from the miry clay,
                    Placed them on higher ground.
Yes, he's taken my feet from the miry clay,
                    Placed them on higher ground.   (FJS)

Rock-A My Soul

Rock-a my soul in the bosom of Abraham,
Rock-a my soul in the bosom of Abraham,
Rock-a my soul in the bosom of Abraham,
Oh, rock-a my soul.

I never shall forget the day,
When Jesus washed my sins away,
I know my God is a man of war,
He fought my battle at hell's dark door;
If you don't believe I'm a child of God,
Follow me where the road is hard.

One day, one day I was walking nigh,
Yes, I heard a reason from on high;
I remember the day, I remember it well,
My sins were forgiven and my soul saved from hell.
I went down to the valley and didn't go to stay,
My soul got happy and I stayed all day;
Just look up yonder what I see,
A band of angels coming after me,
If you get there before I do,
Tell my Lord I'm coming too.
When I get to heaven and sit right down,
Oh, rock-a my soul,
I'll ask my Lord for my starry crown,
Oh, rock-a my soul.   (BDWS) (Variant)

Rock Of Jubilee

O rock of jubilee, poor fallen soul,
Rock to the mercy seat, to the corner of the world,
O, Lord, the rock of jubilee.

O, rock of jubilee,
And I rock them all about;

Stand back, Satan, let me come by;
O come, titty Katy, let me go,
I have no time for to stay at home;
My Father's door is open wide now.
Mary girl, you know my name,
Look this way and you look that way
The wind blows east, it blows from Jesus.   (Allen)

Room Enough In The Heaven

Oh, there's room enough,
Oh, there's room enough,
There's room enough in the heaven,
I know there's room enough,
I can't stay behind.

I can't stay behind, my Lord,
I can't stay behind,
I can't stay behind, my Lord,
I can't stay behind.

Oh, the lilies bloom,
Oh, the lilies bloom,
The lilies bloom in the heaven, I know;
Oh, the lilies bloom,
I can't stay behind.

Oh, the roses bloom,
Oh, the roses bloom,
The roses bloom in the heaven, I know;
Oh, the roses bloom,
I can't stay behind.

Oh, the angels sing,
Oh, the angels sing,
The angels sing in the heaven, I know;
Oh, the angels sing,
I can't stay behind.   (St. Helena)

Sing-A Ho That I Had The Wings Of A Dove

Sing-a ho that I had the wings of a dove,
Sing-a ho that I had the wings of a dove,
Sing-a ho that I had the wings of a dove,
I'd fly away and be at rest.

Virgin Mary had one son,
The Jews and the Romans had him hung;
Zion's daughters wept and mourned,
When their dying Savior groaned;
Sinner man, see what a shame,
To trample down your Savior's name.   (ANS)

Soon I Will Be Done

Soon I will be done with the troubles of the world,
Troubles of the world, the troubles of the world,
Soon I will be done with the troubles of the world,
Going home to live with God.

No more weeping and wailing,
No more weeping and wailing,
No more weeping and wailing,
I'm going to live with God.

I want to meet my mother,
I want to meet my mother,
I want to meet my mother,
I'm going to live with God.

I want to meet my Jesus,
I want to meet my Jesus,
I want to meet my Jesus,
I'm going to live with God.   (ANS)

Sun Don't Set In The Morning

Sun don't set in the morning,
Sun don't set in the morning, Lord,
Sun don't set in the morning,
Light shines 'round the world.

Pray on, praying sister,
Pray on, praying sister,
Pray on, praying sister,
Light shines around the world.

Pray on, praying brother,
Pray on, praying brother,
Pray on, praying brother,
Light shines 'round the world.

Sun don't set in the morning,
Sun don't set in the morning, Lord,
Sun don't set in the morning,
Light shines 'round the world.   (Hampton)

Sun Shine Into My Soul

Sun shine, sun shine,
Sun shine into my soul,
          in the morning.
Sun shine, sun shine,
O, the sun shine into my soul.

Have a good ol' aunty in the kingdom,
Have a good ol' mother in the kingdom,
Have good ol' sister in the kingdom,
An' you may say how-r I know,

But the las' time I heard from her
She's rappin' at Mercy's do'.
Lordy, sun shine in my soul.

Sun shine, sun shine,
Sun shine into my soul,
        in the morning.

Sun shine, sun shine,
O, the sun shine into my soul.   (Calhoun)

Sweet Heaven

Heaven, sweet heaven,
Oh Lord, I want to go to heaven,
Heaven, sweet heaven,
Oh Lord, I want to go to heaven.

You lie on me,
They lie on you,
Lie on everybody;
The last lie you told on me,
It's going to raise me higher in heaven.

Ezekiel saw the mighty big wheel,
In the big wheel there was a little wheel,
The big wheel represents God Himself,
And the little wheel represents Jesus Christ.   (BDWS)

Thank God I'm In The Feel

Lord, I never knowed the battle was so hard,
Lord, I never knowed the battle was so hard,
Lord, I never knowed the battle was so hard,
Thank God I'm in the field.

Thank God I've got religion,
Thank God I've got religion,
Thank God I've got religion,
Thank God I'm in the field.

Thank God I've been converted,
Thank God I've been converted,
Thank God I've been converted,
Thank God I'm in the field.

The heaven is a-raging higher,
The heaven is a-raging higher,
The heaven is a-raging higher,
Thank God I'm in the field.
An' hell is a-sinking deeper,
An' hell is a-sinking deeper,
an' hell is a-sinking deeper,
Thank God I'm in the field.   (Calhoun)

This Is A Sin-Trying World

O, this is a sin-trying world,
This is a sin-trying world,
This is a sin-trying world,
This is a sin-trying world.

O, heaven's so high,
    High heaven!
And I am so low,
    Hard trials!

I don't know whether I'll ever get to heaven or no--
    Crown of Life!

Jordan's stream is chilly and wide,
    Cold Jordan!
    Deep and wide!
None can cross but the sanctified--
    Can't you cross it?

Way over yonder in the harvest fields,
    O, the harvest!
The angels shoving at the chariot wheels--
    Few laborers!
    Won't you join them?
You may bury me in the East,
    In the heavens!
You may bury me in the West,
    With my mother!
But in the morning my soul will be at rest--
    And my Savior!   (ANS)

'Tis Jordan's River

'Tis Jordan's river,
  And I must go 'cross,
'Tis Jordan's river,
  And I must go 'cross,
'Tis Jordan's river,
  And I must go 'cross,
Poor sinner, fare you well.

Am I a soldier of the Cross?
Yes, my Lord!
Or must I count this soul as lost?
Yes, my Lord!

As I go down the stream of time,
I leave this sinful world behind;
Old Satan thinks he'll get us all,
Because in Adam we did fall;
If you want to see old Satan run,
Just shoot him with a Gospel-gun,
Yes, my Lord!
Yes, my Lord!

'Tis Jordan's river,
    And I must go 'cross,
'Tis Jordan's river,
    And I must go 'cross,
'This Jordan's river,
    And I must go 'cross,
Poor sinner, fare you well.

(FJS)

Way Over Jordan

Oh, way over Jordan,
View the land, view the land,
Way over Jordan,
Oh, view the heavenly land;
I want to go to heaven when I die!
View the land, view the land,
To shout salvations as I fly,
Oh, view the heavenly land.

Old Satan's mad, and I am glad,
He missed that soul he thought he had;
You say you're aiming for the skies,
Why don't you stop your telling lies?
You say your Lord has set your free,
Why don't you let your neighbors be?

Oh, way over Jordan,
View the land, view the land,
Way over Jordan,
Oh, view the heavenly land;
I want to go to heaven when I die!
View the land, view the land;
To shout salvation as I fly,
Oh, view the heavenly land.

(FJS)

Way Up The Mountain

Way up on the mountain, Lord!
Mountain top, Lord!
I heard God talking, Lord!
Children, the chariot stop.
Lord! Lord!

One day, one day, Lord,
Was walking along, Lord!
With a hung down head, Lord!
Children, a aching heart, Lord!

O Satan is a liar, Lord!
An' a conjurer, too, Lord!
An' if you don't min', Lord!
Children, he'll conjure you, Lord!

Devil is a making, Lord!
Iron shoes, Lord!

An' if you don't min', Lord!
Children, he'll slip 'em on you, Lord!

Rich man Divey, Lord!
He live' so well, Lord!

An' when he die, Lord!
He had a home in hell, Lord!

Po' man Lazarus, Lord!
Po' as I, Lord!
An' when he die', Lord!
He had a home on high, Lord!   (Calhoun)

When The Train Comes Along

When the train comes along,
When the train comes along,
I will meet you at the station
When the train comes along.

If my mother asks for me,
Tell her Death summons me;
If my brother asks for me,
Tell him Death summons me;
Oh, I may be blind and cannot see.

When the train comes along,
When the train comes along,
I will meet you at the station
When the train comes along.   (CD)

Who Is On The Lord's Side

Let me tell you what is naturally the fact,
Who is on the Lord's side,
None of God's children never look back,
Who is on the Lord's side.

Way in the valley--
Weeping Mary,
Mourning Martha,
Risen Jesus.

Who is on the Lord's side,
None of God's children never look back.   (Allen)

Wish I Was In Heaven Sitting Down (1)

Wish I was in heaven sitting down,
Wish I was in heaven sitting down,
O, Mary, O, Martha,
Wish I was in heaven sitting down.

Wouldn't get tired no more, tired no more,
Wouldn't get tired no more, tired no more;
Wouldn't have nothing to do, nothing to do,
Wouldn't have nothing to do, nothing to do;
Try on my long white robe, long white robe,
Try on my long white robe, long white robe;
Sit at my Jesus' feet, my Jesus' feet,
Sit at my Jesus' feet, my Jesus' feet.

Wish I was in heaven sitting down,
Wish I was in heaven sitting down,
O, Mary, O, Martha,
Wish I was in heaven sitting down.   (ANS)

Wish I Was In Heaven Sittin' Down

I wish I was in Heaven sittin' down, sittin' down,
I wish I was in Heaven sittin' down;
Wish I was in Heaven--Oh, yes! Oh, yes!
I wish I was in Heaven sittin' down.

In Heaven I wouldn't have nothin' a-'tall to do, 'tall to do,
In Heaven I wouldn't have nothin' a-'tall to do;
Just' sit down an' rest--Oh, yes! Oh, yes!
In Heaven I wouldn't have nothin' a-tall to do.

I'd walk about in Heaven an' tell the news, tell the news,
I'd walk about in Heaven an tell the news;
Walk about in Heaven--Oh, yes! Oh, yes!
I'd walk about in Heaven an' tell the news.   (Grissom)

SELECT BIBLIOGRAPHY: SONG COLLECTIONS _____

Allen, William Francis, Charles Pickard Ware, and Lucy McKim Garrison. SLAVE SONGS OF THE UNITED STATES. New York: A. Simpson Co., 1867.

Ballanta-Taylor, Nicholas G. J. SAINT HELENA ISLAND SPIRITUALS. New York: G. Schirmer, 1925.

Barton, William E. OLD PLANTATION HYMNS: A COLLECTION OF HITHERTO UNPUBLISHED MELODIES OF THE SLAVE AND THE FREEDMAN, WITH HISTORICAL AND DESCRIPTIVE NOTES. New York: AMS Press, 1972.

Brown, Sterling A., Arthur P. Davis and Ulysses Lee, eds.. THE NEGRO CARAVAN. New York: Arno Press, 1941, 1969.

Bryan, Ashley, ed. WALK TOGETHER CHILDREN: BLACK AMERICAN SPIRITUALS. New York: Atheneum Press, 1974.

Burleigh, Harry T., ed. PLANTATION MELODIES OLD AND NEW. New York: G. Schirmer, 1901.

Burlin, Natalie Curtis. NEGRO FOLK SONGS, 4 vols. New York: G. Schirmer, 1918-19.

Carawan, Guy and Candie Carawan. AIN'T YOU GOT A RIGHT TO THE TREE OF LIFE?--THE PEOPLE OF JOHNS ISLAND: THEIR FACES, THEIR WORDS AND THEIR SONGS. New York: Simon and Shuster, 1966.

Chambers, Herbert A., ed. THE TREASURY OF NEGRO SPIRITUALS. London: Blanford Press, 1963.

Cohen, Lily Y. LOST SPIRITUALS. New York: Walter Neale, 1928.

Courlander, Harold. A TREASURY OF AFRO-AMERICAN FOLKLORE. New York: Crown Publishers, 1976.

Cox, John H., ed. FOLK-SONGS OF THE SOUTH: COLLECTED UNDER THE AUSPICES OF THE WEST VIRGINIA FOLK-LORE SOCIETY. Cambridge: Harvard University Press, 1936.

Dett, R. Nathaniel. THE DETT COLLECTION OF NEGRO SPIRITUALS. Chicago: Hall and McCreary, 1936.

-------, ed. NEGRO SPIRITUALS. London: Blanford Press, 1959.

-------, ed. RELIGIOUS FOLK SONGS OF THE NEGRO. Hampton, Virginia: Hampton Institute Press, 1927.

Diton, Carl, ed. THIRTY-SIX SOUTH CAROLINA SPIRITUALS. New York: G. Schirmer, 1928.

Edet, Edna S., ed. THE GRIOT SINGS: SONGS FROM THE BLACK WORLD. New York: Medgar Evers College Press, 1978.

Emerson, William C. STORIES AND SPIRITUALS OF THE NEGRO SLAVE. Boston: Richard C. Badger, 1930.

Fenner, Thomas P., Frederic G. Rathburn, and Bessie Cleaveland, eds. CABIN AND PLANTATION SONGS AS SUNG BY THE HAMPTON STUDENTS. New York: G.P. Putnam's Sons, 1890.

Fisher, William Arms, ed. SEVENTY NEGRO SPIRITUALS. Boston: AMS, 1974.

Grissom, Mary Allen. THE NEGRO SINGS A NEW HEAVEN. Chapel Hill: University of North Carolina Press, 1930.

Hallowell, Emily, ed. CALHOUN PLANTATION SONGS. Boston: C.W. Thompson and Company, 1907.

Hughes, Langston and Arna Bontemps, eds. THE BOOK OF NEGRO FOLKLORE. New York: Dodd, Mead, 1958.

Jackson, George Pullen. WHITE AND NEGRO SPIRITUALS. New York: J. J. Augustin, 1944.

Jessye, Eva A. MY SPIRITUALS. New York: Robbins-Engel, 1927.

Johnson, James Weldon and J. Rosamond Johnson, eds. THE BOOK OF AMERICAN NEGRO SPIRITUALS. New York: Viking Press, 1925.

-------, eds. THE SECOND BOOK OF NEGRO SPIRITUALS. New York: Viking Press, 1927.

Logan, William A., ed. ROAD TO HEAVEN: TWENTY-EIGHT NEGRO SPIRITUALS. University, Ala.: University of Alabama Press, 1960.

Lomax, John and Alan Lomax, eds. FOLK SONG U.S.A. New York: Duell, Sloan and Pearce, 1947.

McIlhenny, Edward A., ed. BEFO' DE WAR SPIRITUALS: WORDS AND MELODIES. Boston: Christopher Publishing House, 1933.

Parrish, Lydia A., ed. SLAVE SONGS OF THE GEORGIA SEA ISLANDS. New York: Creative Age Press, 1942.

Sandilands, Alexander, ed. A HUNDRED AND TWENTY NEGRO SPIRITUALS, SELECTED BY ALEXANDER SANDILANDS PARTICULARLY FOR USE IN AFRICA. Morija, Basutoland: Morija Sesuto Books Depot, 1964.

White, Clarence Cameron, ed. FORTY NEGRO SPIRITUALS. Philadelphia: Theodore Presser, 1927.

White, Newman I. AMERICAN NEGRO FOLK-SONGS. Cambridge: Harvard University Press, 1928.

Work, John Wesley, ed. AMERICAN NEGRO SONGS: A COMPREHENSIVE COLLECTION OF 230 FOLK SONGS, RELIGIOUS AND SECULAR. New York: Crown Publishers, 1940.

------. FOLK SONGS OF THE AMERICAN NEGRO. Nashville: Fisk University Press, 1915.

SELECT BIBLIOGRAPHY: HISTORY AND INTERPRETATION _____

Battle, Michael A. "The Kerygmatic Ministry of Black Song and Sermon." THE JOURNAL OF BLACK SACRED MUSIC, Vol. 1, No. 2 (Fall 1987), pp.17-20.

Bowman, Thea, F.S.P.A. "The Gift Of African American Sacred Song." In LEAD ME, GUIDE ME: THE AFRICAN AMERICAN CATHOLIC HYMNAL. Chicago: G.I.A. Publications, 1987.

Bowyer, O. Richard, Betty L. Hart, and Charlotte A. Meade. PRAYER IN THE BLACK TRADITION. Nashville: The Upper Room, 1986.

Cone, James. THE SPIRITUALS AND THE BLUES: AN INTERPRETATION. New York: Seabury Press, 1972.

Courlander, Harold. NEGRO FOLK MUSIC, U.S.A. New York: Columbia University Press, 1963.

De Lerma, Dominique-Rene. BIBLIOGRAPHY OF BLACK MUSIC, 2 Vols. Westport, CT: Greenwood Press, 1981.

Dixon, Christa K. NEGRO SPIRITUALS: FROM BIBLE TO FOLK SONG. Philadelphia: Fortress Press, 1976.

Djeje, Jacqueline C. AMERICAN BLACK SPIRITUAL AND GOSPEL SONGS FROM SOUTHWEST GEORGIA: A COMPARATIVE STUDY. Los Angeles: UCLA Center For Afro-American Studies, 1978.

Epstein, Dena J. SINFUL TUNES AND SPIRITUALS: BLACK FOLK MUSIC TO THE CIVIL WAR. Urbana: University of Illinois Press, 1977.

Fisher, Miles Mark. NEGRO SLAVE SONGS IN THE UNITED STATES. Ithaca: Cornell University Press, 1953.

Friedel, L. M. THE BIBLE AND THE NEGRO SPIRITUAL. Bay St. Louis, Mississippi: St. Augustine Seminary, 1947.

Grissom, Mary Allen. THE NEGRO SINGS A NEW HEAVEN. Chapel Hill: University of North Carolina Press, 1930.

Jackson, Clyde Owen. THE SONGS OF OUR YEARS: A STUDY OF NEGRO FOLK MUSIC. New York: Exposition Press, 1968.

Jackson, Irene V. AFRO-AMERICAN MUSIC: A BIBLIOGRAPHY AND A CATALOGUE OF GOSPEL MUSIC. Westport, CT: Greenwood Press, 1979.

Joyner, Charles W. FOLK SONG IN SOUTH CAROLINA. Columbia: University of South Carolina Press, 1971.

Krehbiel, Henry E. AFRO-AMERICAN FOLKSONGS: A STUDY IN RACIAL AND NATIONAL MUSIC. New York: G. Schirmer, 1914.

Lehmann, Theo. NEGRO SPIRITUALS: GESCHICHTE UND THEOLOGIE. Berlin: Eskart-Verlag, 1965.

Levine, Lawrence W. "Slave Songs and Slave Consciousness." In AMERICAN NEGRO SLAVERY, edited by Allen Weinstein and Frank Otto Gatell, 153-182. 2nd ed. New York: Oxford University Press, 1973.

Lovell, John. BLACK SONG, THE FORGE AND THE FLAME: THE STORY OF HOW THE AFRO-AMERICAN SERMON WAS HAMMERED OUT. New York: Macmillan, 1972.

Maultsby, Portia K. AFRO-AMERICAN RELIGIOUS MUSIC: A STUDY IN MUSICAL DIVERSITY. Springfield, Ohio: The Hymn Society of America. The Papers of the Hymn Society of America, no.35, 1981.

Odum, Howard W. and Guy B. Johnson. THE NEGRO AND HIS SONGS: A STUDY OF NEGRO SONGS IN THE SOUTH. Chapel Hill: University of North Carolina Press, 1925.

Oliver, Paul. SONGSTERS AND SAINTS: VOCAL TRADITIONS ON RACE RECORDS. Cambridge: Harvard University Press, 1984.

Scarborough, Dorothy. ON THE TRAIL OF NEGRO FOLK-SONGS. Cambridge: Harvard University Press, 1925.

Spencer, Jon Michael. SACRED SYMPHONY: THE CHANTED SERMON OF THE BLACK PREACHER. Westport, Ct.: Greenwood Press, 1987.

Stuckey, Sterling. "Through the Prism of Folklore," MASSACHUSETTS REVIEW, 9 (1968), reprinted in Jules Chametzky and Sidney Kaplan, eds., BLACK AND WHITE IN AMERICAN CULTURE: AN ANTHOLOGY FROM THE MASSACHUSETTS REVIEW (New York, 1971), 172-191.

Thurman, Howard. DEEP RIVER: REFLECTIONS ON THE RELIGIOUS INSIGHTS OF CERTAIN OF THE NEGRO SPIRITUALS. New York: Harper,1955.

-------. THE NEGRO SPIRITUAL SPEAKS OF LIFE AND DEATH. New York, Harper, 1947.

Walker, Wyatt Tee. "SOMEBODY'S CALLING MY NAME": BLACK SACRED MUSIC AND SOCIAL CHANGE. Valley Forge: Judson Press, 1979.

ALPHABETICAL INDEX TO FIRST LINES

ALPHABETICAL INDEX TO TITLES

GENERAL INDEX

About the Editor

ERSKINE PETERS is Professor of English and African-American Studies at the University of Notre Dame. His current areas of specialization are Afro-poetics in the United States and philosophical concerns in early African-American writing. His books include *William Faulkner: The Yoknapatawpha World and Black Being*; *African Openings to the Tree of Life*; and *Fundamentals of Essay Writing*.